Oh! 444 Homemade Lamb Recipes

(Oh! 444 Homemade Lamb Recipes - Volume 1)

Nancy Woods

Copyright: Published in the United States by Nancy Woods/ © NANCY WOODS

Published on October, 12 2020

All rights reserved. No part of this publication may be reproduced, stored in retrieval system, copied in any form or by any means, electronic, mechanical, photocopying, recording or otherwise transmitted without written permission from the publisher. Please do not participate in or encourage piracy of this material in any way. You must not circulate this book in any format. NANCY WOODS does not control or direct users' actions and is not responsible for the information or content shared, harm and/or actions of the book readers.

In accordance with the U.S. Copyright Act of 1976, the scanning, uploading and electronic sharing of any part of this book without the permission of the publisher constitute unlawful piracy and theft of the author's intellectual property. If you would like to use material from the book (other than just simply for reviewing the book), prior permission must be obtained by contacting the author at author@tempehrecipes.com

Thank you for your support of the author's rights.

Content

CHAPTER 1: RACK OF LAMB RECIPES ...9

1. Cardamom Scented Lamb With Mashed Sweet Potatoes 9
2. Crown Roast Of Lamb.............................9
3. Feta Stuffed Rack Of Lamb With Pumpkin Seed Crust And Chipotle Sauce 10
4. Grill Roasted Rack Of Lamb In Red Mole 11
5. Grilled Saffron Rack Of Lamb 11
6. Herb Crusted Rack Of Lamb With New Potatoes 12
7. Herbed Rack Of Lamb With Parsley, Mint, And Walnut Sauté 12
8. Lamb Rack With Cucumber Yogurt 13
9. Mustard And Herb Crusted Rack Of Lamb 14
10. Pistachio Crusted Rack Of Lamb 15
11. Provencal Lamb With Mediterranean Vegetables..15
12. Rack Of Lamb And Cherry Tomatoes 16
13. Rack Of Lamb With Pecan Chipotle Sauce 16
14. Rack Of Lamb With Port And Black Olive Sauce..17
15. Rack Of Lamb With Swiss Chard 17
16. Roast Rack Of Lamb 18
17. Roast Rack Of Lamb With Mint Sauce 19
18. Roast Rack Of Lamb With Natural Jus 20
19. Roast Rack Of Lamb With Orange Chipotle Purée..20
20. Roasted Racks Of Lamb With Artichokes, Red Onions, And Garlic Cloves 21
21. Sausage Wrapped Lamb Chops With Tapanade Butter 22
22. Sun Dried Tomato And Garlic Crusted Rack Of Lamb 22

CHAPTER 2: LAMB SHANK RECIPES 23

23. Beer Braised Lamb Shanks 23
24. Chef John's Braised Lamb Shanks 24
25. Flavorful Persian Braised Lamb Shanks 25
26. Grandmother's Lamb Recipe 25
27. Heavenly Lamb Shanks 26
28. Jinx Proof Braised Lamb Shanks...............27
29. Lamb Casserole 28
30. Lamb Osso Buco Slow Cooked................28
31. Lamb Shank 29
32. Lamb Shank Braised In White Wine With Rosemary 29
33. Lamb Shank Vindaloo 30
34. Lamb Shanks With Cilantro Sauce 31
35. Meat Gravy...31
36. Moroccan Style Lamb Shanks With Apricots 32
37. Pressure Cooker Lamb Shanks With White Beans 33
38. Pulled Lamb Sizzlin' Sliders.......................34
39. Rogan Josh, Lamb Shanks 34
40. Superb Lamb Shanks..............................35

CHAPTER 3: GROUND LAMB RECIPES 36

41. A Scotsman's Shepherd Pie 36
42. Armenian Pizzas (Lahmahjoon) 37
43. Authentic Turkish Doner Kebab 37
44. Baby Red Mashed Potatoes And Peas With Spring Meatloaf 38
45. Best Greek Stuffed Turkey 38
46. Bobotie From Boschendal Manor House .39
47. Bry's Chocolate Lamb Chili......................40
48. Eggplant Stuffed With Lamb And Feta.....40
49. Forfar Bridies 41
50. Green Curry Lamb Balls 41
51. Gyros 42
52. Healthy Lamb Meatballs 42
53. Hyderabadi Nargisi Kofta........................43
54. Kebab Massalam 44
55. Keema Matar..44
56. Kibbee Lebanese Style...........................45
57. Lamb Barley Soup..................................45
58. Lamb Black Bean Chili 46
59. Lamb Cobbler 46
60. Lamb Loaf 47
61. Lamb Meatballs 48
62. Lamb Meatballs Over Tandoori Naan.......48
63. Lamb Meatballs And Sauce 49
64. Lamb Patties 50
65. Lamb Puff Pastry Bite Appetizer...............50
66. Lamb Spaghetti.....................................51
67. Lamb And Black Bean Chili 52
68. Lamb And Potato Skillet..........................52

69. Lamb And Rice Stuffed Cabbage Rolls 53
70. Lamb And Rice Stuffed Grape Leaves 54
71. Lamb And Squash 54
72. Lamb, Carrot, And White Bean Curry Stew 55
73. Leek And Meat Fritters 55
74. Little Lamb Meatballs In A Spicy Eggplant Tomato Sauce 56
75. Make Ahead Moroccan Lamb Stew 57
76. Mama's Oh So Savory Lamb And Eggplant Casserole 57
77. Mandy's Lamb Enchiladas 58
78. Marvelous Mongolian Meatballs 59
79. Mediterranean Lamb Meatball Sandwiches With Yogurt Sauce 59
80. Mediterranean Orzo Spinach Salad 60
81. Mediterranean Stuffed Zucchini 61
82. Middle Eastern Kibbeh 61
83. Middle Eastern Stuffed Zucchini 62
84. Minced Lamb Bake 62
85. Mom's Irish Ziti 63
86. No Eggplant Moussaka 64
87. Paul's Fat Tire® Lamb Chili 64
88. Roasted Eggplant Pastitsio 65
89. Spicy Lamb Patties 66
90. Stuffed Bell Peppers, Greek Style 66
91. Stuffed Grape Leaves (Dolmades) 67
92. Three Meat Loaf 67
93. Tikka Masala Skillet Shepherd's Pie 68
94. Tina's Greek Stuffed Peppers 69
95. Traditional Gyro Meat 69
96. Traditional Gyros 70
97. Turkish Meatballs (Kofta) 71
98. Turkish Rissoles 71
99. White Bean And Lamb Soup 72
100. World's Greatest Grape Leaves (Armenian) 72

CHAPTER 4: LAMB STEW RECIPES 73

101. Chanakhi (Georgian Lamb Stew) 73
102. Chef John's Irish Stew 74
103. Couscous De Mouton Tout Simple (Moroccan Mutton Couscous) 74
104. Greek Lamb Stew 75
105. Irish Lamb Stew With Roasted Root Veg.76
106. Irish Style Lamb Stew 77
107. Lamb And Asparagus Stew 77

108. Mediterranean Lamb And Lentil Stew......77
109. One Pot Irish Stew 78
110. Tas Kebab (Persian Lamb And Vegetable Stew) 79
111. Thick Irish Stew 79

CHAPTER 5: BBQ & GRILLED LAMB RECIPES 80

112. Armenian Shish Kabob 80
113. Asian Barbequed Butterflied Leg Of Lamb 80
114. Aussie Barbequed Boneless Leg Of Lamb 81
115. Barbecued Lamb Chops 82
116. Barbecued Lamb Kabobs 82
117. Basil Grilled Mediterranean Lamb Chops .83
118. Best Burgers Ever 83
119. Big M's Grilled Orange Lamb Kabobs 84
120. Champion Lamb Burgers 84
121. Champion Lamb Burgers For Two 85
122. Chef John's Grilled Lamb Steaks 85
123. Chef John's Grilled Lamb With Mint Orange Sauce 86
124. Chris' Best Burgers 87
125. Dale's Lamb 87
126. Dijon Leg Of Lamb 88
127. Dirty Piggy Back Lamb 88
128. Feta And Olive Lamburgers 89
129. Goat Cheese Stuffed Lamb Burgers 89
130. Greek Lamb Kabobs 90
131. Greek Lamb Kabobs With Yogurt Mint Salsa Verde 90
132. Greek Lamb Feta Burgers With Cucumber Sauce 91
133. Grilled "Tandoori" Lamb 92
134. Grilled Lamb Burgers 92
135. Grilled Lamb Chops 93
136. Grilled Lamb Chops With Curry, Apple And Raisin Sauce 93
137. Grilled Lamb Chops With Pomegranate Port Reduction 94
138. Grilled Lamb Chops With Wine Sauce 95
139. Grilled Lamb Kabobs 95
140. Grilled Lamb Shoulder Chops With Fresh Mint Jelly 96
141. Grilled Lamb With Tomato Basil Marinade 97
142. Grilled Lamb With Veggies 97

143. Grilled Leg Of Lamb Steaks 98
144. Grilled Lemon And Rosemary Lamb Chops 98
145. Grilled Mediterranean Lamb Sandwich 99
146. Grilled Pastrami Spiced Lamb Top Sirloin 100
147. Grilled Rack Of Lamb 100
148. Grilled Spicy Lamb Burgers 101
149. Gyros Burgers 101
150. Herb Marinated Lamb Chops 102
151. Herbed Lamb Chops 102
152. Herbed Lamb Chops With Crispy Potatoes 103
153. Herbed Lamb Kabobs 103
154. Indian Style Sheekh Kabab 104
155. Kabab Barg 104
156. Kofta Kebabs 105
157. Korean Barbecued Rack Of Lamb 106
158. Lamb & Chicken Kabobs 106
159. Lamb Burgers 107
160. Lamb Chops With Preserved Lemon (Moroccan Style) 107
161. Lamb Kabobs With Bulgur Pilaf 108
162. Lamb Kabobs With Yogurt Sauce 108
163. Lamb Sliders 109
164. Lamb And Beef Kabobs 110
165. Lamb With Spinach And Onions 110
166. Lemon And Thyme Lamb Chops 111
167. Lemon Honey Lamb Skewers 111
168. Lime Glazed Leg Of Lamb 112
169. Marinated Grilled Lamb 112
170. Marinated Lamb Chops 113
171. Minted Lamb 'n' Veggie Kabobs 113
172. Mixed Grill Of Sausage, Chicken And Lamb With Tandoori Flavorings 114
173. Moroccan Lamb Kabobs 115
174. Papa Wolf's Grilled Lamb Shoulder Chops 115
175. Portobello Lamb Chops 116
176. Rocky Mountain Grill 117
177. Rosemary Thyme Lamb Chops 117
178. Rubbed Sage Lamb Chops 118
179. Serbian Cevapcici 118
180. Sharon's Scrumptious Souvlaki 119
181. Simple Grilled Lamb Chops 119
182. Skewered Lamb With Blackberry Balsamic Glaze 120
183. South African Lamb Sosaties(Kebabs) 120
184. Southwestern Grilled Lamb 121
185. Southwestern Lamb Chops 121
186. Spicy Barbequed Chops 122
187. Spicy Chinese Cumin Lamb Skewers 122
188. Spicy Lamb Kabobs 123
189. Summer Lamb Kabobs 124

CHAPTER 6: LAMB FOR MAIN DISH RECIPES **124**

190. Braised Lamb Shanks & Eggplant 124
191. Braised Lamb Shanks With Butternut Squash Puree 125
192. Braised Lamb With A Garden Vegetable Medley 126
193. Braised Lamb With A Sour Orange Marinade 127
194. Dragan's Leg Of Lamb With Garlic And Beer 127
195. Feta And Olive Meatballs 128
196. Garam Masala Lamb Chops With Apricot Couscous 128
197. Grandma Me's Clove Studded Leg Of Lamb 129
198. Greek Lamb Meatballs 129
199. Grilled Leg Of Lamb With Mint Garlic Rub 130
200. Holiday Leg Of Lamb 131
201. Kashmiri Lamb 131
202. Keema (Indian Style Ground Meat) 132
203. Kefta 132
204. Lahmacun Turkish Pizza 133
205. Lahmahjoon (Armenian Pizza) 134
206. Lahmahjoon Pizza 135
207. Lamb & Rice Stuffed Grape Leaves 135
208. Lamb & Spinach One Pot Pasta 136
209. Lamb & White Bean Chili 137
210. Lamb Chops With Balsamic Reduction .. 137
211. Lamb Chops With Lebanese Green Beans 138
212. Lamb Chops With Mint Pan Sauce 139
213. Lamb Feta Peppers 139
214. Lamb Shanks With Ancho Chile Honey Glaze 140
215. Lamb Tagine With Preserved Lemon 141
216. Lamb For Lovers 142
217. Lamb, Fig & Olive Stew For Two 142

218. Lebanese Cabbage Rolls 143
219. Leg Of Lamb With Raspberry Sauce 144
220. Maple Glazed Chipotle Goat Cheese Lamb Burgers 145
221. Mediterranean Lamb Salad 145
222. Mediterranean Meat Pies (Sfeeha) 146
223. Middle Eastern Lamb Stew 146
224. Moroccan Lamb Chops With Tomato Olive Relish 147
225. Moroccan Lamb With Shiraz Honey Sauce 148
226. Moroccan Tagine 148
227. Mustard Rosemary Grilled Lamb 148
228. Nana's Leg Of Lamb 149
229. North African Orange & Lamb Kebabs .150
230. Orzo With Lamb, Olives & Feta For Two 150
231. Plum Lamb Casserole..............................151
232. Quick Shepherd's Pie...............................151
233. Rack Of Lamb With A Cilantro Mustard Seed Crust 152
234. Roasted Rack Of Lamb.............................152
235. Rosemary Braised Lamb Shanks.............153
236. Rosemary Lemon Lamb Chops With Potato And Fennel Latkes 154
237. Saba Braised Lamb Shanks....................154
238. Seven Hour Leg Of Lamb 155
239. Spicy Lamb Meatballs In Tomato Sauce .156
240. Spicy Sweetbreads 157
241. Stout Braised Lamb Shanks.....................157
242. Tandoori Leg Of Lamb With Fresh Mango Chutney 158
243. Vietnamese Aromatic Lamb Chops 159

CHAPTER 7: LAMB DINNER RECIPES 159

244. Basic Braised Lamb Shanks 159
245. Beef And Lamb Stew 160
246. Best Leg Of Lamb 160
247. Best Ever Lamb Chops..............................161
248. Best Ever Lamb Chops For 2 161
249. Braised Lamb Shanks 162
250. Breaded Rack Of Lamb 162
251. Caribbean Chutney Crusted Chops..........163
252. Cheesy Lamb Cups 163
253. Classic Cottage Pie 164
254. Crusty Roast Leg Of Lamb 164
255. Curried Lamb Chops 165

256. Curried Lamb Stew 165
257. Curried Lamb Stir Fry 166
258. Curried Lamb And Barley Grain 167
259. Curried Lamb And Potatoes 167
260. Curry Lamb Stir Fry.................................168
261. Favorite Irish Stew...................................168
262. Festive Rack Of Lamb 169
263. Flavorful Lamb Chops 170
264. Glazed Racks Of Lamb.............................170
265. Greek Shepherd's Pie 171
266. Herb Crusted Rack Of Lamb....................171
267. Herb Crusted Rack Of Lamb With Mushroom Sauce......................................172
268. Hungarian Lamb Stew..............................173
269. Irish Lamb Stew 173
270. Irish Stew 174
271. Italian Leg Of Lamb 174
272. Italian Leg Of Lamb With Lemon Sauce 175
273. Lamb Broccoli Strudel 176
274. Lamb Chops With Mint Stuffing..............176
275. Lamb Chops With Prunes 177
276. Lamb Fajitas...177
277. Lamb Noodle Stroganoff..........................178
278. Lamb Ratatouille 178
279. Lamb And Potato Stew............................179
280. Lamb With Apricots 179
281. Lamb With Raspberry Sauce 180
282. Leg Of Lamb 180
283. Leg Of Lamb Dinner 181
284. Lemon Herb Lamb Chops 181
285. Lemon Herb Leg Of Lamb 182
286. Mediterranean Rack Of Lamb 182
287. Mint Lamb Stew 183
288. Mint Pesto Lamb Chops..........................183
289. Old Fashioned Lamb Stew.......................184
290. Orange Blossom Lamb 184
291. Pasta Lamb Skillet...................................185
292. Plum Glazed Lamb 185
293. Rack Of Lamb 186
294. Rack Of Lamb With Figs..........................186
295. Rack Of Lamb With Fresh Herbs 187
296. Roast Lamb With Plum Sauce 187
297. Roast Leg Of Lamb 188
298. Roast Leg Of Lamb With Rosemary 188
299. Roast Rack Of Lamb With Herb Sauce ..189
300. Rosemary Leg Of Lamb............................190
301. Rosemary Roasted Lamb 190

302. Rosemary Seasoned Lamb 190
303. Rosemary Rubbed Lamb Chops 191
304. Sauerbraten Lamb Shanks 191
305. Skillet Lamb Chops 192
306. Slow Cook Lamb Chops 193
307. Slow Cooked Lamb Chops 193
308. Spice Rubbed Lamb Chops 194
309. Spiced Lamb Stew With Apricots 194
310. Spinach Stuffed Lamb 195
311. Spring Lamb Supper 195
312. Squash And Lentil Lamb Stew 196
313. Tangy Lamb Tagine 196
314. Tender Lamb With Mint Salsa 197
315. Traditional Lamb Stew 197
316. Vegetable Stew 198
317. West Virginia Shepherd's Pie 199
318. Wyoming Lamb Stew 199
319. Zesty Herbed Lamb Chops 200

CHAPTER 8: EASTER LAMB RECIPES .200

320. Bacon Wrapped Leg Of Lamb With Red Wine Reduction 201
321. Baked Lamb Chops 201
322. Braised Lamb Shank With Vegetables 202
323. Braised Lamb With Radishes And Mint .. 202
324. Broiled And Slow Roasted Butterflied Leg Of Lamb With Cumin And Garlic 203
325. Cassandra's Yummy Lamb Chops 204
326. Chef John's Roasted Leg Of Lamb 204
327. Easter Leg Of Lamb 205
328. Easy Leg Of Lamb 205
329. Easy Roast Leg Of Lamb 206
330. Farikal 206
331. Grecian Lamb Caesar Salad 207
332. Greek Orange Roast Lamb 207
333. Grilled Lamb With Brown Sugar Glaze .. 208
334. Lamb Chops In Duck Sauce 208
335. Lamb Chops With Mint Oil 209
336. Lamb L'Arabique 209
337. Lamb Ribs With Honey And Wine 210
338. Leg O' Lamb With Lemon And Rosemary 210
339. Mint Crusted Rack Of Lamb 211
340. Nita's Lamb, Green Beans And Tomatoes 212
341. Paddy's Chile Verde 212
342. Pistachio Crusted Rack Of Lamb 213
343. Portofino Lamb And Artichoke Risotto .213
344. Rack Of Lamb With Strawberry Mint Sauce 214
345. Roast Leg Of Lamb With Orange Juice And White Wine 215
346. Roasted Lamb With Root Vegetables 215
347. Slow Roast Leg Of Lamb 216
348. Spice Crusted Roast Rack Of Lamb With Cilantro Mint Sauce 217
349. Stuffed Leg Of Lamb 217
350. Stuffed Leg Of Lamb With Balsamic Fig Basil Sauce 218

CHAPTER 9: AWESOME LAMB RECIPES
.... 219

351. A Vegetable Stew Tabakh Rohoo 219
352. Algerian Couscous 220
353. American Gyros 221
354. Anna's Amazing Goulash 221
355. Ash E Anar (Persian Pomegranate Soup) 222
356. Atlas Mountain Soup 223
357. Aunt Louise's Baked Kibbeh 223
358. Awesome Herb Roast Leg Of Lamb 224
359. Bacon Wrapped Mushroom Meatloaf 225
360. Bamieh (Middle Eastern Okra Stew) 225
361. Bhuna Gosht 226
362. Boxty With Liver And Bacon 226
363. Braised Lamb Shoulder Chops 227
364. Butter Lamb Gravy 228
365. Candice's Lamb Cannelloni With Mint Pesto 228
366. Cephalonian Meat Pie 229
367. Chalau 230
368. Chef John's Lamb Moussaka Burger 230
369. Crostini Alla Fiorentina 231
370. Curried Ground Lamb With Quinoa, Swiss Chard, And Fiddle Ferns 232
371. Curried Stew With Lamb 232
372. Diced Lamb With Roasted Vegetables And Couscous 233
373. Eggplant And Lamb Stew 234
374. Egyptian Bamia 234
375. Fasolia (Green Bean Stew) 235
376. Gigot D'Agneau Au Four (Roast Lamb With Beans) 235
377. Grape Leaves Aleppo 236

378. Greek Burgers 236
379. Greek Hamburgers 237
380. Gyroll 237
381. H'rira Onctueuse A L'Agneau (Rich And Creamy Harira Soup) 238
382. Helga's Russian Borscht 238
383. Irish Shepherd's Pie 239
384. Irish Stew, My Way 240
385. Italian Lamb Stew 241
386. JG's Irish Lamb Stew 241
387. Juggernauts Meatloaf 242
388. Kentucky Burgoo 243
389. Kreatopita Argostoli 243
390. Lamb (Gosht) Biryani 244
391. Lamb Braised In Pomegranate 245
392. Lamb Chops With Minted Yogurt Sauce 246
393. Lamb Korma 246
394. Lamb Lover's Pilaf 247
395. Lamb Madras Curry 247
396. Lamb Merguez Sausage Patties 248
397. Lamb Shoulder Vindaloo 249
398. Lamb Stew In An Hour 249
399. Lamb Stew With Green Beans 250
400. Lamb Tagine 250
401. Lamb And Bulgur Soup (Shorba Freek) . 251
402. Lamb And Okra Stew 252
403. Lamb And Winter Vegetable Stew 252
404. Lancashire Hot Pot 253
405. Low Carb Lamb Burgers 253
406. Mama's Lamb Roast 254
407. Margaret's Keftedes (Greek Meatballs) ... 254
408. Marinated Lamb Chislick 255
409. Marinated, Breaded Lamb Chops With Rosemary And Garlic 255
410. McIntire's Lamb Stew 256
411. Mediterranean Lamb Burgers 256
412. Mellas Family Lamb Stuffed Zucchini (Koosa) 257
413. Mensaf (Jordanian Lamb Stew) 258
414. Moroccan Lamb Tagine (Mrouzia) 258
415. Moroccan Shepherd's Pie 259
416. Mozzarella Stuffed Leg Of Lamb 260
417. Mum's Mutton Curry 261
418. NO YOLKS® Lamb Stew 261
419. Never Fail Boneless Leg Of Lamb 262
420. Nova Scotia Style Donair 262
421. Oven Roasted Boneless Leg Of Lamb 263

422. Oven Roasted Lamb Ribs 264
423. Pakistani Lamb Curry 265
424. Pastry Wrapped Lamb Rack 265
425. Paul's Apple, Lamb And Lentil Soup 266
426. Punjabi Lamb Korma With Onion Cilantro Salad 267
427. Rack Of Lamb With Blueberry Sauce 267
428. Roasted Orange Leg Of Lamb 268
429. Rob's Lamb Curry Pie 269
430. Rosemary And Lamb Crispy Roast Potatoes 270
431. Scotch Broth II 270
432. Simplified Cassoulet 271
433. Slow Cooker Lamb Chops 272
434. Slow Cooker Leg Of Lamb 272
435. Slow Cooker Roasted Leg Of Lamb 273
436. Special Mutton Leg Roast For Eid Ul Azha 273
437. Spring Lamb Sliders 274
438. Stuffed Greek Leg Of Lamb 275
439. The Shorba Freekeh Of Algeria 275
440. Tim's Lamb Stew 276
441. Tomato Bredie 276
442. Tunisian Lamb With Saffron (Keleya Zaara) 277
443. Upside Down (Maqluba) 277
444. Whitechapel Shepherd's Pie 278

INDEX 280
CONCLUSION 284

Chapter 1: Rack Of Lamb Recipes

***

1. Cardamom Scented Lamb With Mashed Sweet Potatoes

Serving: Makes 4 servings | Prep: | Cook: | Ready in:

Ingredients

- 1 tablespoon butter
- 2 tablespoons tomato paste
- 6 garlic cloves, minced
- 2 teaspoons chopped fresh thyme
- 2 cups dry red wine
- 1 cup canned beef broth
- 1 cup canned low-salt chicken broth
- 2 tablespoons shelled cardamom seeds
- 2 1 1/4- to 1 1/2-pound racks of lamb, trimmed
- 2 tablespoons olive oil
- 1/4 cup (1/2 stick) chilled unsalted butter, cut into pieces
- 4 teaspoons coarse-grained mustard
- Mashed Sweet Potatoes with Maple Syrup

Direction

- Sauce: Melt 1 tbsp. butter in a medium heavy saucepan on medium high heat then add thyme, garlic and tomato paste; sauté for 1 minute. Add wine; boil for 8 minutes till reduced by half. Add both broths; boil for 10 minutes till reduced to 1 1/4 cups. You can make it 1 day ahead, refrigerated, covered.
- Lamb: Preheat an oven to 450°F. In small heavy skillet, toast cardamom seeds on medium heat for 2 minutes till fragrant; cool. Put in a spice grinder; coarsely grind.
- Sprinkle pepper, salt and cardamom on lamb. Heat oil in a big heavy skillet on high heat and add 1 lamb rack; sear for 6 minutes till brown, occasionally turning. Put lamb on a baking sheet, meat side up; repeat using 2nd lamb rack. Roast for 18 minutes till inserted meat thermometer in the middle reads 125°F to get medium-rare. Stand for 5 minutes; between bones, cut lambs into chops.
- Simmer the sauce. Lower the heat to low then add mustard and butter; whisk till butter melts. Use pepper to season; put sauce on plates. Put lamb and sweet potatoes on top. Serve.

Nutrition Information

- Calories: 1136
- Saturated Fat: 45 g(224%)
- Sodium: 493 mg(21%)
- Fiber: 1 g(6%)
- Total Carbohydrate: 8 g(3%)
- Cholesterol: 211 mg(70%)
- Protein: 36 g(73%)
- Total Fat: 100 g(154%)

2. Crown Roast Of Lamb

Serving: Serves 6 | Prep: | Cook: | Ready in:

Ingredients

- a 16-chop frenched and trimmed crown roast of lamb (about 4 pounds), at room temperature
- 2 tablespoons balsamic vinegar
- 1 cup dry red wine
- 2 1/2 cups beef broth
- 2 tablespoons arrowroot
- 3 tablespoons water
- mint sprigs for garnish
- Accompaniments:

- Minted Saffron Rice with Currants and Pine Nuts
- Glazed Baby Turnips and Carrots
- Garlic Rosemary Jelly

Direction

- Preheat an oven to 425°F. Rub lamb with pepper and salt to taste well; use foil to cover bones' ends.
- Put lamb in oiled roasting pan; roast for 25-30 minutes in center of oven till inserted meat thermometer in thickest meat part inside crow reads 130-135°F to get medium-rare meat. Put lamb on platter. Let stand for 15 minutes, loosely covered.
- Take out extra fat from pan juices as lamb stands. Put pan on medium high heat. Add wine and vinegar; deglaze pan, scraping brown bits up and boiling liquid till reduced to 1/4 cup. Add broth then boil.
- Whisk water and arrowroot till smooth in small bowl. Whisk and add to boiling broth mixture. Simmer sauce till slightly thick for 2 minutes, whisking. Season with pepper and salt; keep sauce warm, covered.
- Remove foil from bones; put some rice in crown using spoon. Serve leftover rice on the side. Put glazed veggies around roast. Strain sauce through fine sieve into sauceboat. Use mint sprigs to garnish platter, then serve with jelly.

Nutrition Information

3. Feta Stuffed Rack Of Lamb With Pumpkin Seed Crust And Chipotle Sauce

Serving: Serves 4 | Prep: | Cook: | Ready in:

Ingredients

- 16 garlic cloves, peeled, halved
- 4 teaspoons corn oil
- 1 cup shelled pumpkin seeds
- 2 1 1/4- to 1 1/2-pound racks of lamb, trimmed, halved
- 1/2 cup crumbled feta cheese (about 3 ounces)
- 1/2 cup chopped drained oil-packed sun-dried tomatoes
- 1/2 cup chopped brine-cured olives (such as Kalamata)
- 1/4 cup chopped fresh cilantro
- 1/4 cup Dijon mustard
- Chipotle Sauce

Direction

- Set the oven to 425°F for preheating. Coat the heavy large baking sheet with oil. In a small bowl, toss the garlic and 2 tsp. of corn oil. Spread the mixture into the baking sheet. Roast for 6 minutes. Add the pumpkin seeds and toss them until coated. Roast for 5 minutes, stirring once until the garlic and seeds turn golden brown. Transfer them onto a rack and allow them to cool. Make sure that the temperature of the oven is maintained.
- Pour the garlic and pumpkin seed mixture into the processor. Grind the mixture until it forms a coarse puree. Stir in 2 tsp. of corn oil.
- Starting at one end of the lamb, cut a slit into the center of each lamb rack half using the long sharp knife, letting the slit extend to the opposite end of the lamb. Insert the wooden spoon's handle into the slit and enlarge the slit into a hole with a size of 3/4-inch. In a large bowl, mix the cilantro, sun-dried tomatoes, feta, and olives. Spoon the feta mixture into the hole of each lamb rack, dividing the mixture equally.
- Lay the lamb into the prepared baking sheet. Spread the rounded side of the lamb with the mustard. Spread 1/4 of the pumpkin seed coating into the mustard-coated side of each lamb rack half, making sure the seed coatings are pressed well. Roast the lamb for 25 minutes until the inserted meat thermometer near the center of the lamb reads 135°F (for

medium-rare). Allow the lamb to rest for 15 minutes. Drizzle each plate with 1/3 cup of the Chipotle Sauce. Top each sauce with one of the lamb rack half. Serve the plates while passing separately the remaining sauce.

Nutrition Information

- Calories: 1198
- Cholesterol: 192 mg(64%)
- Protein: 48 g(96%)
- Total Fat: 107 g(165%)
- Saturated Fat: 42 g(208%)
- Sodium: 646 mg(27%)
- Fiber: 4 g(16%)
- Total Carbohydrate: 13 g(4%)

4. Grill Roasted Rack Of Lamb In Red Mole

Serving: Makes 4 servings | Prep: | Cook: | Ready in:

Ingredients

- Two 7- to 8-bone racks of lamb, trimmed and Frenched (the butcher can do this)
- 2 1/2 cups Red Mole
- 1 to 2 tablespoons canola or grapeseed oil
- Kosher salt and freshly ground black pepper to taste

Direction

- Halve rack of lamb to get 3-4-boned meat sections.
- Put onto platter/baking dish; cover meat with 1 1/2 cups mole (don't put mole on bones). Cover; refrigerate for minimum of 4 hours – no longer than overnight. Refrigerate leftover mole for serving.
- Prep medium fire in the grill. Preheat an oven to 475°.
- Brush extra marinade off lamb. Oil grill rack then lay racks of lamb onto it; grill till browned nicely on all sides, flipping 1-2 times. Flip lamb or move lamb away from hottest flames if lamb's fat drip and make flare ups.
- Put meat into small roasting pan; put into oven. Check lamb after 10 minutes; discard accumulated fat in bottom of pan. Cook lamb till it reaches desired doneness. Best served when medium rare; other doneness can be too dry or springy. Around 130° is the ideal internal temperature. It rises when you take it out of oven, for several degrees. Rest lamb for several minutes.
- Meanwhile, in a small saucepan, warm reserved mole.
- Serve half-racks as they are or cut lamb to chops; offer mole alongside with pepper and salt.

Nutrition Information

5. Grilled Saffron Rack Of Lamb

Serving: Makes 6 servings | Prep: | Cook: | Ready in:

Ingredients

- 2 racks of lamb (3-3 1/2 pounds total), rib bones frenched
- Kosher salt, freshly ground pepper
- 2 garlic cloves, crushed
- 1 cup plain 2% fat Greek yogurt
- 2 tablespoons olive oil
- 1 teaspoon finely grated lemon zest
- 1/2 teaspoon saffron threads, finely crumbled

Direction

- Season lamb with pepper and salt; put every lamb rack in big plastic resealable plastic bag. Whisk saffron, lemon zest, oil, yogurt and garlic in small bowl; divide to bags. Seal bags and press excess air out; turn to coat. Refrigerate lamb overnight.

- Prep grill for indirect medium high heat; bank coals on 1 grill side for charcoal grill or leave 1 burner turned off for gas grill. Take lamb from marinade; wipe excess off. Put lamb above direct head; cook for 8-10 minutes till browned all over, flipping and moving to grill's cooler part as needed to prevent flare-ups.
- Put lamb on grill's cooler part. Cover grill, cook lamb for 15 minutes more till an inserted instant-read thermometer in middle reads 125° to get medium rare, occasionally turning.
- Rest lamb for 10 minutes. Slice to individual chops.

Nutrition Information

- Calories: 1281
- Total Carbohydrate: 2 g(1%)
- Cholesterol: 352 mg(117%)
- Protein: 70 g(141%)
- Total Fat: 108 g(166%)
- Saturated Fat: 35 g(174%)
- Sodium: 1131 mg(47%)
- Fiber: 0 g(0%)

6. Herb Crusted Rack Of Lamb With New Potatoes

Serving: Makes 4 servings | Prep: | Cook: | Ready in:

Ingredients

- 1 1/2 pounds small new or Yukon Gold potatoes, scrubbed
- Kosher salt
- 2 racks of lamb (about 2 pounds total)
- Freshly ground black pepper
- 4 tablespoons olive oil, divided
- 2 garlic cloves, chopped
- 1/2 cup chopped fresh flat-leaf parsley
- 1/4 cup chopped fresh dill
- 1 tablespoon Dijon mustard
- 2 teaspoons cumin seeds, crushed
- 6 cups watercress leaves with tender stems
- 2 teaspoons Sherry vinegar

Direction

- Cover potatoes in 1-in. cold water in a big saucepan; season with salt. Boil. Lower heat; simmer for 10-15 minutes till tender. Drain.
- Meanwhile, preheat an oven to 400°F. Use pepper and salt to season lamb. Heat 2 tbsp. oil on medium high heat in a big skillet; cook lamb, occasionally turning, for 6-8 minutes till golden brown all over. Put it, fat side up, onto foil-lined baking sheet.
- In a small bowl, mix 1 tbsp. oil, cumin, mustard, dill, parsley and garlic; season with pepper and salt.
- Spread herb mixture on lamb; roast for 18-22 minutes till inserted instant-read thermometer in thickest meat part reads 130°F for medium rare. Put onto cutting board; rest before cutting to double chops for 5 minutes.
- Heat leftover 1 tbsp. oil on medium heat in a medium skillet as lamb rests. Add watercress and potatoes; cook, tossing, for 1 minute till watercress just wilts. Mix in vinegar; season with pepper and salt. Serve potatoes and watercress with lamb.

Nutrition Information

- Calories: 3224
- Total Fat: 287 g(441%)
- Saturated Fat: 122 g(611%)
- Sodium: 2435 mg(101%)
- Fiber: 5 g(21%)
- Total Carbohydrate: 34 g(11%)
- Cholesterol: 602 mg(201%)
- Protein: 121 g(241%)

7. Herbed Rack Of Lamb With Parsley, Mint, And Walnut Sauté

Serving: Makes 6 servings | Prep: | Cook: | Ready in:

Ingredients

- 3 1 1/4-pound racks of lamb, frenched
- 5 tablespoons olive oil
- 2 teaspoons coarse kosher salt
- 1/2 cup finely chopped fresh Italian parsley
- 1/4 cup finely chopped fresh rosemary
- 1/4 cup finely chopped fresh mint
- 2 tablespoons extra-virgin olive oil
- 1/2 cup finely chopped shallots
- 6 cups (packed) fresh Italian parsley leaves (from 2 large bunches)
- 3/4 cup very coarsely chopped fresh mint leaves
- 1/2 cup water
- 2 teaspoons grated lemon peel
- 3/4 cup coarsely chopped toasted walnuts (about 2 1/2 ounces)
- 2 tablespoons walnut oil
- 1 tablespoon fresh lemon juice

Direction

- Lamb: Put lamb racks onto big heavy rimmed baking sheet; brush 1 tbsp. oil on lamb. Sprinkle pepper and 2 tsp. coarse salt. In small bowl, mix all herbs; firmly press to adhere on meat side of lamb. Stand in room temperature for 2 hours. You can make it 6 hours ahead. Cover; refrigerate.
- Preheat an oven to 425°F. Heat leftover 4 tbsp. oil on medium high heat in big heavy nonstick skillet. Add lamb in batches, herb-and-meat side down; cook for 4 minutes till brown. Put racks, herb-and-meat side up, on baking sheet; roast lamb for 13 minutes till inserted meat thermometer in middle reads 125°F for medium rare. Remove from oven; stand for 15 minutes.
- Meanwhile, prep sauté: Heat olive oil on medium heat in big heavy skillet. Add shallots; sauté for 4 minutes till soft. Add parsley; sauté for 2 minutes till wilted. Add lemon peel, 1/2 cup water and mint; cook for 3 minutes till parsley is tender. Mix in lemon juice, walnut oil and walnuts; season with pepper and salt.
- Between bones, cut lamb to individual chops and divide parsley sauté to 6 plates. Put lamb chops over.

Nutrition Information

- Calories: 1067
- Saturated Fat: 35 g(174%)
- Sodium: 786 mg(33%)
- Fiber: 4 g(18%)
- Total Carbohydrate: 10 g(3%)
- Cholesterol: 157 mg(52%)
- Protein: 35 g(69%)
- Total Fat: 100 g(154%)

8. Lamb Rack With Cucumber Yogurt

Serving: Serves 4 | Prep: | Cook: | Ready in:

Ingredients

- 1 1/2 cups plain Greek-style yogurt
- 2 cucumbers
- Salt
- 2 teaspoons lemon juice
- 1 tablespoon olive oil
- 1/2 clove garlic
- 1 1/2 tablespoons chopped dill
- 1 tablespoon canola oil
- 1 lamb rack (about 2 1/4 pounds), frenched and tied
- Salt
- 2 tablespoons butter
- 5 sprigs thyme
- 1 clove garlic, crushed but kept whole

Direction

- Cucumber yogurt: Line quadruple cheesecloth layer on a colander; put yogurt into cheesecloth. Suspend above a big bowl; refrigerate, letting moisture drain from yogurt, for 48 hours.

- Peel then grate cucumbers on box grater; season using 1 tsp. salt. To drain extra moisture, hand for 1 hour in quadruple cheesecloth layer. Get 1 cup drained yogurt; put leftover aside for another time. Mix drained cucumbers and 1 cup yogurt in a medium bowl; mix in olive oil and lemon juice. Grate garlic on Microplane grater into mixture; fold in chopped dill. Stir well; season to taste with salt.
- Roasted lamb rack: Preheat an oven to 300°F. Heat big cast-iron skillet on high heat. Generously use salt to season lamb rack. Put rack, fat side down, in skillet; sear on high heat for 2 1/2-3 minutes till browned. Flip; sear bottom for 1 minute. Flip rack onto fat side; add garlic, thyme and butter. Baste rack for 2 1/2-3 minutes with butter. Put lamb rack onto wire rack in rimmed baking sheet, fat side up; roast for 10 minutes in oven. Flip rack; baste with butter. Put in oven for 10 minutes. Take lamb rack from oven; flip. Baste again. Roast in oven till internal temperature is 130-135°F for 10-15 minutes. Rest lamb rack before slicing for 10-15 minutes. Serve with heirloom tomatoes and cucumber yogurt.

Nutrition Information

- Calories: 928
- Protein: 36 g(73%)
- Total Fat: 83 g(127%)
- Saturated Fat: 36 g(181%)
- Sodium: 1247 mg(52%)
- Fiber: 1 g(5%)
- Total Carbohydrate: 11 g(4%)
- Cholesterol: 171 mg(57%)

9. Mustard And Herb Crusted Rack Of Lamb

Serving: Makes 8 servings | Prep: 25mins | Cook: 1.5hours | Ready in:

Ingredients

- 1 1/2 cups fine fresh bread crumbs
- 3 tablespoons finely chopped fresh flat-leaf parsley
- 1 tablespoon finely chopped fresh mint
- 1 1/2 teaspoons minced fresh rosemary
- 1/2 teaspoon salt
- 1/4 teaspoon black pepper
- 3 1/2 tablespoons olive oil
- 3 frenched racks of lamb (8 ribs and 1 1/2 lb each rack), trimmed of all but a thin layer of fat, then brought to room temperature
- 2 tablespoons Dijon mustard
- an instant-read thermometer

Direction

- Mix together the parsley, salt, rosemary, mint, bread crumbs, and pepper in the bowl. Drizzle with 2 1/2 tablespoons of oil and toss to blend well.
- Set oven to 400°F and position oven rack at the center.
- Season the lamb with pepper and salt. On moderately high heat, place a large heavy skillet and heat the remaining tablespoon of oil until hot but not smoking. Brown the lamb 1 rack at a time, flipping once, about 4 minutes on each rack. Prepare a 13x9x2 inch roasting pan and place browned lamb; arrange with the fatty sides up.
- Spread 2 teaspoons of mustard on each rack with fatty sides. In 3 portions, distribute the bread crumbs and per portion, pat over coating each rack with mustard. Press slowly to stick.
- Roast lamb until a thermometer inserted diagonally 2 inches at the middle shows 130°F (medium-rare) for 20-25 minutes. Prepare a chopping board; transfer roasted lambs. Set aside for 10 minutes. Slice into chops.

Nutrition Information

- Calories: 1750
- Sodium: 579 mg(24%)

- Fiber: 1 g(5%)
- Total Carbohydrate: 15 g(5%)
- Cholesterol: 330 mg(110%)
- Protein: 66 g(132%)
- Total Fat: 156 g(241%)
- Saturated Fat: 67 g(334%)

10. Pistachio Crusted Rack Of Lamb

Serving: Makes 4 servings | Prep: 25mins | Cook: 1hours15mins | Ready in:

Ingredients

- 1 cup pomegranate juice
- 1/4 cup dried currants
- 1 garlic clove, peeled
- 3 tablespoons chilled butter, cut into 1/2-inch cubes
- 1/2 teaspoon ground cinnamon
- 1/4 teaspoon ground cumin
- 1 large rack of lamb (2 1/4 pounds), well trimmed
- 1/4 cup chopped natural unsalted pistachios
- 1/4 cup panko (Japanese breadcrumbs)*

Direction

- Preheat an oven to 400°F. Boil garlic, currants and pomegranate juice for 10 minutes till reduced to 1/4 cup and liquid is syrupy in medium skillet, mixing often. Put mixture in mini processor. Add cumin, cinnamon and butter; blend till coarse puree foams. Put processor bowl in freeze to slightly firm butter for 10 minutes.
- Line foil on small rimmed baking sheet. Put lamb on sheet, bone side down; sprinkle pepper and salt. Spread over with pomegranate butter; sprinkle panko and pistachios, pressing to adhere.
- Roast the rack of lamb for 30 minutes till inserted instant-read thermometer into side reads 135°F for medium rare. Put on work surface; rest for 10 minutes. Between bones, cut lamb; drizzle juices from foil.

Nutrition Information

11. Provencal Lamb With Mediterranean Vegetables

Serving: Makes 4 servings | Prep: | Cook: | Ready in:

Ingredients

- 2 teaspoons coriander seeds
- 2 teaspoons fennel seeds
- 2 teaspoons dried thyme
- 1 teaspoon salt
- 1/2 teaspoon ground black pepper
- 1 teaspoon olive oil
- 1 8-rib rack of lamb (about 1 1/2 pounds), well trimmed
- Mediterranean Vegetables

Direction

- Grind initial 3 ingredients coarsely in a spice grinder/blender; put into small bowl. Stir in pepper and salt. Rub oil on lamb then spice mixture. Put lamb on baking sheet; sit for 1 hour.
- Preheat an oven to 425°F. Roast the lamb for 25 minutes till inserted thermometer in middle of meat reads 130°F for medium-rare. Sit for 10 minutes. Between ribs, cut lamb to chops; on each plate, put 2 chops. Put Mediterranean veggies alongside.

Nutrition Information

12. Rack Of Lamb And Cherry Tomatoes

Serving: Makes 4 servings | Prep: 10mins | Cook: 50mins | Ready in:

Ingredients

- 1 2-pound rack of lamb (about 8 ribs)
- 3 tablespoons olive oil, divided
- 3 teaspoons chopped fresh rosemary, divided
- 2 12-ounce containers cherry tomatoes

Direction

- Preheat an oven to 425°F. Rub 1 tbsp. oil on lamb; sprinkle 1 1/2 tsp. rosemary then pepper and salt. Put on big rimmed baking sheet. In a big bowl, put tomatoes, 1 1/2 tsp. rosemary and 2 tbsp. oil. Sprinkle pepper and salt; toss to coat then scatter around lamb. Roast tomatoes and lamb for 30 minutes till inserted thermometer in thickest lamb part reads 135°F for medium rare. Allow to rest for 10 minutes. Between bones, cut lamb to individual chops; put onto platter with the tomatoes.

Nutrition Information

- Calories: 737
- Sodium: 102 mg(4%)
- Fiber: 2 g(8%)
- Total Carbohydrate: 7 g(2%)
- Cholesterol: 126 mg(42%)
- Protein: 26 g(51%)
- Total Fat: 67 g(104%)
- Saturated Fat: 27 g(133%)

13. Rack Of Lamb With Pecan Chipotle Sauce

Serving: Makes 4 servings | Prep: | Cook: | Ready in:

Ingredients

- 2 tablespoons olive oil
- 1/2 small white onion, chopped
- 1 garlic clove, chopped
- 1/2 cup chopped pecans
- 4 cups water
- 8 fresh cilantro sprigs
- 1 teaspoon finely chopped canned chipotle chiles plus 2 tablespoons adobo sauce
- 1/4 cup chile seeds (from any dried but not smoked chile, such as ancho or pasilla)
- 3/4 teaspoon aniseed
- 1/2 teaspoon ground allspice
- 1 (1-inch piece) canela* or cinnamon stick
- 2 whole cloves
- 2 (1 1/4- to 1 1/2-pound) racks of lamb, fat trimmed, frenched (trimmed between bones)

Direction

- In medium saucepan, heat oil over medium-high heat. Put in onion, sauté for 2 minutes or until translucent. Put in garlic, sauté for 1 minute. Put in cilantro, pecans and 4 cups water. Boil for 10 minutes. Mix in adobo sauce and chipotle chiles. Take the cilantro out. In blender, puree the mixture. Put back to the saucepan, boil for 20 minutes or until reduced to one and a half cups. Season salt to the sauce. (You can make one day in advance. Chill, with cover. Reheat to use.)
- Start preheating the oven to 350°F. In large skillet, toast chile seeds for 3 minutes over medium-high heat, until aromatic, shaking the pan constantly. Place the seeds into spice grinder. Put in spices and grind very finely. Sprinkle salt over the lamb. Add spice mixture to coat. Arrange the lamb on the heavy rimmed baking sheet, bone side down. Roast lamb on medium-rare for 25 minutes or until thermometer reads 125°F when inserted into the thickest part of the meat. Allow the lamb to stand for 5 minutes. Chop the lamb. Add the sauce over top and enjoy.

Nutrition Information

- Calories: 1016
- Total Fat: 95 g(146%)
- Saturated Fat: 36 g(182%)
- Sodium: 238 mg(10%)
- Fiber: 2 g(9%)
- Total Carbohydrate: 5 g(2%)
- Cholesterol: 173 mg(58%)
- Protein: 35 g(70%)

14. Rack Of Lamb With Port And Black Olive Sauce

Serving: Serves 4 | Prep: | Cook: |Ready in:

Ingredients

- 2 cups beef stock or canned beef broth
- 2 cups chicken stock or canned low-salt chicken broth
- 2/3 cup ruby Port
- 1/3 cup minced shallots
- 2 teaspoons minced fresh thyme
- 2 tablespoons (1/4 stick) unsalted butter, room temperature
- 1 tablespoon all purpose flour
- 2 1 1/4- to 1 1/2-pound racks of lamb, trimmed
- 1/4 cup Dijon mustard
- 3/4 cup (packed) fresh breadcrumbs from crustless French bread
- 3/4 cup freshly grated Parmesan cheese (about 2 1/4 ounces)
- 6 tablespoons chopped fresh parsley
- 3 tablespoons unsalted butter, melted
- 1 1/2 tablespoons minced garlic
- 1/2 cup chopped pitted Kalamata olives

Direction

- Preparation: Boil the first 5 ingredients for around 35 minutes in a large, heavy saucepan on medium-high heat, or till the mixture is reduced to 1 1/2 cups. In a small bowl, combine flour and 2 tablespoons of butter till a paste forms. Whisk the paste into the sauce; simmer for around 3 minutes, or till thickened slightly. Strain into a heavy, small saucepan. Set the oven at 450°F and start preheating. Arrange lamb on a baking sheet. Spread with mustard. In a small bowl, combine garlic, butter, parsley, cheese and breadcrumbs; press onto the lamb. Bake the lamb to the desired doneness, for around 25 minutes for medium-rare. Simmer the sauce. Stir in olives. Cut the lamb between the ribs into chops. Serve accompanied with the sauce.

Nutrition Information

- Calories: 1255
- Cholesterol: 231 mg(77%)
- Protein: 49 g(99%)
- Total Fat: 102 g(157%)
- Saturated Fat: 48 g(239%)
- Sodium: 1215 mg(51%)
- Fiber: 3 g(11%)
- Total Carbohydrate: 30 g(10%)

15. Rack Of Lamb With Swiss Chard

Serving: Makes 8 servings | Prep: 1hours | Cook: 2hours | Ready in:

Ingredients

- 1/2 cup sweet (red) vermouth
- 1/2 cup golden raisins
- 1 medium onion, chopped
- 2 tablespoons extra-virgin olive oil
- 2 large bunches green Swiss chard (1 pound total), stems and center ribs reserved for another use and leaves coarsely chopped
- 2 tablespoons pine nuts, toasted
- 4 (8-rib) frenched racks of lamb (each about 1 1/2 pound), trimmed of all but a thin layer of fat
- 1/2 cup Dijon mustard

- 2 teaspoons finely chopped thyme
- 1 teaspoon finely chopped rosemary
- Equipment: kitchen string
- Accompaniment: roasted red peppers

Direction

- Swiss chard stuffing: Boil raisins and vermouth in a small saucepan; take off heat. Steep for 15 minutes till raisins are plump and soft.
- Cook onion in oil in a big heavy skillet on medium low heat for 5-8 minutes till onion is tender yet not brown, occasionally mixing. Add 1/4 tsp. pepper, 1/2 tsp. salt, raisins with any leftover vermouth and chard; cook on medium heat for 12 minutes till liquid evaporates and chard is tender, constantly turning chard with tongs. Put in a bowl; mix nuts in. Cool.
- Lamb: create 1 long incision, cutting as near to bones as possible, to separate meat of every rack from bones, don't cut all the way through, stop 1/2-in. from the bottom. Roll away meat from bones to make long opening; season inside with pepper and salt. Use stuffing to fill; roll back meat over the stuffing. Use string to tie the meat to bones between every 2 ribs.
- Preheat an oven with rack in the center to 400°F.
- Mix rosemary, thyme and mustard; spread on both sides of every rack. Put lamb racks in a big heavy shallow baking pan; pair racks so they stand up with bones interlocking yet leave space between them at the base.
- Roast lamb for 25-35 minutes till inserted instant-read thermometer in the middle of the meat without touching the bone reads 130°F to get medium-rare; stand for 15 minutes, loosely covered.
- Cut every rack for 4 double chops; discard the string. Serve over roasted red peppers.
- You can make stuffing 1 da ahead, covered, chilled.

Nutrition Information

- Calories: 3122
- Total Fat: 284 g(437%)
- Saturated Fat: 123 g(614%)
- Sodium: 640 mg(27%)
- Fiber: 1 g(5%)
- Total Carbohydrate: 10 g(3%)
- Cholesterol: 624 mg(208%)
- Protein: 121 g(241%)

16. Roast Rack Of Lamb

Serving: 8 | Prep: 20mins | Cook: |Ready in:

Ingredients

- 2 1-pound French-style lamb rib roasts (8 ribs each)
- 1 cup merlot or other dry red wine
- 2 cloves garlic, minced, divided
- ½ teaspoon ground nutmeg
- 3 tablespoons olive oil, divided
- 1 tablespoon butter
- 1 tablespoon snipped fresh rosemary
- 2 cups soft breadcrumbs
- 3 tablespoons dried cranberries
- 1 tablespoon dried lavender
- ½ teaspoon salt
- ½ teaspoon ground black pepper

Direction

- Peel off fell/membrane and fat layer on roast if present, down to the silver skin; put lamb in big sealable plastic bag in the shallow baking dish. Add nutmeg, 1 garlic clove and wine; seal bag. Marinate for 4-24 hours in the fridge, occasionally turning bag.
- Heat 1 tbsp. each butter and oil on medium heat in a medium skillet. Add leftover 1 garlic clove and rosemary; cook for 1 minute. Add the breadcrumbs; mix and cook for 3 minutes; take off heat. Add pepper, salt, lavender and cranberries; mix in leftover 2 tbsp. oil.

- Preheat an oven to 450°F. Take lamb from marinade; put marinade aside. Put lamb into foil-lined shallow roasting pan, bone-side down; evenly pat crumb mixture on lamb. Put reserved marinade into roasting pan.
- Roast for 25-30 minutes till an instant-read thermometer reads 140°F for medium rare or to 155°F for medium, uncovered. Loosely cover with foil at final 5 minutes of roasting to avoid overbrowning; stand for 15 minutes.

Nutrition Information

- Calories: 212 calories;
- Total Fat: 11
- Saturated Fat: 3
- Sodium: 255
- Fiber: 1
- Cholesterol: 36
- Total Carbohydrate: 9
- Sugar: 0
- Protein: 11

17. Roast Rack Of Lamb With Mint Sauce

Serving: Serves 6 | Prep: | Cook: | Ready in:

Ingredients

- 3 8-chop racks of lamb, trimmed
- 6 tablespoons Dijon mustard
- 3 cups fresh white breadcrumbs
- 6 tablespoons chopped fresh mint
- Fresh mint sprigs
- 1 cup plus 2 tablespoons chopped fresh mint
- 1/2 cup canned beef broth
- 1/3 cup minced shallots
- 6 tablespoons red wine vinegar
- 1/4 cup sugar
- 2 teaspoons cornstarch

Direction

- For the lamb: Turn the oven to 450°F to preheat. Sprinkle pepper and salt over the lamb. Spread over each lamb rack on each side with 1 tablespoon mustard. In a medium-sized bowl, combine mint and breadcrumbs. Press onto the lamb with the breadcrumb mixture to fully coat.
- On a large rimmed baking sheet, place the lamb with the meat-side turning up. Roast the lamb for 10 minutes. Lower the oven heat to 350°F. Roast for another 20 minutes until a thermometer displays 130°F for medium-rare when you insert it into the lamb.
- Remove the lamb to a work surface. Make a tent with foil and let sit for 5 minutes. Slice the lamb racks between the bones into chops. On dishes, place the chops. Use mint sprigs to garnish, passing Mint Sauce separately.
- For the sauce: In a heavy small non-aluminum saucepan, mix together sugar, vinegar, shallots, broth, and 1 cup mint. Whisk over medium heat until the sugar melts. Simmer for 2 minutes. Take away from heat. Put a cover on and let sit for 2 hours.
- Drain the sauce into a big glass measuring cup. In the same saucepan, put cornstarch. Slowly stir in the sauce. Simmer over medium heat, whisking continually. Whisk for 2 minutes until the sauce is translucent and partially thickens. Take away from heat. Let cool to room temperature. (You can prepare 1 day in advance. Put a cover on and chill. Let come to room temperature before continuing). Mix in the leftover 2 tablespoons mint. Use pepper and salt to season. Prepare approximately 1 cup.

Nutrition Information

- Calories: 3221
- Saturated Fat: 121 g(604%)
- Sodium: 1084 mg(45%)
- Fiber: 4 g(15%)
- Total Carbohydrate: 51 g(17%)
- Cholesterol: 602 mg(201%)
- Protein: 124 g(247%)

- Total Fat: 276 g(425%)

18. Roast Rack Of Lamb With Natural Jus

Serving: 4 main-course servings | Prep: | Cook: | Ready in:

Ingredients

- 1 american rack of lamb or 2 new zealand racks of lamb
- salt and pepper to taste
- trimmings from the rack or 1 pound (450 grams) lamb stew meat cut into 1/2-inch (1 cm) pieces
- broth or water as needed

Direction

- Season lamb; let it reach room temperature. Preheat an oven to 230°C/450°F.
- Spread lamb trimmings/stew meat on bottom of roasting pan just big enough to hold rack; roast for 30 minutes till lightly browned.
- Put rack over trimmings (trimming base is called foncage). Slide into oven; roast for 25 minutes till springy to touch. Rest for 15 minutes, covered loosely with aluminum foil.
- Put roasting pan over stove; put 250-ml/1cup broth over. Boil; boil till caramelized juices make brown crust on roasting pan. Pour liquid fat floating on the top out. Use 250-ml/1 cup broth to deglaze pan; scrape juices up. Repeat caramelization as many times as needed before deglazing the last time. Pass jus at the table in a sauce boat.

Nutrition Information

19. Roast Rack Of Lamb With Orange Chipotle Purée

Serving: Makes 6 servings | Prep: | Cook: |Ready in:

Ingredients

- 2 medium-size red bell peppers
- 2 tablespoons rice vinegar
- 4 teaspoons sugar
- 2 teaspoons ground coriander
- 1 teaspoon grated orange peel
- 1/2 teaspoon minced canned chipotle chili*
- 1/2 teaspoon ground cumin
- 3 racks of lamb (about 1 pound each)

Direction

- Char red bell peppers till blackened on all sides in broiler/above gas flame. In paper bag, enclose peppers; stand for 10 minutes. Peel peppers and seed; coarsely chop. In blender, mix peppers with next 6 ingredients; puree.
- Preheat an oven to 450°F. Sprinkle pepper and salt on lamb; put into roasting pan. Roast for 25 minutes to get medium-rare or to desired doneness. In medium saucepan, cook orange-chipotle puree on medium heat, occasionally mixing, till heated through. Cut lamb to double chops then serve with sauce.

Nutrition Information

- Calories: 643
- Sodium: 100 mg(4%)
- Fiber: 1 g(5%)
- Total Carbohydrate: 6 g(2%)
- Cholesterol: 126 mg(42%)
- Protein: 25 g(49%)
- Total Fat: 57 g(88%)
- Saturated Fat: 25 g(126%)

20. Roasted Racks Of Lamb With Artichokes, Red Onions, And Garlic Cloves

Serving: Serves 4 | Prep: | Cook: | Ready in:

Ingredients

- 1 lemon, quartered
- 4 artichokes
- 1 pound Jerusalem artichokes (sunchokes)*, peeled and cut into 1-inch wedges
- 4 medium red onions (about 1 1/2 pounds total), each cut into 6 wedges, leaving enough of root ends attached to keep wedges intact
- 16 unpeeled large garlic cloves plus 1 tablespoon finely chopped garlic
- 2 tablespoons plus 2 teaspoons extra-virgin olive oil
- 1 teaspoon vegetable oil
- 2 frenched racks of lamb** (8 ribs, about 1 1/4 pounds each), trimmed of all but a thin layer of fat
- 3 tablespoons fresh oregano leaves or 2 teaspoons dried oregano, crumbled
- 1 1/2 teaspoons coarse salt
- 1/2 teaspoon freshly ground black pepper
- 1/2 cup chicken broth
- *available at specialty produce markets and many supermarkets
- **available by request from butchers

Direction

- Squeeze juice from the 2 lemon quarters, putting squeezed quarters into water, into bowl of water. Break off 1 artichoke's stem; discard. Bend back outer leaves till they snap off near the base; remove several more leaf layers till you reach pale inner leaves. Trim sides and base of artichoke using very sharp and stainless-steel knife; cut top 1 1/2-in. off. Cut artichoke to quarters; cut spiky purple-tipped leaves and choke away. Rub leftover lemon quarter all over artichoke quarters; drop into bowl with water. In same manner, prep leftover 3 artichokes; if needed, use other lemon quarter.
- Preheat an oven to 475°F.
- Blanch artichokes for 3 minutes in saucepan with boiling salted water; put into bowl with a slotted spoon. Blanch Jerusalem artichokes for 5 minutes in boiling salted water; drain.
- Toss 2 tbsp. olive oil, pepper and salt to taste, garlic cloves, onions, Jerusalem artichokes and artichokes in a 17x11 1/2x2-in. flameproof roasting pan; roast veggies for 20 minutes in center of oven.
- Heat a 12-in. heavy skillet till hot on medium high heat as veggies roast. Season lamb racks with pepper and salt as skillet heats. Put vegetable oil in skillet; brown lamb for 2 minutes, meaty sides down. Flip lamb; brown for 2 minutes. Put lamb onto plate; slightly cool.
- Mix 2 leftover 2 tsp. olive oil, freshly ground pepper, coarse salt, oregano and chopped garlic in a small bowl; rub all over the lamb.
- Take pan from oven; mix veggies. Put lamb, rib sides down, on veggies; roast till meat thermometer in the fleshy section reads 130°F for medium-rare for 20 minutes.
- Take 8 cloves of garlic from pan; squeeze garlic from skins into blender. Add broth; blend till smooth. Put leftover veggies and lamb onto heated platter; keep juices in pan. Rest for 10 minutes, loosely covered.
- Add pepper and salt to taste and garlic broth to pan; deglaze over stove on medium high heat, scraping brown bits up. Boil sauce till slightly thicken; put into sauceboat.
- Halve lamb racks or to individual chops; serve with sauce and veggies.

Nutrition Information

- Calories: 3487
- Protein: 133 g(265%)
- Total Fat: 296 g(456%)
- Saturated Fat: 127 g(636%)
- Sodium: 1279 mg(53%)
- Fiber: 10 g(42%)

- Total Carbohydrate: 72 g(24%)
- Cholesterol: 630 mg(210%)

21. Sausage Wrapped Lamb Chops With Tapanade Butter

Serving: Makes 4 servings | Prep: | Cook: | Ready in:

Ingredients

- 1 8-rib rack of lamb, frenched, trimmed of all fat, cut into 4 double chops
- 1 tablespoon olive oil
- 1 teaspoon butter
- 1/4 cup chopped shallots
- 2 garlic cloves, minced
- 3/4 teaspoon ground cumin
- 4 ounces ground lamb
- 4 ounces ground pork
- 1 large egg
- 1/2 teaspoon salt
- 1/4 teaspoon ground black pepper
- 1 teaspoon brandy
- 1 teaspoon Madeira
- Nonstick vegetable oil spray
- Tapanade Butter

Direction

- Sprinkle pepper and salt on chops. Heat oil on high heat in a big nonstick skillet. Add chops; sear for 1 minute per side till just brown. Put onto plate; cool.
- Melt butter on medium heat in small nonstick skillet. Add garlic and shallots; sauté for 3 minutes till soft. Add cumin; mix for 30 seconds. Put into medium bowl; cool. Mix Madeira, brandy, 1/4 tsp. pepper, 1/2 tsp. salt, egg, pork and ground lamb into shallot mixture; divide to meat mixture to 4 even portions. Press every meat mixture portion around every lamb chop, fully covering meat, leaving bones exposed, pressing to adhere. You can make it 6 hours ahead. Cover; refrigerate.
- Preheat an oven to 450°F. Spray nonstick spray on rimmed baking sheet. On sheet, put lamb chops; roast for 20 minutes till inserted thermometer in middle of chops reads 125-130°F for medium rare. On each of the 4 plates, put 1 double chop. Put 2 slices tapanade butter on each.

Nutrition Information

- Calories: 1759
- Protein: 69 g(138%)
- Total Fat: 161 g(248%)
- Saturated Fat: 67 g(335%)
- Sodium: 565 mg(24%)
- Fiber: 0 g(2%)
- Total Carbohydrate: 3 g(1%)
- Cholesterol: 391 mg(130%)

22. Sun Dried Tomato And Garlic Crusted Rack Of Lamb

Serving: Makes 6 servings | Prep: | Cook: | Ready in:

Ingredients

- 2 6- to 7-ounce jars oil-packed sun-dried tomatoes with herbs, drained well, oil reserved
- 8 large garlic cloves, peeled
- 2 large shallots, peeled, halved
- 1 tablespoon dried oregano
- 3 tablespoons olive oil
- 4 garlic cloves, peeled
- 3 large fresh rosemary sprigs
- 2 2-pound racks of lamb (8 chops each), trimmed, frenched

Direction

- For tomato and garlic crust: Set oven to 350F to preheat. Arrange shallots, garlic, and 1/4 cup reserved tomato oil in a small baking dish; scatter pepper and salt over and tent with

aluminum foil. Bake for about 45 minutes in the preheated oven until garlic is tender.
- Pour garlic mixture into a food processor. Put in oregano and tomatoes. Process until mixture forms a paste. Season mixture with pepper and salt. Mixture can be prepared 2 days in advance. Pour mixture into a bowl; chill, covered.
- For lamb: Heat oil over medium-high heat in a heavy large skillet. Put in rosemary and garlic. Sauté in heated oil for about 5 minutes or until garlic is browned. Remove and discard rosemary and garlic. Scatter pepper and salt over all sides of lamb. Place 1 lamb rack, rounded side down, to the skillet. Sear for about 5 minutes until golden brown. Remove lamb rack to a large rimmed baking sheet, rounded side up. Do the same with the rest of lamb rack.
- Set oven to 450°F to preheat. Roast lamb in the preheated oven for 18 minutes. Take out of the oven. Distribute 1/3 cup of tomato-garlic paste into a thin layer over top of each lamb rack. Place lamb back into the oven; roast for about 3 minutes more or until a thermometer pinned into the center reads 134°F. Allow lamb to sit for 10 minutes. Slice between bones into separate chops; serve right away.

Nutrition Information

- Calories: 1051
- Protein: 37 g(73%)
- Total Fat: 92 g(141%)
- Saturated Fat: 36 g(178%)
- Sodium: 293 mg(12%)
- Fiber: 5 g(22%)
- Total Carbohydrate: 23 g(8%)
- Cholesterol: 168 mg(56%)

Chapter 2: Lamb Shank Recipes

***

23. Beer Braised Lamb Shanks

Serving: 2 | Prep: 15mins | Cook: 3hours10mins | Ready in:

Ingredients

- 2 lamb shanks
- 1 teaspoon salt, divided, or to taste
- freshly ground black pepper to taste
- 1 tablespoon olive oil
- 1 onion, chopped
- 2 large carrots, cut into 1-inch pieces
- 1 large stalk celery, cut into 1-inch pieces
- 3 cloves garlic, finely chopped
- 2 teaspoons tomato paste
- 1 (12 fluid ounce) can or bottle beer
- 2 sprigs rosemary
- 1 pinch cayenne pepper

Direction

- Season lamb shanks with pepper and salt.
- In a deep-sided pan/pot, heat olive oil on moderately high heat. Put in lamb; cook for 5 minutes till browned, flipping as necessary. Take out of pan; lower heat to moderate.
- Put garlic, celery, carrot and chopped onion in pan; season with big pinch of salt. Mix and cook for 2 minutes till veggie juices begin to come out. Add tomato paste; mix for 1 minute to coat. Add beer; mix in rosemary. Put heat on high; simmer sauce mixture.
- Toss lamb shanks in sauce mixture. Lower heat to low; cover. Simmer, turning lamb after 1 hour, for 2 hours till lamb is almost fork-tender. Take off heat; cool for 30 minutes

minimum to room temperature. Refrigerate for 8 hours – overnight.
- If desired, skim fat off top of sauce; cover. Simmer lamb on low heat. Flip; simmer for 45 minutes till meat is nearly falling off bone and is fork tender. To keep warm, put lamb shanks into a bowl.
- Boil sauce on high heat; boil for 3 minutes till reduced by half yet not too thick. Season with cayenne pepper and salt. Plate lamb shanks; put sauce over.

Nutrition Information

- Calories: 387 calories;
- Total Fat: 14.4
- Sodium: 1363
- Total Carbohydrate: 22.4
- Cholesterol: 82
- Protein: 29.8

24. Chef John's Braised Lamb Shanks

Serving: 4 | Prep: 15mins | Cook: 2hours10mins | Ready in:

Ingredients

- 4 lamb shanks
- salt and ground black pepper to taste
- 1 tablespoon vegetable oil
- 1 onion, sliced
- 4 cloves garlic, sliced
- 1 pinch salt
- 1 teaspoon tomato paste
- 1 teaspoon chipotle chile powder
- 1 teaspoon ancho chile powder
- 1/4 teaspoon ground cinnamon
- 1 cup chicken broth
- 3 jalapeno peppers, seeded and sliced
- 1 red bell pepper, seeded and sliced
- 1/2 cup chicken broth
- 1/4 cup chopped cilantro
- 1 pinch salt and ground black pepper to taste

Direction

- Set oven to 325°F (165°C) to preheat. Liberally season lamb shanks with black pepper and salt.
- Heat vegetable oil over medium-high heat in a large Dutch oven. Arrange seasoned lamb shanks in the Dutch oven; cook for about 10 minutes, turning, until all sides are browned. Remove lamb shanks to a plate. Drain off any remaining oil and grease, retaining 1 tablespoon grease in the Dutch oven.
- Sauté garlic, onion, and a dash of salt in the Dutch oven; reduce heat to medium-low, then cook and stir for about 5 minutes or until onions are tender and transparent. Stir in ground cinnamon, ancho chile powder, chipotle chile powder, and tomato paste until well incorporated.
- Stream 1 cup chicken broth over onion mixture. Turn heat to high; once liquid comes to a boil, put lamb shanks into the Dutch oven. Cook in the preheated oven, covered, for 1 1/2 hours.
- Take the Dutch oven out of the oven and mix in 1/2 cup chicken stock, red bell pepper, and jalapeno pepper; bring mixture to a boil on the stovetop. Place the pan back into the oven; cook without covering for about 20 minutes or until lamb shanks is easily flaked using a fork. Remove lamb to a plate.
- Set the Dutch oven over high heat on the stovetop; boil liquid, cook for about 5 minutes until liquid is reduced and thickened, skimming off any foam. Mix in cilantro; sprinkle with pepper and salt to season. Ladle sauce over lamb shanks to serve.

Nutrition Information

- Calories: 289 calories;
- Sodium: 82
- Total Carbohydrate: 9.5
- Cholesterol: 89
- Protein: 28

- Total Fat: 15

25. Flavorful Persian Braised Lamb Shanks

Serving: 4 | Prep: 20mins | Cook: 3hours30mins | Ready in:

Ingredients

- 4 lamb shanks
- 1/4 cup olive oil, divided
- 4 tablespoons salt
- 2 teaspoons ground turmeric
- 1 teaspoon ground cinnamon
- 1 teaspoon ground cardamom
- 1 teaspoon ground black pepper
- 1 teaspoon ground cumin
- 1/2 teaspoon ground nutmeg
- 1 large onion, chopped
- 3 cloves garlic
- 1/3 cup hot water
- 2 limes, juiced
- 2 teaspoons rosewater
- 1/4 teaspoon crumbled saffron
- 1/2 cup red wine
- 1 tablespoon chopped fresh parsley
- 3 sprigs thyme, leaves picked
- 1/2 teaspoon grated lime zest
- 2 bay leaves
- 6 cups hot chicken broth

Direction

- Brush lamb shanks with one tablespoon of olive oil and then cover with salt.
- In a small bowl, combine together turmeric, nutmeg, cinnamon, cumin, black pepper, and cardamom. Drizzle over the lamb shanks. Leave the lamb shanks to marinate for one hour at room temperature.
- In a large pot, heat one tablespoon of olive oil and add onion. Cook while stirring for 10 to 15 minutes until browned. Mix in the garlic and then cook while stirring for about 1 minute until fragrant. Take out from the heat.
- In a small bowl, whisk together saffron, hot water, rose water, and lime juice. Cover the bowl and allow to steep for 10 minutes.
- Over medium-high heat, heat the remaining two tablespoons of olive oil in a large pot. Then cook the lamb shanks in batches for 5 to 8 minutes per batch until browned. Place the lamb shanks onto a plate.
- Whisk the wine into pot and scrape off any browned bits from the bottom. Add in the onion and garlic mixture, parsley, steeped saffron mixture, bay leaves, thyme, and lime zest. Place lamb shanks back into the pot. Add chicken broth to cover and heat to boil. Decrease the heat to medium-low and let to simmer while covered for about 2 1/2 hours until the lamb shanks become tender.
- Preheat the oven to 120 degrees C (250 degrees F).
- Uncover the pot and let to simmer for about 20 minutes until the broth decrease a bit. Place the lamb shanks into an oven-safe dish.
- Transfer the lamb shanks into the preheated oven to keep them warm.
- Heat the broth to boil and let to simmer for about 10 minutes until thickened. Scoop the broth on top of lamb shanks.

Nutrition Information

- Calories: 432 calories;
- Total Fat: 27.2
- Sodium: 8488
- Total Carbohydrate: 12.6
- Cholesterol: 97
- Protein: 28.9

26. Grandmother's Lamb Recipe

Serving: 6 | Prep: 25mins | Cook: 1hours50mins | Ready in:

Ingredients

- Grandmother's Chile Paste:
- 1 teaspoon cumin seeds
- 6 dried red chile peppers (preferably Kashmiri)
- 1/4 cup apple cider vinegar
- 1 clove garlic, coarsely chopped - or more to taste
- 3 tablespoons vegetable oil
- 2 onions, finely chopped
- 2 teaspoons ginger garlic paste
- 5 tablespoons tomato paste
- 1 teaspoon ground red pepper (cayenne) or to taste
- 1/4 teaspoon ground turmeric
- 1/4 teaspoon ground cinnamon
- 1/4 teaspoon ground cloves
- 2 pounds lamb shanks, cut into 1 1/2-inch pieces
- 1/2 teaspoon salt
- 3 cups water
- 1 tablespoon chopped fresh cilantro

Direction

- Put cumin seeds into a dry skillet over medium heat. Toast for one minute until they are darker brown and give off the roasted fragrance, stirring constantly. Scrape seeds into the bowl, let it cool. Grind with a clean spice grinder or a mortar and pestle when cool. Put ground seed aside.
- If necessary, discard the stems of the chiles. In a bowl, soak the pods in apple cider vinegar at least 60 mins until soft. In a food processor or blender, put softened chiles with garlic, cumin, and vinegar. Pulse for 30-60 seconds until ground into paste or as needed.
- In a large pot, heat vegetable oil over the medium heat, cook while stirring onions for 10 mins until lightly browned. Mix in one teaspoon Grandmother's Chile Paste mixture (Or as preferred) and ginger garlic paste. Lower the heat to medium-low, fry onions for 5 mins with spice pastes to blend the flavors. Mix in cloves, cinnamon, turmeric, ground red pepper and tomato paste, then simmer. Cook for 20 mins to blend the flavors.
- Mix in lamb shank pieces, stir to taste in salt. Simmer about 20 mins, stir in water. Boil sauce and lamb. Lower the heat to a simmer, simmer for 45 mins longer until the sauce has thickened and the lamb is very tender. Scatter on top with the chopped cilantro. Then serve.

Nutrition Information

- Calories: 262 calories;
- Total Carbohydrate: 10.8
- Cholesterol: 59
- Protein: 19.1
- Total Fat: 15.4
- Sodium: 409

27. Heavenly Lamb Shanks

Serving: 4 | Prep: 20mins | Cook: 3hours | Ready in:

Ingredients

- 1/2 cup olive oil
- 4 (1 pound) lamb shanks
- 2/3 cup all-purpose flour
- 1 leek, halved and cut into 1/2-inch pieces
- 2 stalks celery, chopped
- 2 carrots, chopped
- 2 onions, cut into chunks
- 12 cloves garlic, unpeeled
- 1 bay leaf
- 1 teaspoon whole black peppercorns
- 1 sprig thyme
- 1 sprig rosemary
- 1 1/2 cups red wine
- 3 cups chicken stock
- 1 pinch Sea salt to taste

Direction

- Preheat an oven to 150 °C or 300 °F.

- In heavy, metal roasting pan, heat olive oil on stove over moderately-high heat. To coat thoroughly, toss shanks along with flour; then throw away excess. In hot oil, scorch shanks till nicely browned on every side, then take away from pan and reserve.
- Into roasting pan, put garlic, onion, carrot, celery and leek. Cook till softened and lightly browned, mixing continuously; for about 5 minutes. Add the rosemary sprigs, thyme, peppercorns and bay leaf to taste. Add chicken stock and red wine, raise heat to high, and simmer. Season with sea salt to taste, and top vegetables with lamb shanks.
- Place heavy aluminum foil on roasting pan to tightly cover, and put into preheated oven. Bake slowly for 2 1/2 to 3 hours till meat is softened and falls off the bone. Get rid of herb stems and bay leaf then serve shanks along with sauce and vegetables.

Nutrition Information

- Calories: 824 calories;
- Sodium: 793
- Total Carbohydrate: 34.8
- Cholesterol: 173
- Protein: 60.8
- Total Fat: 41.3

28. Jinx Proof Braised Lamb Shanks

Serving: 6 | Prep: 20mins | Cook: 2hours30mins | Ready in:

Ingredients

- 5 1/2 pounds lamb shanks
- 2 tablespoons olive oil
- salt and freshly ground black pepper to taste
- 1/2 teaspoon dried rosemary
- 1/2 teaspoon dried thyme
- 1 tablespoon butter
- 1 onion, diced
- 1 rib celery, diced
- 1 large carrot, diced
- 1 1/2 tablespoons all-purpose flour
- 4 cloves garlic, minced
- 1/2 cup red wine
- 1 cup chicken broth
- 1 cup water
- 1 tablespoon balsamic vinegar
- 1/8 teaspoon ground cinnamon
- 1 teaspoon minced fresh rosemary leaves

Direction

- Preheat an oven to 230°C/450°F.
- Put lamb shanks into roasting pan. Drizzle olive oil; season using thyme, dried rosemary, black pepper and salt. Toss lamb shanks with seasonings and oil to coat.
- In preheated oven, roast for 30 minutes till lamb is browned.
- Lower oven heat to 165°C/325°F.
- Melt butter on medium high heat in a saucepan; mix and cook carrot, celery and onion in hot butter for 10 minutes till onion is browned. Mix flour into veggies till mixed; stir in garlic. Mix and cook for 1 minute.
- Put red wine into veggie mixture; stir to mix. Mix in cinnamon, balsamic vinegar, water and chicken stock; put sauce on lamb shanks in roasting pan. Use aluminum foil to cover roasting pan, loosely sealing foil to sauce can slightly reduce while cooking.
- Bake the lamb shanks for 1 hour; turn over. Put foil back onto dish; bake for 1 hour till fork easily inserts into meat. Put lamb shanks into big bowl; cover with foil. Rest lamb for 10 minutes.
- Put braising liquid into saucepan on high heat; boil, skim fat as it slightly thickens and reduces, for 10 minutes. Mix chopped rosemary into sauce; check the levels of pepper and salt. Serve pan sauce with lamb shanks.

Nutrition Information

- Calories: 502 calories;

- Cholesterol: 169
- Protein: 49.6
- Total Fat: 27.3
- Sodium: 153
- Total Carbohydrate: 8.2

- Total Fat: 34.3
- Sodium: 1540
- Total Carbohydrate: 38.5
- Cholesterol: 166
- Protein: 52.7

29. Lamb Casserole

Serving: 6 | Prep: 20mins | Cook: 1hours30mins | Ready in:

Ingredients

- 2 sprigs fresh parsley
- 2 sprigs fresh thyme
- 2 bay leaves
- 2 pounds lamb shank, cooked and diced
- 1 pound cubed ham steak
- 10 small onions
- 5 tomatoes - blanched, peeled and chopped
- 2 cloves garlic, chopped
- 4 cups chicken stock
- 2 (15 ounce) cans cannellini beans, drained and rinsed
- 6 links pork sausage links, halved

Direction

- Tie together the sprigs of thyme and parsley with bay leaves or arrange them in a cheesecloth, then tie closed, because you can easily discard the herbs later. In a large saucepan, place stock, garlic, tomato, onion, ham, lamb and the herb bundle over medium-high heat.
- Bring to a boil. Lower the heat to low and simmer for about 60 minutes. Mix in sausage and beans and keep simmering about 15 minutes. If you prefer thicker consistency, simmer for a few more minutes.

Nutrition Information

- Calories: 683 calories;

30. Lamb Osso Buco Slow Cooked

Serving: 4 | Prep: 15mins | Cook: 6hours20mins | Ready in:

Ingredients

- 1/2 cup all-purpose flour
- 2 1/2 pounds lamb shanks
- salt and freshly ground black pepper to taste
- 2 tablespoons unsalted butter
- 1 cup dry white wine
- 1 (14.5 ounce) can diced tomatoes
- 1 1/2 cups chopped onion
- 3/4 cup chicken broth
- 1/2 cup chopped celery
- 5 sprigs fresh thyme, leaves removed

Direction

- Into shallow wide bowl, put flour. Season lamb shanks with pepper and salt all over. Dredge through flour till coated; shake extra flour off.
- Heat a big skillet on medium heat. Add butter; heat till foaming. Cook lamb shanks in hot butter for 5 minutes per side till golden. Put lamb shanks into a cooker.
- Add wine into skillet; boil while using a wooden spoon to scrape browned food bits off bottom of pan. Put into slow cooker. Add thyme leaves, celery, chicken broth, onion and tomatoes with juice in slow cooker.
- Cook on low for 6-8 hours till lamb is nearly falling off bone and very tender. Put lamb shanks onto platter; use aluminum foil to cover.
- Put sauce in slow cooker into a big skillet; simmer for 10-15 minutes on high heat till

sauce reduces to 2 cups. Season sauce with pepper and salt.

Nutrition Information

- Calories: 479 calories;
- Sodium: 439
- Total Carbohydrate: 23.3
- Cholesterol: 128
- Protein: 36.7
- Total Fat: 20.2

31. Lamb Shank

Serving: 6 | Prep: 15mins | Cook: 1hours | Ready in:

Ingredients

- 1 (4 pound) lamb shank
- Marinade:
- 3 tablespoons olive oil
- 1 teaspoon dried rosemary
- 1/4 teaspoon ground thyme
- 1/4 teaspoon dried basil
- 1/4 teaspoon dried parsley
- 1/2 teaspoon dried mint
- 2 tablespoons ground black pepper
- salt to taste (optional)
- 1 pinch cayenne pepper, or to taste (optional)
- Basting Sauce:
- 1/4 cup lemon juice
- 3 tablespoons honey

Direction

- Cut slits in a crisscross pattern (approximately 1 inch apart and 1/2-inch deep) into lamb shank; arrange in a shallow dish.
- In a mixing bowl, combine cayenne pepper, salt, black pepper, mint, parsley, basil, thyme, rosemary, and olive oil; brush oil mixture over the lamb shank evenly. Chill lamb in the fridge for a minimum of 1 hour.
- Prepare grill for medium heat and lightly grease the grate with oil.
- In a small mixing bowl, mix honey and lemon juice together until smooth.
- Cook lamb shank in the preheated grill until center is red and outside is browned, basting with lemon juice mixture every 15 minutes, for about half an hour on each side. An instant-read thermometer pinned into the center should register 125°F (52°C).

Nutrition Information

- Calories: 342 calories;
- Total Carbohydrate: 11.2
- Cholesterol: 110
- Protein: 36.3
- Total Fat: 16.5
- Sodium: 93

32. Lamb Shank Braised In White Wine With Rosemary

Serving: 4 | Prep: 10mins | Cook: 2hours50mins | Ready in:

Ingredients

- 3 tablespoons olive oil
- 4 lamb shanks
- 5 cloves garlic, sliced
- 1 small onion, chopped
- 2 teaspoons chopped fresh rosemary, plus sprigs for garnish
- 1 pinch salt and freshly ground black pepper
- 1 cup dry white wine

Direction

- Heat oil in a big frying pan on medium-high heat. Put shanks in hot pan. Brown all sides for about 12 minutes. Put on a plate.
- Lower heat to medium-low. Add garlic to the pan. Cook for 30-40 seconds. Mix in onion.

Sauté for 6-8 minutes continue cooking until translucent. Put shanks in pan. Season with pepper, salt to taste and 2 tsp. fresh rosemary. Put wine. Bring heat to medium-high. Simmer. Lower heat to low. Simmer, tightly covered, until shanks are very tender when poked with a knife for 2-2 1/2 hours. Flip 1-2 times while cooking. Add water as needed to keep original liquid level. Garnish with rosemary sprigs. Serve shanks.

Nutrition Information

- Calories: 369 calories;
- Protein: 27
- Total Fat: 21.5
- Sodium: 69
- Total Carbohydrate: 4.6
- Cholesterol: 89

33. Lamb Shank Vindaloo

Serving: 4 | Prep: 30mins | Cook: 3hours50mins | Ready in:

Ingredients

- 4 lamb shanks
- 1/2 cup cider vinegar
- 1/4 cup vegetable oil
- 2 teaspoons salt
- 1 tablespoon tamarind concentrate
- 1 1/2 tablespoons garam masala
- 1 onion, chopped
- 8 cloves garlic, peeled
- 1/3 cup sliced fresh ginger
- 1 cup cherry tomatoes
- 1/2 cup water
- 1 1/2 teaspoons cayenne pepper
- 1 1/2 teaspoons paprika
- 1 teaspoon ground cinnamon
- 1 teaspoon ground cumin
- 1 teaspoon ground mustard
- 1 teaspoon ground black pepper
- 3 tablespoons ghee (clarified butter)
- 1 large onion, chopped
- salt and ground black pepper to taste
- 4 teaspoons brown sugar
- 1/2 cup fresh cilantro, for garnish (optional)

Direction

- In a big resealable plastic bag, put lamb shanks. In a bowl, mix garam masala, tamarind concentrate, salt, oil and cider vinegar. Put it in the bag. Squeeze excess air out. Seal bag. Marinade in the fridge for 8 hours to overnight.
- Preheat oven to 230 degrees C/450 degrees F. Get a foil-lined baking sheet and grease it.
- Take out marinated lamb shanks. Put on prepped baking sheet. Season salt on all sides. Roast in preheated oven for 15-20 minutes until well-browned. Keep marinade in bag.
- In a blender, pulse water, cherry tomatoes, ginger, garlic and 1 onion on and off until smooth. Put aside.
- In a small bowl, mix black pepper, dried mustard, cumin, cinnamon, paprika and cayenne pepper.
- In a big stockpot, melt clarified butter on medium-high heat. Sauté 1 onion for 30 minutes until well-browned and soft. Lower heat to medium. Put in cayenne pepper mixture. Stir and cook for 2 minutes until spices are aromatic.
- Put marinade from bag in stockpot. Mix in brown sugar and onion-tomato mixture. Simmer. Put lamb shanks in pan. Lower heat to low. Cook, covered, for 3-4 hours, occasionally turn, until meat is tender and pierced easily with a fork.
- Take lamb from pot. Cover with foil. Bring up heat. Simmer sauce for several minutes. Skim fat from top. Taste and put salt if needed. Put sauce spooned over the top of lamb shanks. Garnish using cilantro. Serve.

Nutrition Information

- Calories: 523 calories;

- Total Fat: 37
- Sodium: 1288
- Total Carbohydrate: 19.7
- Cholesterol: 114
- Protein: 28.7

34. Lamb Shanks With Cilantro Sauce

Serving: 4 | Prep: 15mins | Cook: 3hours30mins | Ready in:

Ingredients

- 1 tablespoon olive oil
- 1/2 red onion, coarsely chopped
- 1 aji amarillo pepper, seeded and coarsely chopped
- 4 cloves garlic
- 1/2 teaspoon ground cumin
- salt and ground black pepper to taste
- 1 bunch cilantro, coarsely chopped
- 1 (10.5 ounce) can beef broth
- 1 cup Riesling wine
- 1 tablespoon olive oil
- 2 lamb shanks
- 1 extra-large baking potato, cut into large chunks
- 1 (1.5 fluid ounce) jigger Peruvian pisco liquor
- 1/2 cup frozen peas

Direction

- Start preheating the oven to 300°F (150°C).
- In a Dutch oven or large oven-safe pot, heat one tablespoon of the olive oil over medium heat. In hot oil, cook while stirring black pepper, salt, cumin, garlic, aji pepper and red onion for 10 mins or until onion starts to brown. Place the cooked onion mixture into a blender. Put in Riesling wine, cilantro, and beef broth. Blend for about 1-2 mins into a smooth sauce.
- In same pot, heat one tablespoon olive oil more over medium heat. In hot oil, brown lamb shanks on all sides, 2 mins each side. Add the cilantro sauce over the lamb shanks. Place on the lid.
- Bake for 120 mins in prepared oven. Put potato chunks into the pot. Add pisco over the vegetables and lamb. Keep baking for 60 more mins or until sauce is thickened slightly and lamb becomes very tender. Discard from the oven. Sprinkle the lamb with peas. Allow peas to heat through for 10 mins with a cover. Allow lamb shanks to cool for 15 mins before enjoying.

Nutrition Information

- Calories: 333 calories;
- Sodium: 311
- Total Carbohydrate: 20.1
- Cholesterol: 45
- Protein: 17.3
- Total Fat: 12.9

35. Meat Gravy

Serving: 30 | Prep: 1hours30mins | Cook: 5hours | Ready in:

Ingredients

- 1/4 cup extra virgin olive oil
- 1 (2 1/2 pound) pork shoulder roast
- 24 cloves garlic, peeled and lightly cracked into large pieces (divided)
- 2 pounds pork spareribs
- 2 pounds beef oxtails, cut into pieces
- 1 lamb shank (optional)
- 8 (28 ounce) cans Italian-style whole peeled tomatoes
- 1 pound hot Italian sausage, casings removed
- 1 pound sweet Italian sausage, casings removed
- 3 (6 ounce) cans tomato paste
- 2 teaspoons salt, or to taste
- fresh ground black pepper to taste

- 1 pinch crushed red pepper flakes
- 1/2 cup Burgundy wine or other dry red wine
- 8 leaves basil, chopped

Direction

- In a large pot over medium-low heat, heat olive oil. In the center of the pot, put pork shoulder, and place 4-5 garlic cloves on edges around the pork.
- Brown all sides of the pork roast; remove to a large baking dish. Use a slotted spoon to take garlic cloves out of the pot and put into a bowl. Do the process again; browning lamb shank, oxtails and pork spareribs, adding 4 cloves of cracked garlic to each batch of meat and putting them into a baking dish. Take each batch of garlic cloves to the bowl when cooked.
- While cooking the meat, strain the cans of tomatoes and their juice. Press the tomatoes through a colander or use a food mill to discard extra pulp and all of seeds. Pour the strained tomatoes into a large bowl and set aside.
- In the same pot over medium heat, cook sausage in olive oil until it is browned, about 10-12 minutes; meanwhile, use a wooden spoon to break up lumps until no longer pink. Pour them into a large bowl and put into the refrigerator while finishing the next steps. When the sausage is well-browned, put the reserved cooked garlic cloves into the pot and whish in red pepper flakes, black pepper, salt, and tomato paste.
- Use a wooden spoon to stir the tomato paste, scraping up the browned bits of meat in the pot. Pour the buildup of juices in the baking dish that is used to cook the meats into the pot. Pour in Burgundy wine; cook while stirring occasionally for about 15 minutes until the liquid is almost evaporated.
- Put in strained tomatoes and juices; add basil and stir well. Heat the sauce while stirring sometimes until it boils with a cover. Take off the lid, put in cooked lamb shank, oxtails, pork ribs and pork shoulder. Lower the heat to low and simmer while stirring sometimes for 4-5 hours.
- Take out the lamb shank, oxtails, pork spareribs and pork shoulder. When cool enough to handle, take the meat away from the bone and chop it finely. Transfer the meat to the pot of sauce, discard the bones.
- Add cooked sausage to the sauce and stir well; simmer for another 1 hour. Taste and adjust the seasonings to your liking.

Nutrition Information

- Calories: 277 calories;
- Cholesterol: 62
- Protein: 19.1
- Total Fat: 16.7
- Sodium: 944
- Total Carbohydrate: 11.7

36. Moroccan Style Lamb Shanks With Apricots

Serving: 2 | Prep: | Cook: | Ready in:

Ingredients

- 2 tablespoons extra-virgin olive oil
- 1 teaspoon cumin seeds
- 1 onion, thinly sliced
- 4 cloves garlic, crushed
- 1 sweet potato, peeled and diced
- 2 (1 pound) lamb shanks
- 1 (14.4 ounce) can chopped canned tomatoes
- 1 1/4 cups chopped dried apricots
- 1 1/2 teaspoons harissa
- salt and pepper to taste
- 2 tablespoons slivered almonds
- 1 cup quick-cooking couscous
- 2 tablespoons extra-virgin olive oil

Direction

- In a heavy pot, heat 2 tablespoons of olive oil on medium heat. Put cumin seeds and let it cook for about 1 minute until they release their aroma. Mix in the sweet potatoes, garlic and onions. Turn down the heat to medium-low and cook for 5 minutes with cover, mixing from time to time, to prevent the potatoes from sticking.
- In the pot, place the lamb shanks and cook for about 8 minutes until it browns on all sides. Put Harissa, apricots and tomatoes. Sprinkle pepper and salt to season. Add a splash of water if the mixture looks slightly dry. Let it boil, then turn down the heat and put cover. Let it simmer for 1 hour or more, depending on the size of the shanks, until the meat falls off the bone and becomes tender. Mix it from time to time.
- On low heat, heat a small pan then put the slivered almonds. Stir and cook for about 5 minutes, until the almonds are a bit browned. Take it out of the heat and put aside.
- In a big bowl, put the couscous and pour in lukewarm water slowly, until just covered. Allow it to sit for about 10 minutes until the water has been absorbed. Toss the couscous together with toasted almonds and 2 tablespoons of olive oil. Move to a serving dish and spoon the lamb on top of the couscous, then serve.

Nutrition Information

- Calories: 1249 calories;
- Total Fat: 54.6
- Sodium: 811
- Total Carbohydrate: 119.5
- Cholesterol: 179
- Protein: 70

37. Pressure Cooker Lamb Shanks With White Beans

Serving: 4 | Prep: 30mins | Cook: 1hours5mins | Ready in:

Ingredients

- 1 cup dry cannellini beans
- 2 lamb shanks
- 1/4 teaspoon freshly ground black pepper
- 2 tablespoons all-purpose flour
- 2 tablespoons olive oil
- 2 large shallots, chopped
- 2 carrots, chopped
- 2 celery ribs, chopped
- 6 cloves garlic, thinly sliced
- 2 teaspoons chopped fresh rosemary
- 1 cup dry red wine
- 2 cups low-sodium beef broth
- 1 cup water
- 1 tablespoon tomato paste
- 1/2 teaspoon salt
- 2 teaspoons lemon zest
- 1/4 cup chopped Italian flat leaf parsley, divided

Direction

- In a big bowl filled with cold water, soak the cannellini beans for a minimum of 4 hours to overnight; drain.
- Pat dry the lamb shanks; season using ground black pepper then dust in flour. On medium-high heat, heat oil in the pressure cooker; place in the lamb shanks. Cook in batches for 10 minutes for each piece until all sides are brown. Move to a plate and let it rest.
- In the same cooker, stir in garlic, shallots, celery, and carrots. Cook for approximately 15 minutes until the shallot becomes golden. Pour in red wine and rosemary. Cook for another 2 minutes while continuously stirring to scrape the browned bits off the base of the pan. Pour water, beef broth, and drained beans; season with black pepper. Add the reserved lamb shanks back in the pot.

- Secure with a lid and set the cooker on maximum pressure as specified in its manual; cook for 35 minutes. Remove from heat and naturally let the pressure out for 10 minutes.
- Uncover, mix in 1/2 of chopped parsley, tomato paste, lemon zest, and salt.
- Ladle vegetable and bean mix into shallow, big bowls. Place the lamb shanks and sauce on top; garnish with the leftover parsley.

Nutrition Information

- Calories: 474 calories;
- Sodium: 557
- Total Carbohydrate: 51.2
- Cholesterol: 41
- Protein: 30.8
- Total Fat: 12

38. Pulled Lamb Sizzlin' Sliders

Serving: 8 | Prep: 30mins | Cook: 1hours17mins | Ready in:

Ingredients

- 3 pounds lamb shanks, on the bone
- 2/3 cup water
- 1 jalapeno, cut in half width-wise
- 8 ciabatta bread dinner rolls
- 2 tablespoons extra-virgin olive oil
- 2 green bell pepper, sliced
- 1 onion, sliced
- salt and ground black pepper to taste
- 1 cup mayonnaise
- 3 tablespoons Sriracha sauce
- 5 ounces fresh spinach
- 1 jalapeno, seeded and sliced

Direction

- In a slow cooker, add lamb shanks; pour in water. Stir in stem side of the halved jalapeno, reserving the other end.
- Set the slow cooker to High; cook for 1 - 2 hours, till the lamb is tender and can be easily pulled apart using a fork. An instant-read thermometer inserted near the bone should read 165°F (74°C).
- Preheat oven to 375°F (190°C). On a baking sheet, arrange ciabatta rolls.
- Bake in the prepped oven for 10 - 15 minutes, until browned and crisp.
- Take away jalapeno half from the slow cooker; dice with the reserved jalapeno half.
- In a skillet, heat oil over medium-high heat. Mix in pepper, salt, diced jalapeno, onion and bell peppers; cook and stir for 7 - 10 minutes, until onion is translucent and bell peppers are tender.
- In a small bowl, mix chile-garlic sauce and mayonnaise; mix till sauce is mixed.
- Take away lamb from the cooker. Separate meat of the lamb from the bone; discard bones. Shred lamb using a fork; separate into 8 equal portions.
- Spread sauce on half of the ciabatta on top; cover up with spinach leaves. Spoon vegetable mixture and lamb on the bottom half of ciabatta; add sliced jalapeno on top.

Nutrition Information

- Calories: 1646 calories;
- Total Fat: 49.8
- Sodium: 3132
- Total Carbohydrate: 233.5
- Cholesterol: 77
- Protein: 61.2

39. Rogan Josh, Lamb Shanks

Serving: 2 | Prep: 40mins | Cook: 8hours | Ready in:

Ingredients

- 2/3 cup sour cream
- 1 tablespoon all-purpose flour

- 1/2 teaspoon chili powder
- 1 teaspoon ground coriander
- 1/2 teaspoon ground ginger
- 2 cubes chicken bouillon
- 4 whole cardamom pods, broken
- 1 (14.5 ounce) can diced tomatoes
- 1 cup water
- ground nutmeg to taste
- salt and ground black pepper to taste
- 2 tablespoons cornstarch
- 1/4 cup water
- 1 large onion, cut into wedges
- 3 lamb shanks
- 1 (15 ounce) can carrots, drained
- 1 (15 ounce) can whole new potatoes, drained
- 1/2 pound button mushrooms, quartered (optional)

Direction

- In a small bowl, mix all-purpose flour and sour cream together till smooth; set aside. Combine water and cornstarch together in a separate small bowl till the mixture forms a paste.
- In a medium saucepan, mix pepper, salt, nutmeg, water, tomatoes, cardamom, bouillon cubes, ginger, coriander and chili powder; boil the mixture over high heat. Gradually include in the cornstarch paste, stirring constantly; simmer for 2 minutes. Take the saucepan away from the heat; gradually combine in the flour and sour cream mixture.
- Distribute onions across the bottom of a slow cooker; place shanks atop the onions; transfer the prepared tomato mixture on top of the meat. Arrange mushrooms, potatoes and carrots over the top.
- Cook with a cover on high in the slow cooker, 8 hours.

Nutrition Information

- Calories: 811 calories;
- Total Fat: 38.2
- Sodium: 2378
- Total Carbohydrate: 65.3
- Cholesterol: 158
- Protein: 51.2

40. Superb Lamb Shanks

Serving: 6 | Prep: 10mins | Cook: 1hours50mins | Ready in:

Ingredients

- 6 (1 pound) lamb shanks
- 1/4 cup all-purpose flour for coating
- 1 cup water
- 1 onion, finely chopped
- salt and pepper to taste
- 1 cup evaporated milk
- 1 (10.75 ounce) can condensed tomato soup

Direction

- Over medium-high heat, heat a large deep skillet and spray with cooking spray. Lightly coat lamb shanks with the flour. In the hot pan, brown on all sides. Drain off the fat.
- Put in pepper, salt, onion and the water. Cover and lower the heat and cook for roughly 1 1/2 hours or until tender. While cooking, turn the shanks occasionally, and if necessary, pour in more water. Stir in tomato soup and evaporated milk when the shanks are done. Cook, covered for 10 more mins.

Nutrition Information

- Calories: 548 calories;
- Total Fat: 26.7
- Sodium: 456
- Total Carbohydrate: 16.6
- Cholesterol: 191
- Protein: 57.5

Chapter 3: Ground Lamb Recipes

***

41. A Scotsman's Shepherd Pie

Serving: 8 | Prep: 45mins | Cook: 25mins | Ready in:

Ingredients

- 5 cups mashed, boiled potatoes
- 1/2 cup sour cream
- 2 ounces cream cheese
- 2 tablespoons butter, softened, divided
- 1 egg yolk
- 1/2 teaspoon kosher salt
- 1/2 teaspoon freshly ground black pepper
- 1 1/2 teaspoons olive oil
- 1 pound ground lamb
- 1 pinch salt and ground black pepper to taste
- 1 (16 ounce) can stewed tomatoes with juice, chopped
- 1 small onion, chopped
- 1 small carrot, peeled and chopped
- 1/2 cup peas
- 1 cup Irish stout beer (such as Guinness®)
- 1 cube beef bouillon
- 1 tablespoon all-purpose flour
- 1 tablespoon Worcestershire sauce
- 3/4 cup shredded sharp Cheddar cheese
- 2 teaspoons chopped fresh parsley
- 2 teaspoons smoked paprika

Direction

- In a bowl, mix together half teaspoon black pepper, half teaspoon salt, egg yolk, a tablespoon of butter, cream cheese, sour cream and potatoes. Stir until smooth.
- Over medium high heat, heat olive oil in a nonstick pan or cast iron skillet. Put ground lamb and adjust the heat to medium. Cook while stirring occasionally for 4 to 5 minutes until it is crumbly and brown. Drain out extra grease and sprinkle lamb with black pepper and salt for added taste.
- Mix carrot, tomatoes with juice, onion into ground lamb. Simmer for about 5 to 10 minutes until veggies becomes tender. Add peas and adjust heat to low. Cook while stirring frequently for 2 to 3 minutes until peas become warm.
- Over medium heat, heat beer in a saucepan. Put in beef bouillon. Cook and stir for 5 minutes the beer mixture until bouillon dissolves.
- In a separate pan, heat the leftover 1 tablespoon butter over medium low heat until it sizzles. Whisk flour into butter for 1 minute until it is paste-like and thick. Mix Worcestershire sauce and beer mixture into the flour mixture for 2 to 3 minutes until gravy is smooth and thickened. Stir gravy into lamb mixture and simmer at least five minutes until the mixture thickens.
- Place oven rack 6 inches away from heat. Preheat the oven's broiler. Grease a 9inx12in baking dish.
- Put the lamb mixture into the prepared baking dish. Slowly cover the lamb mixture with mashed potatoes like a crust. Season mashed potatoes with parsley, paprika, and Cheddar cheese.
- Broil in the preheated oven for 4 to 5 minutes until cheese melts and crust turns brown in color. Let it cool for 5 minutes. Serve.

Nutrition Information

- Calories: 386 calories;
- Total Fat: 21.4
- Sodium: 561
- Total Carbohydrate: 30.4
- Cholesterol: 96
- Protein: 17

42. Armenian Pizzas (Lahmahjoon)

Serving: 3 | Prep: 20mins | Cook: 30mins | Ready in:

Ingredients

- 1 pound lean ground lamb
- 1/2 teaspoon salt
- 1/4 teaspoon ground black pepper
- 1 tablespoon extra-virgin olive oil
- 1/2 cup chopped red onion
- 3 cloves garlic, minced
- 1/2 green bell pepper, chopped
- 1 tablespoon freshly ground cumin seed
- 1 teaspoon ground turmeric
- 1 teaspoon paprika
- 1 pinch fenugreek seeds, finely crushed (optional)
- 1 lemon wedge
- 1 (14.5 ounce) can diced tomatoes
- 2 tablespoons ketchup
- 1 cup chopped flat-leaf parsley
- 6 (6 inch) pita bread rounds
- 1/3 cup crumbled feta cheese (optional)
- 1 lime, cut into wedges
- 1 tablespoon chopped fresh mint

Direction

- Start by preheating the oven at 230°C (450°F). Then season the lamb with some salt and pepper and set aside.
- In a large skillet, heat some olive oil over medium high heat. Put in garlic, onion and bell pepper and stir. Once the vegetables begin to brown, add in the turmeric, cumin, paprika and fenugreek; stir well.
- Add in the ground lamb immediately and squeeze the juice out of the lemon wedge on the lamb. Take the peel into the mixture. Make sure to break up the meat and mix thoroughly until it has evenly browned. Take out the lemon peel.
- Add in the tomatoes, parsley and ketchup, stir and continue to simmer the mixture for 10 to 15 minutes or until the liquid has reduced. Make sure that the mixture does not have too much liquid left else it can make the pitas soggy.
- If you prefer to bake the pitas on a baking sheet instead of baking it directly in the oven rack, you can start to arrange them on a large baking sheet now. Spread a spoonful of the meat mixture onto the pita and make sure to evenly spread it out, leaving 1/8 of an inch border at the edge of each pita. To finish, sprinkle some feta cheese over the top of the meat.
- Put the pitas in the oven and bake until the edges should are lightly crisp and meat must be slightly browned, but not too dry, for 10-20 minutes. Cooking time varies if you used a baking tray or not. It is served with a squeeze of lime on top and garnished with chopped mint.

Nutrition Information

- Calories: 771 calories;
- Sodium: 1663
- Total Carbohydrate: 74.6
- Cholesterol: 126
- Protein: 42.3
- Total Fat: 33.1

43. Authentic Turkish Doner Kebab

Serving: 4 | Prep: 10mins | Cook: 1hours20mins | Ready in:

Ingredients

- 1 teaspoon all-purpose flour
- 1 teaspoon dried oregano
- 1/2 teaspoon salt
- 1/2 teaspoon garlic powder
- 1/2 teaspoon onion powder
- 1/2 teaspoon dried Italian herb seasoning
- 1/4 teaspoon ground black pepper
- 1/4 teaspoon cayenne pepper
- 1 1/4 pounds ground lamb

Direction

- Preheat the oven to 350°F (175°C).
- In a large bowl mix flour, salt, garlic powder, oregano, onion powder, Italian seasoning, cayenne pepper, and black pepper. Add the ground lamb to the mixture and knead thoroughly for about 3 minutes, until evenly combined.
- Shape the seasoned meat and transfer it to a loaf pan placed on the baking sheet.
- Bake for about 1 hour and 20 minutes in the preheated oven, turning the loaf halfway to allow even browning.
- Once done, wrap loaf in tinfoil, set aside and let it rest for about 10 minutes. Cut as thinly as possible, making the kebab pieces.

Nutrition Information

- Calories: 283 calories;
- Total Fat: 19.3
- Sodium: 370
- Total Carbohydrate: 1.5
- Cholesterol: 95
- Protein: 24.4

44. Baby Red Mashed Potatoes And Peas With Spring Meatloaf

Serving: 4 | Prep: 15mins | Cook: 15mins | Ready in:

Ingredients

- Idahoan Baby Reds with Peas:
- 1 (4 ounce) package Idahoan® Baby Reds Flavored Mashed Potatoes
- 1/4 cup half and half
- 1 tablespoon butter, softened
- Scallions, green parts, finely chopped
- 1 cup fresh peas or frozen peas, thawed
- Spring Meatloaf:
- 1 1/2 pounds ground lamb or ground beef
- Salt and pepper
- 2 slices white bread, crusts trimmed
- 1/4 cup milk
- 1 bunch scallions, white parts finely chopped
- 1/4 cup fresh parsley, finely chopped
- 1/4 cup fresh mint, finely chopped
- 2 cloves garlic, finely chopped
- 1 egg, lightly beaten
- 1 tablespoon lemon zest
- Extra virgin olive oil for drizzling

Direction

- Place a rack in the middle of the oven and set 400 °F to preheat. Use parchment paper to line a baking sheet.
- In a large bowl, place the meat and season generously with pepper and salt. In a small bowl, put the bread into milk and soak, then break the bread up into meat. Combine a healthy drizzle of olive oil, lemon zest, egg, garlic, mint, parsley, and scallion whites into the meat. Form 4 mini loaves with your hands, about 1 1/2-inch thick or form into one large loaf.
- On the lined baking sheet, place the meatloaf and roast in the oven for 15-18 minutes until cooked throughout. Follow package instructions to prepare Idahoan Baby Reds. Mix in half and half, peas, scallions and butter. Serve hot with meatloaf.

Nutrition Information

- Calories: 517 calories;
- Protein: 36.3
- Total Fat: 30.8
- Sodium: 384
- Total Carbohydrate: 23.4
- Cholesterol: 175

45. Best Greek Stuffed Turkey

Serving: 18 | Prep: 30mins | Cook: 4hours | Ready in:

Ingredients

- 1 (12 pound) whole turkey, thawed
- 3 lemons, juiced
- 1/4 cup butter
- 4 medium onions, chopped
- 2 turkey livers, finely chopped
- 1 pound ground lamb
- 2 1/2 cups long grain white rice
- 1 tablespoon ground cinnamon
- 1/4 cup chopped fresh mint leaves
- 2 tablespoons tomato paste
- 3 cups water
- salt and pepper to taste
- 1/2 cup butter, melted

Direction

- Preheat an oven to 230°C or 450°F. Wash turkey inside and out, and pat it dry using paper towels. Massage lemon juice on the entire outer part of turkey and inside the cavity. Reserve.
- In a big skillet, liquify a quarter cup of butter over moderate heat. Put in onion, and cook for 5 minutes, till soft. Put in ground lamb and chopped livers. Cook, mixing to break up, till equally browned. Mix in tomato paste, mint, cinnamon and rice. Stir in 1 cup water, and add pepper and salt to season. Allow to cook for 10 minutes over low heat, mixing continuously.
- Stuff the turkey with filling mixture, and truss. In shallow roasting pan, put on a rack, and add the leftover 2 cups water into pan. Combine together the melted butter and the rest of the lemon juice. It will be the basting sauce.
- In the prepped oven, bake for an hour, then lower oven temperature to 175°C or 350°F and keep roasting for 2 hours longer, or till the inner temperature of chunkiest part of the thigh reads 80°C or 180°F. Baste from time to time with lemon juice and liquified butter.

Nutrition Information

- Calories: 703 calories;
- Total Fat: 33.7
- Sodium: 240
- Total Carbohydrate: 26.7
- Cholesterol: 246
- Protein: 69.8

46. Bobotie From Boschendal Manor House

Serving: 8 | Prep: 35mins | Cook: 1hours25mins | Ready in:

Ingredients

- 1 slice day-old bread
- 1 cup milk
- 2 tablespoons vegetable oil
- 2 large onions, chopped
- 2 cloves garlic, minced
- 1 tablespoon curry powder
- 2 pounds ground lamb
- 1/2 cup raisins
- 4 (2 inch) pieces lemon zest
- 12 blanched almonds, chopped
- 1/4 cup lemon juice
- 3 tablespoons mango chutney, chopped
- 1 egg
- 1 tablespoon white sugar
- 1 teaspoon salt
- 1/2 teaspoon ground black pepper
- 1/2 teaspoon ground turmeric
- 1 egg

Direction

- Preheat an oven to 175°C/350°F. Butter 2-qt. baking dish. Put bread into shallow dish; put milk on it, letting it soak in.
- Heat vegetable oil on medium high heat in a skillet. Mix in garlic and onion; cook for 5 minutes till lightly browned. Lower heat to medium low; mix in curry powder. Mix and cook for 2 minutes. Put aside skillet; cool.

- As onion mixture cools, mix 1 egg, chutney, lemon juice, almonds, lemon zest, raisins and ground lamb in a big bowl. Squeeze extra milk from a bread slice. Add bread to lamb mixture; reserve leftover milk. Season with turmeric, pepper, salt and sugar. Add onions to lamb mixture; mix till combined well. Scrape mixture into prepped baking dish; level top.
- In preheated oven, bake for 1 hour. Beat leftover milk and leftover egg; evenly put on top of casserole. Put casserole into oven; bake for 15-20 minutes till top is golden brown and custard is set.

Nutrition Information

- Calories: 371 calories;
- Total Fat: 21.8
- Sodium: 409
- Total Carbohydrate: 20.8
- Cholesterol: 122
- Protein: 23.5

47. Bry's Chocolate Lamb Chili

Serving: 6 | Prep: 10mins | Cook: 30mins | Ready in:

Ingredients

- 1 medium onion, chopped
- 1 pound lean ground lamb
- 2 tablespoons olive oil
- 1/2 teaspoon red pepper flakes
- 1/2 tablespoon dried basil
- 1 teaspoon cumin
- 1/8 teaspoon cinnamon
- 2 large cloves garlic, minced
- 3 1/2 tablespoons chili powder
- 1/2 teaspoon dried oregano
- 1 teaspoon unsweetened cocoa powder
- 1 teaspoon white sugar
- 1 bay leaf
- salt and pepper to taste
- 1 (14.5 ounce) can diced tomatoes with juice
- 4 cups red beans, with liquid

Direction

- Cook ground lamb and onions in the olive oil in a large pot on medium heat.
- Flavor with pepper, salt bay leaf, sugar, cocoa powder, dried oregano, chili powder, garlic, cinnamon, cumin, basil, and red pepper flakes to taste once meat is browned and onions are soft. Cook for 1 or 2 minutes. Stir in beans and tomatoes. Turn up the heat to boil the soup. Turn down the heat and let simmer for 15 minutes.

Nutrition Information

- Calories: 366 calories;
- Sodium: 1052
- Total Carbohydrate: 33.8
- Cholesterol: 51
- Protein: 22.6
- Total Fat: 16.4

48. Eggplant Stuffed With Lamb And Feta

Serving: 4 | Prep: 35mins | Cook: 1hours5mins | Ready in:

Ingredients

- 2 large eggplants, halved lengthwise
- 1/4 cup olive oil
- 1 pound ground lamb
- 1 small onion, chopped
- 1/2 green bell pepper, chopped
- 3 cloves garlic, minced
- 1 teaspoon ground cinnamon
- 1/2 teaspoon ground allspice
- 1 teaspoon ground black pepper
- 1 1/4 cups marinara sauce
- 1 (8 ounce) package crumbled feta cheese
- 2 eggs, beaten

- 1/2 cup dry bread crumbs
- 1/2 cup shredded mozzarella cheese

Direction

- Set the oven to 400°F (200°C) for preheating. Use an aluminum foil to line the baking sheet.
- Coat the cut sides of the eggplant halves with half of the olive oil. Arrange them onto the baking sheet, cut-side up. Place the baking sheet inside the oven and bake for 30 minutes until tender. Remove from the oven once done and allow it to cool slightly. Scoop the flesh out, making sure to leave the shells with a thickness of 1/2-inch. Get all of its seeds, as many as you can. Chop the flesh coarsely and put them into the large mixing bowl.
- In the meantime, pour the remaining olive oil into the skillet and heat it over medium-high. Add the ground lamb. Cook it for several minutes until it starts to crumble. Mix in cinnamon, black pepper, onion, garlic, allspice, and bell pepper. Cook for 5 minutes until the lamb is not anymore pinkish and the onion turns soft. Pour the mixture into the bowl with eggplant. Mix in feta cheese, bread crumbs, egg, and marinara sauce until well-blended.
- Divide the lamb mixture evenly into the eggplant shells. Place the eggplant into the oven and bake for 10 minutes. Sprinkle the eggplant with mozzarella. Adjust the oven's temperature to 375°F (190°C). Bake for 25 more minutes until the mozzarella turns golden brown and the filling is already set.

Nutrition Information

- Calories: 782 calories;
- Total Fat: 49.3
- Sodium: 1247
- Total Carbohydrate: 46.8
- Cholesterol: 230
- Protein: 41.2

49. Forfar Bridies

Serving: 6 | Prep: 30mins | Cook: 35mins | Ready in:

Ingredients

- 12 ounces ground lamb
- 1 onion, chopped
- 2 tablespoons beef broth
- 1 teaspoon Worcestershire sauce
- 1/4 teaspoon salt, or to taste
- 1/4 teaspoon ground black pepper, or to taste
- 1 recipe pastry for double-crust pie
- 1 egg white, lightly beaten

Direction

- Preheat an oven to 175°C/350°F.
- Cook lamb in a big heavy skillet on medium heat till evenly brown; drain extra fat. Take off heat. Mix in Worcestershire sauce, beef broth and onion; season with pepper and salt.
- Roll out pastry to 1/8-in. thick on lightly floured surface; cut to 6-in. rounds. Put 1/2 cup filling on 1/2 of each; fold pastry on filling. To seal, crimp edges. Lightly brush beaten egg white; to let steam escape, cut 3 slits on top. Put onto baking sheet.
- In preheated oven, bake till golden brown for 30-35 minutes.

Nutrition Information

- Calories: 474 calories;
- Protein: 14
- Total Fat: 33.2
- Sodium: 478
- Total Carbohydrate: 29.2
- Cholesterol: 41

50. Green Curry Lamb Balls

Serving: 4 | Prep: 15mins | Cook: 15mins | Ready in:

Ingredients

- 1/2 pound ground lamb
- 1/2 cup bread crumbs
- steak seasoning to taste
- 1 (10 ounce) can coconut milk
- 1 1/2 tablespoons green curry paste

Direction

- Combine steak seasoning, bread crumbs and ground lamb together in a medium bowl until well mixed. Shape into meatballs of about one inch in diameter. Over medium-high heat, heat a skillet that is greased and then fry lamb balls for about 5 minutes until they're a bit crusty and black. Take out the balls from the pan and reserve.
- Mix curry paste into hot skillet and then fry for about 1 minute. Add in the whole can of coconut milk and then decrease the heat. Allow mixture to simmer while stirring often for about 5 to 10 minutes. You can serve the curry sauce and meatballs on top of rice.

Nutrition Information

- Calories: 348 calories;
- Sodium: 249
- Total Carbohydrate: 12.6
- Cholesterol: 41
- Protein: 14.5
- Total Fat: 31.4

---

51. Gyros

Serving: 8 | Prep: 20mins | Cook: 1hours15mins | Ready in:

Ingredients

- 1/4 cup chopped red onion
- 1 tablespoon minced garlic
- 1 tablespoon dried marjoram
- 1 tablespoon ground dried rosemary
- 2 teaspoons kosher salt
- 1/2 teaspoon freshly ground black pepper
- 1 pound 93%-lean ground beef
- 1 pound ground lamb

Direction

- Start preheating the oven to 350°F (175°C).
- In a food processor, process the red onion until it is minced finely. Put the onion into a piece of the cheesecloth; squeeze as much moisture from onion as you can. Put the onion back to the food processor. Put in garlic. Process until garlic is integrated well. Blend black pepper, kosher salt, rosemary and marjoram into onion mixture.
- Blend ground lamb and ground beef gradually with seasoning and onion mixture; alternately put in small amounts of each meat to mixture and process until well incorporated after each addition.
- Pack meat mixture firmly into the loaf pan, making sure no air pockets are trapped in meat.
- Bake in prepared oven for 75 mins or until no longer pink in middle. An instant-read thermometer should register at least 175°F (80°C) when inserted into middle. Drain the grease. Thinly slice to enjoy.

Nutrition Information

- Calories: 224 calories;
- Total Fat: 14
- Sodium: 538
- Total Carbohydrate: 1.3
- Cholesterol: 80
- Protein: 21.7

---

52. Healthy Lamb Meatballs

Serving: 4 | Prep: 20mins | Cook: 30mins | Ready in:

Ingredients

- 1 pound ground lamb, or more to taste
- 1/2 cup shredded cabbage, or more to taste
- 1/3 cup diced onion
- 1 egg
- 1 1/4 tablespoons ground allspice
- 1 tablespoon freshly ground cardamom
- 1/4 teaspoon ground turmeric (optional)
- 1/4 teaspoon ground sumac (optional)
- salt and ground black pepper to taste

Direction

- Start preheating the oven at 350°F (175°C).
- In a pot of water, heat lamb to a boil, crumbling into small chunks, using a spoon, until cooked completely, for 5 to 10 minutes. Discard fat from the water by a spoon and drain water from meat.
- Combine pepper, salt, sumac, turmeric, cardamom, allspice, egg, onion, cabbage, and cooked lamb in a bowl; roll to form into 1 1/2-inch balls. Put meatballs on a baking sheet.
- Bake in the prepared oven until meatballs are cooked thoroughly and turn brown on the outside, for 25 to 30 minutes.

Nutrition Information

- Calories: 256 calories;
- Sodium: 123
- Total Carbohydrate: 4
- Cholesterol: 122
- Protein: 21.4
- Total Fat: 16.9

53. Hyderabadi Nargisi Kofta

Serving: 8 | Prep: 25mins | Cook: 45mins | Ready in:

Ingredients

- 1 1/4 pounds ground lamb
- 1 cup water
- 1 cinnamon stick
- 1/4 teaspoon ground turmeric
- salt to taste
- 1 onion, minced
- 1 egg, beaten
- 3 tablespoons chickpea flour
- 1 tablespoon ginger garlic paste
- 3 green chile peppers, minced
- 1 teaspoon ground coriander
- 1 teaspoon garam masala
- 1/2 teaspoon ground cumin
- 1/2 teaspoon ground red pepper
- 8 eggs
- oil for deep frying
- 1 teaspoon chaat masala
- 1/2 cup chopped fresh cilantro
- 8 wedges lime, as garnish

Direction

- Over medium heat, mix salt, turmeric, cinnamon stick, water and lamb in a large skillet. Let it cook for about 20 minutes while breaking lamb into small pieces until the liquid is evaporated and meat is no longer pink. Put aside until cooled enough to work on. Take out and get rid of cinnamon stick.
- In a large bowl, combine together ground red pepper, cumin, garam masala, coriander, green chile peppers, ginger garlic paste, chickpea flour, beaten egg, onion and cooked lamb until combined evenly. Chill for at least 30 minutes.
- Put eggs in a single layer into a saucepan and then cover with water by 1 inch. Cover pan and heat water to a boil on high heat. When water boils, take out of the heat and leave eggs to sit for 15 minutes in hot water. Drain the hot water, and cool eggs with cold running water in sink. Then peel when cold.
- Separate lamb mixture into eight even parts. Pick one portion of the meat and then flatten with your palm just like a cutlet. Place one hard-boiled egg in the middle and then tightly wrap meat around it. Then tie a piece of food-safe string all around the wrapped egg. Repeat this with the remaining meat and eggs. Chill eggs for 8 hours or overnight.

- Heat the oil in a large saucepan or deep-fryer to 175 degrees C (350 degrees F). Fry each kofta for 10 to 15 minutes in hot oil until they are slightly crispy outside. Chop and take out the string. Cut koftas lengthwise in half and drizzle with cilantro and chaat masala. You can serve along with lime wedges.

Nutrition Information

- Calories: 353 calories;
- Total Fat: 26.6
- Sodium: 267
- Total Carbohydrate: 7.5
- Cholesterol: 256
- Protein: 20.5

54. Kebab Massalam

Serving: 5 | Prep: 20mins | Cook: 10mins | Ready in:

Ingredients

- 1 pound ground lamb
- 2 cloves garlic, minced
- 2 green Thai chili peppers, finely chopped
- 1 onion, chopped
- 2 tablespoons coriander seeds, crushed
- 2 tablespoons plain yogurt
- 1/2 teaspoon ground turmeric
- 1 tablespoon lemon juice
- 1 teaspoon salt
- 5 (6 inch) bamboo skewers, soaked in water for 20 minutes
- 2 red bell peppers, seeded and cut into 2-inch pieces

Direction

- Preheat an oven's broiler and position oven rack to around 6 inches away from heat source. Oil a broiling pan lightly.
- Use hands to combine together salt, lemon juice, turmeric, yogurt, coriander, onion, chili peppers, garlic and lamb until combined well. Then roll mixture to form 15 meatballs. Thread three meatballs onto each skewer and separate with chunks of red bell pepper. Transfer onto the greased broiling pan.
- Let to broil for five minutes, flip skewers over and continue to broil for about 5 minutes longer until no pink color remains in the middle anymore.

Nutrition Information

- Calories: 223 calories;
- Total Fat: 13
- Sodium: 525
- Total Carbohydrate: 9.4
- Cholesterol: 61
- Protein: 17.1

55. Keema Matar

Serving: 4 | Prep: 10mins | Cook: 30mins | Ready in:

Ingredients

- 1 pound ground lamb
- 1 teaspoon vegetable oil
- 1 small onion, chopped
- 1 clove garlic, pressed
- 1 (6 ounce) can tomato paste
- 3 tablespoons mild curry paste
- 1 1/2 cups water
- 1 cup fresh or frozen peas, thawed
- 3 sprigs cilantro, for garnish

Direction

- Heat a skillet over medium-high heat. Put in the ground lamb, stir and cook for about 5 minutes until browned and crumbly. Let the excess grease drain off, set the meat aside. In the same skillet, heat vegetable oil and stir in onion; continue to cook and stir for about 3

minutes or until the onion starts to brown. Stir in garlic and keep cooking for 1 minute longer.
- Add the cooked lamb back into the skillet, stir along with water, curry paste, and the tomato paste. Boil, then lower the heat to medium-low; simmer, covered, for 15 minutes. Stir in peas, continue to simmer while covered for 5 minutes longer. Then, pour into a serving plate and decorate with cilantro.

Nutrition Information

- Calories: 312 calories;
- Protein: 23.4
- Total Fat: 16.9
- Sodium: 658
- Total Carbohydrate: 16.7
- Cholesterol: 76

56. Kibbee Lebanese Style

Serving: 4 | Prep: 15mins | Cook: 30mins | Ready in:

Ingredients

- 1/2 cup bulgur
- 1/2 cup hot water
- 1/2 teaspoon dried mint
- 1/4 teaspoon ground allspice
- 1/4 teaspoon ground black pepper
- 1/8 teaspoon ground cinnamon
- 1/4 teaspoon salt
- 1 onion, minced
- 2 tablespoons chopped fresh parsley
- 1 pound ground lamb
- 2 tablespoons pine nuts

Direction

- Preheat oven to 175°C/350°F; grease 8-in. square baking dish.
- In hot water, soak bulgur for 10 minutes till bulgur cools and expands. Process lamb, parsley, onion, salt, cinnamon, pepper, allspice, bulgur and mint for 1 minute till well mixed in a food processor. Divide lamb mixture; layer 1/2 in baking dish, making a big patty. Sprinkle meat with pine nuts; layer leftover lamb over, firmly patting. Cut kibbee to 1 1/2-in. squares.
- In preheated oven, bake for 30-35 minutes till lamb isn't pink in center. An inserted instant-read thermometer in middle should read 70°C/160°F.

Nutrition Information

- Calories: 417 calories;
- Cholesterol: 83
- Protein: 22.4
- Total Fat: 29
- Sodium: 219
- Total Carbohydrate: 16.8

57. Lamb Barley Soup

Serving: 8 | Prep: 20mins | Cook: 1hours | Ready in:

Ingredients

- 1 pound ground lamb
- 1/2 large onion, chopped
- 1 (28 ounce) can diced tomatoes
- 2 cups water
- 3 (10.5 ounce) cans beef consomme
- 1 (10.75 ounce) can condensed tomato soup
- 4 medium carrots, chopped
- 3 stalks celery, chopped
- 1/2 cup barley
- 1/2 teaspoon chili powder
- 1/2 teaspoon ground black pepper

Direction

- Set a large skillet on medium-high heat and start heating, stir in onion and ground lamb. Stir and cook until the onions become

translucent and the lamb is browned evenly. Drain off the excess grease and discard.
- Stir in tomato soup, consomme, water, tomatoes, and their liquid. Add barley, celery, and carrots, and flavor with pepper and chili powder. Let simmer for 45 minutes on medium heat.

Nutrition Information

- Calories: 225 calories;
- Total Fat: 8.9
- Sodium: 800
- Total Carbohydrate: 21.1
- Cholesterol: 38
- Protein: 14.4

58. Lamb Black Bean Chili

Serving: 4 | Prep: 10mins | Cook: 30mins | Ready in:

Ingredients

- 1 pound ground lamb
- 1/2 cup onion, chopped
- 1 clove garlic, minced
- 2 (15 ounce) cans black beans, rinsed and drained
- 3 cups canned tomato sauce
- 1 (14.5 ounce) can diced tomatoes
- 1/2 (15 ounce) can refried black beans
- 1 (7 ounce) can chopped green chilies
- 2 tablespoons cocoa powder
- 1 1/2 tablespoons chili powder
- 2 teaspoons ground cumin
- 1 cube chicken bouillon, crushed
- 1/2 teaspoon cayenne pepper

Direction

- Place a large skillet over medium-high heat. Cook while stirring in garlic, onion and lamb in hot skillet for 5-7 minutes, till the lamb completely turns brown.
- Mix in cayenne pepper, chicken bouillon, cumin, chili powder, cocoa powder, green chiles, refried black beans, diced tomatoes, tomato sauce and black beans; cook for 20-30 minutes, till the beans become tender.

Nutrition Information

- Calories: 571 calories;
- Protein: 40.1
- Total Fat: 18.5
- Sodium: 3049
- Total Carbohydrate: 65.1
- Cholesterol: 76

59. Lamb Cobbler

Serving: 12 | Prep: 50mins | Cook: 55mins | Ready in:

Ingredients

- Scones:
- 3 cups self-rising flour
- 2 teaspoons baking powder
- 1/4 cup grated Parmesan cheese
- 1/4 teaspoon salt
- 1/4 cup butter, chilled
- 7 ounces milk
- Filling:
- 1/4 cup butter
- 2 onions, finely chopped
- 4 cloves garlic, crushed
- 2 pounds ground lamb
- 1 teaspoon Worcestershire sauce
- 1 tablespoon brandy
- 1 tablespoon port wine
- salt and pepper to taste
- 1 (10 ounce) package frozen green peas, thawed
- 1 cup water
- 1/4 cup all-purpose flour
- 2 tablespoons milk
- 1/4 cup grated Parmesan cheese

Direction

- To prepare scone topping: In a big bowl, mix together salt, 1/4 cup Parmesan, baking powder and flour; combine thoroughly. Cut in butter till the mixture is crumbly. Pour in milk and mix until the dough just forms a ball.
- On a floured surface, place the dough; knead a couple of times until smooth. Pat dough to around 3/4-in. thickness; cut into 4-in. circles. Gather dough scraps; press together and repeat. There should be a total of 12 rounds. Arrange circles on a slightly floured baking sheet or a plate; chill in the fridge.
- Set oven to 200° C (400° F) and start preheating. Slightly grease a 9x11-in. baking dish.
- To prepare filling: In a skillet, heat butter on medium heat. Mix in onion; stir and cook for 5 minutes till onion becomes translucent and soft. Put in garlic, cook for 2 minutes longer, mixing, being careful not to burn garlic. If using curry paste and garam masala, add them at this point.
- Add pepper, salt, port, brandy, Worcestershire sauce, and lamb. Stir and cook, mixing often, till the lamb is cooked through and browned. Place peas into the skillet, mix.
- Pour in 1 cup red wine or water; heat to a boil. Beat in 1/4 cup flour. Simmer until sauce is thickened, mixing often, about 5 minutes.
- Arrange lamb mixture in the prepared casserole dish. Use circles of scone dough to cover, allowing circles just meet at the edges yet letting space for steam to escape. Brush milk on dough; use Parmesan cheese to sprinkle.
- Place in the preheated oven and bake for 25-30 minutes, till the filling is bubbly and scones are golden brown.

Nutrition Information

- Calories: 459 calories;
- Total Fat: 27.2
- Sodium: 718
- Total Carbohydrate: 32
- Cholesterol: 80
- Protein: 19.5

60. Lamb Loaf

Serving: 4 | Prep: 30mins | Cook: 35mins | Ready in:

Ingredients

- 1/2 teaspoon vegetable oil
- 2 slices dry bread, diced
- 1/2 teaspoon vegetable oil, or as needed
- 1/4 cup milk
- 1 pound ground lamb
- 1 egg
- 4 cloves minced garlic
- 2 tablespoons chopped fresh thyme
- 1 tablespoon Worcestershire sauce
- 1 tablespoon lemon zest
- 1 teaspoon ground coriander
- 1 teaspoon dried basil
- 1 teaspoon dried rosemary, crushed
- 3/4 teaspoon salt
- 1/4 teaspoon ground black pepper
- 1/4 cup tomato sauce
- 5 leaves fresh mint, finely chopped
- 2 tablespoons balsamic vinegar

Direction

- Turn oven to 400°F (200°C) to preheat. Lightly oil a 9x5-inch loaf pan.
- Combine milk and bread in a small mixing bowl. Press bread using a fork to soak up the milk.
- In a medium mixing bowl, combine lamb with pepper, salt, rosemary, basil, coriander, lemon zest, Worcestershire sauce, thyme, garlic, and egg. Put in soaked bread; dispose the leftover milk. Combine everything with your hands until incorporated well. Remove meatloaf to the greased pan.
- Mix mint, and tomato sauce together; distribute evenly over the meatloaf. Drizzle balsamic vinegar over top.

- Bake meatloaf for about 35 minutes in the preheated oven until center is no longer pink. An instant-read thermometer pinned into the center should register at least 160°F (70°C). Take meat out of the oven; allow to cool for 5 minutes before serving.

Nutrition Information

- Calories: 409 calories;
- Sodium: 735
- Total Carbohydrate: 12.2
- Cholesterol: 125
- Protein: 22.3
- Total Fat: 29.7

61. Lamb Meatballs

Serving: 24 | Prep: 25mins | Cook: 20mins | Ready in:

Ingredients

- 1 tablespoon unsalted butter
- 5 shallots, minced
- 2 pounds ground lamb
- 1 cup fresh bread crumbs
- 1/4 cup chopped fresh parsley
- 1 egg, lightly beaten
- 2 tablespoons lemon zest
- 1/2 teaspoon dried marjoram
- salt and freshly ground black pepper to taste
- 1/2 cup unsalted butter
- 1 tablespoon olive oil
- 2 1/2 tablespoons tomato sauce
- 1/4 cup wine
- 1 small garlic clove, minced
- 1 dash ground cinnamon
- toothpicks

Direction

- In a skillet, melt the 1 tablespoon butter over medium heat. Cook and stir the shallots in the skillet until tender. Place into a large bowl.
- In a bowl, combine lemon zest, egg, parsley, bread crumbs and lamb with the shallots. Season with pepper, salt and marjoram. Allow to sit in the fridge for 60 minutes.
- In a skillet, melt 1/2 cup butter then heat olive oil medium-high heat. Shape the lamb mixture into small meatballs; then cook in batches in the skillet until brown evenly. Leave the skillet without draining. On paper towels, drain meatballs then arrange in a serving dish.
- Combine cinnamon, garlic, wine and tomato sauce in the skillet. Cook and stir till heated through and well blended. Drizzle the sauce over the meatballs. Serve with toothpicks.

Nutrition Information

- Calories: 136 calories;
- Protein: 7.2
- Total Fat: 10.3
- Sodium: 145
- Total Carbohydrate: 3.1
- Cholesterol: 45

62. Lamb Meatballs Over Tandoori Naan

Serving: 4 | Prep: 20mins | Cook: 30mins | Ready in:

Ingredients

- Lamb Meatballs:
- 1/4 cup Italian-seasoned bread crumbs
- 1/4 teaspoon garlic powder
- 1/4 teaspoon ground paprika
- 1/4 teaspoon dried mint
- 1/4 teaspoon dried basil
- 1/4 teaspoon dried parsley
- 1 pound ground lamb
- 1 egg
- 2 tablespoons finely chopped onion
- 2 cloves garlic, minced
- 1/2 teaspoon olive oil
- salt and ground black pepper to taste

- Sauce:
- 1 (26 ounce) jar tomato sauce
- 1 tablespoon capers
- 4 leaves fresh basil leaves, torn
- 1/4 teaspoon dried mint
- salt and ground black pepper to taste
- Remaining Ingredients:
- 4 pieces tandoori naan bread
- 8 slices Muenster cheese, or as needed

Direction

- Set the oven for preheating to 400°F (200°C). Prepare by greasing a baking sheet.
- Combine garlic powder, bread crumbs, paprika, a quarter teaspoon mint, parsley and dried basil together in a big bowl. Mix in the egg, ground lamb, onion, olive oil, garlic, pepper and salt together until equally distributed. Shape the lamb mixture into an inch balls and put on the prepared baking sheet, arranging them in a single layer.
- Let it bake inside the oven for 15 minutes. Turn the meatballs and continue to cook for additional 10 minutes until completely cooked. Take the meatballs out from the oven and adjust the oven temperature to 350°F (175°C).
- Put the tomato sauce in a saucepan placed over low heat; drop the fresh basil, capers, a quarter teaspoon mint, pepper and salt. Cook and occasionally stir the sauce for roughly 5 to 10 minutes, until heated completely and the flavors blended together.
- Put the naan bread on a baking sheet. Scoop the tomato sauce using a spoon and place the meatballs on the naan; cover with slices of Muenster cheese.
- Let it bake inside the oven for roughly 5 to 10 minutes until the cheese has melted.

Nutrition Information

- Calories: 771 calories;
- Total Fat: 38
- Sodium: 1885
- Total Carbohydrate: 61
- Cholesterol: 187
- Protein: 47.9

63. Lamb Meatballs And Sauce

Serving: 4 | Prep: 20mins | Cook: 1hours | Ready in:

Ingredients

- 1/2 cup dry bread crumbs
- 1/2 cup milk
- 1 1/4 pounds ground lamb
- 1 egg, beaten
- 3 cloves fresh garlic, minced
- 2 tablespoons olive oil
- 1 tablespoon tomato paste
- 1 tablespoon chopped fresh rosemary
- 1 tablespoon ground cumin
- 1 1/2 teaspoons salt
- 1 teaspoon dried oregano
- 1/2 teaspoon freshly ground black pepper
- 1/4 teaspoon ground cinnamon
- 1 pinch cayenne pepper
- 3 cups tomato sauce
- 1 cup chicken stock
- 2 tablespoons chopped fresh mint
- 1 pinch red pepper flakes, or to taste

Direction

- Set oven to 230° C (450° F) and start preheating
- Use aluminum foil to line a baking tray; oil slightly.
- In a small bowl, mix together milk and bread crumbs. Soak bread crumbs for 30 minutes until milk has been absorbed.
- In a big bowl, combine cayenne pepper, cinnamon, black pepper, oregano, salt, cumin, rosemary, tomato paste, olive oil, garlic, egg, lamb, and bread crumb mixture.
- Shape the lamb mixture into 2-in. meatballs; arrange on the prepared baking tray.
- Put into the preheated oven and cook for 15

minutes until lightly browned. Take out of the oven. Put aside.
- In a big saucepan on medium heat, combine red pepper flakes, fresh mint, chicken stock, tomato sauce, and meatballs, cook about 45 minutes till meatballs are not pink inside anymore.

Nutrition Information

- Calories: 610 calories;
- Total Fat: 43.5
- Sodium: 2323
- Total Carbohydrate: 24.4
- Cholesterol: 154
- Protein: 31.3

64. Lamb Patties

Serving: 18 | Prep: 15mins | Cook: 30mins | Ready in:

Ingredients

- 1 pound ground lamb
- 5 green chile peppers, diced
- 3 onions, peeled and chopped
- 1 tablespoon dark soy sauce
- 1 tablespoon Worcestershire sauce
- 2 tablespoons ginger paste
- 2 tablespoons garlic paste
- 1/2 teaspoon ground white pepper
- 1/2 teaspoon ground cinnamon
- 1/2 teaspoon ground cardamom
- 1/2 teaspoon ground cloves
- 2 tablespoons chopped fresh cilantro
- 1 (17.5 ounce) package frozen puff pastry sheets, thawed
- 1 egg, beaten

Direction

- Combine ground lamb with Worcestershire sauce, soy sauce, chilies, and onion in a large pot. Season lamb mixture with cloves, cardamom, cinnamon, white pepper, garlic and ginger pastes. Cook for about 15 minutes over medium heat, stirring sometimes, until onions are soft and meat is evenly browned. Stir in cilantro, cover the pot and put to one side.
- Turn oven to 375°F (190°C) to preheat. Flatten sheets of puff pastry on a work surface lightly coated with flour. Divide each pastry into 9 squares and roll out to a thickness of 1/4 inch. Place about 1 1/2 tablespoons of meat mixture into the middle of each square. Brush water around the edges, fold corner over filling to make a triangle, and press edges to seal. (Avoid overstuffing because triangles will burst in the oven when baking). Arrange patties about 1 inch apart on a baking sheet lined with foil. Lightly brush beaten egg over tops.
- Bake patties in the preheated oven until all sides are golden brown, for 12 to 15 minutes. Serve right away for the best flavor.

Nutrition Information

- Calories: 222 calories;
- Total Fat: 14.1
- Sodium: 247
- Total Carbohydrate: 15.7
- Cholesterol: 27
- Protein: 7.2

65. Lamb Puff Pastry Bite Appetizer

Serving: 10 | Prep: 30mins | Cook: 20mins | Ready in:

Ingredients

- 1 tablespoon diced garlic
- 1/2 teaspoon salt
- 1/2 teaspoon ground black pepper
- 1/4 teaspoon ground cumin
- 1/4 teaspoon ground coriander
- 1/4 teaspoon ground allspice

- 1 pound ground lamb
- 1 egg
- 2 teaspoons water
- 2 (10x15-inch) sheets of frozen puff pastry, thawed
- 1/2 cup tzatziki sauce

Direction

- In a bowl, mix allspice, coriander, cumin, pepper, salt and garlic; add lamb. Shape lamb mixture to 10-in. logs, thick as hotdogs.
- Whisk water and egg to make egg wash in a small bowl.
- Lay puff pastry sheets onto slightly floured work surface; gently roll to smooth creases. Cut pastry to 10x4-in. strips; brush pastry with egg wash. On each pastry strip, put 1 lamb log; wrap dough around lamb. To seal, pinch edges. Wrap in plastic wrap; chill for 1 hour.
- Preheat an oven to 220°C/425°F; line parchment paper on a baking sheet.
- Remove plastic wrap; use a sharp knife to cut each pastry piece to 8 pieces. Put onto lined baking sheet in 1 layer; brush egg wash on each piece.
- In preheated oven, bake for 20 minutes till golden brown. Serve with tzatziki sauce.

Nutrition Information

- Calories: 375 calories;
- Total Fat: 35
- Sodium: 279
- Total Carbohydrate: 23
- Cholesterol: 49
- Protein: 12.4

66. Lamb Spaghetti

Serving: 10 | Prep: 25mins | Cook: 1hours | Ready in:

Ingredients

- 2 tablespoons olive oil
- 4 pounds ground lamb
- 1 whole head garlic, peeled and crushed
- 1 tablespoon onion powder
- 3 tablespoons lemon juice
- 1/2 teaspoon ground cinnamon
- 1/2 teaspoon dried oregano
- 1 1/2 cups water
- 4 small potatoes, peeled and cut into 1/2-inch dice
- salt and pepper to taste
- 1 (16 ounce) package linguine pasta

Direction

- Heat olive oil in a large skillet; cook ground lamb, onion powder, and garlic, stirring and crumbling meat while cooking, until no pink remains in the lamb. Whisk in oregano, cinnamon, and lemon juice; keep cooking for about 20 minutes, stirring from time to time, until all the liquid in the skillet vaporizes and garlic and lamb turn brown nicely.
- Add potatoes and water; bring to a boil; turn heat to medium-low. Simmer for about 20 minutes or until potatoes are very soft and starting to break apart. Mash potatoes against the side of the skillet using a spoon to thicken the sauce. Season with pepper and salt. Simmer for 10 minutes longer (and up to 1 hour) until flavors have combined and gravy is thickened. Stir from time to time while cooking.
- Bring lightly salted water in a large pot to a rolling boil; add linguine and cook, about 11 minutes, until al dente. Drain off water. Remove cooked pasta to serving plates; spoon lamb gravy over pasta to serve.

Nutrition Information

- Calories: 604 calories;
- Cholesterol: 122
- Protein: 38.8
- Total Fat: 28.5
- Sodium: 110
- Total Carbohydrate: 47.4

67. Lamb And Black Bean Chili

Serving: 4 | Prep: 10mins | Cook: 2hours10mins | Ready in:

Ingredients

- 1 pound ground lamb
- 1 yellow onion, diced
- 2 garlic cloves, minced
- 1 (14.5 ounce) can diced tomatoes, undrained
- 1 (14.5 ounce) can black beans, rinsed and drained
- 2 teaspoons hot pepper sauce (such as Tabasco®), or to taste
- 2 cups beef stock

Direction

- Heat a stockpot on medium high heat; mix and cook garlic, onion and ground lamb in hot skillet for 5-7 minutes till lamb is crumbly and fully browned. Drain the grease; discard.
- Mix beef stock, hot pepper sauce, black beans and tomatoes with lamb mixture; boil. Lower heat to medium low; simmer for 2 hours maximum.

Nutrition Information

- Calories: 383 calories;
- Total Fat: 16.3
- Sodium: 679
- Total Carbohydrate: 27.9
- Cholesterol: 76
- Protein: 29.2

68. Lamb And Potato Skillet

Serving: 4 | Prep: 25mins | Cook: 35mins | Ready in:

Ingredients

- 1 tablespoon vegetable oil
- 1 leek, chopped
- 1 cup chopped fresh mushrooms
- 1 pound ground lamb
- 1 clove garlic, minced
- 3/4 cup beef broth
- 1 tablespoon chopped fresh dill
- 1/2 teaspoon garlic and herb seasoning blend
- 1/4 teaspoon ground black pepper
- 1/4 teaspoon onion powder
- 1 bay leaf
- 3 cups chopped potatoes
- 1 (6.5 ounce) can tomato sauce
- 1/2 head cabbage, cored and shredded

Direction

- In a frying pan, heat oil over medium heat. Mix in mushrooms and leeks for 8 minutes until they start to get tender. Add lamb to the frying pan and break into small pieces; add garlic and cook, tossing sometimes, for 8 minutes until the lamb is not pink anymore. Strain the liquid from the pan.
- Mix in potatoes, bay leaf, onion powder, pepper, herb seasoning blend, garlic, dill, and broth. Boil it, then lower the heat to low. Put a cover on and simmer for 12 minutes until the potatoes are nearly soft. Add shredded cabbage and tomato sauce. Raise the heat to medium and simmer with a cover for 5-7 minutes until the potatoes are soft and the cabbage is cooked.
- Take out the bay leaf and enjoy.

Nutrition Information

- Calories: 412 calories;
- Cholesterol: 76
- Protein: 25.7
- Total Fat: 19.4
- Sodium: 493
- Total Carbohydrate: 35.6

69. Lamb And Rice Stuffed Cabbage Rolls

Serving: 4 | Prep: 30mins | Cook: 1hours45mins | Ready in:

Ingredients

- 1/4 cup butter
- 2 tablespoons olive oil
- 1/2 onion, diced
- 4 cloves garlic, crushed
- 1 teaspoon ground black pepper
- 1 teaspoon ground cumin
- 1/2 teaspoon ground cinnamon
- 1/4 teaspoon cayenne pepper
- 1 pinch dried oregano
- 1 pound ground lamb
- 1 cup white rice
- 2 teaspoons salt
- 1/4 cup packed chopped Italian parsley
- 2 tablespoons sliced almonds
- 1 tablespoon dried currants
- 1 head cabbage
- salt and ground black pepper to taste
- 2 bay leaves
- 1 cup tomato puree
- 3 1/2 cups chicken broth
- 1/2 onion, sliced
- 1/4 cup crumbled feta cheese (optional)
- 2 tablespoons chopped Italian parsley (optional)

Direction

- In a big frying pan, melt butter over medium heat. In the melted butter, heat oil. Stir and cook 1/2 diced onion for 8 minutes until turning translucent. Add garlic and stir and cook for 1 minute. Take away from heat. Mix in oregano, cayenne pepper, cinnamon, cumin, and 1 teaspoon black pepper. Put aside to cool until reaching room temperature.
- In a big bowl, mix together currants, almonds, 1/4 cup parsley, 2 teaspoons salt, rice, and lamb. Add the cooled onion mixture and combine until blended. Put a cover on and put in the fridge until using it.
- Add water to a big pot until halfway full and boil it. Chop the core off the cabbage head and in the boiling water, put the head. Put a cover on and simmer for 5 minutes until the leaves start to fall off. Transfer the 2 outer layers of leaves to a dish lined with paper towels, put a cover on and keep cooking for another 1-2 minutes. Transfer the leftover big leaves to the dish. You should prepare approximately 7 smaller and 8 large leaves.
- Turn the oven to 350°F (175°C) to preheat.
- Working with 1 cabbage leaf, discard the root end. On the bottom edge of the cabbage leaf, put approximately 1/2 cup of the lamb mixture and roll to form a log. Continue with 7 other big leaves and the rest of the lamb mixture to make 8 cabbage rolls.
- Line 4-5 smaller cabbage leaves into the bottom of a Dutch oven or a big casserole dish. Top with the cabbage rolls, use black pepper and salt to season. Add tomato puree and bay leaves. Add chicken broth. Sprinkle over the top with 1/2 sliced onion and put on 3-4 additional cabbage leaves to cover. Put a cover on the casserole.
- Bake in the preheated oven until the rice has been cooked and the lamb is soft, 75 minutes to 90 minutes. Take out of the oven and let sit for 30 minutes. Pour over the top with the pan juices and use 2 tablespoons parsley and feta cheese to garnish and enjoy.

Nutrition Information

- Calories: 740 calories;
- Sodium: 2564
- Total Carbohydrate: 69.6
- Cholesterol: 119
- Protein: 31.5
- Total Fat: 38.6

70. Lamb And Rice Stuffed Grape Leaves

Serving: 8 | Prep: 45mins | Cook: 45mins |Ready in:

Ingredients

- 1/2 pound ground lamb
- 1/2 cup uncooked long grain rice
- 1/4 cup olive oil
- 2 tablespoons chopped fresh mint
- 1 tablespoon dried currants
- 1 tablespoon pine nuts
- 1 1/2 teaspoons kosher salt
- 1 teaspoon ground black pepper
- 1/2 teaspoon ground cumin
- 1/4 teaspoon ground cinnamon
- 1/4 teaspoon dried oregano
- 1 large egg
- 1 (16 ounce) jar grape leaves
- 1 tablespoon olive oil
- juice of one lemon
- 4 cups hot chicken broth
- 2 teaspoons olive oil, or as desired

Direction

- In a bowl, place the egg, oregano, cinnamon, cumin, pepper, salt, pine nuts, currants, mint, 1/4 cups olive oil, rice, and ground lamb. Use a fork to mix thoroughly. Cover and chill until ready to use.
- Unroll and separate grape leaves gently. Wash in cold water to remove the saline. Let drain. Store the less-than-perfect or broken leaves to line the pot.
- Put grape leaves on the work surface with rib side up (smooth side down). Place a rounded tablespoon of the lamb-rice filling close to the bottom-center of the grape leaf. Next, fold the bottom part of the leaf over the filling, fold over sides and roll toward the top of leaf to make a firm cylinder. Do not roll too tightly or these leaves may be torn when cooking.
- In the pot, drizzle a tablespoon olive oil; apply 1 or 2 layers of the reserved grape leaves to line the bottom of pot. Put in the dolmas by placing them along the sides, then moving toward the center to cover the bottom. To allow for expansion, set enough space between dolmas, but close enough to keep their shapes when cooking. Stack another layer on top of the first so that they're all fit, if necessary. Then pour in 2 teaspoons olive oil and lemon juice.
- Overturn a small dish and then a larger one over the dolmas to weigh them down while cooking and to prevent them from slipping. Then add the hot chicken broth. Simmer over medium-high heat, uncovered. Reduce the heat to low as soon as the liquid is heated through and starting to bubble (about 2-4 minutes), cover the pot, and keep cooking for about 35 minutes. Next, take away the dishes and check for doneness. A completely one should be pierced easily with a fork, and a little puffed up. Keep cooking without the weights if they're not done yet: cover the pot and simmer for 10 to 15 minutes longer, or until the rice is softened.
- Serve chilled or warm. If desired, garnish with curls of lemon zest.

Nutrition Information

- Calories: 250 calories;
- Protein: 9.8
- Total Fat: 16.1
- Sodium: 2485
- Total Carbohydrate: 18.1
- Cholesterol: 45

71. Lamb And Squash

Serving: 8 | Prep: 15mins | Cook: 45mins |Ready in:

Ingredients

- 3 cups water
- 1 1/2 cups uncooked white rice
- 1 pound ground lamb

- 1 cup finely chopped onion
- 1 clove garlic, minced
- 1/2 teaspoon dried thyme
- 1/2 teaspoon dried basil
- 1 teaspoon ground mustard
- 1 acorn squash, halved and seeded
- salt and pepper to taste

Direction

- Boil a medium saucepan with water. Add rice; mix. Lower heat; cover. Simmer it for 20 minutes.
- Preheat an oven to 175°C/350°F.
- Cook ground mustard, basil, thyme, garlic, onion and ground lamb in a big skillet on moderately high heat till onion is soft and lamb is evenly brown; mix rice into mixture.
- Use ground lamb mixture to stuff acorn squash halves; season with pepper and salt.
- Put stuffed squash onto medium baking sheet; in preheated oven, bake till squash is tender for 30 minutes.

Nutrition Information

- Calories: 323 calories;
- Sodium: 38
- Total Carbohydrate: 36.4
- Cholesterol: 41
- Protein: 12.8
- Total Fat: 13.7

72. Lamb, Carrot, And White Bean Curry Stew

Serving: 6 | Prep: 25mins | Cook: 35mins | Ready in:

Ingredients

- 1 pound ground lamb
- 1 onion, grated
- 1 egg
- 3 tablespoons minced fresh dill
- 1/4 cup minced fresh cilantro
- 2 teaspoons coarse salt
- 1 tablespoon ground cumin
- 1/2 teaspoon ground turmeric
- 1/4 teaspoon ground cinnamon
- 1 teaspoon ground black pepper
- 1/4 cup olive oil
- 1 (8 ounce) package baby carrots
- 2 (15.5 ounce) cans cannellini beans
- 1 cup water
- 1 tablespoon sour cream

Direction

- Combine the ground lamb with egg, onion, cilantro, dill, cumin, salt, cinnamon, pepper, and turmeric in a bowl. Make sure to mix everything well.
- Heat olive oil in a pan over medium-high heat. Crumble the meat mixture into the pan. Cook for 5 to 10 minutes or until it is no longer pink. Mix carrots in. Lower heat to medium. Pour in 2 cans of beans and water. Mix well. Let it simmer for 25 minutes. Add the sour cream and stir it through the mixture. Cook for 5 to 10 minutes until the liquid is thick.

Nutrition Information

- Calories: 457 calories;
- Sodium: 1186
- Total Carbohydrate: 27.9
- Cholesterol: 105
- Protein: 26.4
- Total Fat: 26.1

73. Leek And Meat Fritters

Serving: 8 | Prep: 10mins | Cook: 8mins | Ready in:

Ingredients

- 4 leeks
- 1 pound ground lamb

- 2 eggs
- 1 cup matzo meal
- salt to taste
- 1/2 teaspoon white pepper
- 1 clove garlic, crushed
- 1/2 cup oil for frying

Direction

- Cut white part of leek stalks to 4-5 pieces each; cook in water till tender, uncovered. Drain. Grind, best done in a meat grinder.
- Mix lamb and ground leeks in a big bowl. Add eggs; stir well. Add matzo meal till it's stable yet not too hard. Add another egg if you add too much matzo meal. Add garlic, pepper and salt.
- Make small patties; put on tray to fry. Bite size is the best patty size.
- Heat oil in a big skillet; pan fry till golden. Serve in room temperature/hot.

Nutrition Information

- Calories: 385 calories;
- Sodium: 61
- Total Carbohydrate: 20.1
- Cholesterol: 88
- Protein: 13.2
- Total Fat: 28.5

74. Little Lamb Meatballs In A Spicy Eggplant Tomato Sauce

Serving: 4 | Prep: 25mins | Cook: 1hours30mins | Ready in:

Ingredients

- 1 eggplant, cubed
- 2 tablespoons olive oil
- salt and freshly ground black pepper to taste
- 1/3 cup finely minced onion
- 1 pinch crushed red pepper flakes, or to taste
- 1 1/2 cups chicken broth
- 1 cup marinara sauce
- 1/4 cup plain dry bread crumbs
- 1 large egg
- 1 1/2 tablespoons Greek yogurt
- 1/4 cup finely minced onion
- 4 cloves garlic, finely minced
- 1 1/2 teaspoons kosher salt
- 1 teaspoon freshly ground black pepper
- 1 teaspoon ground cumin
- 1/2 teaspoon ground cinnamon
- 1/4 teaspoon ground coriander
- 1 pound ground lamb
- cayenne pepper to taste
- 1 tablespoon chopped fresh mint

Direction

- Preheat oven to 450 degrees F (230 degrees C).
- Line silicone baking mats or parchment paper on the baking sheet.
- In a large skillet, combine black pepper, salt, olive oil, and eggplant over medium-high heat. Cook and stir for 5 minutes, or until eggplant starts to soften.
- Mix in red pepper flakes and minced onion. Reduce heat to medium and continue to cook and stir for 4 minutes until onions soften.
- Stir in marinara sauce and chicken broth, then reduce heat to medium-low. Simmer sauce mixture for 30 minutes, or until it has reduced by half.
- In a large bowl, whisk Greek yogurt, egg, and bread crumbs. Whisk for 3 minutes until bread crumbs absorb all liquid.
- Add coriander, cinnamon, cumin, black pepper, Kosher salt, garlic, and onions into the bread crumb mixture and mix thoroughly.
- Crumbled lamb into bread crumb spice mixture and stir in cayenne pepper.
- Shape mixture into small meatballs and place on the prepped baking sheet. Bake meatballs in preheated oven for 10 minutes. Meatballs should be browned but still pink inside.
- Remove meatballs from oven and mix into the simmering sauce. Simmer for 30 to 45 minutes over low heat until sauce thickens.

- Serve with a garnish of chopped fresh mint.

Nutrition Information

- Calories: 420 calories;
- Sodium: 1284
- Total Carbohydrate: 21.5
- Cholesterol: 123
- Protein: 24.9
- Total Fat: 26.4

75. Make Ahead Moroccan Lamb Stew

Serving: 6 | Prep: 30mins | Cook: 50mins | Ready in:

Ingredients

- 1 teaspoon ground cinnamon
- 1 teaspoon ground cumin
- 1/2 teaspoon ground ginger
- 1/4 teaspoon ground cloves
- 1/4 teaspoon ground nutmeg
- 1/4 teaspoon ground turmeric
- 1/8 teaspoon curry powder
- 1 teaspoon kosher salt
- 1 pound ground lamb
- 1 tablespoon butter
- 1 sweet onion, chopped
- 1 (14.5 ounce) can organic beef broth
- 1 (14.5 ounce) can organic chicken broth
- 2 (14.5 ounce) cans beef consomme
- 1 (14.5 ounce) can diced tomatoes, undrained
- 1 tablespoon honey
- 3 large carrots, chopped
- 2 sweet potatoes, peeled and diced
- 1 (15 ounce) can garbanzo beans, drained and rinsed
- 1/2 cup chopped dried apricots
- 1 cup dried lentils, rinsed
- ground black pepper, to taste

Direction

- In a big bowl, mix the salt, curry powder, turmeric, nutmeg, cloves, ginger, cumin, and cinnamon. Stir in the ground lamb. Let the mixture rest, chilled in the fridge overnight for the most delicious result.
- In a big pot, melt the butter on medium heat. Cook the onion in the butter for 5-10 minutes until just starting to brown and tender. In the onions, mix in the spiced lamb mixture. Let it cook and stir for about 5 minutes until the meat browns.
- In the pot, pour the consommé, chicken broth and beef broth. Stir in the lentils, dried apricots, garbanzo beans, sweet potatoes, carrots, honey and tomatoes then boil; Turn down heat to low.
- Simmer the stew until the lentils and veggies are soft and cooked, or for 30 minutes. Sprinkle black pepper to taste.

Nutrition Information

- Calories: 465 calories;
- Sodium: 1337
- Total Carbohydrate: 57.3
- Cholesterol: 56
- Protein: 28.2
- Total Fat: 13.9

76. Mama's Oh So Savory Lamb And Eggplant Casserole

Serving: 4 | Prep: 35mins | Cook: 1hours | Ready in:

Ingredients

- 1 (1 pound) eggplant, cut into 1-inch cubes
- salt
- 1 tablespoon olive oil
- 1 large sweet onion, coarsely chopped
- 2 large stalks celery, sliced
- 1/2 teaspoon ground cumin
- 2 pinches dried oregano
- 2 pinches ground dried rosemary

- 2 pinches paprika
- 1/8 teaspoon dried mint
- 1 pinch salt and ground black pepper to taste
- 1 1/2 teaspoons garlic, minced
- 3 tomatoes, coarsely chopped
- 1 cup chicken broth
- 1 (15 ounce) can tomato sauce
- 1 pound ground lamb
- 1 tablespoon olive oil
- 1 lemon, juiced, or to taste

Direction

- Put the eggplant in a colander by the sink; toss with a teaspoon of salt to coat. Set the eggplant aside for a minimum of an hour. Rinse with water to remove the extra salt and bitter liquid; drain thoroughly.
- On medium heat, heat a tablespoon olive oil in a pan; add celery and onion. Cook and stir for 5 mins until the celery is aromatic and the onion is translucent and soft.
- Meanwhile, prepare the lamb seasoning. In a mortar and pestles or small bowl, combine black pepper, ground cumin, salt, oregano, mint, rosemary, and paprika; stir well and set aside.
- In the pan, mix in garlic and eggplant cubes; cook for another 5 mins. Put in 1/2 of the lamb seasoning mixture then the chopped tomatoes; stir and cook for another 5 mins. Save the leftover seasoning.
- Preheat the oven to 190°C or 375°F. Oil a two-quart casserole dish.
- Add the chicken broth and 1/2 can of the tomato sauce in the pan and let it simmer for 10 mins. If the sauce is getting dry, pour in a little water. Pour sauce in the greased casserole dish.
- Place the pan back in a stove on medium-high heat. Pour the saved tablespoon of oil and heat on medium heat. Add ground lamb and the leftover seasoning mixture in the pan; cook and stir until the ground lamb resembles imperfect meatballs and are equally brown.
- Move lamb to the casserole dish. Press the lamb in the vegetable mixture until a bit submerged. Combine fresh lemon juice and the leftover tomato sauce; pour the mixture on the dish.
- Bake for 45 mins to an hour without cover until the veggies reach the preferred tenderness.

Nutrition Information

- Calories: 385 calories;
- Total Fat: 23.2
- Sodium: 1471
- Total Carbohydrate: 22.6
- Cholesterol: 77
- Protein: 24

77. Mandy's Lamb Enchiladas

Serving: 6 | Prep: 15mins | Cook: 30mins | Ready in:

Ingredients

- 2 pounds ground lamb
- 1 onion, chopped
- 1 (14.5 ounce) can diced tomatoes, drained
- 1 (15.25 ounce) can red kidney beans, drained
- 1 (8 ounce) package sliced fresh mushrooms
- 1 (8 ounce) jar salsa
- 12 (8 inch) flour tortillas
- 2 cups shredded Cheddar cheese

Direction

- Preheat an oven to 175°C/350°F.
- Sauté onion and lamb for 4-5 minutes in a big skillet on medium high heat; mix in mushrooms, beans and tomatoes when lightly browned. Add 1/2 salsa; cook all together till heated through.
- Put it onto tortillas, evenly dividing; roll up tortillas. Put into 9x13-in. lightly greased baking dish. Spread leftover salsa on top; sprinkle cheese.

- Bake for 30 minutes at 175°C/350°F till cheese is bubbly and melted.

Nutrition Information

- Calories: 897 calories;
- Total Carbohydrate: 79.9
- Cholesterol: 142
- Protein: 49.6
- Total Fat: 40.7
- Sodium: 1394

78. Marvelous Mongolian Meatballs

Serving: 12 | Prep: 30mins | Cook: 2hours35mins | Ready in:

Ingredients

- Mongolian Sauce:
- 1/2 cup hoisin sauce
- 4 cloves garlic, minced
- 2 tablespoons red wine vinegar
- 1 1/2 tablespoons soy sauce
- 1 tablespoon grated fresh ginger
- 1 tablespoon rice vinegar
- 2 teaspoons sesame oil
- 2 teaspoons white sugar
- 1 1/2 teaspoons hot sauce
- 1/2 teaspoon ground white pepper
- 1/2 teaspoon ground black pepper
- Meatballs:
- 1 pound ground beef
- 1/2 pound ground lamb
- 1/2 head cabbage, chopped
- 1 yellow onion, chopped
- 1/2 cup panko bread crumbs
- 1/2 cup grated carrot
- 1 tablespoon ground ginger
- 1/4 cup chopped green onion
- 6 cloves garlic, chopped
- 1 teaspoon garlic salt
- 1/2 teaspoon ground black pepper

Direction

- Set the oven at 450°F (230°C) and start preheating.
- In a large bowl, whisk together black pepper, white pepper, hot sauce, sugar, sesame oil, rice vinegar, grated ginger, soy sauce, red wine vinegar, 4 cloves of garlic and hoisin sauce.
- In a separate bowl, combine 2 tablespoons of the hoisin sauce mixture, black pepper, garlic salt, 6 cloves of chopped garlic, green onion, ground ginger, carrot, panko, yellow onion, cabbage, ground lamb and ground beef; form into meatballs and place on a jelly roll pan.
- Bake in the preheated oven for around 25 minutes, till not pink in the center anymore. Turn the meatballs by shaking the pan; switch the oven to broil; cook under the broiler for around 10 more minutes, till browned. Set aside and allow to cool slightly.
- Place the warm meatballs into a slow cooker; transfer the hoisin sauce mixture over.
- Cook while stirring intermittently for 2-4 hours, on low.

Nutrition Information

- Calories: 181 calories;
- Total Fat: 8.6
- Sodium: 519
- Total Carbohydrate: 15.6
- Cholesterol: 37
- Protein: 11.7

79. Mediterranean Lamb Meatball Sandwiches With Yogurt Sauce

Serving: 4 | Prep: 25mins | Cook: 18mins | Ready in:

Ingredients

- Lamb Meatballs:
- 1 small onion
- 1 cup fresh mint leaves

- 3 cloves garlic
- 1 pound ground lamb
- 3 tablespoons ground sweet paprika
- 1 tablespoon ground cumin
- 1 teaspoon salt
- 1 teaspoon ground black pepper
- cooking spray
- 1/4 cup vegetable oil, or as needed
- Yogurt Sauce:
- 1 (6 ounce) container Greek yogurt
- 2 tablespoons tahini
- 1 1/2 teaspoons lemon juice
- 4 sheets lavash bread
- 1 (4 ounce) package crumbled feta cheese
- 1 cup shredded lettuce
- 1/2 cup diced fresh tomatoes
- 1/2 cup cucumber matchsticks

Direction

- Process garlic, mint and onion till minced in a food processor. Add pepper, salt, cumin, paprika and lamb; process till smooth.
- Shape 1 1/2 tsp. lamb mixture to ball; to make 20 meatballs, repeat with leftover lamb mixture.
- Preheat an oven to 190°C/375°F; use cooking spray to grease a baking sheet.
- Put 1/4-in. oil in a big skillet; heat till bubbles form around wooden spoon's end dipped into oil on medium heat. Add 1/2 meatballs; cook for 1-2 minutes per side till browned. Put onto prepped baking sheet; repeat with leftover meatballs.
- In preheated oven, bake for 10 minutes till center isn't pink.
- To make yogurt sauce, mix lemon juice, tahini and yogurt in a bowl.
- In a line down the middle of every lavash sheet, put 2-3 tbsp. yogurt sauce; add 5 meatballs, 2 tbsp. cucumber, 2 tbsp. tomato, 1/4 cup lettuce and 2-3 tbsp. feta cheese. Fold sides and 1 end of lavash up, to roll into the wraps.

Nutrition Information

- Calories: 850 calories;
- Total Carbohydrate: 71.2
- Cholesterol: 110
- Protein: 41.2
- Total Fat: 46.5
- Sodium: 1475

80. Mediterranean Orzo Spinach Salad

Serving: 6 | Prep: 15mins | Cook: 20mins | Ready in:

Ingredients

- 1 cup uncooked orzo pasta
- 2 tablespoons extra virgin olive oil, divided
- 1 pound ground lamb
- 2 cloves garlic, chopped
- 1 tablespoon ground coriander
- salt and pepper to taste
- 4 cups fresh spinach leaves, chopped
- 3 tomatoes, seeded and chopped
- 1 lemon, zested and juiced
- 1/4 cup chopped fresh mint leaves
- 1/4 cup chopped fresh parsley
- 5 green onions, chopped
- 1 cup crumbled feta cheese

Direction

- Boil a big pot of lightly salted water. Cook orzo pasta in boiling water for 5mins or until al dente; drain.
- On medium heat, heat a tablespoon of olive oil in a pan; add in garlic and lamb. Sprinkle pepper, salt, and coriander over the lamb to season. Cook the lamb until evenly brown. Take off from heat, then drain.
- Combine the remaining olive oil, green onions, parsley, mint, lemon zest and juice, tomatoes and spinach in a big bowl. Toss with the feta cheese, lamb and orzo. Serve.

Nutrition Information

- Calories: 461 calories;
- Sodium: 535
- Total Carbohydrate: 34.5
- Cholesterol: 88
- Protein: 25.6
- Total Fat: 25

81. Mediterranean Stuffed Zucchini

Serving: 4 | Prep: 20mins | Cook: 50mins | Ready in:

Ingredients

- 1 extra large zucchini, halved lengthwise
- 1 tablespoon olive oil
- 1 sweet onion, chopped
- 1 tablespoon chopped garlic
- 1 pound ground lamb
- coarse salt to taste
- ground black pepper to taste
- 1 (16 ounce) can tomato sauce
- 2 tomatoes, chopped
- 3/4 cup crumbled feta cheese
- 1/2 cup pine nuts
- 1/4 cup mint leaves
- 1/4 cup water
- 1/4 cup mint leaves
- 3/4 cup seasoned bread crumbs
- 3/4 cup shredded mozzarella cheese

Direction

- Set an oven to 230°C (450°F) and start preheating.
- Separate and remove the pulp and seeds from the zucchini using a melon baller, carve each half and leave approximately 1/2-inch shell. Chop the zucchini pulp into 1/4-inch diameter pieces. Dispose the seeds.
- In a large skillet, heat the olive oil on medium heat. In the heated oil, stir and cook the garlic and onion for 5 minutes until they are tender. Add ground lamb; keep on stirring and cooking for 5-7 minutes until the lamb is browned lightly. Add the chopped zucchini into the lamb mixture and stir. Turn down the heat to medium-low. Let the mixture simmer for 3 minutes until the zucchini becomes hot. Drain off the excess grease. Flavor the lamb mixture with black pepper and coarse salt.
- Take the skillet away from the heat. Stir 1/4 cup of the mint leaves, pine nuts, feta cheese, tomatoes, and tomato sauce through the lamb mixture, then put into the zucchini halves. Place the stuffed zucchini halves in a large baking dish. Pour the water to the baking dish.
- In the prepared oven, bake for half an hour. In a bowl, combine mozzarella cheese and breadcrumbs. Dust the zucchini with 1/4 cup of mint leaves and put the breadcrumb mixture on top. Keep on baking for 10 more minutes until the top is browned and crusty.

Nutrition Information

- Calories: 649 calories;
- Protein: 40.6
- Total Fat: 38.7
- Sodium: 1523
- Total Carbohydrate: 38.8
- Cholesterol: 115

82. Middle Eastern Kibbeh

Serving: 12 | Prep: 20mins | Cook: 12mins | Ready in:

Ingredients

- 2/3 cup medium coarse bulgur
- 1 cup fresh mint leaves
- 1 large onion, chopped
- 1 teaspoon ground cumin
- 1 teaspoon ground allspice
- 1 teaspoon salt
- 1/2 teaspoon ground black pepper
- 1 1/2 pounds lean ground lamb
- 3 tablespoons olive oil

Direction

- In a microwaveable bowl, put in the bulgur and fill it with enough water up to the top of the bulgur. Put it inside the microwave and let the bulgur cook on high setting for 1-2 minutes until the bulgur have soaked up the water and have bulged in size. Give it a little mix and let it cool.
- In the food processor bowl, put in the mint leaves. Run the food processor and slowly put in the onion down the feed tube until there are fine chops of onion and mint. Mix the mint-onion mixture, salt, cumin, pepper and allspice in the cooked bulgur. Combine the bulgur mixture and ground lamb and mix well. Use slightly wet hands to form the lamb-bulgur mixture into small patties about the size of a palm.
- In a skillet placed on medium heat setting, put in the olive oil and let it heat up. Put in the kibbeh patties and let it cook for about 6 minutes per side until the patties turn golden brown in color on the outside and cooked thoroughly in the middle; flip the patties once to let it cook on both sides.

Nutrition Information

- Calories: 159 calories;
- Protein: 10.9
- Total Fat: 9.6
- Sodium: 228
- Total Carbohydrate: 7.4
- Cholesterol: 38

83. Middle Eastern Stuffed Zucchini

Serving: 4 | Prep: 15mins | Cook: 45mins | Ready in:

Ingredients

- 1/4 pound ground lamb
- 1/4 cup basmati rice
- 2 cups tomato puree, divided
- 1/2 teaspoon dried mint
- 1/2 teaspoon salt
- 1/8 teaspoon black pepper
- 2 pounds small zucchini or yellow squash
- 1/2 teaspoon salt
- 1 teaspoon minced garlic
- 1 tablespoon lemon juice
- 1/2 teaspoon dried mint

Direction

- Combine pepper, salt, 1/2 teaspoons of mint, 2 tablespoons of tomato puree, basmati rice, and ground lamb together; combine thoroughly and put aside.
- Cut off the ends of the zucchinis and use an apple corer to hollow the centers. Fill with the lamb mixture.
- In a large skillet, stir 1/2 teaspoon of salt with the rest of the tomato puree together. Put the filled zucchini to the sauce and cover the zucchini with enough water. Simmer on medium-high heat; turn down the heat to medium-low, put a cover on and let simmer for half an hour.
- Stir in the remaining 1/2 teaspoon of mint, lemon juice, and garlic. Put a cover on and simmer for 15 more minutes. Slice the zucchini crosswise into rounds and place onto a serving plate to serve. Spread the sauce over the top.

Nutrition Information

- Calories: 183 calories;
- Total Carbohydrate: 28.7
- Cholesterol: 19
- Protein: 10.6
- Total Fat: 4.7
- Sodium: 1119

84. Minced Lamb Bake

Serving: 4 | Prep: 15mins | Cook: 45mins | Ready in:

Ingredients

- 2 tablespoons olive oil
- 1 medium onion, finely chopped
- 1/2 pound ground lamb
- 4 fresh mushrooms, sliced
- 1 cup dried small pasta shells, cooked according to pkg. directions
- 2 cups bottled marinara sauce
- 1 teaspoon butter
- 4 teaspoons all-purpose flour
- 1 cup milk
- 1 egg, beaten
- 1 cup grated Cheddar cheese

Direction

- Preheat an oven to 175 °C or 350 °F.
- In a wok over moderate heat, heat olive oil, put in onion and fry till tender and soft. Mix in mushrooms and lamb; allow to cook till meat has browned, mixing from time to time to crumble the meat. Add marinara sauce and bring to a simmer. Mix in cooked pasta, then transfer to a baking dish that is ovenproof.
- In a small saucepan, liquify butter over low heat. Add flour and combine thoroughly. Add milk, raise heat to moderate, and allow to cook till thickened. Mix quarter cup of thickened milk into the egg, approximately 1 tablespoon at a time to incorporate the egg, then put egg into the rest of the sauce and mix together. Spread this white sauce on top of the pasta and scatter cheese on top.
- In prepped oven, bake for half an hour till crispy and browned.

Nutrition Information

- Calories: 635 calories;
- Protein: 27.4
- Total Fat: 37
- Sodium: 774
- Total Carbohydrate: 47.3
- Cholesterol: 128

85. Mom's Irish Ziti

Serving: 8 | Prep: 15mins | Cook: 45mins | Ready in:

Ingredients

- 3 cups rigatoni
- 1/2 pound bulk sweet Italian sausage
- 1/2 pound ground lamb
- 1 clove garlic, chopped
- 4 1/2 cups tomato sauce
- 1/2 pound provolone cheese, sliced
- 2 teaspoons Italian seasoning
- 1 pinch crushed red pepper, or to taste
- 1/2 pound mozzarella cheese, sliced
- 1/2 cup grated Parmigiano-Reggiano cheese

Direction

- Preheat oven to 175°C/350°F; use cooking spray to prep 1 1/2-qt. baking dish.
- Put a big pot of lightly salted water on a rolling boil on high heat. Mix in rigatoni when water boils; boil. Occasionally mixing, boil for 13 minutes till pasta is cooked yet firm to chew. Drain it well inside colander in sink; put into prepped baking dish.
- Put skillet on medium heat; crumble lamb and sausage into hot skillet. Mix and cook, using a wooden spoon to break meat to small pieces, for 7-10 minutes till fully browned. Mix in garlic; cook for 2-3 minutes. Drain fat from skillet.
- Put 1/2 tomato sauce on pasta; layer with meat mixture and provolone slices. Season with crushed red pepper and Italian seasoning; top with leftover tomato sauce and mozzarella cheese. Sprinkle Parmigiano-Reggiano cheese over dish.
- In preheated oven, bake for 25-35 minutes till bubbly and hot.

Nutrition Information

- Calories: 457 calories;

- Total Fat: 23.6
- Sodium: 1475
- Total Carbohydrate: 31.1
- Cholesterol: 72
- Protein: 30.4

86. No Eggplant Moussaka

Serving: 6 | Prep: 40mins | Cook: 2hours | Ready in:

Ingredients

- 2 tablespoons butter
- 2 onions, chopped
- 1 tablespoon chopped parsley
- 2 pounds ground lamb
- 2 (16 ounce) cans whole peeled tomatoes
- 1 tablespoon Italian seasoning
- salt and pepper to taste
- 2 tablespoons butter
- 2 tablespoons all-purpose flour
- 1 1/2 cups milk
- 1 beaten egg
- 1/2 cup shredded sharp Cheddar cheese
- 4 potatoes, peeled and thinly sliced

Direction

- Set the oven to 375°F (190°C) and start preheating. Grease a large casserole dish.
- In a large heavy skillet, over medium heat, heat 2 tablespoons butter. Sauté parsley and onions until onion becomes translucent and soft. Raise the heat; add lamb; cool until brown evenly. Drain excess fat; put aside.
- Mix pepper, salt, Italian seasoning and tomatoes in a large bowl. Chop tomatoes; combine well with seasonings. Put aside.
- Over medium heat, melt 2 tablespoons of butter in a saucepan. Stir in flour until smooth. Beat egg and milk together; beat into flour mixture gradually. Cook while stirring constantly until smooth and thick. Take out of the heat; stir in grated cheese.
- Place 1/3 of sliced potatoes on the bottom of the casserole dish; cover as well as possible. Place 1/2 of meat mixture on top, then top with 1/2 of tomato mixture. Do again the layers, finishing with a layer of potatoes on top. Evenly spread cheese sauce over top.
- Bake with a cover in 1 1/2 hours in the prepared oven. Remove cover and bake for half an hour or until it turn light brown.

Nutrition Information

- Calories: 613 calories;
- Total Fat: 34.5
- Sodium: 535
- Total Carbohydrate: 39.5
- Cholesterol: 170
- Protein: 36.7

87. Paul's Fat Tire® Lamb Chili

Serving: 4 | Prep: 10mins | Cook: 2hours25mins | Ready in:

Ingredients

- 1 pound ground lamb
- 1 (16 ounce) can tomato sauce
- 1 (16 ounce) can black beans, rinsed and drained
- 1 (12 fluid ounce) can or bottle amber ale (such as Fat Tire®)
- 1 (4 ounce) carton Texas-style chili seasoning kit (such as Carroll Shelby's®)
- 1 red onion, finely chopped
- 3 jalapeno peppers, ribs removed, chopped
- 3 cloves garlic, minced
- 1 habanero pepper, ribs removed and chopped (wear gloves)

Direction

- Bring a large skillet to medium-high heat. Cook lamb for 5 to 7 minutes in the heated skillet, stirring while cooking, until crumbly

and browned; drain lamb and discard drippings.
- Combine amber ale, black beans, and tomato sauce in a large pot. Mix contents of the chili seasoning kit into the tomato mixture, saving the masa flour; add habanero pepper, garlic, jalapeno peppers, and onion. Mix in lamb.
- Heat the pot over low heat until lamb mixture starts to lightly simmer for about 15 minutes, stirring often. Cover the pot and lower heat to lowest setting (warm); cook for 2 to 4 hours, stirring from time to time, until chili flavors meld. If the chili looks too thin, gradually whisk in the reserved masa flour. If the chili looks too thick, pour in more water.

Nutrition Information

- Calories: 430 calories;
- Protein: 29.5
- Total Fat: 16.3
- Sodium: 1471
- Total Carbohydrate: 35.5
- Cholesterol: 76

88. Roasted Eggplant Pastitsio

Serving: 12 | Prep: 25mins | Cook: 1hours45mins | Ready in:

Ingredients

- Meat Sauce:
- 1 large eggplant, halved lengthwise
- 1 tablespoon olive oil
- 1 1/2 cups chopped onions
- 1 pound ground lamb
- 1 clove garlic, minced
- 1 1/2 teaspoons salt
- 1 teaspoon ground cumin
- 1 teaspoon dried oregano
- 1/4 teaspoon freshly ground black pepper
- 1/4 teaspoon ground cinnamon
- 1 (14 ounce) can diced tomatoes
- 1 (14 ounce) can crushed tomatoes
- 1 tablespoon chopped fresh mint
- White Sauce:
- 2 eggs
- 2 tablespoons unsalted butter
- 2 tablespoons all-purpose flour
- 2 cups milk
- 1 clove garlic, lightly crushed
- 1 (8 ounce) package crumbled feta cheese
- 1/2 teaspoon salt
- black pepper to taste
- 1 pinch freshly grated nutmeg
- cooking spray
- 1 (12 ounce) package penne pasta

Direction

- Place the oven rack 6-inches away from the heat source. Set the oven's broiler to preheating. Use an aluminum foil to line the baking sheet. Arrange eggplant halves onto the foil.
- Broil the eggplant for 15 minutes, checking the eggplant frequently and rotating the baking sheet if necessary until the skin has some chars and turns black. Allow it to cool for 5 minutes until handled easily. Peel the skin off the eggplant. Chop its flesh coarsely.
- Put olive oil in a large skillet and heat it over medium heat. Add the onions. Cook and stir over medium heat for 5 minutes until the onion turns translucent. Add the lamb. Cook for 5 minutes while breaking it into small pieces until it is no longer pink. Pour the grease off from the skillet.
- Stir the salt, pepper, cinnamon, minced garlic, cumin, and oregano into the skillet. Cook the mixture for 1 minute. Mix in crushed tomatoes, chopped eggplant, and diced tomatoes. Simmer the sauce and cook for 20 minutes until thickened. Remove from the heat. Mix in chopped mint.
- Put butter in a saucepan and melt it over medium heat. Mix in flour. Cook and stir constantly for 2 minutes. Pour in milk and stir the mixture until smooth. Add the crushed garlic clove. Adjust the heat to high. Boil the

milk. Lower the heat to a simmer and stir frequently for 5 minutes until thickened slightly. Remove from the heat, discarding the garlic clove.
- Beat the eggs in a large heatproof bowl. In a steady stream, pour the hot milk mixture into the beaten eggs while constantly stirring it. Mix in nutmeg, salt, pepper, and feta cheese.
- Set the oven to 425°F (220°C) for preheating. Coat the 9x13-inches baking dish with the cooking spray.
- Boil a large pot of salted water. Add the pasta. Cook for 12 minutes while occasionally stirring it until the pasta is tender yet firm to the bite; drain.
- Divide the pasta between the lamb sauce and white sauce, stirring until well-combined. Add pasta with lamb sauce to the prepared baking dish. Pour white sauce on top of the pasta.
- Let it bake inside the preheated oven for 30 minutes until the pastitsio is bubbling and its top is golden. Allow it to cool for 5 minutes; serve.

Nutrition Information

- Calories: 330 calories;
- Total Fat: 14.7
- Sodium: 747
- Total Carbohydrate: 33.5
- Cholesterol: 78
- Protein: 17

89. Spicy Lamb Patties

Serving: 4 | Prep: 10mins | Cook: 15mins | Ready in:

Ingredients

- 1 pound ground lamb
- 3 green onions, minced
- 4 cloves garlic, minced
- 1 tablespoon curry powder
- 1 teaspoon ground cumin
- 1/4 teaspoon dried red pepper flakes
- salt and pepper to taste

Direction

- Set a grill to high heat to preheat.
- Mix the lamb, pepper, salt, red pepper, cumin, curry powder, garlic, and green onions in a bowl. Shape into 4 patties.
- Grease the grill grate lightly. Grill the patties until done for 5 minutes on each side.

Nutrition Information

- Calories: 237 calories;
- Cholesterol: 76
- Protein: 20.1
- Total Fat: 15.8
- Sodium: 140
- Total Carbohydrate: 3.1

90. Stuffed Bell Peppers, Greek Style

Serving: 6 | Prep: 20mins | Cook: 1hours | Ready in:

Ingredients

- 2 tablespoons extra virgin olive oil
- 1 1/4 cups onion, chopped
- 1 pound ground lamb
- 3/4 cup white rice
- 3/4 teaspoon salt
- 1/2 teaspoon ground black pepper
- 1/2 teaspoon dried mint, crushed
- 1 cup water
- 1/4 cup chopped fresh parsley to taste
- 1 (14.5 ounce) can chicken broth
- 1 (14.5 ounce) can petite diced tomatoes
- 6 green bell pepper, top removed, seeded

Direction

- Turn the oven to 350°F (175°C) to preheat.

- In a big frying pan, heat olive oil over medium-high heat. Mix in ground lamb and onion; stir and cook for 7 minutes until the meat is not pink anymore and the onion is soft. Mix in mint, black pepper, salt, and rice; cook for another 5 minutes. Add parsley and water. Lower the heat to medium-low and keep stirring and cooking for 15 minutes until the rice has fully absorbed the water. In an oven-proof dish that can just hold the peppers, combine diced tomatoes and chicken broth. In the bell peppers, put the lamb mixture, and put them into the dish.
- Bake for 45 minutes in the preheated oven until the tomatoes are bubbling and the peppers are soft.

Nutrition Information

- Calories: 325 calories;
- Sodium: 448
- Total Carbohydrate: 29.7
- Cholesterol: 51
- Protein: 16.6
- Total Fat: 15.2

91. Stuffed Grape Leaves (Dolmades)

Serving: 8 | Prep: 35mins | Cook: 55mins | Ready in:

Ingredients

- 1 1/2 pounds ground lamb
- 2 medium onions, finely chopped
- 2/3 cup long grain white rice
- 2/3 cup pine nuts
- 1 teaspoon salt
- 1/4 teaspoon pepper
- 1 teaspoon chopped fresh mint
- 1 (8 ounce) jar grape leaves, drained and rinsed
- 1 1/2 cups water

Direction

- In a mixing bowl, combine lamb with mint, pepper, salt, pine nuts, rice, and onions until evenly incorporated. Open up a grape leaf gently; arrange grape leaf onto a work surface, rib-side down. In the center of the grape leaf, place a rounded tablespoon of the meat mixture. Fold the leaf's bottom over the meat mixture, fold in the sides, and roll tightly into cylinder. Arrange the rolled grape leaf, seam side down, in a large skillet. Repeat the steps with the rest of the grape leaves, pressing them in a tight, single layer.
- Bring water in a skillet to a simmer. Turn heat to medium-low; simmer, covered, for 50 to 55 minutes until rice is tender. Check once in a while; pour in more water if needed. Remove water before serving.

Nutrition Information

- Calories: 321 calories;
- Protein: 20
- Total Fat: 18
- Sodium: 1152
- Total Carbohydrate: 20.6
- Cholesterol: 57

92. Three Meat Loaf

Serving: 16 | Prep: 20mins | Cook: 1hours | Ready in:

Ingredients

- Sauce:
- 1/4 cup tomato sauce
- 2 tablespoons Worcestershire sauce
- 1 tablespoon spicy mustard
- 1 tablespoon honey
- Meat loaves:
- 1/2 pound ground beef
- 1/2 pound ground turkey
- 1/2 pound ground lamb

- 2 1/4 cups tomato sauce
- 1 1/2 cups rolled oats
- 1 egg
- 1/2 sweet onion, chopped
- 1 teaspoon salt
- 1/2 teaspoon ground black pepper

Direction

- Set oven to 350°F (175°C) to preheat.
- In a bowl, mix together honey, spicy mustard, Worcestershire sauce and 1/4 cup of tomato sauce; put aside.
- In a large bowl, thoroughly mix ground lamb, ground turkey, ground beef, salt, pepper, sweet onion, egg, oats and 2 1/4 cup of tomato sauce; separate into halves and shape 2 loaves. Place loaves into loaf pans.
- Bake for 45 minutes in the prepared oven, top with sauce using a brush, and keep baking for about 15 minutes more until no pink remains in the center. An instant-read thermometer should show at least 160°F (70°C) when inserted into the center. Allow to cool lightly in pans before serving.

Nutrition Information

- Calories: 125 calories;
- Total Carbohydrate: 9.2
- Cholesterol: 40
- Protein: 9.6
- Total Fat: 5.6
- Sodium: 408

93. Tikka Masala Skillet Shepherd's Pie

Serving: 4 | Prep: 20mins | Cook: 1hours | Ready in:

Ingredients

- Lamb Filling:
- 2 teaspoons vegetable oil
- 1 pound lean ground lamb
- 1/4 teaspoon salt
- 1/4 teaspoon freshly ground pepper
- 1 onion, finely chopped
- 1 carrot, finely chopped
- 1 rib celery, finely chopped
- 1 small red bell pepper, finely chopped
- 1 clove garlic, chopped
- 1/2 (400 mL) jar Patak's Tikka Masala Sauce
- 2 tablespoons finely chopped fresh cilantro
- Sweet Potato Topping:
- 2 medium sweet potatoes, peeled and cut into chunks
- 2 medium Yukon Gold potatoes, peeled and cut into chunks
- 1/4 cup milk
- 2 tablespoons butter
- 1/4 teaspoon salt
- 1/4 teaspoon freshly ground pepper

Direction

- Preheat oven to 204°C (or 400°F) in advance to make lamb filling. In the meantime, bring oil to medium-high heat in an ovenproof high-sided 10" skillet.
- Cook and stir frequently to brown the lamb, 8-10 minutes; degrease the pan.
- Mix in garlic, red pepper, celery, carrot and onion. Cook, while stirring every now and then, until vegetables are tender, 5-8 minutes. Add in Patak's Tikka Masala Sauce and stir until thoroughly combined; simmer. Keep on simmering heat for 5 minutes.
- Cook Yukon Gold potatoes and sweet potatoes on medium heat for 18-20 minutes until softened in boiling salted water to make topping.
- Drain off all the water. Put the potatoes back into the pot. Bring in pepper, salt, butter and milk, then mash until no lumps remain.
- Spread sweet potato topping on top of the filling, then smoothen out the surface. Set the skillet on a baking sheet.
- Bake until bubbles appear on top of the filling and the topping is heated and lightly

goldened, 15-20 minutes. Decorate with cilantro.

Nutrition Information

- Calories: 521 calories;
- Sodium: 645
- Total Carbohydrate: 44.2
- Cholesterol: 96
- Protein: 24.6
- Total Fat: 27.6

94. Tina's Greek Stuffed Peppers

Serving: 6 | Prep: 30mins | Cook: 30mins | Ready in:

Ingredients

- 1/2 pound orzo pasta
- 2 tablespoons olive oil
- 1 yellow onion, chopped
- 2 large cloves garlic, chopped
- 1 1/2 pounds ground lamb
- 4 1/2 teaspoons dried oregano
- 1 tablespoon dried basil
- salt and pepper to taste
- 1 (16 ounce) package frozen chopped spinach, thawed and drained
- 2 tomatoes, diced
- 1 (6 ounce) can tomato paste
- 8 ounces crumbled feta cheese
- 6 large green or red bell peppers - tops removed and seeded
- olive oil

Direction

- On high heat, boil a pot of lightly salted water; add orzo. Cook without cover for about 8mins while mixing from time to time, until the orzo is tender but still firm to chew; drain.
- On medium-high heat, heat 2 tbsp. olive oil in a big pan; add garlic and onion. Cook and stir for about a minute, until aromatic. Crumble ground lamb into the mixture; sprinkle pepper, salt, basil and oregano to season. Keep on cooking for 7-10mins, until the lamb is fully browned; take off from heat. Mix in feta cheese, tomato paste, tomatoes, spinach and orzo until evenly combined.
- Preheat the oven to 200°C or 400°F.
- Massage the outside and the tops of the bell peppers evenly with 2 tbsp. olive oil; sprinkle pepper and salt to season. Place the bell peppers in a baking dish that's big enough to fit them, standing upright. Stuff the lamb mixture inside the peppers until full, place back the tops.
- Bake stuffed bell peppers for 30-40mins in the preheated oven, until they start to brown.

Nutrition Information

- Calories: 639 calories;
- Cholesterol: 109
- Protein: 36.2
- Total Fat: 34
- Sodium: 775
- Total Carbohydrate: 51

95. Traditional Gyro Meat

Serving: 10 | Prep: 15mins | Cook: 45mins | Ready in:

Ingredients

- 1/2 onion, cut into chunks
- 1 pound ground lamb
- 1 pound ground beef
- 1 tablespoon minced garlic
- 1 teaspoon dried oregano
- 1 teaspoon ground cumin
- 1 teaspoon dried marjoram
- 1 teaspoon ground dried rosemary
- 1 teaspoon ground dried thyme
- 1 teaspoon ground black pepper
- 1/4 teaspoon sea salt

Direction

- In a food processor, add onion and process until chopped finely. Scoop into the center of a towel with onions then bring up the ends of the towel and squeeze out liquid from onions. Put into a mixing bowl with onions together with beef and lamb. Use salt, black pepper, thyme, rosemary, marjoram, cumin, oregano and garlic to season. Use your hands to mix the mixture until well-blended. Cover and chill for about 1-2 hours to let flavors combine.
- Set the oven to 165°C or 325°F to preheat.
- Put into the food processor with the meat mixture and process for about 1 minute until the mixture feels tacky and chopped finely. Pack into a 4"x7" loaf pan with the meat mixture, being sure there are no air pockets. Use a wet kitchen towel to line a roasting pan. Place on the towel with the loaf pan inside the roasting pan and put into the preheated oven. Fill boiling water into roasting pan until reaching halfway up the sides of loaf pan.
- Bake the gyro meat for 45-60 minutes, until it is not pink in the center anymore and its internal temperature reaches 75°C or 165°F measured by a meat thermometer. Drain any accumulated fat and let the meat cool a bit prior to slicing thinly and serving.

Nutrition Information

- Calories: 179 calories;
- Total Fat: 11.7
- Sodium: 97
- Total Carbohydrate: 1.9
- Cholesterol: 59
- Protein: 15.7

96. Traditional Gyros

Serving: 12 | Prep: 15mins | Cook: 45mins | Ready in:

Ingredients

- 1 small onion, cut into chunks
- 1 pound ground lamb
- 1 pound ground beef
- 1 tablespoon minced garlic
- 1 teaspoon dried oregano
- 1 teaspoon ground cumin
- 1 teaspoon dried marjoram
- 1 teaspoon dried thyme
- 1 teaspoon dried rosemary
- 1 teaspoon freshly ground black pepper
- 1/4 teaspoon sea salt
- boiling water as needed
- 12 tablespoons hummus
- 12 pita bread rounds
- 1 small head lettuce, shredded
- 1 large tomato, sliced
- 1 large red onion, sliced
- 6 ounces crumbled feta cheese
- 24 tablespoons tzatziki sauce

Direction

- In food processor, put onion; blend until chopped finely. Place onion onto a piece of cheese cloth; then squeeze liquid out. Put onion into a large bowl.
- Using hands, mix onion with salt, black pepper, rosemary, thyme, marjoram, cumin, oregano, garlic, beef and lamb until mixed well. Wrap the bowl in plastic wrap. Place in the refrigerator for 120 minutes until the flavors blend.
- Start preheating the oven to 325°F (165°C).
- In food processor, put meat mixture; pulse for one minute, until they are tacky and chopped finely. Pack the meat mixture into a loaf pan (about 7x4 inches), making sure there have no air pockets. Position loaf pan into the roasting pan. Pour around loaf pan with enough of boiling water to reach halfway up sides.
- Bake in prepared oven for 45-60 minutes until middle is no longer pink. The instant-read thermometer should register at least 165°F (74°C) when inserted into middle. Pour off all the accumulated fat. Let cool slightly.
- Slice gyro meat mixture thinly.

- Spread on every pita bread with one tablespoon of the hummus; add tzatziki sauce, feta cheese, red onion, tomato, lettuce and gyro meat mixture over top of each.

Nutrition Information

- Calories: 425 calories;
- Total Carbohydrate: 42.8
- Cholesterol: 61
- Protein: 22.4
- Total Fat: 40.8
- Sodium: 620

97. Turkish Meatballs (Kofta)

Serving: 6 | Prep: 20mins | Cook: 4mins | Ready in:

Ingredients

- 2 slices slightly stale whole wheat bread
- 1 pound lean ground lamb
- 1 egg
- 2 tablespoons chopped fresh parsley
- 2 cloves garlic
- 1 teaspoon ground cumin
- 1 teaspoon dried mint
- 1/2 teaspoon ground allspice
- 1/2 teaspoon salt
- 1/2 teaspoon ground black pepper
- 1 tablespoon olive oil

Direction

- In a food processor, tear up bread slices into a bowl; process into fine crumbs. Put in egg and ground lamb; process till blended. Put in pepper, salt, allspice, mint, cumin, garlic and parsley; process till equally combined.
- Roll the lamb mixture into small meatballs.
- Place a large skillet on medium heat; heat olive oil. Cook the meatballs in batches while turning sometimes for 4-5 minutes per patch, till browned on all sides. Use a slotted spoon to move to a paper towel-lined plate.

Nutrition Information

- Calories: 181 calories;
- Total Carbohydrate: 4.8
- Cholesterol: 74
- Protein: 13.9
- Total Fat: 11.6
- Sodium: 284

98. Turkish Rissoles

Serving: 6 | Prep: 30mins | Cook: 10mins | Ready in:

Ingredients

- 1 pound ground lamb
- 1 pound ground beef
- 1 teaspoon salt
- 1 teaspoon ground black pepper
- 1 tablespoon ground cumin
- 2 teaspoons ground sweet paprika
- 3 tablespoons tomato paste
- 2 onions, peeled and cut into chunks
- 4 cloves garlic, peeled
- 1 tablespoon olive oil
- 1/4 bunch fresh parsley, chopped
- 3 tablespoons all-purpose flour
- 2 small eggs

Direction

- In a large bowl, place cumin, paprika, salt, pepper, tomato paste, lamb and beef (Do not mix, put aside only).
- Blend onions and garlic then slowly add in olive oil until paste-like mixture. Add in chopped parsley and then blend for 5 seconds. Transfer the blended mixture to the meat. Add flour and eggs then gently knead with clean hands. Let it stand for 5 minutes to develop

flavor and lightly knead again to well combine all the ingredients.
- Shape the meat mixture into small balls and press gently between palms to flatten and form patty. Take a small handful of the meat each time. Put on a big plate. Repeat to all remaining meat mixture. Separate patty layers and cover it using plastic wrap then chill on the fridge for at least an hour.
- Preheat broiler and put rack 3 inches away from source of heat. Position rissoles 1/2 inch apart on lined pan with aluminum foil. Broil the rissoles until it changed to golden brown and do the same for the other side.

Nutrition Information

- Calories: 381 calories;
- Total Fat: 25.1
- Sodium: 548
- Total Carbohydrate: 9.9
- Cholesterol: 142
- Protein: 28.2

99. White Bean And Lamb Soup

Serving: 8 | Prep: 45mins | Cook: 2hours | Ready in:

Ingredients

- 1/2 pound dried great Northern beans, sorted and rinsed
- 1 onion, chopped
- 3 tablespoons olive oil
- 3 cloves garlic, chopped
- 1 1/4 pounds ground lamb
- 3 carrots, peeled and diced
- 3 stalks celery, diced
- 1 1/2 cups canned roma tomatoes, with liquid
- 1/4 cup chopped fresh parsley
- 1 teaspoon dried thyme
- 1/2 teaspoon dried oregano
- fresh ground black pepper
- salt to taste
- 6 cups chicken broth
- 1/2 pound baby spinach leaves
- 4 ounces feta cheese, crumbled

Direction

- Put dried beans in water to soak overnight. When done soaking; strain off the leftover water and rinse.
- Cook onion with oil in a big stockpot over low heat for 4 minutes until barely tender. Mix in garlic and cook for 1 minute. Raise the heat to medium, and add lamb, cook for 3-4 minutes. Mix in celery and carrots, and cook for 1 minute. Mix in tomatoes, and use salt, freshly ground pepper, oregano, thyme, and parsley to season to taste. Add broth and beans to the pot. Boil for 5 minutes, and then lower the heat to medium-low. Put a cover on and simmer until the beans are soft, about 1 1/2 hours.
- Rinse spinach, and then put in a saucepan. Heat to medium heat, and cook until wilt. This will only take a little time, and you will not need to add additional water to the pan.
- Put crumbled feta cheese and wilted spinach on top of each serving of soup.

Nutrition Information

- Calories: 332 calories;
- Total Fat: 18.3
- Sodium: 461
- Total Carbohydrate: 21.8
- Cholesterol: 60
- Protein: 21.4

100. World's Greatest Grape Leaves (Armenian)

Serving: 8 | Prep: 50mins | Cook: 1mins | Ready in:

Ingredients

- 1 cup uncooked long-grain white rice
- 1 pound ground lamb
- 3 (10.75 ounce) cans condensed cream of mushroom soup, divided
- 2 (14.5 ounce) cans stewed tomatoes, divided
- 2 large red bell peppers, chopped
- 1 large onion, chopped
- 1/2 cup lemon juice
- 1/4 lime, juiced, or to taste
- 1 tablespoon minced garlic
- salt and ground black pepper to taste
- 1 (8 ounce) jar grape leaves - stemmed, drained, and rinsed, divided

Direction

- Cover rice in a mixing bowl with water; allow to steep for about 60 minutes. Drain off water.
- In a bowl, combine lamb with pepper, salt, garlic, lime juice, lemon juice, onion, rice, red bell peppers, 1 can tomatoes, and 1 can mushroom soup. Combine using your clean hands.
- Arrange grape leaves in 1 layer on the bottom of a 4-quart pot.
- Arrange the rest of grape leaves, smooth side down, on a flat work surface (ribs of the leaves up). In the middle of each grape leaf, place a rounded tablespoon of filling. Fold bottom parts of the leaf over filling mixture, fold over sides, and roll toward the leaf's top into a firm cylinder. Pack stuffed grape leaves firmly in the pot. Pour in any leftover filling mixture, 1 can tomatoes, and leftover 2 cans mushroom soup on top. Place a small plate on top in order to hold the leaves together.
- Cover and cook for about 60 minutes on low heat until lamb is no longer pink and rice is tender. Turn off the heat; allow to sit for 20 minutes before serving.

Nutrition Information

- Calories: 365 calories;
- Sodium: 1827
- Total Carbohydrate: 41.9
- Cholesterol: 38
- Protein: 16.1
- Total Fat: 15.5

Chapter 4: Lamb Stew Recipes

***

101. Chanakhi (Georgian Lamb Stew)

Serving: 4 | Prep: 30mins | Cook: 2hours | Ready in:

Ingredients

- 1 1/4 pounds cubed lamb meat
- 1 onion, chopped
- 2 1/4 potatoes, cubed
- 3 eggplants, cubed
- 2 cloves garlic, finely chopped
- 1 tablespoon tomato paste
- 2 tomatoes, sliced
- 1 red bell pepper, chopped
- 2 tablespoons chopped fresh parsley
- 2 tablespoons chopped fresh dill
- salt and ground black pepper to taste

Direction

- Preheat an oven to 175 degrees C (350 degrees F).
- Layer the following in this order: lamb, onion, potatoes, eggplants, garlic, tomato paste, tomatoes, red bell pepper, parsley, and dill in a heavy casserole dish. Seasoning every layer with pepper and salt. Add some spoonfuls of water on top and then cover with lid.
- Bake for about 2 hours in the preheated oven until the lamb is tender.

Nutrition Information

- Calories: 439 calories;
- Cholesterol: 73
- Protein: 26.4
- Total Fat: 15.8
- Sodium: 140
- Total Carbohydrate: 52.6

102. Chef John's Irish Stew

Serving: 6 | Prep: 20mins | Cook: 2hours25mins | Ready in:

Ingredients

- 3 pounds lamb shoulder chops
- salt and ground black pepper to taste
- 1 tablespoon vegetable oil
- 1 onion, chopped
- 1 tablespoon butter
- 2 tablespoons all-purpose flour
- 3 cups chicken stock
- 1/2 teaspoon dried rosemary
- 2 carrots, chopped
- 2 stalks celery, chopped
- water as needed
- 1 1/2 pounds baby Dutch yellow potatoes
- 1/4 cup chopped green onions

Direction

- Sprinkle salt and black pepper onto lamb shoulder chops to season.
- In a big heavy skillet over high heat, heat oil. Add lamb shoulder chops into hot oil in batches and cook for about 3-5 minutes each side until both sides are browned. Move chops to a stockpot.
- In the same skillet, cook onion over medium heat with a pinch of salt for about 5 minutes until slightly tender and brown on all edges, remember to stir while cooking. Stir in butter until fully melted. Add flour and stir for 1 minute until onions are well coated.
- Pour stock to onion mixture; bring to a boil. Add rosemary and stir for 5 to 10 minutes until thickened.
- Stir celery and carrots into pot with lamb shoulder chops, pour chicken stock over the ingredients. Add enough water until the meat is completely covered. Bring to a simmer, lower the heat to low and cook, covered, for about 90 minutes until meat is nearly falling off the bones.
- Move meat to a plate. Stir potatoes into stew, transfer meat back to stew, arranging on top of vegetables and simmer, covered, for about 30 minutes until meat is falling off the bones and potatoes are softened.
- Use a slotted spoon to move meat to a plate. Bring stew to a boil and cook for 10 to 12 minutes until stew is reduced and thickened, remember to skim off all fat that floats on top.
- Remove meat from bones; throw away the bones and any pieces of fat. Return meat to stew and stir. Stir in green onion and add salt and pepper to season.

Nutrition Information

- Calories: 508 calories;
- Cholesterol: 120
- Protein: 32.1
- Total Fat: 29.1
- Sodium: 466
- Total Carbohydrate: 28.6

103. Couscous De Mouton Tout Simple (Moroccan Mutton Couscous)

Serving: 8 | Prep: 35mins | Cook: 1hours23mins | Ready in:

Ingredients

- 3 tablespoons vegetable oil
- 2 pounds lamb shoulder, chopped into pieces

- 1 (15 ounce) can chickpeas, drained
- 2 tomatoes, diced
- 1/2 (10.75 ounce) can tomato puree
- 1 onion, chopped
- 1 tablespoon ras el hanout
- 1 pinch saffron threads
- salt and freshly ground black pepper to taste
- 1 1/2 quarts water
- 6 (5.8 ounce) boxes couscous
- 4 zucchini, cut into thick slices
- 4 turnips, quartered
- 4 carrots, cut into thick slices
- 2 stalks celery, chopped
- 1/2 cup butter, softened
- 2 tablespoons butter, softened

Direction

- In a big pot, heat the oil on medium heat. Put the lamb and cook and stir for 3-5 minutes until it becomes brown on all sides. Stir in pepper, salt, saffron, ras el hanout, onion, tomato puree, tomatoes and chickpeas. Pour 1 1/2 qt. of water to cover then boil. Minimize the heat and let it simmer for about 30 minutes until the flavors blend.
- In a very big bowl, put the couscous. Pour 1 1/2 cups of water to cover. Allow it to soak for 15 minutes. Drain and place to a couscous steamer insert.
- In the pot, mix the celery, carrots, turnips and zucchini. Place couscous steamer on top then put cover and steam for about 45 minutes until it becomes tender.
- In the bowl, spoon the couscous back. Mix in 1/2 cup plus 2 tbsp. butter then use fork to fluff it. Serve chickpea stew and lamb on top.

Nutrition Information

- Calories: 917 calories;
- Protein: 35.3
- Total Fat: 32.9
- Sodium: 444
- Total Carbohydrate: 119.5
- Cholesterol: 96

104. Greek Lamb Stew

Serving: 4 | Prep: 15mins | Cook: 2hours20mins | Ready in:

Ingredients

- 2 tablespoons olive oil
- 1 pound lamb shoulder blade chops
- salt and pepper to taste
- 1 large onion, chopped
- 3 cloves garlic, minced
- 1/2 cup dry red wine
- 2 cups chopped tomatoes
- 1 (15 ounce) can tomato sauce
- 1 cup lamb stock
- 1/2 lemon, zested and juiced
- 1/2 teaspoon dried oregano
- 1/2 teaspoon ground cinnamon
- 1 bay leaf
- 1 pound fresh green beans, trimmed
- 1/4 cup chopped fresh parsley

Direction

- In a big, heavy bottomed pot, heat olive oil over medium-high heat. Put pepper and salt to season the lamb, put to pot, and let cook for 5 minutes per side till browned deeply. Mix in garlic and onions, and let cook for 2 minutes till browned slightly.
- Into the pot, put the wine, and boil while scratching up browned bits of food off from base of pan using a wooden spoon. Mix in bay leaf, cinnamon, oregano, lemon zest and juice, lamb stock, tomato sauce and tomatoes. Over high heat, return to a boil, then turn heat to medium-low, put cover, and allow to simmer for 1 1/2 hours till lamb is really soft. Mix in green beans and cook for 20 minutes longer till soft.
- Take off any bones and bay leaf from stew. Garnish with chopped fresh parsley.

Nutrition Information

- Calories: 365 calories;
- Total Fat: 20.3
- Sodium: 606
- Total Carbohydrate: 24.4
- Cholesterol: 61
- Protein: 20

105. Irish Lamb Stew With Roasted Root Veg

Serving: 8 | Prep: 30mins | Cook: 1hours21mins | Ready in:

Ingredients

- 2 tablespoons olive oil
- 1 1/2 pounds roasted lamb, cubed
- 2 tablespoons all-purpose flour, or as needed
- 1 tablespoon olive oil
- 2 1/2 cups thinly sliced leeks
- 1 1/2 quarts beef stock
- 1 (19 ounce) can stewed tomatoes, drained
- 2 cups leftover lamb gravy
- 1 (15 ounce) can Irish stout beer (such as Guinness®)
- 2 large russet potatoes, peeled and cut into 1-inch pieces
- 3 large carrots, peeled and cut into 1-inch pieces
- parsnips, peeled and cut into 1-inch pieces
- 1 turnip, peeled and cut into 1-inch pieces
- 4 cloves garlic, halved, or more to taste
- 1/4 cup olive oil
- 1/4 cup balsamic vinegar
- 1 teaspoon ground rosemary
- 1 teaspoon coarse salt
- 1 teaspoon ground black pepper
- 1/2 cup boiling water
- 3 tablespoons beef gravy granules (such as BISTO)
- 1 tablespoon cornstarch
- 2 tablespoons cold water

Direction

- Turn oven to 400°F (200°C) to preheat.
- In a large pot, heat 2 tablespoons olive oil over medium-high heat. Use flour to coat lamb; cook floured lamb in heated oil for 1 to 2 minutes on each side until it starts to turn golden on all sides. Take out and place on a plate. In the same pot, heat 1 tablespoon oil. Sauté leeks in heated oil for about 5 minutes until translucent and some slices turns golden. Add lamb back in the pot and cook for 2 to 3 minutes. Mix in beer, gravy, tomatoes, and beef stock. Turn heat to low, simmer, covered for 1 to 1 1/2 hours until the roasting process of vegetables is finished.
- Arrange garlic, turnip, parsnips, carrots, and potatoes in a large glass baking dish. Add balsamic vinegar and 1/4 cup olive oil and toss to coat. Season the mixture evenly with pepper, salt, and rosemary.
- Roast vegetables for 1 to 1 1/2 hours in the preheated oven until soft and starts browning, stirring every 20-30 minutes.
- Add hot vegetables into the lamb stew, stir gently. Bring to a boil. In a small bowl, combine gravy granules, 1/2 cup boiling water, and 1 cup liquid from the pot until no lumps remain. Mix into the lamb stew. Stir cornstarch with 2 tablespoons water until dissolved and pour into the stew. Mix well for about 5 minutes until the stew has thickened.

Nutrition Information

- Calories: 458 calories;
- Protein: 19.9
- Total Fat: 20.1
- Sodium: 1990
- Total Carbohydrate: 47.9
- Cholesterol: 38

106. Irish Style Lamb Stew

Serving: 4 | Prep: 25mins | Cook: 2hours | Ready in:

Ingredients

- 1 pound cubed lamb meat
- 1 large onion, halved and sliced
- 1 pound baking potatoes, peeled and sliced
- 1 carrot, peeled and sliced
- 1 large stalk celery, sliced
- 2 tablespoons chopped fresh parsley
- salt and pepper to taste
- 2 cups beef stock
- 1 tablespoon chopped fresh parsley, for garnish

Direction

- Set oven at 165°C (325°F) and start preheating.
- Add the celery, carrot, potatoes, onion and lamb meat in reverse order to get layers of ingredients on a casserole dish or an ovenproof pot. Use pepper, salt and parsley to taste each layer. Pour in the beef stock and tightly cover.
- Put it into the prepared oven, bake for 1 1/2 to 2 hours until meat and vegetables get very tender. Distribute into bowls and use more parsley to decorate.

Nutrition Information

- Calories: 303 calories;
- Total Fat: 12.5
- Sodium: 116
- Total Carbohydrate: 27.4
- Cholesterol: 58
- Protein: 19.7

107. Lamb And Asparagus Stew

Serving: 2 | Prep: 20mins | Cook: 35mins | Ready in:

Ingredients

- 3 tablespoons vegetable oil
- 1 onion, chopped
- 1/2 pound cubed lamb stew meat
- 1/2 teaspoon salt
- 1/2 teaspoon ground black pepper
- 1 tablespoon ground turmeric
- 1/2 (6 ounce) can tomato paste
- 1 cup water
- 1 clove garlic, chopped
- 1 bunch fresh asparagus, trimmed and cut into 1 inch pieces

Direction

- In a saucepan over medium high heat, heat vegetable oil. Stir in onions and cook for 2 minutes, remember to stir constantly while cooking. Add turmeric, pepper, salt and lamb; cook for about 3 minutes until the outside of lamb loses its pink color, remember to stir while cooking. Stir in garlic, water and tomato paste. Bring to a simmer, then lower the heat to medium-low, cover the saucepan and simmer for about 25 minutes until the lamb is softened.
- When the lamb is soft, stir in asparagus and keep cooking for 3 minutes until asparagus is tender.

Nutrition Information

- Calories: 503 calories;
- Cholesterol: 64
- Protein: 25.6
- Total Fat: 33.5
- Sodium: 980
- Total Carbohydrate: 30.5

108. Mediterranean Lamb And Lentil Stew

Serving: 4 | Prep: 15mins | Cook: 40mins | Ready in:

Ingredients

- 1 tablespoon olive oil
- 1 1/2 pounds lamb shoulder arm chops, cubed, round bones reserved
- 1 teaspoon salt
- 1/2 teaspoon ground black pepper
- 1 onion, chopped
- 4 cloves garlic, minced
- 1 cup lentils, picked over and rinsed
- 2 cups chicken broth, or more as needed
- 1 (14 ounce) can diced tomatoes
- 3 carrots, peeled and sliced
- 1/2 teaspoon dried thyme
- 1/2 teaspoon dried sage
- 1/2 teaspoon dried basil
- 2 cups coarsely chopped fresh spinach
- 1 lemon, juiced and zested
- 1/2 cup ricotta salata cheese, crumbled

Direction

- In a heavy pot, heat oil on medium high heat. Add bones and lamb cubes; brown for 3 minutes on all sides. Sprinkle pepper and salt. Add garlic and onion; cook for 2 minutes, frequently mixing.
- Mix in basil, thyme, sage, carrots, tomatoes, 2 cups chicken broth and lentils; boil. Lower heat to low; simmer till lentils are tender yet not quite done, occasionally mixing, covered. This can take 15-30 minutes, depending on freshness and type of lentils. Add more broth, 1 cup extra, if stew looks dry; discard lamb bones.
- Add spinach; cook for 5 minutes. Mix in juice and lemon zest; use some crumbled cheese to garnish individual serving.

Nutrition Information

- Calories: 572 calories;
- Sodium: 1049
- Total Carbohydrate: 46.4
- Cholesterol: 103
- Protein: 39.3
- Total Fat: 26.7

109. One Pot Irish Stew

Serving: 4 | Prep: 25mins | Cook: 1hours25mins | Ready in:

Ingredients

- 1 2/3 pounds boneless lamb shoulder, chopped
- 1 quart water
- salt and ground black pepper to taste
- 1 onion, thickly sliced
- 8 potatoes, peeled and quartered, divided
- 2 carrots, peeled and thickly sliced
- 2 tablespoons chopped fresh parsley, or to taste

Direction

- In a large pot, cover lamb with water, add salt. Bring to a boil and skim all fat that floats on the surface of liquid. Lower the heat and simmer for about 30 minutes over low heat.
- Mix in half of potatoes and onion; cook for about 30 minutes until potatoes are tender. To thicken the stew, break up potatoes with wooden spoon.
- Put carrots and the remainder of the potatoes into the stew. Allow to simmer for 20-30 minutes until potatoes become tender. Add salt and pepper to season; stir in parsley.

Nutrition Information

- Calories: 636 calories;
- Sodium: 146
- Total Carbohydrate: 81.2
- Cholesterol: 97
- Protein: 33.7
- Total Fat: 19.9

110. Tas Kebab (Persian Lamb And Vegetable Stew)

Serving: 4 | Prep: 50mins | Cook: 2hours30mins | Ready in:

Ingredients

- 1 tablespoon vegetable oil
- 2 onions, sliced 1/2-inch thick
- 1 pound lamb, cut into 1-inch cubes
- 1/2 teaspoon salt
- 1/2 teaspoon ground black pepper
- 1/4 teaspoon ground turmeric
- 1/4 teaspoon ground cinnamon
- 3 cloves garlic, minced
- 1 (1 inch) piece fresh ginger, sliced (optional)
- 1/2 cup pitted prunes
- 2 carrots, peeled and sliced
- 1 quince, cored and sliced
- 1 large eggplant, peeled and cut into 1-inch slices
- 1 tomato, sliced
- 1 pinch salt
- 1 cup water
- 1/2 cup tomato juice
- 2 tablespoons lemon juice (optional)
- 3 potatoes, peeled and sliced

Direction

- Pour oil in a pot and then add onions on the bottom of pot. Place in lamb. Season with pepper, half teaspoon of salt, cinnamon, and turmeric.
- Onto the seasoned lamb, spread a layer tomato, eggplant, garlic, quince ginger, carrots, and prunes. Drizzle with one pinch of salt. Add in lemon juice, water, and tomato juice.
- Cook while covered on low heat for about 2 to 2 1/2 hours until the lamb becomes tender. Place in potatoes and cover the pot. Cook for about half an hour until the potatoes become soft.

Nutrition Information

- Calories: 467 calories;
- Total Fat: 10.7
- Sodium: 496
- Total Carbohydrate: 71.2
- Cholesterol: 62
- Protein: 26.7

111. Thick Irish Stew

Serving: 8 | Prep: 20mins | Cook: 2hours30mins | Ready in:

Ingredients

- 8 (4 ounce) lamb shoulder blade chops
- 4 carrots, coarsely chopped
- 4 onions, coarsely chopped
- 6 potatoes, coarsely chopped
- 1 pinch salt
- 1/4 teaspoon cracked black pepper
- 4 cups vegetable broth
- water, or amount to cover
- 3 bay leaves
- 1 (14 ounce) bag dry split yellow peas

Direction

- In a big pot over medium heat, put potatoes, onions, carrots and lamb shoulder chops. Mix in cracked black pepper and salt.
- Put in vegetable broth and cover with enough water; add bay leaves. Take to a boil, decrease heat to low and simmer for an hour, mixing occasionally.
- Toss in split peas then take to a boil. Decrease heat to low and simmer for about another 1 1/2 hours until the split peas have cracked apart and the lamb is very tender. Mix occasionally to prevent stew from burning on the bottom.

Nutrition Information

- Calories: 389 calories;
- Total Fat: 10
- Sodium: 312
- Total Carbohydrate: 55
- Cholesterol: 47
- Protein: 21.1

Chapter 5: Bbq & Grilled Lamb Recipes

***

112. Armenian Shish Kabob

Serving: 6 | Prep: 1hours | Cook: 18mins | Ready in:

Ingredients

- 1/2 cup olive oil
- 2 tablespoons fresh lemon juice
- 1 teaspoon dry white wine
- 1 tablespoon minced garlic
- 1/8 teaspoon salt
- 1/8 teaspoon black pepper
- 1/8 teaspoon dried oregano
- 1/8 teaspoon dried rosemary leaves
- 1 bay leaf
- 2 pounds boneless leg of lamb, cut into 1 1/2-inch cubes
- 2 large onions, peeled, cut into 8 wedges each
- 2 large green bell peppers, cut into 8 wedges each
- 12 mushrooms, stems removed
- 2 large tomatoes, cut into 8 wedges

Direction

- Mix together wine, olive oil, garlic, lemon juice, oregano, rosemary, bay leaf, salt and pepper. Add in the lam and toss to coat. Transfer into a zip-top bag and keep in the refrigerator for at least 1 day.
- Set oven to broil. Place rack at topmost level.
- Take the lamb off its marinade, reserving the liquid. Thread onto metal skewers. Thread green peppers, onion wedges, and mushrooms on separate skewers. Brush with reserved marinade.
- Place skewers on a broiler pan and turn frequently while cooking. Cooking times are 12 minutes for the onions, 10 minutes for the lamb, 7 minutes for the peppers, and 3 minutes for the mushrooms. Remove the skewers from the oven and allow to rest until cool enough to handle.
- Slide the pieces off their skewers. Cue them again, this time alternating the lamb, green peppers, onion wedges, mushrooms, and tomatoes. Brush with marinade and arrange on broiler pan. Dispose of remaining marinade.
- Broil the skewers, turning frequently until lamb is cooked medium-rare and the vegetables are blackened in spots, about 5 to 7 minutes.

Nutrition Information

- Calories: 384 calories;
- Sodium: 101
- Total Carbohydrate: 11.8
- Cholesterol: 62
- Protein: 19.7
- Total Fat: 29.3

113. Asian Barbequed Butterflied Leg Of Lamb

Serving: 10 | Prep: 15mins | Cook: 30mins | Ready in:

Ingredients

- 2/3 cup hoisin sauce
- 6 tablespoons rice vinegar
- 1/2 cup minced green onions
- 1/4 cup mushroom soy sauce
- 4 tablespoons minced garlic
- 2 tablespoons honey
- 1/2 teaspoon sesame oil
- 1 tablespoon toasted sesame seeds
- 1/2 teaspoon ground white pepper
- 1/2 teaspoon freshly ground black pepper
- 1 (5 pound) boneless butterflied leg of lamb

Direction

- Combine rice vinegar, mushroom soy sauce, hoisin sauce, sesame oil, honey, garlic, black pepper, green onions, sesame seeds, rice vinegar, and white pepper in a resealable big plastic bag. Add the lamb to bag. Reseal and flip to coat. Keep in refrigerator, 8 hours-overnight.
- Prepare grill and preheat on high heat.
- Transfer the lamb onto grill after oiling the grill grate. Discard the marinade. For 15 minutes per side, grill until internal temperature is at least 145°F (63°C) or cook to desired doneness. On a serving platter put meat, let the meat rest, 20 minutes. Chop and serve.

Nutrition Information

- Calories: 325 calories;
- Protein: 27
- Total Fat: 17.7
- Sodium: 688
- Total Carbohydrate: 13.3
- Cholesterol: 93

114. Aussie Barbequed Boneless Leg Of Lamb

Serving: 10 | Prep: 40mins | Cook: 1hours30mins | Ready in:

Ingredients

- 1 cup vegetable oil
- 1/2 cup distilled white vinegar
- 2 cloves garlic, minced
- 1 tablespoon salt
- 1/2 teaspoon ground black pepper, or to taste
- 1 (3 pound) boneless leg of lamb, trimmed of fat
- 1/2 cup water
- 1/2 cup lemon juice
- 3/4 cup vegetable oil
- 2 1/2 cups tomato puree
- 2 cups chopped onion
- 2 tablespoons distilled white vinegar
- 2 teaspoons hot pepper sauce (e.g. Tabasco™)
- 1 teaspoon minced hot green chile peppers
- 2 cloves garlic, minced
- 1 tablespoon dry mustard powder
- 1 teaspoon salt

Direction

- In a bowl, mix together the black pepper, 1 tablespoon salt, 2 cloves minced garlic, 1/2 cup of vinegar and 1 cup of vegetable oil; then place into a resealable plastic bag. Put in the trimmed lamb leg, cover with the marinade, compress to let the air out, and secure bag. Let it marinate for 2 hours at room temperature.
- In the meantime, combine in a big pot 3/4 cup vegetable oil, onion, water, hot sauce, mustard powder, tomato puree, 2 cloves minced garlic, 1 teaspoon salt, lemon juice, 2 tablespoons vinegar, and minced chile. Heat to a boil on medium-high, the decrease heat to medium-low, and simmer until sauce is thick and onions are soft, 30 minutes.
- Prepare an outdoor grill by preheating to medium low heat and put oil lightly on the grate.

- Take the lamb from marinade and shake off any excess. Get rid of left marinade. Place on the preheated grill and cook for 1 1/2 to 2 hours, flipping and basting often with the hot barbecue sauce.

Nutrition Information

- Calories: 498 calories;
- Total Fat: 43.3
- Sodium: 1228
- Total Carbohydrate: 10.3
- Cholesterol: 53
- Protein: 18.7

115. Barbecued Lamb Chops

Serving: 9 servings. | Prep: 5mins | Cook: 10mins | Ready in:

Ingredients

- 2 to 3 cups olive oil
- 1/4 cup chopped garlic
- 4 teaspoons salt
- 1 teaspoon minced fresh rosemary or 1/2 teaspoon dried rosemary, crushed
- 1 teaspoon salt-free garlic and herb seasoning
- 1 teaspoon pepper
- 18 lamb rib chops (1 inch thick and 4 ounces each)

Direction

- Mix together in a large resealable plastic bag the seasonings, garlic and oil; put in lamb chops. Secure bag and flip to coat; place inside the refrigerator overnight, flipping occasionally.
- Strain get rid of marinade. Place the chops on the grill over medium heat, uncovered for 5-9 minutes per side or until the meat achieves doneness desired (160°F for medium well and 170°F for well done).

Nutrition Information

- Calories:
- Protein:
- Total Fat:
- Sodium:
- Fiber:
- Total Carbohydrate:
- Cholesterol:

116. Barbecued Lamb Kabobs

Serving: 8-10 servings. | Prep: 20mins | Cook: 15mins | Ready in:

Ingredients

- 2-1/2 pounds boneless leg of lamb, cut into 1-inch cubes
- MARINADE:
- 1/2 tablespoon dried parsley flakes
- 1/2 tablespoon dried minced onion
- 1 teaspoon salt
- 1/2 teaspoon black pepper
- 1/2 cup lemon juice
- 1/2 cup white wine or broth of choice
- 2 tablespoons soy sauce
- DIPPING SAUCE:
- 1/2 cup canola oil
- 1/2 cup lemon juice
- 1 large onion, chopped
- 2 garlic cloves, minced
- Salt to taste
- Pepper to taste
- Hot peppers to taste, chopped

Direction

- Take a heavy plastic bag and combine all the marinade ingredients with the lamb. Let marinate overnight or at least 5 hours, turning bag from time to time. Drain, discarding marinade. Skewer the lamb and broil or grill on medium-hot for 7-8 minutes per side or until meat is cooked to liking. A thermometer should read 145 degrees for medium-rare; 160 degrees for medium; and 170 degrees for well-done. Make the sauce by blending together all the sauce ingredients. Put the lid on and blend on high until smooth. Serve lamb with dipping sauce.

Nutrition Information

- Calories:
- Sodium:
- Fiber:
- Total Carbohydrate:
- Cholesterol:
- Protein:
- Total Fat:

117. Basil Grilled Mediterranean Lamb Chops

Serving: 4 | Prep: 10mins | Cook: 10mins | Ready in:

Ingredients

- 4 (8 ounce) lamb shoulder chops
- 2 tablespoons Dijon mustard
- 2 tablespoons balsamic vinegar
- 1 tablespoon chopped garlic
- 1/4 teaspoon ground black pepper
- 1/2 cup olive oil
- 2 tablespoons shredded fresh basil, or to taste

Direction

- Pat dry the lamb chops. Place in a short-sided glass dish in one layer.
- In a small bowl stir balsamic vinegar, pepper, garlic, and Dijon mustard together. Gradually add in oil until smooth. Toss in the basil and pour over the lamb chops, flip to coat each side. For 1-4 hours place in refrigerator with cover.
- For 30 minutes, let chops warm to room temperature.
- Prepare the grill by lightly oiling the grate and preheat at medium heat. Grill, 5-10 minutes each side until lamb chops turn brown. Insert a thermometer at the middle and it must register a temperature of 145 degrees F (63 degrees C) or higher.

Nutrition Information

- Calories: 521 calories;
- Total Fat: 45.9
- Sodium: 256
- Total Carbohydrate: 3.5
- Cholesterol: 90
- Protein: 22.7

118. Best Burgers Ever

Serving: 4 | Prep: 15mins | Cook: 5mins | Ready in:

Ingredients

- 1 pound ground lamb
- 1 tablespoon egg
- 1/2 teaspoon ginger paste
- 1/2 teaspoon garlic paste
- 2 teaspoons garam masala
- 1 teaspoon dried cilantro
- 4 hamburger buns, split and toasted

Direction

- Prepare an outdoor grill by preheating to medium-high heat and lightly grease the grate.
- Into a mixing bowl, combine the cilantro, garam masala, garlic, ginger, egg and lamb. Shape the mixture into 4 patties. Place on the preheated grill and cook according to doneness desired, 3 minutes each side for medium-well. Present on toasted hamburger buns.

Nutrition Information

- Calories: 358 calories;
- Total Fat: 18.2
- Sodium: 334
- Total Carbohydrate: 22.9
- Cholesterol: 90
- Protein: 23.7

119. Big M's Grilled Orange Lamb Kabobs

Serving: 8 | Prep: 30mins | Cook: 30mins | Ready in:

Ingredients

- 2 1/4 pounds lean lamb meat, cubed
- 1 1/3 cups coriander seeds
- 4 1/4 cups fresh orange juice
- 6 orange, peeled, sectioned, and cut into bite-size pieces
- 1 hot chile pepper, minced
- 2/3 cup orange liqueur
- 1 bunch fresh cilantro

Direction

- Take a large, non-metal bowl to put the lamb in. Pound coriander seeds with a mortar and pestle and rub on the meat. Trickle the orange liqueur and orange juice over the meat and add in the chopped chile peppers and oranges. Cover the bowl and let marinate in the fridge for one day, turning the lamb over every 2 hours.
- Set grill on medium to preheat. Take the lamb and the orange pieces from its marinade. Pour the marinade into a small saucepan and set aside. Skewer the lamb cubes alternately with the oranges, starting and ending with an orange piece.
- Place the saucepan with marinade on the grill and let boil until thickened.
- Start grilling the skewers when the marinade has started boiling. Grill slowly until cooked to liking and with char marks on the meat. Place skewers in a warm dish, cover, and let meat rest for 5 minutes. Put out the orange sauce with sprigs of cilantro on top.

Nutrition Information

- Calories: 351 calories;
- Total Fat: 12
- Sodium: 48
- Total Carbohydrate: 39
- Cholesterol: 52
- Protein: 17.8

120. Champion Lamb Burgers

Serving: 6 servings. | Prep: 15mins | Cook: 10mins | Ready in:

Ingredients

- 2 large red onions, thinly sliced
- 2 teaspoons olive oil
- 1 tablespoon red wine vinegar
- 2 teaspoons minced fresh rosemary
- 1-1/2 teaspoons sugar
- 1 teaspoon stone-ground mustard
- 1/4 teaspoon salt
- 1/4 teaspoon pepper
- BURGERS:
- 2 pounds ground lamb
- 2 garlic cloves, minced
- 1 teaspoon salt
- 1/4 teaspoon pepper
- 6 pita pocket halves
- 2 tablespoons olive oil
- 1-1/2 cups spring mix salad greens

Direction

- Sauté the onions in oil in a large skillet until softened. Put in the pepper, salt, mustard, sugar, rosemary and vinegar; then cook for five more minutes. Keep it warm.
- Into A large bowl, crumble the lamb; sprinkle on pepper, salt and garlic and combine well.

Form into six patties. Place the burgers on the grill over medium heat, covered, or broil 4 inches from the heat for 4 to 6 minutes per side or until a thermometer says 160°F and the juices run clear.
- Brush with oil the pita pockets; grill both sides lightly. Present burgers in pita pockets with onions and lettuce.

Nutrition Information

- Calories: 445 calories
- Total Carbohydrate: 23g carbohydrate (4g sugars
- Cholesterol: 100mg cholesterol
- Protein: 29g protein.
- Total Fat: 26g fat (9g saturated fat)
- Sodium: 748mg sodium
- Fiber: 2g fiber)

121. Champion Lamb Burgers For Two

Serving: 2 servings. | Prep: 15mins | Cook: 10mins | Ready in:

Ingredients

- 1 medium red onion, thinly sliced
- 1 teaspoon olive oil
- 1-1/2 teaspoons red wine vinegar
- 1 teaspoon minced fresh rosemary
- 1/2 teaspoon sugar
- 1/2 teaspoon stone-ground mustard
- 1/8 teaspoon salt
- 1/8 teaspoon pepper
- BURGERS:
- 12 ounces ground lamb
- 1 garlic cloves, minced
- 1/2 teaspoon salt
- 1/8 teaspoon pepper
- 2 pita pocket halves
- 2 teaspoons olive oil
- 1/2 cup spring mix salad greens

Direction

- Put the oil and onions in a big skillet and sauté it until the onions have softened. Mix in the rosemary, salt, sugar, pepper, vinegar and mustard and let the mixture cook for 5 more minutes. Make sure to keep the mixture warm.
- In a big bowl, put in the lamb and break it apart then season it with salt, pepper and garlic; mix everything thoroughly. Form the lamb mixture into 2 patties. Put the lamb patties onto the grill over medium heat then cover and let it grill, or put the patties in a broiler and let it broil 4 inches away from the heat for 4 to 6 minutes on every side until the juices are clear and the thermometer inserted on the patties indicate 160°.
- Use a brush to coat the pita pockets with oil then let it grill a little bit on both sides. Put the grilled lamb patties, onions and lettuce inside the pita pockets and serve.

Nutrition Information

- Calories:
- Protein:
- Total Fat:
- Sodium:
- Fiber:
- Total Carbohydrate:
- Cholesterol:

122. Chef John's Grilled Lamb Steaks

Serving: 4 | Prep: 15mins | Cook: 15mins | Ready in:

Ingredients

- Marinade:
- 1 bunch fresh tarragon leaves, torn
- 1/2 bunch fresh mint leaves, torn
- 2 tablespoons plain yogurt
- 1 tablespoon olive oil

- 4 cloves garlic, chopped
- 1 teaspoon ground cumin
- 1 teaspoon freshly ground black pepper
- 4 center-cut lamb leg steaks, 1 1/2-inch thick
- Vinaigrette:
- 1/4 cup olive oil
- 3 tablespoons sherry vinegar
- 2 tablespoons honey
- salt and freshly ground black pepper to taste
- 2 tablespoons chopped fresh mint
- 1 tablespoon olive oil, or as needed
- salt and ground black pepper to taste

Direction

- In a bowl, combine the yogurt, garlic, cumin, tarragon, 1/2 bunch of mint, 1 teaspoon of black pepper, and 1 tablespoon of olive oil; whisk. Transfer the marinade to the plastic resealable bag. Add in the lamb steaks and coat with the marinade, squeeze out any extra air, and seal. Keep in refrigerator to marinate for 8 hours or overnight.
- Set the outdoor grill to high heat; preheat and oil lightly the grill grate.
- In a bowl, beat sherry vinegar, pepper, salt, honey, and 1/4 cup of olive oil. Add in 2 tablespoons of sliced mint; whisk to combine the vinaigrette.
- Take out steaks from the marinade, scraping off the garlic and all of the herbs. Throw away the marinade. Pour 1 tablespoon of olive oil over steaks and sprinkle with pepper and salt.
- Place steaks on heated grill until outside of the steaks turn brown and center is slightly pink, 6 minutes each side. Insert a meat thermometer at the middle and it must register 130°F (54°C). Place the steaks on a plate and pour 1/2 of vinaigrette on top; then use foil to cover the steaks. For 10 minutes, let steaks rest. Place the steaks on individual plates then drizzle the remaining vinaigrette on top of each.

Nutrition Information

- Calories: 467 calories;
- Total Fat: 33.5
- Sodium: 80
- Total Carbohydrate: 11.8
- Cholesterol: 93
- Protein: 29.2

123. Chef John's Grilled Lamb With Mint Orange Sauce

Serving: 5 | Prep: 10mins | Cook: 15mins | Ready in:

Ingredients

- 2 pounds lamb loin chops
- 2 tablespoons olive oil
- 3 cloves garlic, minced
- 1 tablespoon cumin
- 1 teaspoon mixed herbs - Italian, Greek, or French blend
- 1/2 teaspoon black pepper
- 1/2 teaspoon ground coriander
- 1/4 teaspoon cinnamon
- 1 pinch cayenne pepper
- salt as needed
- Sauce:
- 1/4 cup orange marmalade
- 1 pinch hot chili flakes
- 1/2 tablespoon rice vinegar
- 1 tablespoon chopped fresh mint

Direction

- In a large bowl, put lamb chops. Put salt, cayenne, cinnamon, coriander, pepper, cumin, mixed herbs, garlic and olive oil to season. Then toss until well coated with seasonings and oil. Place inside the refrigerator, covered. Let it marinate for at least 4 hours.
- Prepare an outdoor grill by preheating to high heat and oiling the grate lightly. Then put lamb chops on the grill. Sprinkle chops with a little salt. Then grill for 4-7 minutes until brown on the first side depending on size of chops. Turn chops a half turn on the grill about a minute before flipping them. Flip and grill for another 4-7 minutes the other side

reaches doneness desired. An instant read thermometer poked into the middle should read 125 to 130°F (54 degrees C) for medium rare. Put on a serving dish and use foil to tent loosely.
- Put marmalade in bowl. Mix in rice vinegar, mint and chili flakes. Mix together until well combined.
- Over the chops, brush the sauce then serve.

Nutrition Information

- Calories: 438 calories;
- Sodium: 126
- Total Carbohydrate: 12.4
- Cholesterol: 108
- Protein: 27.6
- Total Fat: 30.6

124.   Chris' Best Burgers

Serving: 5 | Prep: 10mins | Cook: 10mins | Ready in:

Ingredients

- 1 teaspoon butter
- 1/2 cup finely diced onion
- 2 pounds ground beef chuck
- 1/2 pound ground lamb
- 5 teaspoons Worcestershire sauce
- salt and ground black pepper to taste

Direction

- Place a skillet on the stove and turn on medium heat add butter to melt then stir and cook onion for about 4 minutes until almost translucent; separate from heat and let it cool at room temperature.
- In a bowl, combine the black pepper, salt, Worcestershire sauce, onion, lamb and beef chuck. Split the mixture into fifths and make each piece into a large burger. In the middle of each burger, press an indentation using your thumb to keep flat the burgers while cooking. Let the patties chill thoroughly for 4 to 8 hours. Before cooking, let the burgers warm to room temperature.
- Prepare an outdoor grill by preheating to high heat and put oil lightly on the grate.
- Place the burgers and cook for about 5 minutes each side until grill marks appear and the meat's pink color fades. Do not use spatula to press burgers while they cook and turn only once. Before serving, let them stand for 1 minute.

Nutrition Information

- Calories: 434 calories;
- Protein: 38.5
- Total Fat: 28.8
- Sodium: 192
- Total Carbohydrate: 2.6
- Cholesterol: 146

125.   Dale's Lamb

Serving: 8 | Prep: 15mins | Cook: 50mins | Ready in:

Ingredients

- 2/3 cup lemon juice
- 1/2 cup brown sugar
- 1/4 cup Dijon mustard
- 1/4 cup soy sauce
- 1/4 cup olive oil
- 2 cloves garlic, minced
- 1 (1/2 inch) piece fresh ginger root, sliced
- 1 teaspoon salt
- 1/2 teaspoon ground black pepper
- 1 (5 pound) leg of lamb, butterflied

Direction

- Combine together Dijon mustard, brown sugar, olive oil, salt, pepper, ginger, lemon juice, soy sauce, and garlic in a bowl. Transfer

lamb to a shallow container. Add lemon juice mixture on top of lamb. Marinate with cover, for 8 hours to overnight in the refrigerator.
- Set the outdoor grill on medium heat; preheat. Drain the marinade and transfer to a small pot; boil. Lower heat to low. Let mixture simmer while constantly stirring until thickened slightly.
- Oil lightly grill grate and grill lamb on indirect heat for 40-50 minutes, flip to grill every side, until the internal temperature is at least 145°F (63°C). Cool before slicing. Add the thickened marinade mixture to cover grilled lamb. Serve.

Nutrition Information

- Calories: 451 calories;
- Total Fat: 27.2
- Sodium: 1015
- Total Carbohydrate: 17.8
- Cholesterol: 115
- Protein: 32.4

126. Dijon Leg Of Lamb

Serving: 9 servings. | Prep: 10mins | Cook: 01hours30mins | Ready in:

Ingredients

- 1 boneless leg of lamb (4 to 5 pounds)
- 1 cup Dijon mustard
- 1/2 cup soy sauce
- 2 tablespoons olive oil
- 1 tablespoon chopped fresh rosemary or 1 teaspoon dried rosemary, crushed
- 1 teaspoon ground ginger
- 1 garlic clove, minced

Direction

- Slice leg of lamb horizontally from one long side to within 1 inch of the opposite side. To make it lie flat, open meat; take out and get rid of fat. In a large resealable plastic bag, place the lamb. Mix together in a small bowl the seasonings, oil, soy sauce and mustard. Over lamb, Place one cup of marinade. Secure the bag and flip to coat; place inside the refrigerator overnight. Place inside the refrigerator the left marinade, covered.
- Strain and get rid of marinade. Moisten a paper towel with cooking oil and coat the grill's rack lightly using long-handled tongs. Using a drip pan, prepare the grill for indirect heat.
- Put lamb over the drip pan and grill, cover, over medium-low heat for 1 to 1/2 to 2 1/2 hours or until meat achieves the doneness desired (a thermometer should read 145°F for medium rare; 160°F for medium; 170°F for well done). For 10 minutes, let it stand before slicing. Heat reserved mustard sauce; present with lamb.

Nutrition Information

- Calories:
- Total Carbohydrate:
- Cholesterol:
- Protein:
- Total Fat:
- Sodium:
- Fiber:

127. Dirty Piggy Back Lamb

Serving: 4 | Prep: 20mins | Cook: 40mins | Ready in:

Ingredients

- 2 tablespoons olive oil
- 1 (8 ounce) package sliced fresh mushrooms
- 8 slices bacon
- 4 lamb blade chops
- 1 teaspoon cracked black peppercorns
- seasoned salt to taste

Direction

- Prepare the grill by preheating to high heat.
- While heating the grill, place a large skillet on the stove and turn to medium heat then put in olive oil. Place the mushrooms; then stir and cook until softened. Reserve.
- Use pepper to season the slices of bacon and put them on the grill. Cook the bacon until it becomes crisp, flipping once, then reserve. Put season salt on the lamb chops to taste and put them on the grill. Cook to doneness desired, 3 minutes per side for medium.
- Present each chop with two bacon slices and sliced mushrooms on top.

Nutrition Information

- Calories: 351 calories;
- Sodium: 531
- Total Carbohydrate: 2.4
- Cholesterol: 77
- Protein: 22.8
- Total Fat: 27.7

128. Feta And Olive Lamburgers

Serving: 4 | Prep: 20mins | Cook: 10mins | Ready in:

Ingredients

- 1 pound ground lamb
- 1 cup crumbled feta cheese
- 1 large egg
- 1/2 cup kalamata olives, pitted and sliced
- 1/8 teaspoon ground cumin
- ground black pepper to taste
- 4 whole-wheat hamburger buns, toasted if desired

Direction

- In a mixing bowl mix the feta cheese, olives, lamb, and egg. Sprinkle black pepper and cumin in to season. Stir until well blended.
- Mold mixture in 4 patty shapes and put on waxed paper. Keep in refrigerator, 15 minutes.
- Prepare the grill by lightly oiling the grate and preheat at medium heat.
- Place the lamb burgers on heated grill. Grill lamb until cooked to your desired doneness. For medium, cook patties 3 minutes each side. Serve over toasted buns and with your desired condiments.

Nutrition Information

- Calories: 537 calories;
- Sodium: 1005
- Total Carbohydrate: 27.4
- Cholesterol: 156
- Protein: 32.6
- Total Fat: 32.1

129. Goat Cheese Stuffed Lamb Burgers

Serving: 6 | Prep: 25mins | Cook: 15mins | Ready in:

Ingredients

- 1 teaspoon olive oil
- 1/2 cup diced onion
- 2 pounds ground lamb
- 1 egg
- 1 cup bread crumbs
- 1 clove garlic, minced
- 4 1/2 teaspoons salt
- 1 tablespoon ground black pepper
- 4 ounces soft goat cheese
- 1 tablespoon extra-virgin olive oil
- 1 tablespoon chopped fresh basil leaves
- 1 tablespoon chopped fresh oregano

Direction

- On medium heat, place a small skillet and cook 1 teaspoon olive oil. Toss in onions; stir and cook for 5 minutes until opaque and soft.

- Knead carefully the lamb, bread crumbs, salt, softened onions, egg, garlic, and pepper together. Split the mixture in 6 pieces and mold in balls. Keep in the refrigerator with cover until needed.
- Combine the basil, oregano, goat cheese, and extra-virgin olive oil until well blended. For 5 minutes chill with cover.
- Set an outdoor grill to medium-high heat; preheat.
- Doing one side of the meat at one time, create a hollow in middle of the ball using your thumb. Add in a heaping tablespoon of goat cheese mixture to fill the hollow. Carefully pull to form meat patty around cheese filling to create a burger patty. Do again with each lamb mixture ball.
- Place patties on preheated grill, 8 minutes a side until color at the center is not pink and cooked through.

Nutrition Information

- Calories: 484 calories;
- Cholesterol: 147
- Protein: 33.7
- Total Fat: 31
- Sodium: 2071
- Total Carbohydrate: 15.8

130. Greek Lamb Kabobs

Serving: 4 servings. | Prep: 10mins | Cook: 10mins | Ready in:

Ingredients

- 1/2 cup lemon juice
- 2 tablespoons dried oregano
- 4 teaspoons olive oil
- 6 garlic cloves, minced
- 1 pound boneless lamb, cut into 1-inch cubes
- 16 cherry tomatoes
- 1 large green pepper, cut into 1-inch pieces
- 1 large onion, cut into 1-inch wedges

Direction

- Combine garlic, oil, oregano, and lemon juice in a small bowl. Transfer 1/4 cup of the mixture into a covered container and refrigerate for basting later. The remaining marinade goes into a large re-sealable plastic bag with the lamb; zip the top and turn several times to coat the lamb with the mixture. Store in the refrigerator for 8 hours or overnight, turning occasionally in the duration of storage. Drain and discard marinade from bag with the lamb. Thread lamb onions, green peppers, and tomatoes alternately on eight metal or water-soaked wooden skewers. Dab an oil-moistened paper towel on the grates to grease lightly; use a pair of long-handle tongs for safety. Cook on a covered grill at medium heat, or broil 4 in. from heat. Turn and baste occasionally within the grilling time, until lamb is at desired doneness and vegetables are cooked inside but still crisp outside, about 5-6 minutes per side.

Nutrition Information

- Calories: 226 calories
- Protein: 25g protein. Diabetic Exchanges: 3 lean meat
- Total Fat: 9g fat (3g saturated fat)
- Sodium: 83mg sodium
- Fiber: 2g fiber)
- Total Carbohydrate: 13g carbohydrate (0 sugars
- Cholesterol: 74mg cholesterol

131. Greek Lamb Kabobs With Yogurt Mint Salsa Verde

Serving: 4 | Prep: 25mins | Cook: 8mins | Ready in:

Ingredients

- Lamb Skewers:
- 8 6-inch rosemary sprigs
- 1 tablespoon minced garlic
- 1 tablespoon chopped fresh thyme
- 1/3 cup extra virgin olive oil
- 1/4 cup sherry vinegar
- 1 teaspoon sea salt
- 1 teaspoon ground white pepper
- 1 1/2 pounds lamb tenderloin, cut into 2-inch pieces
- Salsa Verde:
- 1/4 cup fresh lemon juice
- 1/2 cup extra virgin olive oil
- 1/3 cup Greek yogurt
- 1 crushed garlic clove
- 1/4 teaspoon sea salt
- 2 teaspoons chopped fresh mint
- 1 teaspoon chopped fresh oregano
- 1 teaspoon chopped fresh parsley
- 1 teaspoon small capers
- 1 anchovy filet

Direction

- Immerse the rosemary sprigs in water for half an hour. Whisk together olive oil, garlic, sherry vinegar, thyme, salt, and pepper in a glass bowl. Toss the lamb in the marinade and soak for 30 minutes at room temperature. Skewer onto rosemary sprigs.
- Make the salsa verde: Blend yogurt, lemon juice, olive oil, garlic, mint, oregano, parsley, salt, capers, and anchovy fillet until smooth. Transfer to a serving dish and put aside until serving time.
- Set an outdoor grill on medium to pre-heat.
- Grill the lamb, turning from time to time, until the meat is not pink anymore, about 8 minutes. Serve with salsa verde.

Nutrition Information

- Calories: 688 calories;
- Total Fat: 57.6
- Sodium: 908
- Total Carbohydrate: 4
- Cholesterol: 115
- Protein: 36.1

132. Greek Lamb Feta Burgers With Cucumber Sauce

Serving: 4 | Prep: | Cook: | Ready in:

Ingredients

- 4 large unpeeled garlic cloves
- 1 1/4 pounds ground lamb
- 1/2 cup crumbled feta cheese
- 3/4 teaspoon dried oregano
- 1/2 teaspoon salt
- 1/2 teaspoon black pepper
- 1/2 large cucumber, peeled, grated and squeezed very dry in a clean towel
- 3/4 cup sour cream
- 1 tablespoon minced fresh mint leaves
- 1 teaspoon red or rice wine vinegar
- 1 clove garlic, minced
- 4 large, thin red onion slices
- 4 large, thin tomato slices
- 4 small (4 inch) pita breads

Direction

- Place a small skillet on the stove and turn on medium high heat then add 4 whole garlic cloves; toast for about five minutes until spotty brown in color. Peel, mince, and reserve.
- In a medium bowl, break up lamb. Sprinkle on pepper, salt, oregano, feta and roasted garlic over the meat; use a fork to mix until well combined. Split into four pieces. Form a ball by tossing meat back and forth between cupped hands. Use fingertips to Pat and flatten to 4 inches wide. Then place inside the refrigerator.
- In a small bowl, combine to taste pepper, salt, 1 minced clove of garlic, vinegar, mint, sour cream and cucumber. Place the sauce inside the refrigerator until ready to serve.

- On one side of grill, build a hot fire. Then put the rack back on. Once coals are covered with white ash, put on burgers. Cook and cover, flipping only once, until done, for 4 to 5 minutes each side for medium to medium well burgers.
- Place the pitas on grill for about one minute or so each side becomes spotty brown in color and hot. Divide crosswise. Over for pita halves, spread a couple of tablespoons of the sauce. Place an Onion slice, tomato slice and a burger on top. Drizzle some of the left sauce over each burger. Then place left pita halves on top.

Nutrition Information

- Calories: 650 calories;
- Total Carbohydrate: 25.2
- Cholesterol: 139
- Protein: 31.2
- Total Fat: 46.8
- Sodium: 761

133. Grilled "Tandoori" Lamb

Serving: 10 | Prep: 20mins | Cook: 15mins | Ready in:

Ingredients

- 1 cup plain yogurt
- 1/2 cup lemon juice
- 1/4 cup finely minced onion
- 2 cloves crushed garlic
- 1 tablespoon freshly grated ginger
- 2 teaspoons garam masala
- 2 teaspoons paprika
- 1 teaspoon ground cumin
- 1/2 teaspoon turmeric powder
- 1/2 teaspoon cayenne pepper
- 2 pounds boneless lamb shoulder, cut into 2 inch pieces
- 2 teaspoons kosher salt, divided
- 1 tablespoon vegetable oil
- chopped cilantro (optional)
- fresh lemon wedges (optional)
- medium red onion, sliced (optional)
- spicy cilantro chutney

Direction

- Whisk together yogurt, lemon juice, garlic, onion, ginger, paprika, garam masala, turmeric, cumin, and cayenne pepper in a bowl until well-blended.
- Toss the lamb in the marinade and season with salt, mixing until the lamb pieces are evenly coated. Cling wrap the bowl and marinate in the refrigerator for at least 4 hours.
- Cue the lamb with a small space in between pieces. Take off excess marinade by wiping with a paper towel, then brush the lamb pieces with vegetable oil. Sprinkle with salt.
- Set grill on medium to pre-heat, and lightly grease the grate.
- Grill the lamb skewers until the meat springs back when touched; this is about 5 to 7 minutes per side.
- Garnish the skewers with lemon wedges, red onions, and chopped cilantro, if desired.

Nutrition Information

- Calories: 194 calories;
- Total Fat: 11.8
- Sodium: 430
- Total Carbohydrate: 8.9
- Cholesterol: 58
- Protein: 15.7

134. Grilled Lamb Burgers

Serving: 5 | Prep: 25mins | Cook: 10mins | Ready in:

Ingredients

- 1 1/4 pounds ground lamb
- 1 egg

- 1 teaspoon dried oregano
- 1 teaspoon dry sherry
- 1 teaspoon white wine vinegar
- 1/2 teaspoon crushed red pepper flakes
- 4 cloves garlic, minced
- 1/2 cup chopped green onions
- 1 tablespoon chopped fresh mint, or to taste
- 2 tablespoons chopped fresh cilantro
- 2 tablespoons dry bread crumbs
- 1/8 teaspoon salt
- 1/4 teaspoon ground black pepper
- 5 hamburger buns

Direction

- Prepare an outdoor grill by preheating to medium-high heat and oil lightly the grate.
- In a mixing bowl, combine the pepper, salt, bread crumbs, cilantro, mint, green onions, garlic, red pepper flakes, vinegar, sherry, oregano, egg and lamb by using your hands until equally combined. Shape into 5 patties.
- Place on the preheated grill and cook until burgers reach doneness desired, 4 minutes each side for medium-rare. The instant-read thermometer poked into the middle should read 160 degrees F (70 degrees C). Present on buns.

Nutrition Information

- Calories: 376 calories;
- Total Fat: 18.5
- Sodium: 370
- Total Carbohydrate: 25.4
- Cholesterol: 113
- Protein: 25.5

135. Grilled Lamb Chops

Serving: 3 servings. | Prep: 15mins | Cook: 15mins | Ready in:

Ingredients

- 1/2 cup canola oil
- 1/4 cup finely chopped onion
- 2 tablespoons lemon juice
- 1 teaspoon ground mustard
- 1/2 teaspoon garlic salt
- 1/2 teaspoon dried tarragon
- 1/8 teaspoon pepper
- 6 lamb loin chops (1-1/4 inches thick and 6 ounces each)

Direction

- Mix together the first seven ingredients in a large resealable plastic bag; put in the lamb chops. Secure the bag and flip the coat; place inside of the refrigerator for 10 to 15 minutes.
- Strain and get rid of marinade. Place the chops on the grill, cover, and cook over medium heat for 7 minutes per side or until meat achieves doneness desired (a thermometer should read 145°F for medium rare; 160°F for medium; and 170°F for well done).

Nutrition Information

- Calories: 523 calories
- Total Fat: 37g fat (8g saturated fat)
- Sodium: 314mg sodium
- Fiber: 0 fiber)
- Total Carbohydrate: 2g carbohydrate (1g sugars
- Cholesterol: 136mg cholesterol
- Protein: 43g protein.

136. Grilled Lamb Chops With Curry, Apple And Raisin Sauce

Serving: 6 | Prep: 15mins | Cook: 1hours20mins | Ready in:

Ingredients

- 1/4 cup butter
- 1 tablespoon olive oil

- 3 cups chopped onion
- 1 clove garlic, crushed
- 2 tablespoons curry powder, or to taste
- 1 tablespoon ground coriander
- 1 tablespoon ground cumin
- 2 teaspoons salt, or to taste
- 2 teaspoons white pepper
- 1 teaspoon dried thyme
- 1/2 lemon (including peel), seeded and finely chopped
- 3 cups apples - peeled, cored, and chopped
- 1 cup applesauce
- 2/3 cup dark raisins
- 2/3 cup golden raisins
- 1 tablespoon water, if needed (optional)
- 6 (4 ounce) lamb chops
- 1 teaspoon seasoned salt

Direction

- Place a saucepan on the stove and turn on medium heat, put butter to melt with olive oil, then stir in garlic and onions for about 8 minutes until the onions become translucent. Add in golden raisins, dark raisins, applesauce, apples, lemon, thyme, white pepper, salt, cumin, coriander and curry powder and combine well. Make the mixture boil, lower the heat to gently boil, cover with a lid, and gently boil the sauce for 1 hour until it has the consistency of applesauce and the raisins starts to break apart and are plump. Add in a tablespoon of water if sauce is too thick.
- Prepare an outdoor grill by preheating to medium heat and put oil lightly on the grate. Drizzle the lamb chops with seasoned salt.
- Then cook on the preheated grate until the chops are browned well, cook to desired color of pink inside and grill marks appear,3-5 minutes each side for medium-rare. The instant-read thermometer inserted into the middle of a chop, without touching the bone, should read 145 degrees F (65 degrees C). Present the lamb chops with the sauce on the side.

Nutrition Information

- Calories: 500 calories;
- Total Carbohydrate: 50.5
- Cholesterol: 88
- Protein: 20
- Total Fat: 26.6
- Sodium: 1046

137. Grilled Lamb Chops With Pomegranate Port Reduction

Serving: 4 | Prep: 15mins | Cook: 55mins |Ready in:

Ingredients

- 1 lemon, zested and juiced
- 2 tablespoons chopped fresh oregano
- 2 cloves garlic, minced
- salt and black pepper to taste
- 8 (3 ounce) lamb chops
- 1/2 cup fresh unsweetened pomegranate juice
- 1 cup port wine
- 2 tablespoons pomegranate seeds

Direction

- In a bowl, beat together oregano, salt, black pepper, lemon zest and juice, and garlic. Transfer to resealable plastic bag and place the lamb chops in. Coat the lamb chops with marinade then remove extra air, and seal bag. Put on one side to marinate.
- Set the outdoor grill on medium heat; preheat and oil lightly the grill grate.
- On high heat, in a small pot, allow port wine and pomegranate to simmer. Lower heat to medium-low, continue to simmer mixture until volume has lessened to half, 45 minutes. Add pomegranate seeds and put on one side.
- Take out lamb from marinade, shaking off any excess; discard the rest of the marinade. Place the lamb chops on heated grill and cook until beginning to firm up, are juicy at middle, and reddish-pink, for medium-rare 4 minutes a

side. Present the chops along with the reduction of pomegranate-port.

Nutrition Information

- Calories: 396 calories;
- Total Fat: 23.4
- Sodium: 83
- Total Carbohydrate: 10.2
- Cholesterol: 101
- Protein: 25.9

138. Grilled Lamb Chops With Wine Sauce

Serving: 4 servings. | Prep: 25mins | Cook: 30mins | Ready in:

Ingredients

- 2 tablespoons finely chopped sweet onion
- 3 teaspoons olive oil, divided
- 1 cup dry red wine
- 1 teaspoon butter
- 1 teaspoon minced fresh thyme or 1/4 teaspoon dried thyme
- 1 cup cherry tomatoes
- 6 whole unpeeled garlic cloves
- 2 garlic cloves, minced
- 1/4 teaspoon salt
- 1/4 teaspoon pepper
- 4 lamb rib or loin chops (6 ounces each)

Direction

- Put 1 teaspoon of oil in a small saucepan, then add in the onion and let it cook until the onion has softened; pour in the wine. Let the mixture boil and allow it to cook until the wine has reduced to just 2 tablespoons. Add in the thyme and butter and give it a mix. Remove the pan away from the heat source and let it stay warm.
- In a double thickness durable foil, put in the tomatoes. Pour 1 teaspoon of oil evenly on top of the tomatoes. Fold the foil over the tomatoes to keep it inside then seal it tightly; put it aside. Do the same for the remaining oil and whole garlic cloves. Put the enclosed garlic clove in a covered grill and let it grill for 30 minutes over medium heat.
- While the garlic is grilling, mix the salt, pepper and minced garlic together and massage it onto the chops. Put the coated lamb chops and tomato packet onto the grill over medium heat then cover and let it grill for 6 to 8 minutes on every side until the preferred meat doneness is achieved (a thermometer inserted on the meat should indicate 170° for well-done, 160° for medium and 145° for medium-rare).
- Gently open the grilled tomato packet to let out the steam then put the tomatoes in a small bowl. Crush the grilled softened garlic on top of the grilled tomatoes once the garlic is cool enough to the touch; mix everything together. Serve the grilled lamb chops together with the prepared wine sauce and the tomato-garlic mixture.

Nutrition Information

- Calories: 262 calories
- Total Fat: 11g fat (4g saturated fat)
- Sodium: 221mg sodium
- Fiber: 1g fiber)
- Total Carbohydrate: 6g carbohydrate (2g sugars
- Cholesterol: 70mg cholesterol
- Protein: 22g protein. Diabetic Exchanges: 3 lean meat

139. Grilled Lamb Kabobs

Serving: 4 servings. | Prep: 25mins | Cook: 10mins | Ready in:

Ingredients

- 1-1/4 cups grapefruit juice
- 1/3 cup honey
- 2 tablespoons minced fresh mint
- 3/4 teaspoon salt
- 3/4 teaspoon ground coriander
- 3/4 teaspoon pepper
- 1 pound lamb stew meat, cut into 1-inch pieces
- CITRUS SALSA:
- 4 medium navel oranges, divided
- 2 medium pink grapefruit
- 1/2 cup mango chutney
- 1 to 2 tablespoons minced fresh mint
- 2 medium onions, cut into wedges
- 1 large sweet red pepper, cut into 1-inch pieces

Direction

- Combine the first six ingredients in a large bowl. Pour a cup of the marinade into a large re-sealable plastic bag with the lamb. Close the bag, turn to coat, and let marinate in the fridge for 1-4 hours. Keep remaining marinade covered and refrigerated. Make the salsa: peel and separate the sections of 2 oranges and a grapefruit. Chop the sections and combine with mint and chutney in a large bowl. Cling wrap the bowl and refrigerate. Peel the rest of the oranges and slice into eight wedges. Drain the lamb, discarding its marinade. Take eight metal or pre-soaked wooden skewers, and alternately cue the lamb, onions, red peppers, and orange wedges onto them. Cook on an open grill over medium heat, or broil 4 in. from the heat, for 8-10 minutes or until lamb is cooked to preference: a meat thermometer reading of 145 deg is medium-rare, 160 deg is medium, and 170 deg is well-done. Occasionally turn and baste with reserved marinade. Serve warm kabobs with cold salsa.

Nutrition Information

- Calories: 367 calories
- Total Fat: 7g fat (2g saturated fat)
- Sodium: 282mg sodium
- Fiber: 7g fiber)
- Total Carbohydrate: 56g carbohydrate (0 sugars
- Cholesterol: 65mg cholesterol
- Protein: 24g protein.

140. Grilled Lamb Shoulder Chops With Fresh Mint Jelly

Serving: 2 | Prep: 15mins | Cook: 10mins | Ready in:

Ingredients

- 3 sprigs fresh rosemary
- 2 (8 ounce) lamb shoulder chops
- 1 teaspoon ground black pepper, or to taste
- 4 cloves garlic, crushed
- 2 tablespoons pomegranate juice
- Kosher salt, to taste
- olive oil
- Sauce:
- 1/2 cup orange marmalade
- 1 tablespoon white wine vinegar
- 1 tablespoon water
- 1/2 teaspoon red pepper flakes
- 1/2 bunch fresh mint, leaves only, very thinly sliced

Direction

- Release the rosemary sprigs fragrance by chopping it until bruised with the dull side of the knife; sprinkle lamb chops with pepper. In a plastic resealable bag transfer bruised rosemary sprigs, pomegranate juice, and garlic. Seal the bag and distribute the flavors by gently massaging it. For 1 hour, keep in the refrigerator.
- In a pot, add the orange marmalade. Pour in water and vinegar, allow to boil on medium-high heat, and quickly take from heat. Strain through a fine colander to take out the orange rind. Sprinkle in pepper flakes and for 30 minutes, keep in the refrigerator until cold. Stir in the mint when the jelly is cold until well

blended. (Mint will become black if added to warm jelly.)
- Discard the marmalade after removing the lamb. Add salt on both sides of chops. Drizzle lightly on 1-2 teaspoons of olive oil.
- Set grill to medium-high heat and oil lightly. Grill until chops are browned and doneness is medium-rare, 5 minutes per side. Insert a meat thermometer at the middle and it must register 130°F (54°C).
- Serve alongside the mint jelly.

Nutrition Information

- Calories: 604 calories;
- Cholesterol: 116
- Protein: 30.5
- Total Fat: 28.5
- Sodium: 322
- Total Carbohydrate: 59.6

141. Grilled Lamb With Tomato Basil Marinade

Serving: 8 | Prep: 15mins | Cook: 8mins | Ready in:

Ingredients

- 1 (6 ounce) can tomato paste
- 2/3 cup red wine
- 1 1/2 tablespoons olive oil
- 6 cloves garlic, minced
- 12 leaves fresh basil, cut into ribbons and chopped
- 8 1-inch-thick loin lamb chops
- sea salt and cracked black pepper to taste

Direction

- Preparation for marinade: In a small bowl combine olive oil, basil, garlic, red wine, and tomato paste.
- In a ceramic or glass container put lamb, brush the marinade on both sides thoroughly. Use a plastic wrap to cover and keep in the refrigerator, 4 or more hours.
- Prepare the outdoor grill by lightly oiling the grate and preheat at 475°F (245°C).
- Wipe off most of the marinade, leaving an only light coating on the lamb. Season with pepper and salt.
- For 4-5 minutes a side, grill until lamb becomes firm, color is reddish-pink, and juicy at middle. Insert a meat thermometer at the center and it must not be lower than 130°F (54°C).

Nutrition Information

- Calories: 237 calories;
- Sodium: 251
- Total Carbohydrate: 5.2
- Cholesterol: 56
- Protein: 15.2
- Total Fat: 15.6

142. Grilled Lamb With Veggies

Serving: 2 servings. | Prep: 25mins | Cook: 0mins | Ready in:

Ingredients

- 1/2 cup apple juice
- 1/2 cup honey
- 2 tablespoons dried minced onion
- 2 tablespoons cider or red wine vinegar
- 2 tablespoons tomato paste
- 2 garlic cloves, minced
- 1 teaspoon Worcestershire sauce
- 1/2 teaspoon pepper
- 3 medium potatoes
- 1 each medium green, sweet red and yellow pepper
- 2 sirloin lamb chops (about 1-1/2 pounds), trimmed

Direction

- Mix together the initial 8 ingredients in a saucepan; boil. Lower the heat; let simmer for 5 minutes without a cover. Slice every potato into 16 wedges. Distribute peppers and potatoes among 2 heavy-duty foil pieces, approximately 18-inch squares. Put half a cup of the sauce on top of each; reserve the rest of the sauce. Enclose foil securely. Grill lamb chops and vegetable packets with a cover for 5 minutes on moderately-hot heat. Flip chops over; baste with the rest of the sauce. Grill for an additional of 5 minutes. Flip over and baste once more. Grill for 2 minutes or until meat achieves preferred doneness; a thermometer should register 145° for medium-rare, 160° for medium and 170° for well-done. Serve along vegetables.

Nutrition Information

- Calories: 1051 calories
- Total Carbohydrate: 155g carbohydrate (88g sugars
- Cholesterol: 193mg cholesterol
- Protein: 72g protein.
- Total Fat: 18g fat (7g saturated fat)
- Sodium: 220mg sodium
- Fiber: 10g fiber)

143. Grilled Leg Of Lamb Steaks

Serving: 4 | Prep: 10mins | Cook: 10mins | Ready in:

Ingredients

- 4 bone-in lamb steaks
- 1/4 cup olive oil
- 4 large cloves garlic, minced
- 1 tablespoon chopped fresh rosemary
- salt and ground black pepper to taste

Direction

- In a shallow dish, place lamb steaks in one layer. Add pepper, salt, rosemary, garlic and olive oil to cover. Turn steaks to cover both sides. Let them sit for 30 minutes until steaks absorbed the flavors.
- Prepare an outdoor grill by preheating to high heat and oil lightly the grate. Place the steaks and cook until brown in color on the outside and lightly pink in the middle, 5 minutes each side for medium. The instant-read thermometer poked into the middle should at least read 140 degrees F (60 degrees C).

Nutrition Information

- Calories: 327 calories;
- Total Fat: 21.9
- Sodium: 112
- Total Carbohydrate: 1.7
- Cholesterol: 93
- Protein: 29.6

144. Grilled Lemon And Rosemary Lamb Chops

Serving: 8 | Prep: 10mins | Cook: 15mins | Ready in:

Ingredients

- 1/2 cup plain yogurt
- 1 large lemon, juiced and rind grated
- 1 tablespoon chile paste
- 4 cloves garlic, crushed
- 2 tablespoons minced fresh rosemary
- 1 teaspoon dried oregano
- 1 teaspoon salt
- 1/2 teaspoon ground black pepper
- 1/4 teaspoon ground cinnamon
- 8 lamb loin chops

Direction

- In a small bowl, mix the cinnamon, black pepper, salt, oregano, rosemary, garlic, chile paste, lemon zest, lemon juice and yogurt. Put into a resealable plastic bag. Put in the lamb chops, then cover with the marinade, compress to let the air out, and secure the bag. Place inside the refrigerator to marinate for 4 hours.
- Prepare the grill by preheating to medium heat and put oil on the grate lightly.
- Get the lamb chops from the marinade and shake off excess. Get rid of used marinade. Use black pepper and salt to season the chops. Cook on the preheated grill for 3 to 4 minutes until medium rare on the inside and brown in color. The instant read thermometer poked into the middle should say 130°F (54°C).

Nutrition Information

- Calories: 198 calories;
- Cholesterol: 57
- Protein: 15.3
- Total Fat: 13.6
- Sodium: 362
- Total Carbohydrate: 4.5

145. Grilled Mediterranean Lamb Sandwich

Serving: 4 | Prep: 20mins | Cook: 6mins | Ready in:

Ingredients

- 1 pound ground lamb
- 1 shallot, finely chopped
- 3 tablespoons finely chopped mint
- 1 tablespoon paprika
- 1 tablespoon ground cumin
- 1/2 teaspoon salt
- 1/2 teaspoon ground coriander
- 1/2 teaspoon ground cinnamon
- 1/4 teaspoon ground black pepper
- 1/4 teaspoon adobo seasoning
- Yogurt-Tahini Sauce:
- 1 (5.3 ounce) container fat-free Greek yogurt
- 2 tablespoons tahini
- 1 tablespoon lemon juice
- Sandwich Garnishes:
- 4 pita bread rounds
- 1 tomato, chopped
- 1/2 cup crumbled feta cheese
- 1/2 cup shredded lettuce

Direction

- Prepare an outdoor grill by preheating to high heat and put oil on the grate lightly.
- In a bowl, gently combine adobo, black pepper, cinnamon, coriander, salt, cumin, paprika, mint, shallot and lamb. Using about 3 tablespoons of mixture per cylinder, make lamb mixture into 8 cylinders about 1x3-inch in size.
- Lower the heat of the grill to medium; put lamb on grill and cook for about 3 to 4 minutes each side until the pink in the middle fades and the juices run clear. The instant read thermometer poked into the middle should at least read 165°F (74°C). Take off grill.
- In a bowl, combine the lemon juice, tahini and yogurt until sauce is uniform.
- Put 1/4 of the yogurt sauce down the center of each pita; place lamb, tomato, feta and lettuce on top.

Nutrition Information

- Calories: 564 calories;
- Total Carbohydrate: 38.2
- Cholesterol: 112
- Protein: 33.2
- Total Fat: 31
- Sodium: 1013

146. Grilled Pastrami Spiced Lamb Top Sirloin

Serving: 4 | Prep: 15mins | Cook: 16mins | Ready in:

Ingredients

- 2 (8 ounce) lamb top sirloins
- For the Wet Rub:
- 2 tablespoons olive oil, or more as needed
- 2 tablespoons freshly ground black pepper
- 2 tablespoons ground coriander
- 1 teaspoon paprika
- 1/4 teaspoon cayenne pepper
- 1 tablespoon kosher salt
- For the Sauce:
- 1/4 cup plain yogurt
- 1 tablespoon Dijon mustard
- 1 clove garlic, minced
- 2 teaspoons freshly minced mint

Direction

- In a crosshatch pattern on both sides of the lamb, cut 4 to 5 slashes about 1/4 inch deep.
- Into a bowl, Place 1/2 tablespoon of olive oil. Add kosher salt, cayenne pepper, paprika, coriander and black pepper. Mix together; mix in enough olive oil to create a paste. Massage lamb portions into the spice mixture until well coated. Use plastic wrap to cover and place inside the refrigerator for at minimum 2 to 3 hours or overnight to marinate.
- Prepare an outdoor grill by preheating to medium heat and put oil on the grate lightly.
- Put the lamb on the grate. Grill for 8 minutes each side to doneness between medium and medium-well. The instant-read thermometer poked into the middle should at least read 140°F (60°C).
- Put lamb on a plate and let it cool for five minutes. Thinly cut. Combine the mint, garlic, mustard and yogurt; present sauce with the lamb.

Nutrition Information

- Calories: 304 calories;
- Total Fat: 23.2
- Sodium: 1599
- Total Carbohydrate: 5.9
- Cholesterol: 68
- Protein: 18.5

147. Grilled Rack Of Lamb

Serving: 8 servings. | Prep: 10mins | Cook: 15mins | Ready in:

Ingredients

- 2 cups apple cider or juice
- 2/3 cup cider vinegar
- 2/3 cup thinly sliced green onions
- 1/2 cup canola oil
- 1/3 cup honey
- 1/4 cup steak sauce
- 2 teaspoons dried tarragon
- 2 teaspoons salt
- 1/2 teaspoon pepper
- 4 racks of lamb (1-1/2 to 2 pounds each)

Direction

- Mix first nine ingredients in a big saucepan, allow to boil. Lower heat and simmer for 20 minutes without cover; cool until room temperature. Reserve 1 cup for later basting. Keep in the refrigerator with cover. In a big plastic resealable bag, transfer the rest of the marinade and add the lamb. Seal and turn the bag over to coat. For 2 to 3 hours or overnight, keep in the refrigerator while turning once or twice.
- Drain the marinade; discard. Using foil, cover the ends of the ribs. Use a paper towel to moisten with cooking oil and lightly grease grill rack using tongs with a long handle. On medium heat, grill with a cover or alternatively broil 4 inches from heat, 15 minutes.

- Drizzle the reserved marinade over and broil or grill for an additional of 5 to 10 minutes until meat is cooked to your desired doneness. For doneness of medium rare, the inserted thermometer must register 145 degrees; 160 degrees for medium; 170 degrees for well-done, while occasionally basting.

Nutrition Information

- Calories:
- Total Fat:
- Sodium:
- Fiber:
- Total Carbohydrate:
- Cholesterol:
- Protein:

148. Grilled Spicy Lamb Burgers

Serving: 4 | Prep: 15mins | Cook: 10mins | Ready in:

Ingredients

- 1 pound ground lamb
- 2 tablespoons chopped fresh mint leaves
- 2 tablespoons chopped fresh cilantro
- 2 tablespoons chopped fresh oregano
- 1 tablespoon garlic, chopped
- 1 teaspoon sherry
- 1 teaspoon white wine vinegar
- 1 teaspoon molasses
- 1 teaspoon ground cumin
- 1/4 teaspoon ground allspice
- 1/2 teaspoon red pepper flakes
- 1/2 teaspoon salt
- 1/2 teaspoon ground black pepper
- 4 pita bread rounds
- 4 ounces feta cheese, crumbled

Direction

- Prepare the grill by preheating to medium heat.
- In a large bowl, put the lamb and combine with molasses, vinegar, sherry, garlic, oregano, cilantro and mint. Put black pepper, salt, red pepper flakes, allspice and cumin to season. Form into 4 patties.
- Brush with oil the grate of grill. Cook burgers for 5 minutes per side or until well cooked. Heat pita pocket on grill. Present burgers wrapped in pitas with feta cheese.

Nutrition Information

- Calories: 478 calories;
- Sodium: 1003
- Total Carbohydrate: 38
- Cholesterol: 101
- Protein: 29.4
- Total Fat: 22.4

149. Gyros Burgers

Serving: 4 | Prep: 10mins | Cook: 15mins | Ready in:

Ingredients

- 1/2 pound lean ground beef
- 1/2 pound lean ground lamb
- 1/2 onion, grated
- 2 cloves garlic, pressed
- 1 slice bread, toasted and crumbled
- 1/2 teaspoon dried savory
- 1/2 teaspoon ground allspice
- 1/2 teaspoon ground coriander
- 1/2 teaspoon salt
- 1/2 teaspoon ground black pepper
- 1 dash ground cumin

Direction

- Set the outdoor grill on medium heat; preheat and oil lightly the grill grate.

- Mix together the ground lamb, garlic, ground beef, bread crumbs, and onion in a big bowl. Sprinkle on allspice, salt, cumin, pepper, savory, and coriander. Massage mixture until stiff. Mold mixture in 4 thin patties about 1/8-1/4 inch in thickness.
- For 5-7 minutes per side, cook the patties until thoroughly cooked.

Nutrition Information

- Calories: 338 calories;
- Sodium: 408
- Total Carbohydrate: 5.7
- Cholesterol: 84
- Protein: 20.3
- Total Fat: 25.4

150. Herb Marinated Lamb Chops

Serving: 4 servings. | Prep: 10mins | Cook: 15mins | Ready in:

Ingredients

- 1/4 cup dry red wine or beef broth
- 2 tablespoons reduced-sodium soy sauce
- 1-1/2 teaspoons minced fresh mint or 1/2 teaspoon dried mint
- 1 teaspoon minced fresh basil or 1/4 teaspoon dried basil
- 1/2 teaspoon pepper
- 1 garlic clove, minced
- 4 bone-in lamb loin chops (1 inch thick and 6 ounces each)

Direction

- Mix garlic, pepper, basil, mint, soy sauce and broth or wine together in a big resealable plastic bag; put in lamb chops. Enclose the bag and coat by flipping; chill in the fridge for 8 hours or up to overnight.
- Let drain and put away the marinade. Grill lamb without covering on moderate heat or broil for 5 to 7 minutes per side in a 4- to 6-inch distance away from the heat until meat achieves preferred doneness; a thermometer should register 160° for medium and 170° for well-done.

Nutrition Information

- Calories:
- Sodium:
- Fiber:
- Total Carbohydrate:
- Cholesterol:
- Protein:
- Total Fat:

151. Herbed Lamb Chops

Serving: 4 | Prep: 20mins | Cook: 10mins | Ready in:

Ingredients

- 1/2 cup olive oil
- 1/2 cup red wine vinegar
- 1/4 cup white wine
- 2 tablespoons lemon juice
- 2 cloves garlic, peeled and minced
- 1/4 cup minced onion
- 1 teaspoon dried tarragon
- 1 teaspoon chopped fresh parsley
- 1 teaspoon black pepper
- 4 lamb chops

Direction

- Combine in a large nonreactive container, the onion, garlic, lemon juice, white wine, red wine vinegar and olive oil. Put in pepper, parsley and tarragon the season. Put the lamb chops in mixture. Place inside the refrigerator, covered, to marinate for 2 hours.

- Prepare an outdoor grill by preheating to high heat and put oil on the grate lightly.
- Place the lamb chops on the grill and cook for 5 minutes each side, inside temperature should be 145°F (63°C). Get rid of any left marinade.

Nutrition Information

- Calories: 566 calories;
- Total Fat: 52.4
- Sodium: 56
- Total Carbohydrate: 5.2
- Cholesterol: 70
- Protein: 15.9

152. Herbed Lamb Chops With Crispy Potatoes

Serving: 4 servings. | Prep: 40mins | Cook: 20mins | Ready in:

Ingredients

- 3 tablespoons olive oil
- 2 garlic cloves, halved
- 1/3 cup lightly packed fresh basil leaves
- 1/4 cup fresh parsley leaves
- 1/4 cup fresh oregano leaves
- 1/4 cup coarsely chopped chives
- 2 tablespoons fresh rosemary leaves
- 1 teaspoon salt
- 1 teaspoon pepper
- 8 lamb loin chops (1 inch thick and 3 ounces each)
- POTATOES:
- 2 tablespoons olive oil
- 4 medium red potatoes, cut into 1/2-inch cubes
- 1 teaspoon lemon-pepper seasoning
- 3/4 teaspoon salt
- 1/2 teaspoon paprika
- 4 cups fresh baby spinach
- 2 tablespoons pine nuts, toasted

Direction

- In a food processor, put the first nine ingredients; blend by pulsing until well combined. Scatter over both sides of chops. For 30 minutes, let it stand.
- In the meantime, place a large nonstick skillet on the stove and turn on medium-high heat add oil. Stir in potatoes; cook for 15-20 minutes or until golden brown in color and softened, occasionally stirring. Season with paprika, salt and lemon pepper; take out of pan. Keep it warm.
- Place the chops on the grill, cover, and cook for 3-4 minutes per side over medium heat or until meat reaches doneness desired (a thermometer should read 145°F for medium-rare; 160°F for medium; 170°F for well-done.)
- Then toss spinach with potatoes; sprinkle on pine nuts. Pair with lamb chops when served.

Nutrition Information

- Calories:
- Total Fat:
- Sodium:
- Fiber:
- Total Carbohydrate:
- Cholesterol:
- Protein:

153. Herbed Lamb Kabobs

Serving: 8 servings. | Prep: 15mins | Cook: 20mins | Ready in:

Ingredients

- 1 cup canola oil
- 1 medium onion, chopped
- 1/2 cup lemon juice
- 1/2 cup minced fresh parsley
- 3 to 4 garlic cloves, minced
- 2 teaspoons salt

- 2 teaspoons dried marjoram
- 2 teaspoons dried thyme
- 1/2 teaspoon pepper
- 2 pounds boneless lamb
- 1 medium red onion, cut into wedges
- 1 large green pepper, cut into 1-inch pieces
- 1 large sweet red pepper, cut into 1-inch pieces

Direction

- Mix the first nine ingredients in a small bowl. Transfer a cup of the mixture into a large zip-top bag with the lamb. Seal the bag and turn several times to coat; keep refrigerated for 6-8 hours. Cover the bowl of remaining marinade and store in the refrigerator until ready for basting. Drain the lamb and dispose of the marinade. Alternately thread lamb and vegetables on eight metal or water-soaked wooden skewers. Cook on an uncovered grill at medium heat, basting frequently with reserved marinade, for 8-10 minutes per side or until meat is cooked to liking. A meat thermometer reading of 145 degrees is medium-rare, 160 degrees is medium, and 170 degrees is well-done.

Nutrition Information

- Calories: 366 calories
- Sodium: 591mg sodium
- Fiber: 2g fiber)
- Total Carbohydrate: 6g carbohydrate (3g sugars
- Cholesterol: 69mg cholesterol
- Protein: 22g protein.
- Total Fat: 28g fat (5g saturated fat)

154. Indian Style Sheekh Kabab

Serving: 8 | Prep: 15mins | Cook: 10mins | Ready in:

Ingredients

- 2 pounds lean ground lamb
- 2 onions, finely chopped
- 1/2 cup fresh mint leaves, finely chopped
- 1/2 cup cilantro, finely chopped
- 1 tablespoon ginger paste
- 1 tablespoon green chile paste
- 2 teaspoons ground cumin
- 2 teaspoons ground coriander
- 2 teaspoons paprika
- 1 teaspoon cayenne pepper
- 2 teaspoons salt
- 1/4 cup vegetable oil
- skewers

Direction

- Mix together ground lamb, ginger paste, onions, cilantro, chile paste, and mint in a large bowl. Sprinkle with salt, cumin, cayenne, coriander, and paprika. Cover the bowl and let lamb marinate for 2 hours.
- Mold 1 cup of the lamb mixture to form sausages around the skewers. Even out the thickness all around the skewers. Keep in the fridge until ready to grill.
- Preheat grill on high.
- Generously oil the grates and arrange the kabobs, cooking for 10 minutes for well-done, and turning as necessary to cook evenly.

Nutrition Information

- Calories: 304 calories;
- Total Fat: 22.6
- Sodium: 665
- Total Carbohydrate: 4.7
- Cholesterol: 76
- Protein: 20.1

155. Kabab Barg

Serving: 6 | Prep: 15mins | Cook: 10mins | Ready in:

Ingredients

- 1/2 cup extra-virgin olive oil
- 1/4 cup fresh lime juice
- 2 large onions, grated
- 1 clove garlic, crushed
- 1/2 teaspoon saffron
- 1 teaspoon salt
- 1/4 teaspoon black pepper
- 1 3/4 pounds boneless lamb, cut into 1/2-inch x 1 1/2-inch pieces
- 4 tomatoes
- 1 tablespoon sumac powder (optional)

Direction

- In a large zip bag, mix together lime juice, garlic, onions, salt, pepper, saffron, and olive oil. Put in the lamb pieces, close the bag, and shake or turn to coat the pieces well. Marinate the lamb in the bag under refrigeration overnight or even up to 24 hours.
- Set an outdoor grill at medium-high to pre-heat. Lightly grease the grille.
- Skewer the lamb pieces on long, thin metal skewers. Thread fresh, whole tomatoes on a different skewer. Brush some marinade over the lamb and the tomatoes. Dispose of the remaining marinade.
- Grill lamb to preferred doneness, and the tomatoes until heated through and have grill marks, which is about 5 minutes per side. If desired, sprinkle with sumac before serving.

Nutrition Information

- Calories: 424 calories;
- Total Fat: 33.1
- Sodium: 452
- Total Carbohydrate: 10.1
- Cholesterol: 75
- Protein: 21.6

156. Kofta Kebabs

Serving: 28 | Prep: 45mins | Cook: 5mins | Ready in:

Ingredients

- 4 cloves garlic, minced
- 1 teaspoon kosher salt
- 1 pound ground lamb
- 3 tablespoons grated onion
- 3 tablespoons chopped fresh parsley
- 1 tablespoon ground coriander
- 1 teaspoon ground cumin
- 1/2 tablespoon ground cinnamon
- 1/2 teaspoon ground allspice
- 1/4 teaspoon cayenne pepper
- 1/4 teaspoon ground ginger
- 1/4 teaspoon ground black pepper
- 28 bamboo skewers, soaked in water for 30 minutes

Direction

- Use a mortar and pestle to mash garlic with salt until paste like. Use the flat side of the chef's knife and chopping board as an alternative way to create the paste. Stir garlic, onion, coriander, cumin, parsley, allspice, ginger, cayenne pepper, cinnamon, and pepper with lamb in a bowl. Stir mixture until well incorporated then mold in 28 balls. Make every ball around the tip of skewer and flat each into a 2-inch oval. Repeat with the rest of the skewers. On a baking sheet and transfer kebabs. For 30 minutes to 12 hours, refrigerate with cover.
- Prepare the grill by lightly oiling the grate and preheat at medium heat.
- Place the skewers on heated grill. Grill lamb while flipping occasionally until cooked to your desired doneness. For medium, grill 6 minutes.

Nutrition Information

- Calories: 35 calories;
- Total Fat: 2.3
- Sodium: 78
- Total Carbohydrate: 0.6
- Cholesterol: 11
- Protein: 2.9

157. Korean Barbecued Rack Of Lamb

Serving: 4 | Prep: 15mins | Cook: 25mins | Ready in:

Ingredients

- 2 tablespoons gochujang (Korean hot pepper paste)
- 6 cloves garlic, crushed
- 1/4 cup minced green onions, white and light green parts only
- 1 1/2 tablespoons brown sugar
- 3 tablespoons rice vinegar
- 1 tablespoon sesame oil
- 1/4 cup soy sauce
- 1 teaspoon kosher salt
- 2 (1 pound) racks of lamb, trimmed
- kosher salt to taste

Direction

- Mix together the salt, soy sauce, sesame oil, rice vinegar, brown sugar, green onions, garlic and gochujang. Beat marinade until well combined.
- Along the surface of the lamb, trim any extra fat. Slice a slash about 1 1/2 inches deep between each rib bone, stop cutting above the loin. Put racks in a zip-top bag. Put the bag in a bowl; place marinade inside. Secure the bag and knead the marinade on lamb. Place inside the refrigerator to marinate for 8 to 24 hours, flipping once or twice.
- Put racks of lamb on a plate and put marinade back in the fridge. Remove excess moisture from the fatty side of the lamb. Drizzle more kosher salt on top.
- Prepare an outdoor grill by preheating to 350°F (175°C). Place racks fat down and cook for 7 to 8 minutes until brown in color. Turn and keep on cooking for 12 to 15 minutes until internal temperature is 125°F (52°C).Then plate the lamb and let it rest for 10 minutes.
- Place a saucepan on the stove and turn on medium-high heat then pour in the reserved marinade. Make it boil; keep on cooking for 1 to 2 minutes until lessened to a glaze. Over the lamb, brush glaze.

Nutrition Information

- Calories: 421 calories;
- Sodium: 1626
- Total Carbohydrate: 12.4
- Cholesterol: 97
- Total Fat: 30
- Protein: 24.2

158. Lamb & Chicken Kabobs

Serving: 2 servings. | Prep: 15mins | Cook: 10mins | Ready in:

Ingredients

- 6 ounces sirloin lamb roast, cut into 1-inch pieces
- 1 boneless skinless chicken breast (5 ounces), cut into 1-inch pieces
- 1 large portobello mushroom, quartered
- 1/2 small sweet red pepper, cut into 1-inch pieces
- 2 green onions, cut into 2-inch pieces
- 1/2 teaspoon garlic powder
- 1/8 teaspoon salt
- Dash pepper
- 2 tablespoons lemon juice
- 2 tablespoons olive oil
- 2 fresh basil leaves, thinly sliced

Direction

- Alternately thread chicken, vegetables, and lamb on two metal or pre-soaked wooden skewers. Season with salt, pepper, and garlic powder. Mix lemon juice, basil, and oil in a small bowl. Cook the kabobs in a covered grill over medium heat for 4-5 minutes per side, or until chicken is cooked through. Baste often with the lemon mixture while grilling.

Nutrition Information

- Calories: 332 calories
- Total Fat: 20g fat (4g saturated fat)
- Sodium: 226mg sodium
- Fiber: 2g fiber)
- Total Carbohydrate: 6g carbohydrate (2g sugars
- Cholesterol: 87mg cholesterol
- Protein: 32g protein.

159. Lamb Burgers

Serving: 4 | Prep: 20mins | Cook: 10mins | Ready in:

Ingredients

- 1 pound ground lamb
- 1 4-inch sprig rosemary, chopped
- 4 sprigs thyme, chopped
- 1 tablespoon garlic powder
- 1 pinch salt
- 1 pinch ground black pepper
- 3 tablespoons mayonnaise
- 1 tablespoon Dijon mustard
- 4 hamburger buns, split and toasted
- 4 thick slices tomato
- 1 cup baby mixed salad greens

Direction

- Prepare the grill by preheating to medium heat and put oil on the grate lightly.
- In a bowl, mix together pepper, salt, garlic powder, thyme, rosemary, and ground lamb; form into four patties.
- Then place the burgers on the grill and cook for five minutes a side, until they are starting to become firm and hot and slightly pink in the middle. The instant read thermometer poked into the middle should say 140°F (60°C). Or you can cook the burgers according to doneness desired. While assembling toppings, let the burgers rest.
- In a small bowl, combine mustard and mayonnaise; onto one side of each bun, place 1 tablespoon of the mixture. Place a burger on each bun and put greens and tomato on top. To serve, sandwich with left bun half.

Nutrition Information

- Calories: 439 calories;
- Cholesterol: 80
- Protein: 24
- Total Fat: 25.9
- Sodium: 501
- Total Carbohydrate: 26.1

160. Lamb Chops With Preserved Lemon (Moroccan Style)

Serving: 4 | Prep: 35mins | Cook: 15mins | Ready in:

Ingredients

- 1/4 cup chopped fresh cilantro
- 1/4 cup chopped fresh parsley
- 1/4 cup chopped fresh mint
- 4 cloves garlic, minced
- 1/4 cup chopped Moroccan preserved lemon
- 1 tablespoon olive oil
- ground black pepper to taste
- 1 (7 bone) rack of lamb, trimmed and frenched
- 1/4 cup slivered kalamata olives
- 1 red bell pepper, thinly sliced

Direction

- In a small pot mix together mint, parsley, and cilantro. Reserve half of herb mixture and put to one side. In the left herbs, add lemon, black pepper, garlic, olives, and olive oil. Place 2

tablespoon of mixture on the lamb rack; spread. Using aluminum foil, wrap the lamb's exposed bones to avoid burning them. Toss bell pepper and olives in reserved herb mixture. On low heat, keep mixture warm.
- Set the outdoor grill on medium heat; preheat.
- Place the lamb rack on heated grill; cook until to the desired doneness. For medium rare, grill lamb 4 minutes a side. Use warmed relish for basting lamb occasionally. Take off grill when cooked, allow lamb to rest 5 minutes. Slice lamb rack in single chops.
- Serving: Prepare a platter and arrange on it the chops. Scoop some of warmed relish over the chops and season with reserved sliced herbs.

Nutrition Information

- Calories: 425 calories;
- Sodium: 1027
- Total Carbohydrate: 5.1
- Cholesterol: 95
- Protein: 21.6
- Total Fat: 35

161. Lamb Kabobs With Bulgur Pilaf

Serving: 6 servings. | Prep: 15mins | Cook: 35mins | Ready in:

Ingredients

- 30 garlic cloves, crushed (1-1/2 to 2 bulbs)
- 1/2 cup balsamic vinegar
- 3/4 cup chopped fresh mint or 1/4 cup dried mint
- 1/4 cup olive oil
- 2 pounds lean boneless lamb, cut into 1-1/2-inch cubes
- PILAF:
- 1/2 cup butter, cubed
- 1 large onion, chopped
- 1 cup uncooked mini spiral pasta
- 2 cups bulgur
- 3 cups beef broth

Direction

- Combine garlic, oil, vinegar, mint, and lamb in a large re-sealable plastic bag. Seal the bag, turn several times to coat, and refrigerate for several hours up to overnight. Prepare the pilaf: melt butter in a large skillet, add the onions and the pasta. Sauté until pasta is lightly browned. Add in the bulgur and stir to coat. Pour in broth and bring to a boil. Reduce heat to simmer while covered for 25-30 minutes or until bulgur is tender. Remove from heat and let cool for 5 minutes. Fluff with a fork. Drain the lamb and dispose of its marinade. Skewer lamb onto six metal or water-soaked wooden skewers. Cook the kabob on a grill over medium heat, covered, for 8-10 minutes or until meat is at desired doneness, turning frequently. Serve with bulgur pilaf.

Nutrition Information

- Calories: 626 calories
- Sodium: 644mg sodium
- Fiber: 10g fiber)
- Total Carbohydrate: 52g carbohydrate (4g sugars
- Cholesterol: 132mg cholesterol
- Protein: 38g protein.
- Total Fat: 31g fat (14g saturated fat)

162. Lamb Kabobs With Yogurt Sauce

Serving: 2 servings. | Prep: 20mins | Cook: 10mins | Ready in:

Ingredients

- 1/2 cup white wine or chicken broth

- 2 tablespoons olive oil
- 2 teaspoons ground coriander
- 1 teaspoon ground ginger
- 1/2 teaspoon salt
- 1/4 teaspoon ground cinnamon
- 1/2 pound sirloin lamb roast, cut into 1-inch cubes
- 1/2 cup plain yogurt
- 6 medium fresh mushrooms
- 1 medium zucchini, cut into 1/2-inch slices
- 1-1/2 cups hot cooked couscous

Direction

- Take the first six ingredients and mix together in a small bowl. Pour a third of a cup of the mixture into a large re-sealable plastic bag with the lamb. Close the bag and turn to coat the lamb with the marinade; let it soak in the refrigerator for 15 minutes. Put the yogurt in a small bowl and stir in a tablespoon of marinade. Cover the bowl and refrigerate. Keep the remaining marinade in the refrigerator for basting later. Drain the lamb and discard its marinade. Thread the lamb, zucchini, and mushrooms alternately on two metal or water-soaked wooden skewers. Cook on a covered grill over medium heat for 5-6 minutes per side, or until lamb is cooked to liking, basting often with the reserved marinade. A meat thermometer reading of 145 degrees means medium-rare; 160 degrees is medium, and 170 degrees is well-done. Serve skewers with couscous and yogurt mixture on the side.

Nutrition Information

- Calories: 500 calories
- Sodium: 572mg sodium
- Fiber: 6g fiber)
- Total Carbohydrate: 40g carbohydrate (6g sugars
- Cholesterol: 72mg cholesterol
- Protein: 31g protein.
- Total Fat: 20g fat (5g saturated fat)

163. Lamb Sliders

Serving: 4 | Prep: 20mins | Cook: 5mins | Ready in:

Ingredients

- 1 tablespoon minced garlic
- 1/4 teaspoon ground cumin
- 1/4 teaspoon ground coriander
- 1/4 teaspoon ground allspice
- 1/4 teaspoon salt, or to taste
- 1/4 teaspoon ground black pepper, or to taste
- 1 pound ground lamb
- 8 small slider-size rolls, split
- 1 cup baby spinach
- 1/2 cup tzatziki sauce
- 1/4 cup sliced red onion
- 1/4 cup crumbled feta cheese

Direction

- Prepare an outdoor grill by preheating to medium-high heat and oil lightly the grate.
- In a bowl, combine pepper, salt, allspice, coriander, cumin and garlic; mix in lamb and combine well. Make mixture into 2-ounce patties.
- Place patties on the preheated grill and cook for 2 to 3 minutes each side until cooked enough. The instant-read thermometer poked into the middle should at least read 160 degrees F (70 degrees C). Put rolls on the grill and warm each roll.
- To create sliders, layer each roll with spinach, tzatziki sauce, the lamb burger, red onion, and feta.

Nutrition Information

- Calories: 459 calories;
- Sodium: 646
- Total Carbohydrate: 33.5
- Cholesterol: 86
- Protein: 28.3
- Total Fat: 46.1

164. Lamb And Beef Kabobs

Serving: 8 servings. | Prep: 25mins | Cook: 10mins | Ready in:

Ingredients

- 1/4 cup minced fresh parsley
- 2 tablespoons olive oil
- 4 teaspoons salt
- 2 teaspoons pepper
- 2 teaspoons lemon juice
- 2 pounds boneless lamb, cut into 1-1/2-inch cubes
- 1 pound beef top sirloin steak, cut into 1-1/2-inch cubes
- 6 small onions, cut into wedges
- 2 medium sweet red peppers, cut into 1-inch pieces
- 16 large fresh mushrooms
- 6 pita breads (6 inches), cut into wedges

Direction

- Mix the first five ingredients in a small bowl. In a big plastic resealable bag, add the beef and lamb. Pour in half of marinade. In a separate plastic resealable bag, add the other half of marinade and vegetables. Seal the bags and coat by turning. Keep in the refrigerator for 1 hour.
- On eight soaked wooden or metal skewers, thread the beef, red peppers, lamb, onions, and mushrooms, alternately. Grill meat with cover on medium heat, about 5 to 6 minutes per side until cooked to desired degree of doneness and vegetables turn tender. Serve along with the pita bread.

Nutrition Information

- Calories: 419 calories
- Protein: 40g protein.
- Total Fat: 13g fat (4g saturated fat)
- Sodium: 1524mg sodium
- Fiber: 3g fiber)
- Total Carbohydrate: 34g carbohydrate (5g sugars
- Cholesterol: 105mg cholesterol

165. Lamb With Spinach And Onions

Serving: 6 servings. | Prep: 25mins | Cook: 10mins | Ready in:

Ingredients

- 1/2 cup lime juice
- 1/4 cup dry red wine or 1 tablespoon red wine vinegar
- 1 small onion, chopped
- 2 tablespoons minced fresh rosemary or 2 teaspoons dried rosemary, crushed
- 2 tablespoons olive oil
- 2 tablespoons Worcestershire sauce
- 3 garlic cloves, minced
- 1 tablespoon minced fresh thyme or 1 teaspoon dried thyme
- 1/4 teaspoon pepper
- Dash Liquid Smoke, optional
- 12 rib lamb chops (1 inch thick)
- ONION SAUCE:
- 2 tablespoons finely chopped green onions
- 1 teaspoon butter
- 1 cup balsamic vinegar
- 1 cup dry red wine or 1/2 cup beef broth and grape juice
- 1/2 cup loosely packed fresh mint leaves, chopped
- 1 tablespoon sugar
- 1 large sweet onion, cut into quarters
- Olive oil
- Salt and pepper to taste
- SPINACH:
- 1/4 cup finely chopped green onions
- 3 garlic cloves, minced
- 3 tablespoons olive oil

- 3 tablespoons butter
- 12 cups fresh baby spinach
- Salt and pepper to taste

Direction

- Mix the first ten ingredients in a big plastic resealable bag; put in lamb chops. Seal and turn to coat; chill for 8 hrs. or overnight.
- Sauté green onions in a saucepan with butter until tender. Pour in wine and vinegar or grape juice and broth; boil. Put in sugar and mint. Lower the heat; let it simmer for half an hour without a cover until the sauce reduces to 3/4 cup. Strain then get rid of the mint; set aside.
- Onto soaked wood or metal skewers, thread the onion wedges then rub with pepper and salt. Take the lamb out of the marinade. On medium-hot heat, grill chops for 5-6 minutes per side while covering or until it reaches the preferred doneness. A thermometer should register 170 degrees F for well-done or 160 degrees F for medium. Grill the onion skewers for 2-3 mins or until the onions are tender.
- Sauté garlic and green onions in a big skillet with butter and oil until tender. Put in pepper, salt, and spinach; sauté for 2-3 mins until the spinach is thoroughly heated and just starts to wilt. Move onto a serving platter. Take the onion out of the skewers; lay the lamb chops and onion on the spinach.

Nutrition Information

- Calories:
- Cholesterol:
- Protein:
- Total Fat:
- Sodium:
- Fiber:
- Total Carbohydrate:

166. Lemon And Thyme Lamb Chops

Serving: 12 | Prep: 10mins | Cook: 10mins | Ready in:

Ingredients

- 1/2 cup olive oil
- 1/4 cup lemon juice
- 1 tablespoon chopped fresh thyme
- salt and pepper to taste
- 12 lamb chops

Direction

- In a small bowl, mix together the thyme, lemon juice and olive oil. Put in pepper and salt to taste. In a shallow dish, put lamb chops, and brush with olive oil mixture. Place inside the refrigerator to marinate for 1 hour.
- Prepare the grill by preheating to high heat.
- Then put oil on the grill grate lightly. Put the lamb chops on the grill and get rid of marinade. Grill for 10 minutes, flipping once or to doneness desired.

Nutrition Information

- Calories: 205 calories;
- Total Fat: 17.6
- Sodium: 34
- Total Carbohydrate: 0.5
- Cholesterol: 42
- Protein: 10.8

167. Lemon Honey Lamb Skewers

Serving: 4 | Prep: 45mins | Cook: 10mins | Ready in:

Ingredients

- 1 cup chopped fresh mint
- 3/4 cup dry white wine

- 2 tablespoons lemon juice
- 2 tablespoons honey
- 3 pounds cubed lamb stew meat
- 24 pearl onions, peeled
- 8 bamboo skewers, soaked in water for 30 minutes
- 1 tablespoon apricot preserves
- 2 teaspoons cornstarch
- 1 tablespoon water

Direction

- In a mixing bowl, stir together wine, lemon juice, honey, and mint. Toss in the lamb and onions. Cover the bowl and let lamb and onions marinate for 4 hours to overnight in the refrigerator.
- Set an outdoor grill to medium-high to pre-heat and lightly oil its grates.
- Strain the marinade into a small saucepan. Cue the lamb and 3 pieces of onions per skewer. Grill the skewers until lamb is done to liking; about 8 minutes is medium-well.
- Take the saucepan with reserved marinade and let simmer over medium heat. Add in the apricot preserves, whisking until dissolved, then reduce heat to medium-low to gently simmer for 5 minutes. Add a bit of water as needed to keep from burning. Mix cornstarch in a tablespoon of water and slowly whisk into the sauce, simmering for 30 seconds to thicken the sauce. Serve lamb skewers with warm sauce.

Nutrition Information

- Calories: 386 calories;
- Total Fat: 11
- Sodium: 124
- Total Carbohydrate: 19.5
- Cholesterol: 134
- Protein: 42.4

168. Lime Glazed Leg Of Lamb

Serving: 10 | Prep: 10mins | Cook: 50mins | Ready in:

Ingredients

- 1 (6 ounce) can frozen limeade concentrate
- 1/2 cup dry white wine
- 1 large clove garlic, pressed
- 2 tablespoons butter
- salt and pepper to taste
- 1/2 teaspoon dried thyme
- 1 (4 pound) leg of lamb, butterflied

Direction

- Prepare an outdoor grill by preheating to medium heat.
- Place a saucepan on the stove and turn on medium heat, then place in the thyme, pepper, salt, garlic, white wine, and limeade concentrate. Cook, whisking, until the butter has melted. Separate from heat.
- Onto the preheated grill, place leg of lamb, and cook for 45 to 50 minutes basting often, or until the inside temperature has reached 145°F (62°C) at least.

Nutrition Information

- Calories: 290 calories;
- Total Carbohydrate: 14.1
- Cholesterol: 80
- Protein: 20.4
- Total Fat: 15.4
- Sodium: 70

169. Marinated Grilled Lamb

Serving: 10 servings. | Prep: 10mins | Cook: 01hours30mins | Ready in:

Ingredients

- 1/4 cup lemon juice
- 1/4 cup dry white wine or chicken broth
- 3 tablespoons olive oil
- 8 garlic cloves, minced
- 3 tablespoons minced fresh rosemary
- 1 tablespoon minced fresh thyme
- 1 tablespoon minced fresh oregano
- 1 teaspoon salt
- 1/2 teaspoon coarsely ground pepper
- 1 boneless leg of lamb (3 to 4 pounds), trimmed and untied
- 1 sprig fresh rosemary
- Additional salt and pepper

Direction

- Mix together the first nine ingredients in a large resealable plastic bag; add in lamb. Secure the bag and flip the coat; place inside the refrigerator for 4 hours.
- Prepare the grill for indirect medium heat. Strain lamb, getting rid of marinade. Put rosemary sprig on lamb; roll it up and use kitchen string to tie, keep a piece of the sprig exposed. Season with additional pepper and salt if desired.
- Grill the lamb on the indirect medium heat with cover on for 1-1/2 to 2 hours or until meat is doneness desired (a thermometer should read 145°F for medium rare; 160°F for medium; 170°F for well done). Take from grill; use foil to tent and before slicing, let it stand for 15 minutes. Get rid of rosemary sprig before serving.

Nutrition Information

- Calories: 225 calories
- Total Fat: 12g fat (4g saturated fat)
- Sodium: 304mg sodium
- Fiber: 0 fiber)
- Total Carbohydrate: 2g carbohydrate (0 sugars
- Cholesterol: 82mg cholesterol
- Protein: 26g protein. Diabetic Exchanges: 4 lean meat

170. Marinated Lamb Chops

Serving: Serves 4 | Prep: | Cook: | Ready in:

Ingredients

- 1/4 cup olive oil
- 1 tablespoon balsamic vinegar
- 4 garlic cloves, minced
- 8 frenched 1-inch-thick rib lamb chops (about 1 pound total)

Direction

- Beat together in a small bowl the pepper, salt, garlic, vinegar and oil to taste. Coat lamb chops on both sides with marinade for 30 minutes, and let it sit at room temperature, flipping once, on a plate or in a shallow dish.
- Prepare the broiler by preheating.
- Place chops on rack of broiler pan 2 inches from heat and roast for 7 minutes, flipping after 5 minutes to achieve a medium-rare meat.

Nutrition Information

- Calories: 11920
- Saturated Fat: 482 g(2412%)
- Sodium: 1777 mg(74%)
- Fiber: 0 g(0%)
- Total Carbohydrate: 2 g(1%)
- Cholesterol: 2409 mg(803%)
- Protein: 460 g(921%)
- Total Fat: 1104 g(1698%)

171. Minted Lamb 'n' Veggie Kabobs

Serving: 4 servings. | Prep: 30mins | Cook: 10mins | Ready in:

Ingredients

- 3 tablespoons olive oil
- 2 tablespoons lemon juice
- 4 garlic cloves, minced
- 2 teaspoons dried basil
- 1 teaspoon dried oregano
- 1 teaspoon pepper
- 1/2 teaspoon salt
- 1/2 teaspoon dried thyme
- 1 pound boneless leg of lamb, cut into 1-inch cubes
- 1 medium sweet red pepper, cut into 1-inch pieces
- 1 medium sweet yellow pepper, cut into 1-inch pieces
- 1 medium zucchini, cut into 1/4-inch slices
- 1 small red onion, cut into chunks
- 16 medium fresh mushrooms
- 1 cup fresh mint leaves
- Hot cooked brown rice

Direction

- Mix the salt, pepper, basil, garlic, oregano, thyme, oil, and lemon juice in a large re-sealable bag. Add in the lamb, seal the bag and turn to coat the meat. Let stand in refrigerator for 30 minutes. Alternately skewer lamb and vegetables with mint leaves on eight metal or pre-soaked wooden skewers. Grill with cover over medium heat, or broil 4 in. from the heat, for 4-5 minutes per side or until vegetables are tender and meat is done to liking. Serve with warm rice.

Nutrition Information

- Calories: 305 calories
- Total Carbohydrate: 14g carbohydrate (5g sugars
- Cholesterol: 69mg cholesterol
- Protein: 26g protein.
- Total Fat: 17g fat (4g saturated fat)
- Sodium: 365mg sodium
- Fiber: 5g fiber)

172. Mixed Grill Of Sausage, Chicken And Lamb With Tandoori Flavorings

Serving: 8 | Prep: | Cook: | Ready in:

Ingredients

- 2 pounds spicy or mild Italian pork sausage
- 1/4 cup olive oil
- 3 tablespoons ground cumin
- 1 tablespoon curry powder
- 1 1/2 teaspoons garlic powder
- 3/4 teaspoon ground ginger
- 3/4 teaspoon salt
- 1/2 teaspoon cayenne pepper
- 8 lamb loin chops
- 1/2 cup plain yogurt
- 3 tablespoons red wine vinegar
- 12 chicken drumsticks, skin removed

Direction

- In a big 12-inch skillet, add the sausage and 1/2 cup of water. Steam sausages with cover for 8 minutes until the raw color of sausages is gone throughout. Remove water and put to one side.
- Combine cumin, oil, curry powder, ginger, garlic powder, cayenne, and salt in a medium bowl. Transfer half of spice mixture in a separate medium bowl. Put the lamb chops in one of the bowls, tossing until well coated. Pour the vinegar and yogurt in the other bowl and put chicken legs in, tossing until well coated. Put on one side to marinate.
- 30 minutes before serving, set all the burners on high to preheat fully a gas grill for 10-15 minutes. Clean the grill rack with a wire brush and using the tongs, wipe a rag soaked in oil on the rack. Return the grill to correct temperature with the lid closed. Prepare water for extinguishing flare-ups.
- For all meats to finish at the same time, stagger the meat additions. Place the chicken on the

grill and close the lid. Grill-roast for 20 minutes in total, 8 minutes each side (first side- 8 minutes and second- 8 minutes) and an additional 4 minutes, flipping as necessary towards the end of grilling to assure doneness. Put the lamb on and grill-roast for 8 minutes in total, 4 minutes on each side. Place the sausage on and grill-roast for 4 minutes in total, 2 minutes each side.
- Prepare a platter and transfer on it grilled, lamb, sausage, and chicken. Serve alongside couscous.

Nutrition Information

- Calories: 743 calories;
- Total Fat: 52.5
- Sodium: 1093
- Total Carbohydrate: 4.7
- Cholesterol: 214
- Protein: 59.8

173. Moroccan Lamb Kabobs

Serving: 6 | Prep: 20mins | Cook: 10mins | Ready in:

Ingredients

- 2 pounds ground lamb
- 1 cup raisins
- 5 ounces goat cheese
- 1/3 cup mayonnaise
- 1 red onion, finely chopped
- 2 cloves garlic, finely chopped
- 2 tablespoons chopped fresh cilantro
- 3/4 tablespoon ground cayenne pepper
- 1/2 teaspoon ground cumin
- 1/2 teaspoon ground coriander
- salt to taste
- coarsely ground black pepper to taste

Direction

- Lightly oil the grate of an outdoor grill and preheat on high.
- Mix ground lamb, goat cheese, mayonnaise, garlic, red onion, cilantro, raisins, ground coriander, cumin, cayenne pepper, black pepper, and salt in a medium bowl. Portion out evenly into 6, and press these around skewers.
- Grill skewers for about 4 minutes each side, or until the raisins are soft, the cheese has melted, and the lamb is done according to preference.

Nutrition Information

- Calories: 554 calories;
- Sodium: 280
- Total Carbohydrate: 22.7
- Cholesterol: 125
- Protein: 32.2
- Total Fat: 37.6

174. Papa Wolf's Grilled Lamb Shoulder Chops

Serving: 4 | Prep: 10mins | Cook: 25mins | Ready in:

Ingredients

- 2 cups peach juice
- 3 tablespoons Worcestershire sauce
- 2 tablespoons olive oil
- 2 tablespoons mint sauce
- 1 tablespoon soy sauce
- 1 tablespoon lemon juice
- 1 tablespoon Italian seasoning
- 1/2 teaspoon ground cumin
- 2 teaspoons sea salt
- 2 onions, chopped
- 4 cloves garlic, finely chopped
- 4 (3 ounce) 1-inch thick lamb shoulder chops
- 1 teaspoon butter, or as needed

Direction

- In a large bowl, combine the lemon juice, soy sauce, mint sauce, olive oil, Worcestershire sauce, and peach juice. In another bowl, combine the salt, cumin and Italian seasoning. Gradually add seasoning mixture into the peach juice mixture; beat well. Put garlic and onions in the marinade; combine well.
- In a large resealable plastic bag, put the lamb chops and then the marinade. Gently toss to fully cover lamb chops. Then place inside the refrigerator for at least two hours to marinate.
- Take the onions and lamb from the marinade. In a sheet of aluminum foil that is lightly buttered, wrap onions. Place left marinade into a pot.
- Prepare an outdoor grill by preheating to medium-high heat and put oil on the grate lightly. Put the foil-wrapped onions on the upper grill while preheating.
- Put lamb chops on grill and baste with marinade. Flip onions over and cover with the lid. Cook, flipping the lamb once and basting again, until the thermometer poked into chops at least reads 130°F (54°C), about 5 1/2 minutes each side.
- Boil the marinade in the pot. Gently boil for 5 minutes until warmed through. Scoop on top of the lamb chops.

Nutrition Information

- Calories: 327 calories;
- Sodium: 1290
- Total Carbohydrate: 37.9
- Cholesterol: 49
- Protein: 16.4
- Total Fat: 12.9

175. Portobello Lamb Chops

Serving: 4 servings. | Prep: 10mins | Cook: 20mins | Ready in:

Ingredients

- 3/4 cup peach preserves
- 1 tablespoon balsamic vinegar
- 1/4 teaspoon pepper
- 1/8 teaspoon salt
- 4 lamb loin chops (2 inches thick and 5 ounces each
- 1/4 cup olive oil
- 1 teaspoon dried rosemary, crushed
- 4 large portobello mushrooms

Direction

- Mix all of the first 4 ingredients together in a small bowl. In a big ziplock plastic bag, put in 1/3 cup of the marinade mixture followed by the lamb chops. Seal the ziplock bag and turn it to coat the lamb chops with the marinade mixture; keep it in the fridge for 1-4 hours. Cover the remaining marinade mixture and keep it in the fridge as well.
- Mix the rosemary and oil together in a small bowl then use a brush to coat the mushrooms with the rosemary-oil mixture. Use long-handled tongs to lightly rub a grill rack with a paper towel dampened with cooking oil.
- Put the marinated lamb chops and coated mushrooms onto the prepared grill over medium heat and let it grill without cover, or put the lamb chops and mushrooms in a broiler and let it broil 4 inches away from the heat for 8 to 10 minutes on every side until the preferred meat doneness is achieved (a thermometer inserted on the meat should indicate 170° for well-done, 160° for medium and 145° for medium-rare), use the reserved marinade to baste the lamb chops and mushrooms from time to time.
- Cut the grilled mushrooms into slices and serve it alongside the grilled lamb chops.

Nutrition Information

- Calories: 429 calories
- Protein: 20g protein.
- Total Fat: 19g fat (4g saturated fat)
- Sodium: 131mg sodium
- Fiber: 1g fiber)

- Total Carbohydrate: 44g carbohydrate (38g sugars
- Cholesterol: 57mg cholesterol

176. Rocky Mountain Grill

Serving: 4 servings. | Prep: 5mins | Cook: 10mins | Ready in:

Ingredients

- 2 tablespoons water
- 2 tablespoons red wine vinegar
- 2 tablespoons canola oil
- 1-1/2 teaspoons rubbed sage
- 1 teaspoon grated onion
- 1/2 teaspoon lemon-pepper seasoning
- 1/2 teaspoon Dijon mustard
- 1/8 to 1/4 teaspoon cayenne pepper
- 4 lamb loin chops (1 pound)

Direction

- Mix the first 8 ingredients in a big plastic resealable bag; take out 3 tbsp. for basting then chill. Put the lamb chop into the rest of the marinade then turn to coat; seal then chill overnight.
- Drain then get rid of the marinade. On medium-hot heat, grill chops for 4 mins while covering. Flip then use the reserved marinade to baste; grill for 4 mins. Flip then grill for another minute or until it reaches the preferred doneness. A thermometer should register 170 degrees F for well-done, 160 degrees F for medium, and 145 degrees for medium-rare.

Nutrition Information

- Calories: 233 calories
- Sodium: 86mg sodium
- Fiber: 0 fiber)
- Total Carbohydrate: 0 carbohydrate (0 sugars
- Cholesterol: 78mg cholesterol

- Protein: 24g protein. Diabetic Exchanges: 1 fat
- Total Fat: 15g fat (0 saturated fat)

177. Rosemary Thyme Lamb Chops

Serving: 4 servings. | Prep: 15mins | Cook: 15mins | Ready in:

Ingredients

- 8 lamb loin chops (3 ounces each)
- 1/2 teaspoon pepper
- 1/4 teaspoon salt
- 3 tablespoons Dijon mustard
- 1 tablespoon minced fresh rosemary
- 1 tablespoon minced fresh thyme
- 3 garlic cloves, minced

Direction

- Season lamb chops with salt and pepper. Combine in a small bowl the garlic, thyme, rosemary and mustard.
- Place chops on the grill and cook on a greased rack over medium heat for six minutes, covered. Flip; spread the herb mixture over lamb. Cook for 6-8 minutes or until meat achieves doneness desired (a thermometer should read 135°F for medium rare; 140°F for medium; and 145°F for medium well).

Nutrition Information

- Calories: 231 calories
- Sodium: 493mg sodium
- Fiber: 0 fiber)
- Total Carbohydrate: 3g carbohydrate (0 sugars
- Cholesterol: 97mg cholesterol
- Protein: 32g protein. Diabetic Exchanges: 4 lean meat.
- Total Fat: 9g fat (4g saturated fat)

178. Rubbed Sage Lamb Chops

Serving: 2 servings. | Prep: 10mins | Cook: 10mins | Ready in:

Ingredients

- 2 tablespoons water
- 2 tablespoons red wine vinegar
- 2 tablespoons canola oil
- 1-1/2 teaspoons rubbed sage
- 1 teaspoon grated onion
- 1/2 teaspoon lemon-pepper seasoning
- 1/2 teaspoon Dijon mustard
- 1/8 to 1/4 teaspoon cayenne pepper
- 4 bone-in lamb loin chops (1 inch thick and 4 ounces each)

Direction

- Mix seasonings, oil, vinegar and water together in a small bowl. Pour a quarter cup into a big resealable plastic bag; put in the lamb. Enclose bag and coat by flipping; chill in the fridge overnight. Put on a cover and chill the rest of the marinade in the fridge for basting.
- Let drain and put away the marinade. With cooking oil, dampen one paper towel and coat grill rack lightly using tongs with long handle. Grill chops with a cover over moderate heat or broil for 4 minutes per side 4-inch away from the heat, basting from time to time with reserved marinade.
- Grill for an additional of 1 to 2 minutes or until meat achieves preferred doneness (a thermometer must register 145° for medium-rare, 160° for medium and 170° for well-done).

Nutrition Information

- Calories: 305 calories
- Total Carbohydrate: 1g carbohydrate (0 sugars
- Cholesterol: 90mg cholesterol
- Protein: 29g protein.
- Total Fat: 20g fat (4g saturated fat)
- Sodium: 189mg sodium
- Fiber: 0 fiber)

179. Serbian Cevapcici

Serving: 4 | Prep: 10mins | Cook: 30mins | Ready in:

Ingredients

- 1 1/2 pounds ground pork
- 1 pound lean ground beef
- 1/2 pound ground lamb
- 1 egg white
- 4 cloves garlic, minced
- 1 teaspoon salt
- 1 teaspoon baking soda
- 2 teaspoons ground black pepper
- 1 teaspoon cayenne pepper
- 1/2 teaspoon paprika

Direction

- Prepare the grill by preheating at medium-low heat.
- Mix the ground beef, egg white, ground pork, and the ground lamb in a big bowl. Toss in salt, baking soda, cayenne pepper, paprika, garlic, and black pepper. Use your hands to blend mixture well. Mold mixture into a sausage shapes the length of a finger and 3/4 inch thick.
- On grilling surface, lightly oil. For 30 minutes, grill sausages while flipping as necessary until cooked completely.

Nutrition Information

- Calories: 690 calories;
- Total Fat: 46.1
- Sodium: 1097
- Total Carbohydrate: 2.1
- Cholesterol: 223

- Protein: 62.8

180. Sharon's Scrumptious Souvlaki

Serving: 8 | Prep: 30mins | Cook: 20mins | Ready in:

Ingredients

- 2 pounds lamb, cut into 1 inch square cubes
- 1/2 cup olive oil
- 1 cup red wine
- 1 teaspoon salt
- freshly ground black pepper to taste
- 1 teaspoon dried oregano
- 1 tablespoon dried mint, crushed
- 1 clove garlic, chopped
- 4 cups plain yogurt
- 1 cucumber, shredded
- 4 cloves garlic, minced
- 2 tablespoons olive oil
- 1/2 teaspoon dried dill weed
- salt and pepper to taste
- 8 pita bread rounds
- 2 tablespoons olive oil
- 1 red onion, thinly sliced
- 1 tomato, thinly sliced

Direction

- In a large bowl, put the lamb, red wine, 1/2 cup olive oil, pepper, 1 teaspoon salt, garlic, mint, and oregano. Toss to coat lamb well. Cover the bowl and keep refrigerated for at least 3 hours, or even overnight.
- Lightly grease the grates of a preheating grill. Prepare the yogurt sauce: take a small bowl and mix together 2 tablespoons olive oil, yogurt, minced garlic, and cucumber. Sprinkle with salt, pepper, and dill weed.
- Skewer the meat and grill for 10 minutes, turning the skewers once. Lightly drizzle some olive oil on the pita and grill for a minute or until warm. Slide the meat off the skewers and arrange on warm pita with some sliced tomatoes and red onions, and the prepared yogurt sauce.

Nutrition Information

- Calories: 814 calories;
- Sodium: 766
- Total Carbohydrate: 46.5
- Cholesterol: 91
- Protein: 31.1
- Total Fat: 53.2

181. Simple Grilled Lamb Chops

Serving: 6 | Prep: 10mins | Cook: 6mins | Ready in:

Ingredients

- 1/4 cup distilled white vinegar
- 2 teaspoons salt
- 1/2 teaspoon black pepper
- 1 tablespoon minced garlic
- 1 onion, thinly sliced
- 2 tablespoons olive oil
- 2 pounds lamb chops

Direction

- In a large resealable bag, combine the olive oil, onion, garlic, pepper, salt and vinegar until the salt dissolves. Put in lamb, then coat by tossing, and place inside in the refrigerator for 2 hours to marinate.
- Prepare an outdoor grill by preheating to medium high heat.
- Get the lamb from the marinade and if some onions stick to meat leave them. Get rid of any left marinade. Use aluminum foil to wrap the exposed ends of the lamb bones to avoid any burning. Then grill to doneness desired, about three minutes each side for medium. Broiling the chops in the oven about five minutes each side for medium is another option.

Nutrition Information

- Calories: 519 calories;
- Total Fat: 44.8
- Sodium: 861
- Total Carbohydrate: 2.3
- Cholesterol: 112
- Protein: 25

---

182. Skewered Lamb With Blackberry Balsamic Glaze

Serving: 6 servings. | Prep: 10mins | Cook: 10mins | Ready in:

Ingredients

- 1/2 cup seedless blackberry spreadable fruit
- 1/3 cup balsamic vinegar
- 1 tablespoon minced fresh rosemary or 1 teaspoon dried rosemary, crushed
- 1 tablespoon Dijon mustard
- 1-1/2 pounds lean boneless lamb, cut into 1-inch cubes
- 1/4 teaspoon salt

Direction

- Mix together vinegar, the spreadable fruit, mustard, and rosemary. Take 2/3 cup of this marinade and pour into a large re-sealable plastic bag with the lamb. Zip the bag and turn several times to coat; let marinate in the fridge for at least an hour. Store leftover marinade in a covered container in the refrigerator. Drain the lamb and discard its marinade. Take six metal or pre-soaked wooden skewers and cue the lamb pieces. Arrange the kabobs on greased grill rack, and cook, covered, over medium heat or broil 4 in. from the heat for 10-12 minutes or until lamb is done to liking - for medium-rare, a meat thermometer should read 145 degrees; medium at 160 degrees; well-done at 170 degrees. Turn once but baste often with the reserved marinade. Salt the kabobs before serving.

Nutrition Information

- Calories: 255 calories
- Total Fat: 9g fat (4g saturated fat)
- Sodium: 264mg sodium
- Fiber: 0 fiber)
- Total Carbohydrate: 9g carbohydrate (7g sugars
- Cholesterol: 103mg cholesterol
- Protein: 32g protein. Diabetic Exchanges: 5 lean meat

---

183. South African Lamb Sosaties(Kebabs)

Serving: 8 | Prep: 30mins | Cook: 30mins | Ready in:

Ingredients

- 1 cup plain yogurt
- 2 teaspoons curry powder
- 1 tablespoon white sugar
- 1 tablespoon vegetable oil
- 1 large onion
- 1 cup cubed lamb stew meat
- 12 ounces dried apricots
- 8 kabob skewers

Direction

- To make the sauce, combine in a small bowl the oil, sugar, curry powder and yogurt. Modify the seasonings according to your desire.
- Peel and slice the onions into 1-inch pieces. Alternately thread skewers with Lamb cubes, dried apricot halves and onion. Then put them into a large resealable bag and add in the sauce. Ensure the kabobs are equally coated.

Place inside the refrigerator and let marinate overnight or for a minimum of 8 hours.
- Prepare the grill by preheating to medium heat and put oil lightly on the grate.
- Then place the kabobs on the grill over medium coals and cook for 8 to 10 minutes per side or to doneness desired.

Nutrition Information

- Calories: 172 calories;
- Total Fat: 3.3
- Sodium: 35
- Total Carbohydrate: 31.9
- Cholesterol: 12
- Protein: 6.5

184. Southwestern Grilled Lamb

Serving: 2 servings. | Prep: 10mins | Cook: 20mins | Ready in:

Ingredients

- 1 cup salsa
- 1/2 cup chopped onion
- 1/4 cup molasses
- 1/4 cup fresh lime juice (about 2 limes)
- 1/4 cup chicken broth
- 2 garlic cloves, minced
- 1 to 3 tablespoons chopped seeded jalapeno peppers
- 2 teaspoons sugar
- 4 lamb chops (1 inch thick)
- Sour cream

Direction

- Mix first 8 ingredients in a pot, allow to simmer without cover.
- While waiting, grill the lamb chops, flipping once on medium heat: for medium-rare 10 to 14 minutes, for medium 14 to 16 minutes, or for well-done 16 to 20 minutes. When there is only a few cooking minutes left, brush lamb with the sauce.
- Serve along with the sour cream.

Nutrition Information

- Calories:
- Total Carbohydrate:
- Cholesterol:
- Protein:
- Total Fat:
- Sodium:
- Fiber:

185. Southwestern Lamb Chops

Serving: 4 servings. | Prep: 15mins | Cook: 15mins | Ready in:

Ingredients

- 1 cup orange juice
- 2 jalapeno peppers, seeded and finely chopped
- 1 teaspoon ground cumin
- 1/2 teaspoon salt, optional
- Dash pepper
- 3/4 cup halved sliced sweet onion
- 4 teaspoons cornstarch
- 1/4 cup cold water
- 1 cup fresh orange sections
- 2 tablespoons minced fresh cilantro
- 8 lamb loin chops (1 inch thick and 4 ounces each)

Direction

- Mix the cumin, orange juice, pepper, salt (optional) and jalapeño together in a small saucepan. Let the mixture cook over medium-high heat setting until it is starting to simmer. Add in the onion and give it a mix.

- Mix the water and cornstarch together until it is smooth in consistency then put it slowly into the orange juice mixture. Let the mixture boil and cook it for 2 minutes while stirring it over medium heat until the sauce mixture is bubbling and is thick in consistency. Remove the pan away from the heat. Mix in the cilantro and oranges and keep the temperature of the sauce mixture warm.
- Put the lamb chops onto the grill over medium heat then cover and let it grill, or put the lamb chops in a broiler and let it broil 4-6 inches away from the heat for 4 to 9 minutes on every side until the preferred meat doneness is achieved (a thermometer inserted on the meat should indicate 170° for well-done, 160° for medium and 145° for medium-rare).
- Serve the grilled lamb chops along with the prepared orange sauce.

Nutrition Information

- Calories: 281 calories
- Protein: 30g protein. Diabetic Exchanges: 4 lean meat
- Total Fat: 10g fat (3g saturated fat)
- Sodium: 83mg sodium
- Fiber: 2g fiber)
- Total Carbohydrate: 18g carbohydrate (11g sugars
- Cholesterol: 90mg cholesterol

186. Spicy Barbequed Chops

Serving: 6 | Prep: 15mins | Cook: 10mins |Ready in:

Ingredients

- 1/4 cup tomato sauce
- 2 tablespoons barbeque sauce
- 2 teaspoons Worcestershire sauce
- 1 tablespoon malt vinegar
- 1 teaspoon Dijon mustard
- 2 teaspoons brown sugar
- 2 pounds lamb chops

Direction

- Combine in a large bowl the brown sugar, mustard, vinegar, Worcestershire sauce, barbecue sauce and tomato sauce. Add the lamb chops into the mixture, and place inside the refrigerator for at least 20 minutes to marinate.
- Prepare an outdoor grill by preheating to high heat.
- Grill the lamb chops for 10 minutes, frequently turning and basting often with marinade. Inside temperature of the chops should read at least 145°F (63°C).

Nutrition Information

- Calories: 303 calories;
- Total Fat: 20.7
- Sodium: 221
- Total Carbohydrate: 4.7
- Cholesterol: 90
- Protein: 22.7

187. Spicy Chinese Cumin Lamb Skewers

Serving: 10 | Prep: 20mins | Cook: 6mins |Ready in:

Ingredients

- 1 pound lamb shoulder, cut into 1/2-inch pieces
- 10 skewers
- 2 tablespoons ground cumin
- 2 tablespoons red pepper flakes
- 1 tablespoon salt

Direction

- Thread the lamb onto flat kebab skewers.
- Preheat a grill on medium then oil the rack lightly.

- Place the kebabs on the hot grill. Season with salt, cumin, and red pepper flakes. Frequently turn until evenly browned and not pink in middle, about 6 minutes.

Nutrition Information

- Calories: 77 calories;
- Total Fat: 5.2
- Sodium: 715
- Total Carbohydrate: 1.6
- Cholesterol: 23
- Protein: 6.3

---

188. Spicy Lamb Kabobs

Serving: 8 servings. | Prep: 40mins | Cook: 10mins | Ready in:

Ingredients

- 1 large cucumber
- 2 cups (8 ounces) sour cream or plain yogurt
- 2 teaspoons lemon juice
- 1/2 teaspoon salt
- 1/8 teaspoon garlic powder
- 1/8 teaspoon dill weed
- 1/8 teaspoon pepper
- KABOBS:
- 2 cups buttermilk
- 2 teaspoons ground turmeric
- 2 teaspoons curry powder
- 1 teaspoon coarsely ground pepper
- 1 teaspoon chili powder
- 1 teaspoon minced fresh sage
- 1/2 teaspoon salt
- 2-1/2 pounds lean boneless lamb, cut into 1-inch cubes
- 16 cubes fresh pineapple (1-inch)
- 16 cherry tomatoes
- SALAD:
- 8 cups torn leaf lettuce
- 2 cups torn romaine
- 2 cups torn Bibb or Boston lettuce
- 1/2 large sweet onion, sliced
- 1/2 medium red onion, finely chopped
- 1 medium tomato, chopped
- 1/2 cup bean sprouts
- 1/2 cup green grapes, quartered
- 1/2 cup chopped walnuts
- 1/2 cup crumbled feta cheese
- 1/4 cup butter, softened
- 2 tablespoons honey
- 4 pita breads (6 inches), halved and warmed

Direction

- Peel the cucumber, removing its seeds. Process the peeled and de-seeded cucumbers in a food processor until finely chopped. Set aside half then puree the rest. Stir together the pureed cucumber and the chopped cucumber, then the sour cream, seasonings, and lemon juice. Keep in the refrigerator for at least 60 minutes. Combine the first seven kabob ingredients in a small bowl. Place the lambs in a large zip-top bag and pour 1 1/2 cups of the marinade over the meat. Zip the bag, turn to coat, and refrigerate for at least an hour. Keep the remaining marinade in a covered container in the refrigerator, for use in basting later. Drain and discard marinade from the lamb. Take eight metal or pre-soaked wooden skewers and alternately thread lamb, tomatoes, and pineapples. Put out a large bowl and mix together the lettuces, tomatoes, onions, grapes, sprouts, and walnuts, then scatter cheese over it. Set aside. Cook kabobs in a covered gill over medium heat for 5-6 minutes per side or until lamb is cooked to liking. A meat thermometer should read 145 deg for medium-rare, 160 deg for medium, and 170 deg for well-done. Brush often with reserved marinade. Beat honey and butter until well-blended and brush this over the pitas. Serve kabobs with honey-glazed pita, salad greens, and sauce.

Nutrition Information

- Calories: 610 calories
- Total Fat: 30g fat (15g saturated fat)

- Sodium: 729mg sodium
- Fiber: 5g fiber)
- Total Carbohydrate: 43g carbohydrate (19g sugars
- Cholesterol: 147mg cholesterol
- Protein: 39g protein.

189. Summer Lamb Kabobs

Serving: 20 | Prep: 20mins | Cook: 12mins | Ready in:

Ingredients

- 5 pounds boneless lamb shoulder, cut into 1 inch pieces
- 6 tablespoons Dijon mustard
- 4 tablespoons white wine vinegar
- 4 tablespoons olive oil
- 1/2 teaspoon salt
- 1/2 teaspoon black pepper
- 1/2 teaspoon chopped fresh rosemary
- 1/2 teaspoon crumbled dried sage
- 4 cloves garlic, chopped
- 4 green bell peppers, cut into large chunks
- 1 (10 ounce) package whole fresh mushrooms
- 1 (16 ounce) can pineapple chunks, drained with juice reserved
- 1 pint cherry tomatoes
- 4 onions, quartered
- 1 (10 ounce) jar maraschino cherries, drained and juice reserved
- 1/3 cup melted butter or margarine

Direction

- Put lamb in a big bowl.
- Take another bowl and mix together olive oil, vinegar, mustard, salt, pepper, garlic, sage, and rosemary. Spoon the mixture over the lamb and mix well to coat. Cover the bowl and marinate in the refrigerator overnight.
- Set outdoor grill for direct heat.
- Thread lamb, vegetables, and fruit onto bamboo or stainless steel skewers. Keep some

of the liquid from the cherries and the pineapple chunks.
- Put melted butter in a small bowl and stir in a few splashes of the pineapple and the cherry juices. Use this for basting.
- Arrange the skewers on the grill. Turn and baste with butter mixture during the 12-minute grilling time.

Nutrition Information

- Calories: 406 calories;
- Cholesterol: 90
- Protein: 20
- Total Fat: 30.3
- Sodium: 266
- Total Carbohydrate: 13.2

Chapter 6: Lamb For Main Dish Recipes

***

190. Braised Lamb Shanks & Eggplant

Serving: 4 | Prep: | Cook: 30mins | Ready in:

Ingredients

- 1½ pounds eggplant (see Tip), peeled
- 4 12-ounce lamb shanks (about 3 pounds), trimmed
- 2 tablespoons ground sumac, divided
- 1¼ teaspoons salt
- ½ teaspoon freshly ground pepper
- 2 tablespoons extra-virgin olive oil, divided
- 1 large green bell pepper, diced
- 1 small onion, diced

- 3 cloves garlic, minced, divided
- 5 plum tomatoes, diced
- 1 cup water
- ½ cup finely chopped parsley, divided

Direction

- Slice eggplant lengthwise (1/2 -in. in width), then crosswise (1-in. in width); set aside. Use pepper, salt and 1 tablespoon of sumac to rub the lamb shanks.
- Place a large Dutch oven (or a 5- to 6-qt. pot) on medium-high heat and heat 1 tablespoon of oil. Put in the lamb; cook while turning often for 5-7 minutes till browned on all sides. (Avoid overcrowding the pan; work in batches if needed.) Move to a plate.
- Put the remaining 1 tablespoon of oil into the pot; add in the remaining 1 tablespoon of sumac, 2 minced garlic cloves, onion and bell pepper. Cook while stirring often for 3-5 minutes till the vegetables begin to soften. Put the lamb back to the pot. Mix in water, tomatoes and the eggplant. Allow to boil. Lower the heat to maintain a simmer; cook with a cover while stirring occasionally for around 2 hours, flipping over once halfway through, until the lamb turns very tender.
- Transfer the lamb to a plate, tent with foil to stay warm. Raise the heat to medium-high, cook the sauce for 5-10 minutes or till thickened and slightly reduced.
- In a small bowl, mix the remaining garlic and the remaining 1/4 cup of parsley.
- Top the lamb and veggie sauce with parsley-garlic mixture, serve.

Nutrition Information

- Calories: 321 calories;
- Sodium: 812
- Fiber: 8
- Cholesterol: 94
- Sugar: 10
- Total Fat: 14
- Saturated Fat: 3
- Total Carbohydrate: 20
- Protein: 32

191. Braised Lamb Shanks With Butternut Squash Puree

Serving: 4 | Prep: 25mins | Cook: 6hours29mins | Ready in:

Ingredients

- 1/4 cup melted butter, divided
- 2 tablespoons olive oil
- 4 lamb shanks
- sea salt, divided
- 1 1/2 teaspoons freshly ground black pepper
- 1 large onion, chopped
- 3 carrots, chopped
- 2 stalks celery, chopped
- 6 cloves garlic, minced
- 1 tablespoon dried thyme, divided
- 1 1/2 teaspoons dried rosemary, divided
- 1 teaspoon dried basil
- 3 cups chicken broth, or more as needed
- 1 cup red wine, or more as needed
- 1 (2 1/2 pound) butternut squash, peeled and chopped

Direction

- Set an oven to preheat to 135?°C (275°F).
- In a big oven safe pan, heat 2 tbsp. of butter and olive oil on medium-high heat. Sprinkle 1/2 tsp pepper and 1/2 tsp salt to season the lamb shanks. Let it cook for about 2 minutes on each side, until it becomes brown.
- Into the pan, stir the celery, carrots and onion. Add basil, 1 tsp rosemary, 2 tsp thyme, garlic, 1/2 tsp pepper and 1/2 tsp salt. Pour in wine and chicken broth, then boil. Separate it from the heat then cover.
- Put the covered pan in the preheated oven and let it bake for about 6 hours, until the lamb shanks become tender. Every 2 hours, check the level of liquid, then, add more red wine or chicken broth if too much has evaporated.

- In a big pot of water, put the butternut squash with 1 tsp salt, then boil. Lower the heat and let it simmer for 15-20 minutes until it becomes tender. Let it drain and put it back into the pot.
- Stir 1/2 tsp rosemary, 1 tsp thyme, 1/2 tsp pepper, 1 tsp salt and 2 tbsp. butter. Use a fork to mash it until it becomes smooth. Reheat it over medium heat prior to serving with the lamb shanks.

Nutrition Information

- Calories: 620 calories;
- Sodium: 2177
- Total Carbohydrate: 47.9
- Cholesterol: 124
- Protein: 31.9
- Total Fat: 30.6

192. Braised Lamb With A Garden Vegetable Medley

Serving: 6 | Prep: | Cook: 30mins | Ready in:

Ingredients

- 2½ pounds boneless lamb leg, trimmed and cut into 2-inch cubes
- ½ teaspoon salt
- 1 tablespoon extra-virgin olive oil
- 1 medium carrot, finely chopped
- 1 small onion, finely chopped
- 1 tablespoon all-purpose flour
- 1¾ cups dry red wine
- 1 cup reduced-sodium beef broth
- Freshly ground pepper, to taste
- 4 cloves garlic, minced
- 1 tablespoon finely chopped fresh rosemary
- 1 14-ounce can diced tomatoes
- 1 cup pearl onions, peeled (see Tip), or frozen small onions, rinsed under warm water to thaw
- 1 cup baby turnips, peeled (¼ inch of green left on) and halved, or regular turnips cut into ½-inch wedges
- 1½ cups baby carrots
- 1½ cups peas, fresh or frozen
- 2 tablespoons chopped fresh parsley

Direction

- Put pepper and salt to season lamb. In a big Dutch oven or deep skillet, heat the oil. Put lamb and allow to cook for 6 minutes, flipping occasionally, till all sides are browned. Put to plate.
- To the pan, put onion and carrot; allow to cook for 3 minutes, mixing frequently, till browned lightly. Scatter flour on top of vegetables; coat by mixing. Put wine and scratch up some browned bits. Allow to simmer for 2 to 3 minutes till slightly reduced.
- Put rosemary, garlic, tomatoes, and broth; simmer. Put lamb back to pan. Turn heat to low, put cover and let simmer for 1 1/4 hours, monitor occasionally to ensure it will not boil too rapidly.
- Mix in carrots, turnips and pearl onions. Allow to simmer with cover for half an hour, till vegetables and lamb are soft.
- Put peas and heat through. Scatter parsley on top, serve.

Nutrition Information

- Calories: 420 calories;
- Cholesterol: 126
- Total Carbohydrate: 16
- Sugar: 7
- Total Fat: 14
- Saturated Fat: 4
- Sodium: 529
- Fiber: 4
- Protein: 43

193. Braised Lamb With A Sour Orange Marinade

Serving: 16 | Prep: 15mins | Cook: 5hours | Ready in:

Ingredients

- 6 pounds deboned leg of lamb
- 1 tablespoon dried oregano
- 4 cloves garlic, minced
- 1 large onion, thinly sliced
- 2 bay leaves
- 4 sour oranges
- 1 cup white wine
- 1 teaspoon salt, or to taste
- 1 teaspoon ground black pepper, or to taste
- 2 tablespoons vegetable oil

Direction

- Squeeze the juice from the sour oranges, then in a large bowl, mix white wine, bay leaf, oregano, onion, and garlic. Arrange the meat into the marinade, put a cover on, and store in the fridge for 2-4 hours.
- Heat the oil on medium-high heat in a large pot. Arrange the meat into the pan and sear all the sides. Turn down the heat to low. Pour the marinade on the meat placed in the pan, then put a cover on. Cook for 3 hours until the meat becomes fork tender; if needed, add water into the pot to prevent the meat from scorching.

Nutrition Information

- Calories: 272 calories;
- Total Fat: 9.5
- Sodium: 252
- Total Carbohydrate: 6.7
- Cholesterol: 109
- Protein: 35.6

194. Dragan's Leg Of Lamb With Garlic And Beer

Serving: 6 | Prep: 15mins | Cook: 2hours | Ready in:

Ingredients

- 1 pound new potatoes
- 12 ounces baby carrots
- 1 (5 pound) leg of lamb
- 30 cloves garlic, peeled
- salt and pepper to taste
- 1/4 cup coarse-grain brown mustard
- 1 cup beer

Direction

- Start preheating the oven to 400°F (200°C). Boil water in a big pot. Add carrots and potatoes, then boil for approximately 3 minutes. Drain and put aside.
- Rinse the lamb leg and tap dry. Put it in a roasting pan and use pepper and salt to generously season. Rub into the meat with pepper and salt. Make incisions, using a small knife, large enough to fit a garlic clove in all over the leg. Into the incisions, stuff the garlic cloves. Spoon over the lamb with mustard and also rub it in.
- Roast without a cover for about 30 minutes in the preheated oven. Lower the oven temperature to 375°F (190°C). Add carrots and potatoes to the roasting pan. Use beer to baste the lamb, saving the remaining to baste at 20-minute intervals.
- Keep roasting the lamb for about 1 1/2 more hours until the internal temperature registers a minimum of 140°F (60°C) for medium-rare. Take out of the oven and let sit for a minimum of 5 minutes before carving. Add the pan drippings onto the vegetables and meat when eating.

Nutrition Information

- Calories: 514 calories;
- Sodium: 281

- Total Carbohydrate: 24.8
- Cholesterol: 167
- Protein: 45.5
- Total Fat: 23.9

195. Feta And Olive Meatballs

Serving: 8 | Prep: 10mins | Cook: 10mins | Ready in:

Ingredients

- 1 pound ground lamb
- 1/2 cup chopped fresh parsley
- 2 tablespoons finely chopped onion
- 1/2 cup crumbled feta cheese
- 1/2 cup chopped green olives
- 2 eggs
- 1 teaspoon Italian seasoning

Direction

- Preheat oven broiler.
- Mix Italian seasoning, eggs, green olives, feta cheese, onion, parsley and ground lamb in a big bowl; form to 16 meatballs. Put onto baking sheet, 2-in. apart.
- Broil 3-in. from heat till browned on top. Flip; broil other side.

Nutrition Information

- Calories: 185 calories;
- Total Fat: 13.7
- Sodium: 482
- Total Carbohydrate: 1.5
- Cholesterol: 98
- Protein: 13.8

196. Garam Masala Lamb Chops With Apricot Couscous

Serving: 4 | Prep: | Cook: 35mins | Ready in:

Ingredients

- 1¼ cups water
- 1 teaspoon kosher salt, divided
- 1 tablespoon garam masala
- 4 teaspoons extra-virgin olive oil, divided
- ½ teaspoon freshly ground pepper
- 1 rack of lamb, exterior fat trimmed
- ¾ cup whole-wheat couscous, (see Ingredient note)
- ¼ cup chopped fresh apricots
- ¼ cup golden raisins
- 2 tablespoons pine nuts, toasted if desired
- ¼ cup sliced fresh mint
- ¼ cup lemon juice

Direction

- Set the oven to 450°F for preheating. Boil 1/2 tsp. of salt and water in a small saucepan.
- In a small bowl, mix 1 tsp. of oil, the leftover 1/2 tsp. of salt and pepper, and the garam masala. Rub the mixture into the lamb. In a large and ovenproof nonstick skillet, heat 1 tsp. of oil over high heat. Cook the lamb, skin-side down for 3-5 minutes until that side is browned. Flip it over and transfer the skillet into the oven. Roast the lamb for 6-12 minutes until an inserted instant-read thermometer in the center registers 145°F (medium-rare). Transfer the lamb in a cutting board. Let it rest for 5 minutes before chopping it.
- In the meantime, mix raisins, couscous, and apricots into the boiling water. Bring the mixture to a boil. Adjust the heat to low. Cover and simmer the mixture for 2 minutes. Remove it from the heat. Allow it to stand for 5 minutes while covered. Mix in lemon juice, the leftover 2 tsp. of oil, mint, and pine nuts. Serve the couscous together with the lamb.

Nutrition Information

- Calories: 418 calories;
- Fiber: 8
- Cholesterol: 56
- Protein: 25
- Total Fat: 14
- Saturated Fat: 3
- Sodium: 645
- Total Carbohydrate: 50
- Sugar: 10

197. Grandma Me's Clove Studded Leg Of Lamb

Serving: 8 | Prep: 15mins | Cook: 2hours35mins | Ready in:

Ingredients

- 1 (6 pound) bone-in leg of lamb, trimmed
- 1 tablespoon whole cloves
- 1 (12 ounce) can apricot nectar
- 1 teaspoon salt
- 1 pinch black pepper
- 1/4 teaspoon soy sauce
- 4 slices lemon, for garnish
- 2 teaspoons cornstarch
- 1/2 cup water
- 1 cube vegetable bouillon, crushed

Direction

- Set oven to 165° C (325° F) and start preheating.
- Slice through the narrow end of lamb leg with a sharp knife, about 3 inches from the end. Slice through the meat surrounding the bone. Take out this piece and discard, keeping the clean exposed bone. (You can ask the butcher to do this for you.) Stick an even pattern of cloves into the lamb leg. Arrange in a metal shallow roasting pan.
- Place in the preheated oven and bake 2 hours. Drain to remove drippings and fat. In a small bowl, whisk together soy sauce, pepper, salt and apricot nectar; spread over lamb leg. Bring the lamb back to the oven and bake, basting often, until inserting a meat thermometer into the thickest part and it shows 71° C (160° F) for medium-well doneness. Place lemon slices atop the roast; bake 5 more minutes.
- Transfer lamb to a serving plate, use aluminum foil to cover. Let sit 10-15 minutes, then slice. In the meantime, on the stove over medium heat, place the roasting pan. Put cornstarch in water and dissolve; add to the roasting pan together with the bouillon cube. Cook while stirring for 1 minutes until the sauce clears and thickens, and bouillon is dissolved. Take out lemon slices and cloves. Then slice the lamb and serve with sauce.

Nutrition Information

- Calories: 414 calories;
- Total Carbohydrate: 8
- Cholesterol: 138
- Protein: 38.3
- Total Fat: 24.6
- Sodium: 404

198. Greek Lamb Meatballs

Serving: 6 | Prep: | Cook: 25mins | Ready in:

Ingredients

- 8 ounces mushrooms, chopped
- 1 small onion, chopped
- 1 stalk celery, sliced
- 4 cloves garlic
- 1 tablespoon extra-virgin olive oil
- ½ cup fine dry breadcrumbs
- ¼ cup toasted pine nuts
- ¼ cup crumbled feta cheese
- 1 tablespoon dried mint
- 1 tablespoon dried oregano
- Zest of 1 lemon

- ½ teaspoon salt
- ½ teaspoon ground pepper
- 1 pound lean ground lamb

Direction

- In a food processor, finely chop garlic, celery, onion and mushrooms. Heat oil on medium high heat in a big skillet. Add veggie mixture; cook, occasionally mixing, for 6-8 minutes till liquid is evaporated. Put into big bowl; cool for 10 minutes.
- Preheat an oven to 450°F. Line foil on big rimmed baking sheet; coat using cooking spray.
- Add pepper, salt, lemon zest, oregano, mint, feta, pine nuts and breadcrumbs to cooled veggies; mix till combined. Add lamb. Gently mix to combine; don't overmix. Shape, scant 2 tbsp. each, to 30 meatballs. Put on prepped baking sheet.
- Bake meatballs for 15 minutes till inserted instant-read thermometer in middle reads 165°F.

Nutrition Information

- Calories: 219 calories;
- Sugar: 2
- Protein: 17
- Saturated Fat: 3
- Sodium: 360
- Fiber: 2
- Total Carbohydrate: 12
- Total Fat: 12
- Cholesterol: 44

199. Grilled Leg Of Lamb With Mint Garlic Rub

Serving: 16 | Prep: | Cook: 40mins | Ready in:

Ingredients

- 1 cup fresh mint leaves, loosely packed
- ½ cup flat-leaf parsley leaves, loosely packed
- 3 cloves garlic
- ¼ cup extra-virgin olive oil
- 2 teaspoons kosher salt
- 1 teaspoon freshly ground pepper
- 1 5-pound boneless leg of lamb, butterflied and trimmed (see Tip)

Direction

- In a small bowl, chop garlic, parsley and mint finely and blend. Whisk in pepper, salt and oil.
- Pat lamb to dry. Thread 2 metal skewers horizontally through the lamb (if you own ones) to keep the meat in place and make it easier to turn on the grill (In case you don't own any skewers, make sure you own long and sturdy tongs). Rub lamp evenly with herb mixture. Refrigerate, covered, for 3-24 hours to let flavors penetrate.
- Take lamb out of the fridge 60 minutes before grilling.
- Set a gas grill to medium and begin preheating or set a charcoal grill to medium-hot and arrange all coals to 1 side.
- Grill the lamb for 10-15 minutes each side on direct heat source until an instant-read thermometer reads 125-130 degrees F for medium-rare when inserted horizontally into the thickest area. Move the skewers occasionally to the cooler part of the grill in case meat gets too charred. (Another way is to roast the lamb for 25-35 minutes at 425 degrees F in a roasting pan set in the oven until it registers the desired heat.)
- Transfer lamb to a clean cutting board, tent using foil and allow to rest for 10 minutes; slice to serve.

Nutrition Information

- Calories: 175 calories;
- Sodium: 193
- Fiber: 0
- Cholesterol: 65
- Protein: 21

- Total Fat: 9
- Saturated Fat: 3
- Total Carbohydrate: 1
- Sugar: 0

200. Holiday Leg Of Lamb

Serving: 10 | Prep: 20mins | Cook: 3hours | Ready in:

Ingredients

- 1 teaspoon salt
- 1/2 teaspoon black pepper
- 1 teaspoon seasoned salt
- 1/2 teaspoon dried marjoram
- 1/4 teaspoon dry mustard
- 1/8 teaspoon ground cardamom
- 5 pounds whole leg of lamb
- 1/2 teaspoon dried thyme
- 1 orange peel, cut into slivers
- 2 tablespoons chopped fresh mint, or to taste

Direction

- Set an oven to 165°C (325°F) and start preheating.
- Combine cardamom, mustard, marjoram, seasoned salt, pepper, and salt together in a small bowl. Massage the lamb with the spice mixture. Slice 16 deep slits in the roast. Place a sliver of the orange peel and thyme into the middle of the thickest part of the meat.
- In the prepared oven, roast lamb for 2 1/2-3 hours. The meat is well done once a meat thermometer reads 180°F and medium done at 175°F.
- Take the meat thermometer out. On a warm serving platter, arrange the roast. Place a paper frill around the end of the leg bone, then add fresh mint to the platter to decorate.

Nutrition Information

- Calories: 524 calories;

- Total Fat: 38.8
- Sodium: 451
- Total Carbohydrate: 0.4
- Cholesterol: 156
- Protein: 40.7

201. Kashmiri Lamb

Serving: 6 | Prep: 35mins | Cook: 1hours30mins | Ready in:

Ingredients

- 4 dried red chile peppers (such as cayenne)
- 3 long, green fresh chile peppers (such as Indian Jwala)
- 1 teaspoon cumin seeds
- 1 teaspoon Kashmiri garam masala
- 1 (1 inch) piece fresh ginger root, peeled and grated
- 5 cloves garlic, crushed
- 1/4 cup dried unsweetened coconut
- 3 tomatoes, chopped
- 6 tablespoons vegetable oil
- 2 large onions, thinly sliced
- 2 pounds lamb meat, cut into 1 1/2-inch cubes
- salt to taste
- 1/2 teaspoon ground turmeric
- 1 cup plain yogurt
- 1/2 teaspoon saffron threads
- 20 whole blanched almonds
- 1/4 cup chopped fresh cilantro

Direction

- Put tomatoes, grated coconut, garlic, ginger, garam masala, cumin seeds, green chiles and red chiles in a blender; pulse a few times to chop, blend to smooth paste.
- Heat vegetable oil in big skillet/Dutch oven on medium heat. Mix onion in; mix and cook for 5 minutes till onion is translucent and soft. Lower heat to medium low; mix and cook for 10-15 minutes more till onion is golden brown and very tender.

- Mix spice paste into onion; mix and cook for 3 minutes till oil separates from mixture.
- Mix in salt and lamb pieces. Cook on medium high heat for 8 minutes till lamb pieces are browned on all the sides, frequently mixing.
- Mix in blanched almonds, saffron and yogurt till combined well.
- Lower heat to low; simmer for 1 hour till gravy is thick and meat is tender, covered.
- Before serving, garnish curry using chopped cilantro.

Nutrition Information

- Calories: 489 calories;
- Protein: 28.1
- Total Fat: 35.4
- Sodium: 132
- Total Carbohydrate: 16.1
- Cholesterol: 88

202. Keema (Indian Style Ground Meat)

Serving: 4 | Prep: 5mins | Cook: 20mins | Ready in:

Ingredients

- 1 1/2 pounds ground lamb
- 1 onion, finely chopped
- 2 cloves garlic, minced
- 2 tablespoons garam masala
- 1 teaspoon salt
- 4 teaspoons tomato paste
- 3/4 cup beef broth

Direction

- Cook the ground lamb in a large heavy skillet over medium heat until it turns brown evenly. Use a wooden spoon to break it apart while cooking until it is crumbled. Place the cooked lamb into a bowl, then drain off all but retain a tablespoon of fat. Sauté the onion for 5 minutes until it is translucent and soft. Mix in the garlic, sauté for a minute. Stir in salt and garam masala and cook for a minute. Place the browned lamb back into the pan, then stir in beef broth and tomato paste. Turn down the heat and simmer until the liquid evaporates and the meat is completely cooked through, about 10 - 15 minutes.

Nutrition Information

- Calories: 513 calories;
- Total Fat: 40.7
- Sodium: 885
- Total Carbohydrate: 6.4
- Cholesterol: 124
- Protein: 29.6

203. Kefta

Serving: 10 | Prep: 20mins | Cook: 50mins | Ready in:

Ingredients

- 1 bunch fresh parsley, chopped
- 3 medium onions, finely chopped
- 1 1/2 pounds ground lamb
- 2 teaspoons ground allspice
- 1 1/2 teaspoons grated lemon zest
- 2 teaspoons salt
- 1/4 cup butter, softened
- 1 medium tomato, sliced

Direction

- Preheat an oven to 175°C/350°F.
- Mix butter, salt, lemon zest, allspice, lamb, onions and parsley till well blended in a big bowl; for best results, use your hands. Pat into 2-in. tall round on baking sheets with sides/put in baking dish. Put tomato slices over.
- In the preheated oven, bake with no cover, till internal temperature is 72°C/160°F and not

pink for 50 minutes; serve with rice or pita bread.

Nutrition Information

- Calories: 192 calories;
- Total Fat: 14
- Sodium: 541
- Total Carbohydrate: 4.3
- Cholesterol: 58
- Protein: 12.4

204. Lahmacun Turkish Pizza

Serving: 10 | Prep: 2hours | Cook: 20mins | Ready in:

Ingredients

- For the Lamb Sauce:
- 1 teaspoon chopped garlic
- 1 yellow onion, chopped
- 3 tablespoons chopped fresh basil
- 1/2 cup chopped fresh parsley
- 2 tablespoons chopped fresh mint
- 1/2 teaspoon paprika
- 1/2 teaspoon ground cumin
- 1/2 teaspoon ground coriander seed
- 1/2 cup green bell pepper, diced
- 1/2 cup red bell pepper, diced
- 1/2 lemon, juiced
- 4 teaspoons olive oil
- 4 roma (plum) tomatoes, halved
- 1 pound lean ground lamb
- 6 tablespoons double concentrated tomato paste
- cayenne pepper to taste
- salt to taste
- For the Dough:
- 3 1/4 teaspoons active dry yeast
- 1/2 teaspoon white sugar
- 1 cup warm water (110 degrees F/45 degrees C)
- 5 cups all-purpose flour
- 2 teaspoons salt
- 1/4 cup vegetable oil
- 1/2 cup water
- For the Garlic Sauce:
- 1 cup plain yogurt
- 1/2 teaspoon chopped fresh parsley
- 1/4 teaspoon crushed garlic
- salt and ground black pepper to taste
- For the Garnish:
- 1 cup shredded green cabbage
- 1 cup shredded red cabbage

Direction

- Place a large skillet over medium-high heat. Mix the diced bell peppers, lemon juice, garlic, onion, parsley, basil, paprika, mint, coriander, cumin, and olive oil in a food processor. Pulse until all the vegetables are finely chopped. Toss in halved tomatoes and continue processing until you get a thick puree.
- Add the lamb into the preheated skillet and lower heat to medium. Pour the tomato paste and puree in, stir and combine well. Cook for 10 to 15 minutes, stirring until the lamb is cooked. Add in cayenne pepper and salt to taste. Place the mixture in a shallow baking dish and let it cool to room temperature. Use plastic wrap to cover and place in fridge overnight.
- In 1 cup of warm water dissolve the yeast and sugar. In a separate bowl combine the flour and salt and mix well. Add 1/2 cup of water and vegetable oil to the yeast mixture and pour everything over the flour. Knead the dough using your hands. Transfer the dough onto a lightly floured surface and continue kneading for about 8 minutes, until you get a smooth and elastic dough.
- Shape the dough into a ball and put it in the greased bowl. Cover the bowl with a wet towel and let the dough rise in a warm place for about 1 hour – dough should double. Take out the lamb sauce from the refrigerator and leave on the room temperature. Make the garlic sauce: mix the yogurt, crushed garlic, parsley, salt, and pepper. Mix all the ingredients and set aside.

- Punch down dough. Place the dough on a floured work surface, and make 10 even portions from the dough, shaping each portion into a ball. Gently flatten each round with your hand; using a rolling pin to flatten each piece into a 10-inch circle. Each circle should be thin like a crepe. Place the thinned rounds on baking sheet lined with the parchment paper.
- Preheat the oven to 500°F (260°C).
- Mix the lamb sauce and spread it on each dough round. The filling should be spread in a thin layer, pressing it down gently so it sticks to dough. Bake pizzas for 8 to 10 minutes on the lowest oven rack on the parchment paper-lined baking sheets until the edges are a lightly browned.
- Remove from the oven and place on a wire rack to cool. The pizzas can be stored in refrigerator for three days in an airtight container or in freezer for three months. Can reheat by placing the pizza in the 350°F preheat oven (175°C) for 8 minutes.
- Lahmacun can be served with garlic sauce, sprinkled with shredded cabbage, and rolled up for serving. Other garnish ideas can also apply.

Nutrition Information

- Calories: 480 calories;
- Total Carbohydrate: 57.6
- Cholesterol: 35
- Protein: 17.2
- Total Fat: 20.1
- Sodium: 571

205. Lahmahjoon (Armenian Pizza)

Serving: 4 | Prep: | Cook: | Ready in:

Ingredients

- 1 pound lean ground lamb
- 1 1/2 cups finely chopped onion
- 1/2 cup chopped green bell pepper
- 1 teaspoon minced garlic
- 1 (14.5 ounce) can peeled and diced tomatoes
- 1 (6 ounce) can tomato paste
- 1/2 cup chopped fresh Italian parsley
- 1 teaspoon chopped fresh basil
- 1 tablespoon chopped fresh mint leaves
- 1/2 teaspoon ground cumin
- 1 pinch cayenne pepper (optional)
- 4 pita breads, or fluffy tortillas

Direction

- In a large skillet, arrange the ground lamb on medium-high heat. Cook and break the lamb into small pieces until it is mostly browned. Drain off all the excess grease. Add garlic, green pepper, and onion. Cook until the onion turns translucent. Stir in tomato paste and diced tomatoes, then flavor with cayenne (if using), cumin, mint, basil, and parsley. Let simmer for 5 minutes. Take away from the heat, put a cover and store in the fridge overnight to combine the flavors.
- Set an oven to 230°C (450°F) and start preheating. Evenly distribute the lamb mixture on the tortillas and spread over to the edges. Arrange the tortillas on a baking sheet.
- In the prepared oven, bake for 20 minutes. Take out of the oven, then arrange the lahmahjoons on a large piece of aluminum foil so that two of them are meat side to meat side; stack those two pieces together and place the foil onto the top to keep it warm. Serve cold or hot. Slice into small wedges.

Nutrition Information

- Calories: 476 calories;
- Sodium: 888
- Total Carbohydrate: 52.4
- Cholesterol: 76
- Protein: 28.7
- Total Fat: 16.5

206. Lahmahjoon Pizza

Serving: 6 | Prep: | Cook: 45mins | Ready in:

Ingredients

- 1 tablespoon extra-virgin olive oil
- ½ cup chopped shallots
- 8 ounces ground lamb
- 4 medium plum tomatoes, chopped
- 2 tablespoons minced fresh parsley
- 1 tablespoon pomegranate molasses, (see Shopping Tip)
- 1 teaspoon ground cinnamon
- ½ teaspoon salt
- ½ teaspoon freshly ground pepper
- Yellow cornmeal, for dusting
- 1 pound Easy Whole-Wheat Pizza Dough (recipe follows), or other prepared dough
- ⅓ cup crumbled feta
- 1 tablespoon pine nuts

Direction

- Over medium heat, heat oil in a large nonstick skillet then add shallots. Cook while stirring frequently for about 2 minutes until softened. Place in lamb; cook and stir for about 5 minutes, breaking up using a wooden spoon until browned lightly. Place into a colander to drain the fat. Wipe out the pan and place the shallots and meat back into pan. Mix in tomatoes and cook for about 3 minutes until tomatoes start to break down. Add pepper, salt, cinnamon, pomegranate molasses and parsley. Mix to coat; take off heat.
- Preheat the grill to low.
- Drizzle cornmeal over a large baking sheet or pizza peel. Roll the dough out and place it into prepared baking sheet or peel. Be sure the underside of dough is coated completely with cornmeal.
- Move the crust over the grill rack and cover with lid. Cook for 3 to 4 minutes until browned lightly.
- Turn the crust with a large spatula. Spread lamb mixture over the crust and leave a 1-inch border. Drizzle with pine nuts and feta.
- Cover with lid again then grill for about 8 minutes, until the bottom of the crust is browned and the toppings are hot.

Nutrition Information

- Calories: 341 calories;
- Fiber: 2
- Cholesterol: 35
- Saturated Fat: 6
- Sodium: 498
- Total Carbohydrate: 35
- Sugar: 4
- Protein: 14
- Total Fat: 18

207. Lamb & Rice Stuffed Grape Leaves

Serving: 55 | Prep: | Cook: 1hours30mins | Ready in:

Ingredients

- 1 15- to 16-ounce jar grape leaves (see Note), drained
- 1 pound ground lamb
- 2 cups instant brown rice
- ⅓ cup minced fresh parsley
- 2 tablespoons minced fresh mint or 2 teaspoons dried
- 1 tablespoon dried marjoram leaves
- 1 tablespoon extra-virgin olive oil
- 2 teaspoons ground cinnamon
- 2 teaspoons ground cumin
- 1 teaspoon salt
- ¾ teaspoon freshly ground pepper
- ½ teaspoon ground allspice

- 4 tablespoons lemon juice, plus lemon wedges for serving
- Plain yogurt for serving

Direction

- Boil a large saucepan of water. Take the grape leaves out from the jar and unroll. Divide into 2 piles— one with pieces of leaves or torn leaves and one with whole leaves. The whole leaves are used for rolling. Put the others aside for Step 5.
- In the boiling water, cook the whole grape leaves for 5 minutes; strain in a colander.
- To make the filling: In a medium bowl, blend the allspice, pepper, salt, cumin, cinnamon, oil, marjoram, mint, parsley, rice, and lamb until blended thoroughly.
- To assemble the grape leaves: On a work surface, place a clean kitchen towel. On the towel, arrange at once 4-6 whole grape leaves with the stem end pointing at you and stem-side up. Trim or pinch tough or long stems off. Form 1-2 tablespoons of the filling into a 1 1/2-2-inch log, depending on the leaf size; put it on the leaf that is perpendicular to the stem end. Tuck in the sides and tightly roll the end of the leaf over the filling to form into a cigar shape. Repeat the process with the remaining filling and grape leaves. (You may don't have to use all the grape leaves or filling.)
- In a large saucepan, arrange very small remaining or the torn grape leaves and completely cover the bottom to prevent the filled leaves from sticking when cooking (See tips if you have no leftover leaves). In the pan, stuff one tight layer with approximately half of the stuffed grape leaves and use 2 tablespoons of lemon juice to sprinkle. Create a second layer of grape leaves atop the first one and use the remaining 2 tablespoons of lemon juice to sprinkle.
- Arrange the largest heatproof plate you may find which can fit in the pot atop the grape leaves. Atop the plate, arrange a small-to-medium heatproof bowl and fill 3/4 of it with water (which plays as a weight to keep submerging the grape leaves). Pour the water into the pan until it rises to the rim of the plate.
- Timing: Bring to a boil, then turn down the heat to a simmer. Cook for 45 minutes until the rice becomes tender, pouring additional water to keep submerging the grape leaves. (Take the plate and bowl away gently, then take 1 filled grape leaf out with a slotted spoon and slice it open to check whether the rice is finished or not.)
- Take the plate and bowl away gently, then use a slotted spoon to move the grape leaves from the water. If desired, serve warm along with lemon wedges and yogurt for dipping.

Nutrition Information

- Calories: 46 calories;
- Saturated Fat: 1
- Cholesterol: 7
- Total Carbohydrate: 3
- Total Fat: 3
- Sodium: 167
- Fiber: 1
- Sugar: 0
- Protein: 2

208. Lamb & Spinach One Pot Pasta

Serving: 5 | Prep: 35mins | Cook: |Ready in:

Ingredients

- 8 ounces whole-wheat elbow noodles
- 1 pound ground lamb
- 6 cups chopped spinach
- 1 (14 ounce) can no-salt-added diced tomatoes
- 1 medium onion, chopped
- 4 cloves garlic, thinly sliced
- 2 tablespoons tahini (see Tip)
- 1 teaspoon ground cumin
- 1 teaspoon dried oregano

- ¾ teaspoon salt
- 4 cups water
- 2 tablespoons crumbled feta cheese

Direction

- In a big pot, mix together the salt, oregano, cumin, tahini, garlic, onion, tomatoes, spinach, lamb and pasta. Mix in water, then boil on high heat. Let it boil for 10-12 minutes, mixing often, until the water has nearly evaporated and the pasta is cooked. Take it out of the heat and allow it to stand for 5 minutes, stirring from time to time. Sprinkle feta on top, then serve.

Nutrition Information

- Calories: 400 calories;
- Saturated Fat: 6
- Sodium: 444
- Protein: 24
- Sugar: 3
- Total Fat: 16
- Fiber: 6
- Cholesterol: 60
- Total Carbohydrate: 42

209. Lamb & White Bean Chili

Serving: 6 | Prep: | Cook: 40mins | Ready in:

Ingredients

- 3 tablespoons extra-virgin olive oil or canola oil
- 1 pound lean ground lamb (see Tip)
- 1 large onion, diced
- 4 cloves garlic, minced
- 1 small eggplant (about 1 pound), diced (4 cups)
- ½ cup bulgur
- 3 tablespoons chili powder
- 2 tablespoons paprika
- 2 teaspoons ground cumin
- 1 teaspoon ground cinnamon
- ¼ teaspoon ground allspice
- 1 teaspoon salt
- 1 14-ounce can no-salt-added diced tomatoes
- 2 15-ounce cans no-salt-added small white beans, rinsed
- 4 cups water

Direction

- In a Dutch oven, heat oil over medium-high heat. Put garlic, onion and ground lamb. Let cook for 3 to 5 minutes, mixing and crumbling the meat using a wooden spoon, till meat is not pink anymore.
- Put eggplant, and allow to cook for 5 to 7 minutes, mixing from time to time, till eggplant is beginning to soften.
- Put salt, allspice, cinnamon, cumin, paprika, chili powder and bulgur and let cook for half minute to a minute, mixing, till fragrant.
- Mix in beans and tomatoes.
- Put water and boil. Lower heat to a simmer, partly cover pot and allow to cook for 50 minutes, mixing from time to time, till liquid is thickened and reduced and bulgur is soft.

Nutrition Information

- Calories: 355 calories;
- Sugar: 6
- Protein: 22
- Fiber: 13
- Cholesterol: 39
- Saturated Fat: 3
- Sodium: 597
- Total Carbohydrate: 39
- Total Fat: 13

210. Lamb Chops With Balsamic Reduction

Serving: 4 | Prep: 10mins | Cook: 15mins | Ready in:

Ingredients

- 3/4 teaspoon dried rosemary
- 1/4 teaspoon dried basil
- 1/2 teaspoon dried thyme
- salt and pepper to taste
- 4 lamb chops (3/4 inch thick)
- 1 tablespoon olive oil
- 1/4 cup minced shallots
- 1/3 cup aged balsamic vinegar
- 3/4 cup chicken broth
- 1 tablespoon butter

Direction

- Combine pepper, salt, thyme, basil, and rosemary in a cup or a small bowl. Rub on both sides of the lamb with the mixture. On a dish, put the lamb, put a cover on and put aside for the flavors to soak in, about 15 minutes.
- In a big frying pan, heat olive oil over medium-high heat. In the frying pan, put the lamb chops, and cook for 3 1/2 minutes each side for medium-rare, or keep cooking until reaching your wanted doneness. Take out of the frying pan, and put on a serving dish to keep warm.
- Add shallots to the frying pan, and cook until barely browned, about several minutes. Mix in vinegar, scraping any lamb bits from the bottom of the frying pan, and then mix in chicken broth. Keep stirring and cooking over medium-high heat until the sauce has decreased by 1/2, about 5 minutes. Otherwise, the sauce won't be good and be runny. Take away from heat, and mix in butter. Spread over the lamb chops, and enjoy.

Nutrition Information

- Calories: 255 calories;
- Cholesterol: 64
- Protein: 14.6
- Total Fat: 19.3
- Sodium: 70
- Total Carbohydrate: 5

211. Lamb Chops With Lebanese Green Beans

Serving: 4 | Prep: | Cook: 45mins | Ready in:

Ingredients

- 1 tablespoon plus 1 teaspoon extra-virgin olive oil, divided
- 1 medium yellow onion, chopped
- 2 tablespoons chopped fresh mint, or 2 teaspoons dried, divided
- ½ teaspoon ground cinnamon
- 1 teaspoon salt, divided
- ¼ teaspoon freshly ground pepper, plus more to taste
- 3 cups diced tomatoes, (4-5 medium)
- ⅓ cup water
- 12 ounces green beans, trimmed
- 8 lamb loin chops, trimmed (1½-1¾ pounds total)

Direction

- Turn oven to 400°F to preheat.
- Heat 1 tablespoon oil over medium heat in a large skillet. Sauté onion in heated oil for about 5 minutes until lightly browned and tender, stir from time to time. Add pepper, 1/2 teaspoon salt, cinnamon, 1 tablespoon fresh mint (or 1 teaspoon dried mint); cook for about half a minute, stirring, until aromatic. Add water and tomatoes and turn heat to high. Cook for 2 to 3 minutes, stirring from time to time, until tomatoes start to break down. Add green beans. Lower heat to medium; cook, covered, for about 12 minutes while stirring from time to time until green beans are soft.
- In the meantime, dust lamb chops on both sides with 1/4 teaspoon pepper and leftover 1/2 teaspoon salt. Heat the remaining 1 teaspoon oil over medium-high heat in a large oven-safe skillet. Put in lamb chops; cook for

about 2 minutes or until one side is browned. Flip over; remove the pan to the oven. Roast for 6 to 10 minutes or until medium-rare (an instant-read thermometer reads 140°F when inserted horizontally into the chop); cooking time depends on the thickness of the lamb chops.
- Mix the rest of mint into the green bean mixture. Enjoy lamb chops with green beans.

Nutrition Information

- Calories: 306 calories;
- Saturated Fat: 4
- Sodium: 668
- Cholesterol: 87
- Total Fat: 14
- Total Carbohydrate: 15
- Sugar: 6
- Protein: 31
- Fiber: 5

212. Lamb Chops With Mint Pan Sauce

Serving: 4 | Prep: | Cook: 35mins | Ready in:

Ingredients

- ⅓ cup apple juice
- 1½ teaspoons cornstarch
- 8 lamb loin chops, trimmed of fat (about 1½ pounds total)
- ½ teaspoon kosher salt
- ½ teaspoon freshly ground pepper
- 1 teaspoon canola oil
- 1 shallot, minced
- ⅓ cup reduced-sodium beef broth
- 2 tablespoons cider vinegar
- 2 tablespoons mint jelly
- 2 tablespoons minced fresh mint, divided

Direction

- Preheat an oven to 450°F. In a small bowl, mix cornstarch and apple juice. Reserve.
- Sprinkle the lamb chops with pepper and salt. Over medium-high heat, heat oil in a large ovenproof skillet and then add chops. Cook for about 2 minutes until it turned brown on one side. Flip them over and place the pan into the oven. Roast for 6 to 10 minutes, it depends on the thickness, until an instant-read thermometer inserted horizontally inside a chop reads 140°F for medium-rare. Place chops onto a plate and then tent with foil.
- Set the skillet on top of medium-high heat (be careful since the handle will be hot). Place in shallot and then cook while stirring continuously for about 1 minute until softened and browned. Add jelly, vinegar and broth and heat to boil and whisk to dissolve jelly. Cook while whisking continuously for 2 to 3 minutes until liquid is reduced by half. Mix cornstarch mixture and transfer to pan. Heat to simmer while stirring continuously for about 30 seconds until sauce is thickened. Take out from heat and mix in 1/2 the mint and the accumulated juices from chops. Serve the chops with the remaining mint and the sauce on top.

Nutrition Information

- Calories: 197 calories;
- Sodium: 234
- Cholesterol: 62
- Sugar: 8
- Protein: 20
- Total Fat: 8
- Saturated Fat: 2
- Fiber: 0
- Total Carbohydrate: 11

213. Lamb Feta Peppers

Serving: 6 | Prep: 15mins | Cook: 1hours | Ready in:

Ingredients

- 1 tablespoon olive oil
- 1 medium onion, chopped
- 1 clove garlic, minced
- 6 medium green bell peppers
- 2 tablespoons chopped fresh dill
- 3/4 teaspoon salt
- 1/2 teaspoon ground allspice
- 1/2 teaspoon ground black pepper
- 1 cup cooked rice
- 8 ounces ground lamb
- 1 cup crumbled feta cheese
- 1 cup tomato sauce
- 1 cup cold water
- 1 tablespoon fresh lemon juice
- 1 teaspoon white sugar

Direction

- Preheat the oven to 190°C or 375°Fahrenheit.
- On medium heat, heat oil in a medium pan; add and cook onion for 4 minutes until soft. Mix in garlic then cook for a minute.
- Cut off the tops of peppers then take the seeds out. Place the peppers straight up in a 9-in by 12-in baking dish.
- Combine pepper, onion mixture, allspice, salt, and dill in a big bowl; mix in lamb and rice, then fold feta cheese in. Stuff the mixture into peppers.
- Combine sugar, tomato sauce, lemon juice, and water; drizzle 1/2 on top of the peppers and the other half on the bottom of the dish. Use foil to cover.
- Bake for 45 minutes in the preheated oven; remove the cover. Bake for another 15 minutes until an inserted meat thermometer in the middle of the filling registers 70°C or 160°Fahrenheit, occasionally baste with sauce.

Nutrition Information

- Calories: 273 calories;
- Total Fat: 16.8
- Sodium: 912
- Total Carbohydrate: 19.3
- Cholesterol: 50
- Protein: 12.4

214. Lamb Shanks With Ancho Chile Honey Glaze

Serving: 4 | Prep: 45mins | Cook: 2hours | Ready in:

Ingredients

- 2 tablespoons olive oil
- 4 lamb shanks
- 1 onion, chopped
- 2 cloves garlic, minced
- 2 dried ancho chiles - chopped, stemmed and seeded
- 2 cups chicken broth
- 4 cups tomato puree
- 1 teaspoon ground cumin
- 1 bay leaf
- salt and pepper to taste
- 6 dried ancho chiles, stemmed and seeded
- 4 cups boiling water
- 1/2 cup honey
- 1 teaspoon grated orange zest
- 1 cup plain yogurt
- 2 tablespoons chopped fresh cilantro
- salt to taste

Direction

- Set an oven to 175°C (350°F) and start preheating. In an enamel baking pot or large Dutch oven, heat the oil. Sear all sides of the shanks and put aside. Sauté the garlic and onion for 2-3 minutes in the same pot. Add chicken stock, tomatoes, and 2 ancho chilies. Flavor with pepper, salt, bay leaf, and cumin. Bring to a brief boil, then place the shanks back to the pan.
- Put a cover on and bake in the prepared oven for 2 to 2 1/2 hours. The meat should be just about to fall off the bone.
- For the glaze: Pour boiling water to 6 ancho chilies to cover, soak them for 10 minutes. Mix

orange zest, honey, a cup of water, and chilies in a food processor. Blend until it becomes smooth, then put aside.
- For the topping: Combine salt, cilantro, and yogurt together in a small bowl. Put a cover on and store in the fridge.
- Transfer them from the Dutch oven into a roasting pan coated with oil once the shanks are cooked. Turn up the oven temperature to 200°C (400°F). Spread the glaze on the shanks and place back into the oven for 6-10 minutes until it forms a light crust. Place on large plates surrounded with a tomato base and place the refreshing yogurt mixture on top, then serve.

Nutrition Information

- Calories: 616 calories;
- Sodium: 1135
- Total Carbohydrate: 82.9
- Cholesterol: 86
- Protein: 39.1
- Total Fat: 18.4

215. Lamb Tagine With Preserved Lemon

Serving: 8 | Prep: 50mins | Cook: | Ready in:

Ingredients

- Tagine
- 3 pounds boneless lamb shoulder, trimmed and cut into 2- to 3-inch chunks
- 4 teaspoons ras el hanout
- 1¼ teaspoons kosher salt
- 1 pound carrots, cut into 2-inch chunks
- 1 pound medium turnips or golden beets, peeled and quartered
- 1 large red onion, chopped
- ¼ cup finely chopped rinsed preserved lemon rind
- 4 tablespoons chopped garlic, divided
- 3 tablespoons grated fresh ginger, divided
- ½-1 teaspoon crushed red pepper
- Toppings
- 1 cup whole-milk plain Greek yogurt
- 4 tablespoons lemon juice, divided
- ½ teaspoon smoked paprika
- Pinch of salt
- 1 cup finely chopped fresh mint
- 1 cup finely chopped flat-leaf parsley
- ¼ cup finely chopped rinsed preserved lemon rind
- 2 tablespoons extra-virgin olive oil
- Unsalted chopped pistachios for garnish

Direction

- Preparing the tagine: Sprinkle 1 1/4 tsp. salt and ras el hanout on the lamb to season, then put it in a 5 to 6-quart slow cooker. Stir in 2 tbsp. of ginger, 3 tbsp. garlic, 1/4 cup preserved lemon, onion, turnips or beets and carrots.
- Put a cover and let it cook for 6 hours on Low and 3 hours on High.
- Stir the leftover crushed red pepper, 1 tbsp. ginger and 1 tbsp. garlic into the tagine to taste. Put a cover and let it cook for additional 10 minutes.
- Preparing the toppings: In a small bowl, mix together the salt, paprika, 2 tbsp. lemon juice and yogurt. In a separate small bowl, mix together the leftover 2 tbsp. lemon juice, oil, preserved lemon, parsley and mint.
- Put yogurt and herb mixtures on top of the tagine to serve, then put pistachios to garnish, if preferred.

Nutrition Information

- Calories: 397 calories;
- Sodium: 557
- Cholesterol: 112
- Total Fat: 21
- Saturated Fat: 7
- Fiber: 4
- Total Carbohydrate: 16

- Sugar: 7
- Protein: 35

216. Lamb For Lovers

Serving: 4 | Prep: 30mins | Cook: 8hours30mins | Ready in:

Ingredients

- 2 tablespoons olive oil
- 2 (7 bone) racks of lamb, trimmed, fat reserved
- salt and pepper to taste
- 4 cloves garlic, minced
- 1 large onion, diced
- 4 carrots, diced
- 1 cup celery tops
- 1 cup port wine
- 1 cup red wine
- 1 (14.5 ounce) can low-sodium chicken broth
- 5 sprigs fresh spearmint
- 3 sprigs fresh rosemary
- 1 cup mint apple jelly
- 2 tablespoons olive oil
- salt and pepper to taste
- 1 tablespoon garlic, minced
- 1/4 cup panko bread crumbs
- 2 tablespoons olive oil
- 4 sprigs fresh mint

Direction

- Making Demi-Glace: In a medium skillet, heat two tablespoons of olive oil on medium heat and then place in trimmings from the lamb. Season with pepper and salt, then brown the fat, lower the heat and add chicken broth, red wine, port, celery leaves, carrots, onion and 4 cloves minced garlic. Place mixture into a slow cooker and let it simmer for 8 hours or overnight on Low.
- Over medium-low heat, strain the mixture from slow cooker into saucepan. Stir in mint jelly, rosemary and spearmint. Simmer while adding extra broth, wine or port as needed, until the mixture leaves behind a coating like that of a syrup on the back of a spoon, then strain again and keep it warm as the lamb roasts.
- Roasting the Lamb: Put an oven-proof skillet or a cast iron in an oven and then preheat to 230 degrees C (450 degrees F). Rub the lamb with garlic, pepper, salt and two tablespoons of olive oil, then coat with the panko bread crumbs.
- Gently take out the heated skillet from oven. Heat two tablespoons of olive oil in skillet and then sear the lamb on each side. Place skillet containing the lamb back into the oven and continue to cook for 5 to 10 minutes, until the internal temperature is 63 degrees C (145 degrees F).
- Place a little amount of demi-glace onto a platter and then arrange the lamb crisscrossed. Drizzle with additional demi-glace and stud with fresh mint. Serve.

Nutrition Information

- Calories: 1246 calories;
- Cholesterol: 192
- Protein: 45.3
- Total Fat: 79.4
- Sodium: 422
- Total Carbohydrate: 68.4

217. Lamb, Fig & Olive Stew For Two

Serving: 2 | Prep: | Cook: 40mins | Ready in:

Ingredients

- 8 ounces lean ground lamb, preferably leg (see Tips)
- 1 teaspoon extra-virgin olive oil
- 2 tablespoons plus 1 teaspoon minced garlic, divided
- 1 teaspoon herbes de Provence, (see Tips)

- ¼ cup dry red wine
- 1 14-ounce can reduced-sodium beef broth
- 2 teaspoons cornstarch
- 2 plum tomatoes, diced
- ¼ cup chopped dried figs
- 2 tablespoons finely chopped, pitted green olives, (see Tips)
- ⅛ teaspoon freshly ground pepper
- 2 tablespoons chopped fresh parsley
- 1 teaspoon freshly grated lemon zest

Direction

- Over medium heat, heat a large saucepan, then add lamb and cook for 4 to 6 minutes while breaking up with wooden spoon until browned. Place the lamb onto a sieve that is set over a bowl and drain. Get rid of the fat.
- Wipe the pan out, add oil and then heat on medium-high. Add herbes de Provence and 2 tablespoons of garlic. Cook while stirring continuously for about 30 seconds until fragrant. Pour in wine and cook for about 1 minute while scraping up the browned bits until reduced slightly.
- In a small bowl, combine together cornstarch and broth. Transfer to pan, adjust the heat to high and heat to simmer while stirring continuously. Add pepper, olives, figs and tomatoes and heat to simmer while stirring often. Lower the heat to maintain a simmer and let to cook while stirring sometimes for about 5 minutes until tomatoes are broken down. Add reserved lamb and cook while stirring sometimes for about 2 minutes until heated through.
- In a small bowl, mix the lemon zest, parsley and remaining 1 teaspoon garlic. You can serve the stew with parsley mixture on top.

Nutrition Information

- Calories: 306 calories;
- Sodium: 696
- Fiber: 3
- Protein: 24
- Saturated Fat: 2
- Total Carbohydrate: 23
- Sugar: 12
- Total Fat: 11
- Cholesterol: 69

218. Lebanese Cabbage Rolls

Serving: 4 | Prep: | Cook: 1hours15mins | Ready in:

Ingredients

- ½ cup bulgur
- 1 large head Savoy cabbage
- 2 tablespoons extra-virgin olive oil
- 2 cups finely chopped onion
- 1 cup finely chopped leeks, white and light green parts only
- ¾ teaspoon salt
- ¾ teaspoon freshly ground pepper
- ½ teaspoon ground turmeric
- ¼ teaspoon ground ginger
- ¼ teaspoon ground allspice
- Pinch of ground cinnamon
- 12 ounces ground lamb
- ½ cup chopped flat-leaf parsley
- 2 teaspoons chopped fresh mint
- 1 large egg, lightly beaten
- ½ cup white wine
- ½ cup reduced-sodium chicken broth
- 2 teaspoons grated lemon zest
- 3 tablespoons lemon juice, divided
- 1 egg yolk

Direction

- Prepare bulgur as directed on package; pour into a medium bowl.
- Turn oven to 325°F to preheat.
- In a large skillet, bring 2 1/2 cups water to a boil. Trim bottom of cabbage and separate leaves. Place the 8 largest leaves into boiling water and cover. Lower heat to medium-high and simmer for 5 to 7 minutes until tender. Remove cooked cabbage leaves to a clean

work surface and allow to cool. Reserve the leftover leaves.

- In the meantime, in the large skillet, heat oil over medium heat. Add leeks and onion; stir well. Cook, covered, for 5 to 8 minutes, stirring occasionally until softened. Mix in cinnamon, allspice, ginger, turmeric, pepper, and salt; cook and stir for 1 more minute. Pour the mixture over the bulgur in the bowl and allow to stand for about 5 minutes until cool enough to handle. Add lightly beaten egg, mint, parsley, and lamb. Use your hand to knead the mixture gently until well combined.
- Use some of the uncooked cabbage leaves to line a 9x13-inch baking pan. Add 1/2 cup filling over the root end of each cooked cabbage leaf. Gently fold in the sides and roll up the leaf until a bundle is formed. Place cabbage rolls, seam side facing down, in the pan. Mix together 2 tablespoons lemon juice, lemon zest, broth, and wine. Pour over the cabbage rolls. Tightly cover using foil.
- Bake for 45 to 60 minutes until the thicker ribs of cabbage leaves are really soft and an inserted instant-read thermometer in a roll reads a minimum of 165°F.
- Transfer the cooked rolls and cabbage leaves to a serving platter; tent to keep warm with foil. Cautiously transfer juice from the pan into a small saucepan and bring the juice to a boil over medium-high heat for 6 to 10 minutes until reduced by 1/2. In a small mixing bowl, whisk together egg yolk and the remaining 1 tablespoon lemon juice. Stir reduced liquid into the lemon-egg yolk mixture, and transfer the sauce back into the pan. Cook, stirring constantly, over low heat for 2 to 4 minutes until the sauce is thick enough to coat the back of a spoon. (Do not overheat the sauce to prevent egg from curdling). Serve the cabbage rolls with the sauce.

Nutrition Information

- Calories: 521 calories;
- Fiber: 10
- Cholesterol: 155
- Sugar: 9
- Total Fat: 30
- Saturated Fat: 11
- Sodium: 642
- Total Carbohydrate: 38
- Protein: 24

219. Leg Of Lamb With Raspberry Sauce

Serving: 4 | Prep: 20mins | Cook: 1hours | Ready in:

Ingredients

- 1 1/2 cups vegetable broth
- 2 cups frozen raspberries
- 1/4 cup raspberry jam
- 2 tablespoons red wine vinegar
- 1 (3 pound) boneless leg of lamb
- 1/2 teaspoon dried rosemary

Direction

- Puree red wine vinegar, raspberry jam, raspberries and vegetable broth till smooth in a big food processor/blender's container. Put into a big bowl; put aside.
- Heat nonstick skillet on medium high heat; quickly sear leg of lamb on all sides. Remove from pan; use fork tines to pierce every inch or so of meat. Put into bowl with raspberry sauce then cover; refrigerate to marinate for a minimum of 12 hours. Occasionally turn.
- Preheat an oven to 175°C/350°F. Remove lamb from marinate; pat dry. Put onto roasting rack in roasting pan.
- In the preheated oven, roast lamb till inserted meat thermometer into meat reads 62°C/140°F for 1 hour; stand before carving for 10-15 minutes. Temperature raises while resting by 5-10° for medium rare. Wait till it's 145°F before taking out of oven if you want it more done.

- Put marinade into saucepan as lamb roasts; boil. Add rosemary; boil on medium high heat for 10 minutes till sauce slightly thickens and reduces. Carve lamb; put sauce on it. Serve.

Nutrition Information

- Calories: 559 calories;
- Cholesterol: 131
- Protein: 38.8
- Total Fat: 23
- Sodium: 278
- Total Carbohydrate: 49

220. Maple Glazed Chipotle Goat Cheese Lamb Burgers

Serving: 4 | Prep: 40mins | Cook: 1hours5mins | Ready in:

Ingredients

- 1 head garlic
- 1 pound ground lamb
- 6 ounces soft goat cheese
- 6 tablespoons minced chipotle peppers in adobo sauce
- 2 sprigs chopped fresh rosemary
- 2 tablespoons maple syrup
- 1 1/2 teaspoons salt
- 1/2 teaspoon cracked black pepper
- 1 tablespoon olive oil
- 2 tablespoons maple syrup
- 4 ciabatta buns, split and toasted

Direction

- Set an oven to 150°C (300°F). Remove the top of the head of garlic and put on a small, oven-safe dish.
- Bake the garlic in the prepared oven for about an hour until the cloves turn golden brown and soft. Take away from the oven, and allow to cool. In a mixing bowl, squeeze the roasted garlic when it is cool enough to handle. Mix thoroughly pepper, salt, 2 tablespoons of maple syrup, rosemary, chipotle peppers, goat cheese, and the lamb. Shape into 4 patties.
- In a large skillet, heat the olive oil on medium-high. Sear the lamb patties for 1 minute per side, then turn the heat down to medium-low, and keep on cooking for around 2 minutes on each side for medium-well to the desired doneness. Around a minute before the patties are done, add in the remaining 2 tablespoons of maple syrup; let it glaze and thicken the burgers. Serve together with toasted ciabatta buns.

Nutrition Information

- Calories: 609 calories;
- Total Fat: 33.7
- Sodium: 1482
- Total Carbohydrate: 42
- Cholesterol: 110
- Protein: 33.5

221. Mediterranean Lamb Salad

Serving: 6 | Prep: | Cook: 30mins | Ready in:

Ingredients

- 1 pound boneless leg of lamb steaks, 1-1½ inches thick (see Note)
- 1.5 teaspoons kosher salt, divided
- Freshly ground pepper, to taste
- 2 medium cucumbers, peeled, halved, seeded and diced
- 2 large tomatoes, diced
- 1 15-ounce can chickpeas, rinsed
- ½ cup minced red onion
- ¼ cup crumbled feta cheese
- ¼ cup sliced fresh mint leaves
- ¼ cup lemon juice
- 1 teaspoon extra-virgin olive oil

Direction

- Preheat grill on high. Sprinkle pepper and 1/2 tsp. salt on lamb; grill lamb for 2-4 minutes each side for medium, varies on steak's thickness. Put onto cutting board; rest before thinly cutting across grain for minimum of 5 minutes.
- Meanwhile, mix mint, feta cheese, onion, chickpeas, tomatoes and cucumbers in a big bowl. Add extra pepper to taste, leftover 1 tsp. salt, oil and lemon juice; stir to mix. Put sliced lamb over; serve.

Nutrition Information

- Calories: 255 calories;
- Cholesterol: 54
- Total Carbohydrate: 23
- Sugar: 4
- Total Fat: 9
- Saturated Fat: 3
- Sodium: 824
- Fiber: 5
- Protein: 21

222. Mediterranean Meat Pies (Sfeeha)

Serving: 18 | Prep: 20mins | Cook: 15mins | Ready in:

Ingredients

- 1 pound ground beef
- 1/2 pound ground lamb
- 1 white onion, finely chopped
- 3/4 cup pine nuts
- 1/8 teaspoon ground cinnamon
- salt and ground black pepper to taste
- 1/3 cup lemon juice
- 1 egg, beaten
- 2 (17.3 ounce) packages frozen puff pastry, thawed

Direction

- Place the large skillet over medium-high heat. Stir in chopped onion, ground beef and ground lamb, salt, black pepper, pine nuts, and cinnamon. Cook until the meat is browned all over, crumbly, and no longer pink. Let it drain and remove any excess grease.
- Mix in lemon juice. Taste the mixture to adjust the seasonings. Allow the meat mixture to cool.
- Set the oven to 350°F (175°C) for preheating. Grease the baking sheet lightly, or you can line it with a parchment paper.
- Roll the thawed pastry sheets into 1/8-inch thick. Cut each sheet to at least 9 rounds using the sharp 3-inches round cookie cutter. Coat each inside edges with a little water. Spoon 2 teaspoons of the filling into the center of each round. Fold each round in half to cover the filling, sealing the edges tightly. Arrange them onto the prepared baking sheet. Do the same with the remaining dough circles.
- Coat each pie with a little egg wash. Let it bake inside the preheated oven for 15-20 minutes until golden brown.

Nutrition Information

- Calories: 412 calories;
- Sodium: 162
- Total Carbohydrate: 26.4
- Cholesterol: 34
- Protein: 12.7
- Total Fat: 28.7

223. Middle Eastern Lamb Stew

Serving: 8 | Prep: | Cook: 40mins | Ready in:

Ingredients

- 1½ pounds boneless lamb stew meat, (shoulder cut) or 2½ pounds lamb shoulder chops, deboned, trimmed and cut into 1-inch chunks
- 1 tablespoon olive oil, or canola oil
- 4 teaspoons ground cumin
- 1 tablespoon ground coriander
- ¼ teaspoon cayenne pepper
- ¼ teaspoon salt
- Freshly ground pepper, to taste
- 1 large or 2 medium onions, chopped
- 1 28-ounce can diced tomatoes
- ¾ cup reduced-sodium chicken broth
- 4 cloves garlic, minced
- 1 15- or 19-ounce can chickpeas, rinsed
- 6 ounces baby spinach

Direction

- In a 4-qt. or bigger slow cooker, put lamb. In a small bowl, stir together pepper, salt, cayenne, coriander, cumin, and oil. Put the lamb into the spice paste to coat and toss to thoroughly coat. Put onion on top.
- In a medium-sized saucepan, simmer garlic, broth, and tomatoes over medium-high heat. Add to the onion and lamb. Put the lid on and cook on low for 5 1/2-6 hours or on high for 3-3 1/2 hours, until the lamb is fully tender.
- Blot or skim any fat that forms on the top of the stew. In a small bowl, use a fork to mash 1/2 cup of chickpeas. Mix whole and mashed chickpeas into the stew together with spinach. Put the lid on and cook for 5 minutes on high until the spinach wilts.

Nutrition Information

- Calories: 253 calories;
- Total Carbohydrate: 12
- Protein: 19
- Total Fat: 14
- Sodium: 412
- Sugar: 3
- Saturated Fat: 5
- Fiber: 5
- Cholesterol: 59

224. Moroccan Lamb Chops With Tomato Olive Relish

Serving: 4 | Prep: 20mins | Cook: |Ready in:

Ingredients

- 1 cup chopped seeded tomatoes
- ¼ cup chopped oil-cured olives
- ¼ cup chopped flat-leaf parsley
- 2 tablespoons extra-virgin olive oil, divided
- Pinch of ground pepper
- 8 lamb rib chops, trimmed (about ½ inch thick; 1¼ pounds total)
- 1 tablespoon ras el hanout (see Tips)

Direction

- Set a grill to high.
- In a small bowl, combine pepper, 1 tablespoon oil, parsley, olives, and tomatoes.
- Brush the remaining 1 tablespoon oil on the lamb and sprinkle with the ras el hanout. Grill each side for 2 - 3 minutes for medium-rare. Serve with relish.

Nutrition Information

- Calories: 427 calories;
- Total Fat: 27
- Saturated Fat: 8
- Sodium: 296
- Sugar: 1
- Protein: 37
- Fiber: 1
- Cholesterol: 125
- Total Carbohydrate: 3

225. Moroccan Lamb With Shiraz Honey Sauce

Serving: 4 | Prep: 20mins | Cook: 30mins | Ready in:

Ingredients

- 1 (7 bone) rack of lamb, trimmed and frenched
- coarse sea salt to taste
- 2 1/2 tablespoons ras el hanout
- 1 cup Shiraz wine
- 1/3 cup honey

Direction

- Set the oven to 400°F (200°C) and start preheating.
- Season lamb with sea salt; rub ras el hanout over it. Sear lamb on all sides in a medium cast iron skillet over medium-high heat until evenly browned.
- Put the skillet with lamb in the prepared oven; roast for half an hour or until the internal temperature reached 145°F (63°C) as the minimum.
- Take the lamb out of the skillet; reserve the juices; let stand for 10-15 minutes before you slice the ribs. Put the skillet with juices over medium heat; stir in honey and wine. Cook until the liquid reduces by about 1/2. Drizzle over ribs; serve.

Nutrition Information

- Calories: 907 calories;
- Total Carbohydrate: 26.6
- Cholesterol: 166
- Protein: 35
- Total Fat: 69.3
- Sodium: 136

226. Moroccan Tagine

Serving: 6 | Prep: 15mins | Cook: 45mins | Ready in:

Ingredients

- 1 tablespoon olive oil
- 2 skinless, boneless chicken breast halves - cut into chunks
- 1/2 onion, chopped
- 3 cloves garlic, minced
- 1 small butternut squash, peeled and chopped
- 1 (15.5 ounce) can garbanzo beans, drained and rinsed
- 1 carrot, peeled and chopped
- 1 (14.5 ounce) can diced tomatoes with juice
- 1 (14 ounce) can vegetable broth
- 1 tablespoon sugar
- 1 tablespoon lemon juice
- 1 teaspoon salt
- 1 teaspoon ground coriander
- 1 dash cayenne pepper

Direction

- In a big pan, heat the oil on medium heat and cook garlic, onion and chicken for about 15 minutes until it turns brown.
- In the pan, stir in the lemon juice, sugar, broth, tomatoes with juice, carrot, garbanzo beans and squash. Sprinkle cayenne pepper, coriander and salt to season. Let the mixture boil and keep on cooking until the veggies are soft, or for 30 minutes.

Nutrition Information

- Calories: 265 calories;
- Total Carbohydrate: 44.7
- Cholesterol: 20
- Protein: 14.1
- Total Fat: 4.3
- Sodium: 878

227. Mustard Rosemary Grilled Lamb

Serving: 4 | Prep: 20mins | Cook: | Ready in:

Ingredients

- 8 lamb rib or loin chops, cut 1 inch thick (about 2 pounds)
- ¼ cup stone-ground mustard
- 2 green onions, thinly sliced (¼ cup)
- 2 tablespoons dry white wine
- 1 tablespoon balsamic vinegar or rice vinegar
- 3 cloves garlic, minced
- 1 teaspoon snipped fresh rosemary
- 1 teaspoon honey
- ½ teaspoon salt
- ½ teaspoon freshly ground pepper

Direction

- Trim fat off chops; put aside the chops. Mix pepper, salt, honey, rosemary, garlic, vinegar, wine, green onions and mustard in small bowl. Evenly scatter the mixture on each side of chops. On a big plate, put the chops and use plastic wrap to loosely cover. Refrigerate for 2 up to 3 hours.
- Let chops grill on grill rack with no cover right over moderate coals till preferred doneness, flipping one time midway through grilling. For medium-rare, 145°F, let 12 to 14 minutes and for medium 160°F, 15 to 17 minutes.

Nutrition Information

- Calories: 194 calories;
- Sodium: 557
- Cholesterol: 64
- Sugar: 2
- Total Fat: 9
- Saturated Fat: 3
- Fiber: 0
- Total Carbohydrate: 4
- Protein: 21

228. Nana's Leg Of Lamb

Serving: 6 | Prep: 15mins | Cook: 3hours | Ready in:

Ingredients

- 1 (4 pound) leg of lamb
- salt to taste
- 1 clove garlic, cut into slivers
- 2 teaspoons vegetable oil
- 2 lemons, sliced and seeded
- 2 cups hot water
- 2 tablespoons butter
- 2 tablespoons Worcestershire sauce

Direction

- Let oven warm up to 300°F or 150°C.
- Get rid of fat and skin from the lamb leg and rub with salt. Use a knife to make a hole in the meat and then insert slices of garlic.
- In a big skillet, warm oil over medium-high fire. When skillet is already warm, cook the lamb leg until it becomes brown on the outside; turn as necessary. Place in a big roasting pan. Assemble cut pieces of lemon and place toothpicks to secure lemons over the roast.
- Let butter, Worcestershire sauce and water boil in a small saucepan. Decant sauce over the meat then wrap roasting pan with a foil.
- Let it roast in the warmed up oven for 2 and half hours and basting every half an hour. Take off the aluminum foil and lemon slices. Throw away. Allow to roast for another half an hour until lamb's internal temperature achieves at least 145°F or 68°C. Take off from the oven and lightly cover with aluminum foil. Let it stand for 15 to 20 minutes and then carve and serve.

Nutrition Information

- Calories: 756 calories;
- Total Fat: 57.2
- Sodium: 256
- Total Carbohydrate: 5.1
- Cholesterol: 219
- Protein: 54.7

229. North African Orange & Lamb Kebabs

Serving: 4 | Prep: | Cook: 20mins | Ready in:

Ingredients

- ½ cup loosely packed fresh cilantro leaves
- ½ cup loosely packed fresh parsley leaves
- 3 cloves garlic, crushed and peeled
- 1 teaspoon paprika
- 1 teaspoon ground cumin
- ½ teaspoon salt
- ¼ teaspoon freshly ground pepper
- ¼ cup nonfat plain yogurt
- 2 tablespoons lemon juice
- 1 pound lean leg of lamb, trimmed of fat and cut into 1-inch cubes
- 2 seedless oranges, unpeeled, quartered and cut into ¼-inch-thick slices

Direction

- Preheat the grill on high.
- In a food processor, mix then process pepper, salt, cumin, paprika, garlic, parsley and cilantro until herbs are chopped finely. Add lemon juice and yogurt. Process it until smooth. Scrape mixture into a medium bowl. Put lamb. Toss until coated. Use plastic wrap to cover. Marinate for 20 minutes in the fridge.
- Alternately, thread orange slices and lamb on 8 skewers. Throw out marinade.
- Oil grill rack. Grill kebabs, occasionally turning, for 7-10 minutes for medium-rare or to your desired doneness. Immediately serve.

Nutrition Information

- Calories: 200 calories;
- Sodium: 380
- Sugar: 7
- Total Carbohydrate: 12
- Protein: 25
- Total Fat: 6
- Saturated Fat: 2
- Fiber: 2
- Cholesterol: 73

230. Orzo With Lamb, Olives & Feta For Two

Serving: 2 | Prep: | Cook: 30mins | Ready in:

Ingredients

- ½ cup orzo
- 4 ounces lean ground lamb, or ground beef or ground turkey
- 2 teaspoons extra-virgin olive oil
- 1 small onion, finely chopped
- 1 clove garlic, minced
- ¼ teaspoon ground cinnamon
- ¼ teaspoon crumbled dried rosemary, or oregano
- Pinch of crushed red pepper, (optional)
- 1 8-ounce can no-salt-added tomato sauce
- 1 tablespoon pitted, chopped black olives
- ⅛ teaspoon salt
- ⅛ teaspoon freshly ground pepper, or to taste
- 2 tablespoons crumbled feta cheese

Direction

- Boil a big saucepan of water; follow package to cook orzo or for 8 minutes till tender. Drain.
- Meanwhile, cook turkey/beef/lamb in a medium nonstick skillet on medium heat, mixing, for 2-3 minutes till browned. Drain in sieve above bowl. Clean pan; dry.
- Add oil to pan; heat on medium heat. Add onion; cook, mixing, for 3-5 minutes till soft. Add crushed red pepper (optional), oregano/rosemary, cinnamon and garlic; cook, mixing, for 1 minute till fragrant. Add tomato sauce and turkey/beef/lamb; cook, occasionally mixing, for 5-7 minutes till sauce is thick. Take off heat; mix in pepper, salt and olives. Toss sauce with orzo. Garnish with feta; serve.

Nutrition Information

- Calories: 503 calories;
- Saturated Fat: 7
- Sodium: 399
- Cholesterol: 63
- Protein: 25
- Total Fat: 20
- Fiber: 4
- Total Carbohydrate: 56
- Sugar: 4

231. Plum Lamb Casserole

Serving: 4 | Prep: 25mins | Cook: 1hours30mins | Ready in:

Ingredients

- 1 tablespoon butter
- 1 onion, sliced
- 2 tablespoons all-purpose flour
- salt and ground black pepper to taste
- 2 pounds lamb shoulder chops, trimmed
- 1 carrot, sliced
- 1/2 cup sliced celery
- 1/2 cup low-sodium vegetable stock
- 1/4 cup plum jam
- 2 tablespoons tomato sauce
- 2 teaspoons Worcestershire sauce

Direction

- Set an oven to preheat to 175°C (350°F).
- In a big pot, heat the butter on medium heat until it melts. Add the onion and let it cook and stir for around 5 minutes, until it becomes soft.
- In a shallow dish, sprinkle pepper and salt to season the flour. In the flour mixture, dredge the lamb chops on both sides.
- In a casserole dish, layer the lamb chops with the celery, carrot and onion.
- In a small bowl, combine the Worcestershire sauce, tomato sauce, plum jam and stock, then pour it on top of the lamb in the casserole dish.
- Let it bake for around 1 hour 30 minutes in the preheated oven, until the lamb becomes tender.

Nutrition Information

- Calories: 557 calories;
- Total Fat: 34.1
- Sodium: 283
- Total Carbohydrate: 25.8
- Cholesterol: 142
- Protein: 35.3

232. Quick Shepherd's Pie

Serving: 4 | Prep: | Cook: 35mins | Ready in:

Ingredients

- 1 pound Yukon Gold potatoes, cut into 1-inch chunks
- ¼ cup low-fat milk
- 2 tablespoons butter
- ½ teaspoon salt, divided
- ½ teaspoon freshly ground pepper, divided
- 1 tablespoon extra-virgin olive oil
- 1 pound lean ground lamb
- 1 medium onion, finely chopped
- 2 cups chopped carrots
- 3 tablespoons all-purpose flour
- 1 tablespoon chopped fresh oregano
- 1 14-ounce can reduced-sodium chicken broth
- 1 cup frozen corn, thawed

Direction

- Boil 2 inches of water in a big pot fitted with a steamer basket. Put in potatoes, steam for 10-12 minutes until tender. Drain, bring potatoes back to the pot. Add in 1/4 teaspoon each pepper and salt, butter, and milk. Mash

together till it reaches a chunky consistency. Cover to retain warmness.
- At the same time, in a big nonstick skillet on medium-high heat, heat oil. Add the remaining 1/4 teaspoon each pepper and salt, carrots, onion, and lamb; cook for 6-8 minutes while mixing until the lamb is not pink anymore. Sprinkle the mixture with oregano and flour, cook for 1 minute while mixing. Add corn and broth; heat to a simmer; cook for 3-5 minutes longer while mixing until thickened.
- With a ladle, distribute lamb stew into 4 bowls, put potatoes on top.

Nutrition Information

- Calories: 410 calories;
- Saturated Fat: 6
- Sodium: 630
- Fiber: 5
- Cholesterol: 74
- Total Fat: 16
- Total Carbohydrate: 43
- Sugar: 7
- Protein: 25

233. Rack Of Lamb With A Cilantro Mustard Seed Crust

Serving: 2 | Prep: | Cook: 45mins | Ready in:

Ingredients

- 2 tablespoons chopped fresh cilantro
- 1 tablespoon Dijon mustard
- 1½ teaspoons mustard seeds
- 1 clove garlic, minced
- 1 1-pound rack of lamb, trimmed of fat
- Salt & freshly ground pepper, to taste
- 1 teaspoon canola oil
- New Mexico Chile Sauce, (recipe follows), heated

Direction

- Preheat an oven to 425°F.
- In a small bowl, mix garlic, mustard seeds, mustard and cilantro.
- Season lamb with pepper and salt. Evenly brush oil on small cast-iron/other ovenproof skillet. Heat a skillet on medium high heat. Add the lamb, meat side down; cook for 2-3 minutes, till browned. Take off heat. Spread mustard mixture on browned side. Put skillet in oven; roast lamb till lamb reaches desired doneness (for rare, instant read thermometer reads 140°F) for 15-20 minutes.
- Put lamb onto cutting board; rest for 5 minutes. Between ribs, carve rack. Onto 2 plates, put some New Mexico Chile Sauce; put lamb over. Immediately serve.

Nutrition Information

- Calories: 352 calories;
- Total Fat: 15
- Saturated Fat: 4
- Sodium: 1,323
- Sugar: 5
- Fiber: 6
- Cholesterol: 82
- Total Carbohydrate: 23
- Protein: 33

234. Roasted Rack Of Lamb

Serving: 4 | Prep: 20mins | Cook: 20mins | Ready in:

Ingredients

- 1/2 cup fresh bread crumbs
- 2 tablespoons minced garlic
- 2 tablespoons chopped fresh rosemary
- 1 teaspoon salt
- 1/4 teaspoon black pepper
- 2 tablespoons olive oil
- 1 (7 bone) rack of lamb, trimmed and frenched

- 1 teaspoon salt
- 1 teaspoon black pepper
- 2 tablespoons olive oil
- 1 tablespoon Dijon mustard

Direction

- Preheat an oven to 230 degrees C (450 degrees F). Set the oven rack into the middle position.
- Mix 1/4 teaspoon pepper, 1 teaspoon salt, rosemary, garlic and bread crumbs in a large bowl. Toss in two tablespoons of olive oil in order to moisten the mixture. Reserve.
- Season all over the rack with pepper and salt. Over high heat, heat two tablespoons of olive oil in a large heavy oven proof skillet, then sear the rack of lamb for 1 to 2 minutes on all sides. Reserve for several minutes. Use mustard to brush the rack of lamb, then roll in bread crumb mixture until coated evenly. To prevent charring, cover the ends of bones with foil.
- Arrange the rack in the skillet with bone side down, then roast lamb in the preheated oven for 12 to 18 minutes depending on your desired doneness. Measure the temperature in the middle of meat using a meat thermometer after 10 to 12 minutes and take out the meat or cook for longer to suit your taste. Leave it to rest for 5 to 7 minutes while loosely covered, prior to carving in between the ribs.

Nutrition Information

- Calories: 481 calories;
- Total Fat: 40.8
- Sodium: 1369
- Total Carbohydrate: 5.6
- Cholesterol: 94
- Protein: 22.2

235. Rosemary Braised Lamb Shanks

Serving: 6 | Prep: 30mins | Cook: 2hours | Ready in:

Ingredients

- 6 lamb shanks
- salt and pepper to taste
- 2 tablespoons olive oil
- 2 onions, chopped
- 3 large carrots, cut into 1/4 inch rounds
- 10 cloves garlic, minced
- 1 (750 milliliter) bottle red wine
- 1 (28 ounce) can whole peeled tomatoes with juice
- 1 (10.5 ounce) can condensed chicken broth
- 1 (10.5 ounce) can beef broth
- 5 teaspoons chopped fresh rosemary
- 2 teaspoons chopped fresh thyme

Direction

- Scatter pepper and salt on shanks. In Dutch oven or heavy big pot, heat the oil over medium-high heat. Let the shanks cook in batches for 8 minutes till all sides are brown. Put shanks to a plate.
- To pot, put garlic, carrots and onions, and sauté for 10 minutes till golden brown. Mix in beef broth, chicken broth, tomatoes and wine. Put thyme and rosemary to season. Put shanks back to pot, forcing down to soak. Boil, then lower heat to medium-low. Put cover, and allow to simmer for 2 hours till meat is soft.
- Uncover pot. Let simmer for 20 minutes more. To a platter, put the shanks, put in a warm oven. Allow juices in pot to boil for 15 minutes till thickened. Scoop on top of shanks.

Nutrition Information

- Calories: 481 calories;
- Total Fat: 21.8
- Sodium: 759
- Total Carbohydrate: 17.6
- Cholesterol: 93

- Protein: 30.3

236. Rosemary Lemon Lamb Chops With Potato And Fennel Latkes

Serving: 4 | Prep: 20mins | Cook: | Ready in:

Ingredients

- 2 medium medium russet potatoes (about 10 ounces total) (see Tip)
- 1 medium bulb fennel (see Tip)
- ¼ cup finely chopped onion
- 1 tablespoon snipped fresh rosemary
- 4 cloves garlic, minced
- 1 teaspoon finely shredded lemon peel
- ¼ teaspoon salt
- ⅛ teaspoon black pepper
- 8 lamb rib chops, cut about 1 inch thick (2 to 2½ pounds total)
- Nonstick cooking spray
- 1 egg white, lightly beaten
- ¼ teaspoon salt
- ⅛ teaspoon black pepper
- 1 tablespoon canola oil

Direction

- Remove the skin and shred coarsely potatoes. Trim off fennel bulb and chop out core; shred coarsely shred fennel bulb as the Tip. You are about to have 1.5 cups each of fennel and potato. In the medium-sized microwave-safe bowl, mix the onion, fennel, and potato. Use the vented plastic wrap to cover.
- Microwave on High till the veggies just soften or for 4-5 minutes, whisking one or two times. Drain any liquid and put the potato mixture aside to let cool down to the room temperature.
- In the small-sized bowl, mix 1/8 tsp. of the pepper, a quarter tsp. of the salt, lemon peel, garlic, and rosemary. Trim the fat out of the lamb chops and drizzle chops equally with rosemary mixture, rubbing them in using fingers.
- Using the cooking spray to coat the grill pan, heat on medium heat. Put in lamb chops. Cook to doneness that you want, flipping one time half-way through the cooking process. Cook for 15-17 minutes for medium-cooked at 160 degrees F or 12-14 minutes for medium-rare at 145 degrees F.
- At the same time, put 1/8 tsp. of the pepper, a quarter tsp. of the salt and egg white into potato mixture. Whisk till well-combined. Separate the mixture among eight even parts. Heat the oil on medium high heat in the big nonstick skillet. Pour the potato portions into hot skillet and flatten each of the portions into the circle that is approximately half an in. in thickness.
- Cook potato latkes till turning golden brown or for 5 minutes, flipping one time half-way through the cooking process. Serve latkes along with lamb chops.

Nutrition Information

- Calories: 276 calories;
- Fiber: 4
- Total Carbohydrate: 19
- Protein: 23
- Sodium: 400
- Cholesterol: 64
- Sugar: 1
- Total Fat: 12
- Saturated Fat: 3

237. Saba Braised Lamb Shanks

Serving: 4 | Prep: 20mins | Cook: 3hours30mins | Ready in:

Ingredients

- 4 lamb shanks
- 2 tablespoons olive oil
- 2 teaspoons kosher salt
- 1 teaspoon freshly ground black pepper
- 1 teaspoon smoked paprika
- 1 teaspoon ground cinnamon
- 1/2 teaspoon dried rosemary
- 1 large onion, sliced
- 6 cloves garlic, crushed
- 1 cup chicken broth
- 1/3 cup saba
- 1/2 teaspoon chopped fresh rosemary

Direction

- Set an oven to 230°C (450°F) and start preheating.
- Put lamb shanks in a large bowl; spray with olive oil. Dust with rosemary, cinnamon, smoked paprika, black pepper, and salt. Toss the lamb shanks to distribute the seasonings and oil over the meat.
- Spread the garlic cloves and onion slices over the bottom of a heavy 9x12-inch baking dish. Place lamb shanks on top of the garlic and onions.
- In the prepared oven, bake the lamb for half an hour. Turn down the oven temperature to 95°C (200°F).
- In a bowl, mix saba and chicken broth. Pour the mixture on the lamb shanks. Use foil to tightly cover the dish and arrange the baking dish onto a baking sheet.
- In the oven, bake the lamb for 2 1/2-3 hours until the meat becomes fork-tender. The meat will become tender without falling off the bone. In the pan sauce, flip over the shanks with tongs. Turn up the temperature to 175°C (350°F).
- Place the shanks back into the oven, remove the cover and bake for 10-15 minutes until the sauce is slightly thickened and the meat can be pierced easily with a fork. After 10 minutes, flip over the shanks in the sauce and test the tenderness; place back into the oven for 10-15 minutes more if they are not tender enough and check again.
- Put the lamb shanks into a bowl and keep them warm. Strain the pan juices into a saucepan and arrange over medium heat. Boil, cook and stir frequently for 5 minutes until thickened. Remove all the excess grease from the surface of the sauce. Season to taste with salt; mix in the fresh rosemary. Drizzle the sauce on the lamb shanks to serve.

Nutrition Information

- Calories: 338 calories;
- Total Carbohydrate: 10.1
- Cholesterol: 84
- Protein: 26.2
- Total Fat: 20.6
- Sodium: 1275

238. Seven Hour Leg Of Lamb

Serving: 12 | Prep: | Cook: 55mins | Ready in:

Ingredients

- 1 6-pound bone-in leg of lamb, trimmed
- 2 tablespoons olive oil (not extra-virgin)
- 2 teaspoons kosher salt
- ½ teaspoon freshly ground pepper, plus more to taste
- 2 lemons, halved
- 1 bottle (750-ml) dry white wine
- 2 medium leeks, white and light green parts only, sliced (see Tip)
- 1 head garlic, cloves separated and peeled
- 5 bay leaves, preferably fresh
- 4 sprigs fresh rosemary
- 4 sprigs fresh thyme
- 4 cups reduced-sodium chicken broth

Direction

- Preheat an oven to 300°F.
- Rub oil on lamb; season with pepper and salt. Put a big roasting pan on 2 burners over

medium high heat. Add lamb; cook, sometimes turning, for 10-12 minutes till all sides brown. Add lemons after 5 minutes; cook, cut side down, till browned well. Put onto plate; cool.

- Squeeze juices from lemons on lamb when it is browned. Add juiced lemons with thyme, rosemary, bay leaves, garlic, leeks and wine into pan; use foil to tightly cover pan.
- Roast lamb, flipping every hour or so, for 3 hours. When you check roast, carefully uncover pan; watch for steam that escapes.
- Flip lamb one more time after 3 hours. Into pan, put broth; mixing to blend with liquid, herbs and veggies. Use foil to cover and keep roasting, turning and basting lamb, about additional 4 hours, every hour or so.
- Put lamb onto warmed platter after cooking for 7 hours; to keep warm, tent with foil. At this point, lamb should be falling off bone.
- On medium high heat, put roasting pan on 2 burners. Boil; lower heat. Simmer as lamb rests for 10 minutes. Strain cooking liquid, pressing on solids, into a bowl. Discard solids. If desired, season jus with pepper. Serve with lamb.

Nutrition Information

- Calories: 268 calories;
- Sugar: 1
- Protein: 25
- Total Fat: 12
- Sodium: 382
- Fiber: 0
- Total Carbohydrate: 4
- Saturated Fat: 4
- Cholesterol: 80

239. Spicy Lamb Meatballs In Tomato Sauce

Serving: 12 | Prep: | Cook: 45mins | Ready in:

Ingredients

- 12 ounces ground lamb
- 12 ounces 93%-lean ground turkey
- 1 cup fresh whole-wheat breadcrumbs, (see Tip)
- 1 large egg white
- 1 cup minced onion, divided
- 6 cloves garlic, minced, divided
- 4 tablespoons chopped fresh mint, divided
- 1 teaspoon ground coriander
- ½ teaspoon ground cumin
- ½ teaspoon kosher salt, divided
- 1 tablespoon extra-virgin olive oil
- ½ cup red wine
- ¼ teaspoon cayenne pepper
- 1 28-ounce can crushed tomatoes

Direction

- Preheat an oven to 350°F; use cooking spray to coat a baking sheet.
- Gently mix 1/4 tsp. salt, cumin, coriander, 2 tbsp. mint, 1/2 garlic, 1/2 cup onion, egg white, breadcrumbs, turkey and lamb to combine in a big bowl; form, 1 tbsp. each, to 48 small meatballs. Put on prepped baking sheet.
- Bake meatballs for 10 minutes; put aside.
- Meanwhile, heat oil on medium heat in a big saucepan. Add leftover 1/2 cup onion; cook, mixing, for 3-5 minutes till golden. Mix in leftover 1/4 tsp. salt, cayenne, wine and leftover garlic; simmer on medium low heat for 3-5 minutes till wine reduces significantly. Add tomatoes; simmer. Lower heat to low; simmer for 20 minutes, partially covered.
- Add meatballs to sauce; cook for 5 minutes till heated through. Garnish with leftover 2 tbsp. mint.

Nutrition Information

- Calories: 178 calories;
- Total Carbohydrate: 14
- Sugar: 4
- Protein: 13
- Total Fat: 7

- Sodium: 275
- Fiber: 2
- Saturated Fat: 2
- Cholesterol: 35

240. Spicy Sweetbreads

Serving: 4 | Prep: 15mins | Cook: 34mins | Ready in:

Ingredients

- 16 ounces lamb sweetbreads
- 7 tablespoons butter, divided
- 1/2 lemon, juiced
- salt to taste
- 2 large portobello mushrooms, diced
- 1 tablespoon all-purpose flour
- 1 teaspoon ground paprika
- 1/2 teaspoon cayenne pepper
- 1 cup warmed milk, or to taste
- 2 cups frozen peas
- 1 jalapeno pepper, thinly sliced

Direction

- In a large bowl with water, soak the sweetbreads for an hour; then drain the sweetbreads.
- In a saucepan, arrange the sweetbreads and add cold water to cover; then boil. Drain the sweetbreads. Cool the sweetbreads under cold water.
- Place the sweetbreads back into the saucepan and add cold water again to cover. Add salt, lemon juice, and a tablespoon of butter; then boil. Bring to a simmer for 10 minutes. Take away from the heat and allow to cool.
- In a heavy-bottomed skillet, melt 3 tablespoons of butter over medium heat. Add the mushrooms; stir and cook for 5 minutes until they are tender. Place into a plate.
- In the skillet, melt the remaining 3 tablespoons of butter. Add the flour; stir and cook for a minute until a paste is formed. Flavor with cayenne and paprika. Then slowly pour in the milk, beating for 3-5 minutes until the sauce is smooth.
- Stir peas, mushrooms, and sweetbreads into the sauce; cook for 5 minutes until the peas are heated through. Flavor the sweetbreads with salt. Add jalapeno pepper to decorate to serve.

Nutrition Information

- Calories: 375 calories;
- Sodium: 242
- Total Carbohydrate: 4.8
- Cholesterol: 326
- Protein: 17.8
- Total Fat: 31.6

241. Stout Braised Lamb Shanks

Serving: 4 | Prep: 25mins | Cook: 2hours25mins | Ready in:

Ingredients

- 1 tablespoon vegetable oil
- 4 lamb shanks
- 1 onion, chopped
- 4 cloves garlic, chopped
- 2 carrots, chopped
- 2 celery ribs, chopped
- 2 tablespoons tomato paste
- 1 (12 fluid ounce) bottle stout (such as Guinness®) or porter
- 1 (14 ounce) can beef broth
- 3 sprigs fresh thyme
- 3 sprigs fresh parsley
- 1 bay leaf
- 1 sprig fresh rosemary
- salt and pepper to taste

Direction

- In a big, wide pot or Dutch oven, heat oil over medium-high heat till oil starts to smoke. In

hot oil, brown all sides of lamb shanks for 10 minutes till well browned. Take off lamb shanks and reserve. Put extra grease from Dutch oven, turn heat to medium, and mix in garlic and onions. Let cook and mix for 5 minutes till onions have become translucent and softened. Mix in tomato paste, celery and carrots; keep cooking for 5 minutes longer.
- Put lamb shanks back to Dutch oven, and put in beef broth and stout beer. Simmer over high heat. Meanwhile, with kitchen twine, in a secure bundle, bind the bay leaf, parsley sprigs and thyme sprigs together; put to lamb shanks.
- When lamb shanks start to simmer, lower heat to medium-low, put cover, and allow to simmer for 2 to 3 hours till lamb is really soft and almost falling off form bone. As it cooks, mix the lamb from time to time, and put water if necessary, to maintain cooking liquid from turning very thick. By the time lamb shanks are done, cooking liquid should reduce into a nice sauce. On the final 10 minutes of cooking, mix in rosemary sprig, and pepper and salt to taste. Take off rosemary herb bundle and sprig prior serving.

Nutrition Information

- Calories: 348 calories;
- Total Fat: 15.3
- Sodium: 544
- Total Carbohydrate: 16.2
- Cholesterol: 89
- Protein: 30.2

242. Tandoori Leg Of Lamb With Fresh Mango Chutney

Serving: 10 | Prep: | Cook: 40mins | Ready in:

Ingredients

- 1 5-pound bone-in leg of lamb, trimmed
- 1 cup nonfat plain yogurt
- ¼ cup lime juice, (2 limes)
- 2 tablespoons minced fresh ginger
- 3 cloves garlic, crushed
- 1½ teaspoons salt
- ¼ teaspoon freshly ground pepper
- 1 tablespoon ground coriander
- ½ teaspoon cayenne pepper
- ½ teaspoon ground cinnamon
- ½ teaspoon ground cloves
- ½ teaspoon ground cardamom
- Fresh Mango Chutney, (recipe follows)

Direction

- Make a quarter to half-inch deep crisscross patterns on all sides of the lamb using a sharp knife; put in a plastic bag. In a bowl, mix pepper, yogurt, salt, lime juice, garlic, and ginger; pour in the plastic bag. Turn the bag to cover the lamb. Place in the refrigerator for at least 2hrs or overnight to marinate.
- Preheat the oven to 450 degrees F. Grease the rack lightly then place over a roasting pan; put the lamb on the rack. In a small bowl, mix cardamom, coriander, cloves, cinnamon, and cayenne together; evenly spread all over the lamb.
- Roast for 15mins then reduce heat to 325°F. Roast for another 55-60mins until an inserted thermometer in the lamb reads 140 degrees F for medium-rare. Let it sit for 10mins then slice.
- Prepare the Fresh Mango Chutney. Serve chutney with lamb slices.

Nutrition Information

- Calories: 390 calories;
- Total Fat: 14
- Saturated Fat: 5
- Fiber: 2
- Sodium: 718
- Cholesterol: 152
- Total Carbohydrate: 14
- Sugar: 11

- Protein: 50

---

243. Vietnamese Aromatic Lamb Chops

Serving: 5 | Prep: 10mins | Cook: 20mins | Ready in:

Ingredients

- 15 (3 ounce) lamb loin chops (1-inch thick)
- 2 cloves garlic, sliced
- 1 teaspoon garlic powder, or to taste
- 1 pinch chili powder
- 2 tablespoons white sugar
- freshly ground black pepper to taste
- 1 tablespoon fresh lime juice
- 1 tablespoon soy sauce
- 2 tablespoons olive oil
- 1/4 cup chopped fresh cilantro
- 2 lime wedges
- 2 lemon wedges

Direction

- Arrange the lamb chops in a roasting pan and spice it up evenly with the chili powder, garlic, pepper, garlic powder, salt and sugar. Sprinkle with a tablespoon of lime juice, olive oil and soy sauce. Chill in the fridge with cover overnight.
- Set the oven for preheating to 400°F (200°C). While preheating, let the lamb sit at room temperature.
- Remove the cover and allow to roast in the preheated oven to your preferred degree of doneness, about 20 minutes for medium, or half an hour for well done. Squeeze a lemon and lime juice over and top with cilantro before serving.

Nutrition Information

- Calories: 555 calories;
- Total Fat: 40.4

- Sodium: 301
- Total Carbohydrate: 7.4
- Cholesterol: 151
- Protein: 38.6

Chapter 7: Lamb Dinner Recipes

***

---

244. Basic Braised Lamb Shanks

Serving: 2 servings. | Prep: 10mins | Cook: 01hours30mins | Ready in:

Ingredients

- 2 lamb shanks (1 pound each)
- 1 cup beef broth
- 1/4 cup soy sauce
- 2 tablespoons brown sugar
- 1 garlic clove, minced
- 2 teaspoons prepared mustard

Direction

- Arrange lamb in an oiled 2 1/2-quart baking dish. Stir mustard, garlic, brown sugar, soy sauce, and broth together; pour over lamb in the baking dish. Bake, covered, for 90 to 120 minutes at 325° until meat is tender.

Nutrition Information

- Calories: 451 calories
- Total Fat: 21g fat (9g saturated fat)
- Sodium: 2419mg sodium
- Fiber: 0 fiber)

- Total Carbohydrate: 15g carbohydrate (14g sugars
- Cholesterol: 159mg cholesterol
- Protein: 48g protein.

245. Beef And Lamb Stew

Serving: 12 servings (3 quarts). | Prep: 50mins | Cook: 08hours30mins | Ready in:

Ingredients

- 1/2 cup dry red wine or beef broth
- 1/2 cup olive oil
- 4 garlic cloves, minced, divided
- 1-1/2 teaspoons salt, divided
- 1-1/2 teaspoons dried thyme, divided
- 1-1/4 teaspoons dried marjoram, divided
- 3/4 teaspoon dried rosemary, crushed, divided
- 3/4 teaspoon pepper, divided
- 1 pound beef stew meat, cut into 1-inch cubes
- 1 pound lamb stew meat, cut into 1-inch cubes
- 10 small red potatoes, halved
- 1/2 pound medium fresh mushrooms, halved
- 2 medium onions, thinly sliced
- 2 cups fresh cauliflowerets
- 1 can (16 ounces) kidney beans, rinsed and drained
- 1-1/2 cups cut fresh green beans
- 3 medium carrots, cut into 1/2-inch slices
- 1 celery rib, thinly sliced
- 1 cup beef broth
- 2 tablespoons minced fresh parsley
- 2 teaspoons sugar
- 3 tablespoons cornstarch
- 1/4 cup cold water
- 6 cups hot cooked brown rice

Direction

- Combine 1/4 teaspoon pepper, 1/2 teaspoon rosemary, 3/4 teaspoon marjoram. 1 teaspoon thyme, 1/2 teaspoon salt, 2 minced garlic cloves, oil, and wine in a large resealable plastic bag; add lamb and beef. Close the bag and shake well to coat; chill for 8 hours.
- Layer celery, carrots, green beans, kidney beans, cauliflower, onions, mushrooms, and potatoes in a 5- or 6-quart slow cooker.
- Drain beef and discard marinade; transfer meat to the slow cooker. Combine pepper, rosemary, marjoram, thyme, salt, remaining garlic, sugar, parsley, and the broth; pour the mixture over the meat.
- Cook, covered on low setting until meat and vegetables are softened, or for 8 to 10 hours. Whisk together water and cornstarch until no lumps remain; mix into stew. Cook, covered until thickened, or for 30 minutes longer. Serve warm with rice.

Nutrition Information

- Calories: 377 calories
- Total Carbohydrate: 44g carbohydrate (5g sugars
- Cholesterol: 48mg cholesterol
- Protein: 22g protein. Diabetic Exchanges: 2-1/2 starch
- Total Fat: 12g fat (3g saturated fat)
- Sodium: 499mg sodium
- Fiber: 7g fiber)

246. Best Leg Of Lamb

Serving: 12 servings. | Prep: 15mins | Cook: 02hours30mins | Ready in:

Ingredients

- 1/3 cup minced fresh rosemary
- 2 tablespoons Dijon mustard
- 2 tablespoons olive oil
- 8 garlic cloves, minced
- 1 teaspoon reduced-sodium soy sauce
- 1/2 teaspoon salt
- 1/2 teaspoon pepper
- 1 bone-in leg of lamb (7 to 9 pounds), trimmed

- 1 cup chicken broth

Direction

- Mix the first 7 ingredients in a small bowl; rub over lamb leg. Cover; refrigerate overnight.
- Put lamb onto a rack into a shallow roasting pan, fat side up; bake for 1 1/2 hours at 325°, uncovered.
- Put broth into pan; loosely cover using foil. Bake for 1-1 1/2 hours till meat gets desired doneness (170° for well-done, 160° for medium and 145° for medium-rare on a thermometer); stand for 10-15 minutes then slice.

Nutrition Information

- Calories: 246 calories
- Sodium: 320mg sodium
- Fiber: 0 fiber)
- Total Carbohydrate: 2g carbohydrate (0 sugars
- Cholesterol: 120mg cholesterol
- Protein: 33g protein. Diabetic Exchanges: 5 lean meat
- Total Fat: 11g fat (4g saturated fat)

247. Best Ever Lamb Chops

Serving: 4 servings. | Prep: 10mins | Cook: 10mins | Ready in:

Ingredients

- 1 teaspoon each dried basil, marjoram and thyme
- 1/2 teaspoon salt
- 8 lamb loin chops (3 ounces each)
- Mint jelly, optional

Direction

- Mix salt and herbs; rub over the lamb chops. Refrigerate, covered, for 1 hour.
- Broil 4-6 in. from the heat for 5-8 minutes on each side or until meat is done as desired (for those who like well-done, thermometer should read 170°, for medium, 160°, for medium-rare, 145°). If preferred, serve with mint jelly.

Nutrition Information

- Calories: 157 calories
- Total Fat: 7g fat (2g saturated fat)
- Sodium: 355mg sodium
- Fiber: 0 fiber)
- Total Carbohydrate: 0 carbohydrate (0 sugars
- Cholesterol: 68mg cholesterol
- Protein: 22g protein. Diabetic Exchanges: 3 lean meat.

248. Best Ever Lamb Chops For 2

Serving: 2 servings. | Prep: 10mins | Cook: 10mins | Ready in:

Ingredients

- 1/2 teaspoon each dried basil, marjoram and thyme
- 1/4 teaspoon salt
- 4 lamb loin chops (3 ounces each)
- Mint jelly, optional

Direction

- Mix salt and herbs together; rub all over the lamb chops. Refrigerate, covered, for 60 minutes.
- Broil for 5 to 8 minutes per side in a 4-6"-distance from heat source until meat achieves desired doneness (the thermometer should register 145 degrees for medium-rare, 160 degrees for medium and 170 degrees for well-done). Serve alongside jelly as preferred.

Nutrition Information

- Calories: 157 calories

- Sodium: 355mg sodium
- Fiber: 0 fiber)
- Total Carbohydrate: 0 carbohydrate (0 sugars
- Cholesterol: 68mg cholesterol
- Protein: 22g protein. Diabetic Exchanges: 3 lean meat
- Total Fat: 7g fat (2g saturated fat)

249. Braised Lamb Shanks

Serving: 4 | Prep: 20mins | Cook: 3hours | Ready in:

Ingredients

- 2 large white onions, chopped
- 4 lamb shanks
- 2 cups dry red wine
- 1 cup balsamic vinegar
- 1/3 cup olive oil
- 4 cloves garlic, pressed
- 2 lemons, quartered
- 2 (14.5 ounce) cans diced tomatoes
- 1 bunch fresh basil, chopped
- 1 tablespoon kosher salt
- 1 tablespoon cracked black pepper

Direction

- Set the oven to 350°F (175°C) and start preheating.
- Arrange onions in 1 layer in the bottom of a medium roasting pan with a lid or Dutch oven. Top over onions with lamb shanks. Pour the olive oil, balsamic vinegar and wine over the lamb. Put a clove of pressed garlic next to each shank, and 1/4 of a lemon on each side. Top over everything with tomatoes, season with basil, pepper and salt.
- Cover and transfer into the prepared oven. Cook for 3 hours. Make a nice flavorful gravy with the juices from the pan.

Nutrition Information

- Calories: 572 calories;
- Total Fat: 25.2
- Sodium: 1851
- Total Carbohydrate: 34.4
- Cholesterol: 86
- Protein: 32.5

250. Breaded Rack Of Lamb

Serving: 2 servings. | Prep: 5mins | Cook: 40mins | Ready in:

Ingredients

- 1 rack of lamb (1 pound), trimmed
- 3 garlic cloves, minced
- 1/8 teaspoon salt
- 1/8 teaspoon pepper
- 1/2 cup dry bread crumbs
- 3 tablespoons butter, melted
- 1 tablespoon dried parsley flakes
- 1/4 teaspoon dried thyme

Direction

- Put lamb onto greased rack in greased roasting pan; rub with pepper, salt and garlic. Bake at 375°, uncovered, for 20 minutes.
- Mix thyme, parsley, butter and breadcrumbs in a small bowl; press onto meat.
- Bake till meat gets desired doneness for 20-30 minutes; thermometer should read 170° for well done, 160° medium and 145° for medium rare.

Nutrition Information

- Calories: 441 calories
- Total Carbohydrate: 21g carbohydrate (2g sugars
- Cholesterol: 112mg cholesterol
- Protein: 24g protein.
- Total Fat: 29g fat (15g saturated fat)
- Sodium: 530mg sodium

- Fiber: 2g fiber)

251. Caribbean Chutney Crusted Chops

Serving: 4 servings. | Prep: 10mins | Cook: 20mins | Ready in:

Ingredients

- 1 cup soft bread crumbs
- 1-1/2 teaspoons Caribbean jerk seasoning
- 1/4 cup mango chutney
- 1/2 teaspoon salt
- 1/2 teaspoon pepper
- 4 lamb loin chops (2 inches-thick and 8 ounces each)

Direction

- Preheat an oven to 450°. Mix jerk seasoning and breadcrumbs in shallow bowl; put aside. Mix pepper, salt and chutney; spread over both sides of the lamb chops. Coat using crumb mixture.
- Put lamb chops onto a rack coated with cooking spray in a shallow baking pan; bake for 20-25 minutes till meat gets desired doneness (thermometer should read 170° for well-done, 160° medium and 145° for medium-rare).

Nutrition Information

- Calories: 296 calories
- Total Carbohydrate: 20g carbohydrate (9g sugars
- Cholesterol: 91mg cholesterol
- Protein: 30g protein. Diabetic Exchanges: 4 lean meat
- Total Fat: 10g fat (3g saturated fat)
- Sodium: 711mg sodium
- Fiber: 0 fiber)

252. Cheesy Lamb Cups

Serving: 6 servings. | Prep: 15mins | Cook: 20mins | Ready in:

Ingredients

- 1 envelope onion soup mix
- 1/3 cup dry bread crumbs
- 1 cup evaporated milk
- 2 pounds ground lamb
- 4 ounces cheddar cheese, cut into 12 cubes
- 1 can (10-3/4 ounces) condensed cheddar cheese soup, undiluted
- 1/2 cup milk
- 1 teaspoon Worcestershire sauce

Direction

- Whisk together evaporated milk, bread crumbs and soup mix in a small bowl. Crumble lamb over the mixture and stir well.
- Divide the mixture into half and fill 12 greased muffin cups half full with the first portion of the lamb mixture. Insert one cheese cube into the middle of each cup. Layer the remaining portion on top of the cup while mound each lightly. Bake for 20-25 minutes at 375 degrees or until a thermometer registers 160 degrees.
- In the meantime, in a small saucepan, stir Worcestershire sauce, milk and soup together, heat through and stirring until it smooth. Spoon over the lamb cups to serve.

Nutrition Information

- Calories: 507 calories
- Sodium: 1112mg sodium
- Fiber: 1g fiber)
- Total Carbohydrate: 17g carbohydrate (6g sugars
- Cholesterol: 142mg cholesterol
- Protein: 36g protein.
- Total Fat: 34g fat (16g saturated fat)

253. Classic Cottage Pie

Serving: 6 servings. | Prep: 45mins | Cook: 20mins | Ready in:

Ingredients

- 1 pound ground lamb or beef
- 2 medium carrots, finely chopped
- 1 medium onion, finely chopped
- 2 tablespoons all-purpose flour
- 2 tablespoons minced fresh parsley
- 1 tablespoon Italian seasoning
- 3/4 teaspoon salt
- 1/4 teaspoon pepper
- 1-1/2 cups reduced-sodium beef broth
- 2 tablespoons dry red wine or additional reduced-sodium beef broth
- 1 tablespoon tomato paste
- 1 teaspoon brown sugar
- 1/2 cup frozen peas
- TOPPING:
- 4 medium potatoes, peeled and cubed
- 1/2 cup 2% milk
- 1/4 cup butter, cubed
- 3/4 cup shredded cheddar cheese, divided
- 1/4 teaspoon salt
- 1/8 teaspoon pepper

Direction

- Cook onion, carrots and lamb in a big skillet on medium heat till veggies are tender and meat isn't pink; drain. Mix in pepper, salt, Italian seasoning, parsley and flour till blended. Add wine and broth slowly; mix in brown sugar and tomato paste. Boil. Lower heat; simmer, uncovered, occasionally mixing, till thick for 10-15 minutes. Mix in peas.
- Meanwhile, cover potatoes in water in a big saucepan. Boil. Lower heat; cover. Cook till tender for 10-15 minutes.
- Preheat an oven to 400°. Put meat mixture into 9-in. deep-dish greased pie plate. Drain the potatoes; mash with butter and milk. Mix in pepper, salt and 1/2 cup cheese. Spread on mixture; sprinkle leftover cheese.
- Put pie plate onto foil-lined baking sheet; the plate will get full. Bake till top is golden brown for 20-25 minutes.

Nutrition Information

- Calories: 408 calories
- Sodium: 728mg sodium
- Fiber: 3g fiber)
- Total Carbohydrate: 31g carbohydrate (7g sugars
- Cholesterol: 88mg cholesterol
- Protein: 20g protein.
- Total Fat: 22g fat (12g saturated fat)

254. Crusty Roast Leg Of Lamb

Serving: 10 servings. | Prep: 20mins | Cook: 02hours00mins | Ready in:

Ingredients

- 1 boneless leg of lamb (4 to 5 pounds)
- 1 cup soft bread crumbs (about 2 slices)
- 2 tablespoons butter, melted
- 1/2 teaspoon herbes de Provence
- Dash salt and pepper
- 1 large onion, finely chopped
- 1 can (14-1/2 ounces) chicken broth
- 2-1/2 pounds medium potatoes, peeled and cut into wedges
- 1 large tart apple, sliced

Direction

- Put lamb leg onto a rack in the roasting pan. Mix seasonings, butter and breadcrumbs in a small bowl; spread over meat. Put onion in pan; put broth over onion. Bake for 1 hour at 325°, uncovered.

- Add potatoes; bake for 30 minutes more. Add apple; bake for 30 minutes longer or till potatoes are tender and the meat gets desired doneness (170° for well-done, 160° for medium, 145° for medium-rare on a thermometer).
- Remove apple and veggies; keep warm. Stand roast for 10-15 minutes; slice.

Nutrition Information

- Calories: 349 calories
- Cholesterol: 116mg cholesterol
- Protein: 36g protein.
- Total Fat: 13g fat (6g saturated fat)
- Sodium: 316mg sodium
- Fiber: 2g fiber)
- Total Carbohydrate: 21g carbohydrate (4g sugars

255. Curried Lamb Chops

Serving: 2 servings. | Prep: 20mins | Cook: 15mins | Ready in:

Ingredients

- 4 bone-in loin lamb chops (about 3/4 pound)
- 1 tablespoon vegetable oil
- 1/2 cup chopped onion
- 1/2 cup diced peeled tart apple
- 1/2 teaspoon curry powder
- 4 teaspoons all-purpose flour
- 1/2 teaspoon salt
- 1/2 teaspoon sugar
- 1/4 teaspoon ground mustard
- 1-1/3 cups chicken broth
- 2 tablespoons lemon juice
- Hot cooked rice

Direction

- Brown both sides of lamb chops in oil in a big skillet. Remove; keep warm. Sauté curry, apple and onion till tender in the same skillet. Mix mustard, sugar, salt and flour; add to pan. Mix in lemon juice and broth slowly till blended; boil on medium heat. Mix and cook for 2 minutes; lower heat.
- Put chops in skillet; cover. Simmer, flipping once, for 15 minutes till meat gets desired doneness; 170° well done, 160° medium and 145° for medium rare on a thermometer. Serve on rice.

Nutrition Information

- Calories: 345 calories
- Protein: 34g protein.
- Total Fat: 16g fat (4g saturated fat)
- Sodium: 1287mg sodium
- Fiber: 2g fiber)
- Total Carbohydrate: 15g carbohydrate (8g sugars
- Cholesterol: 97mg cholesterol

256. Curried Lamb Stew

Serving: 6 servings. | Prep: 15mins | Cook: 01hours25mins | Ready in:

Ingredients

- 2 pounds lean lamb stew meat, cut into 3/4-inch cubes
- 4 teaspoons olive oil
- 1 medium onion, chopped
- 2 garlic cloves, minced
- 1 tablespoon curry powder
- 1 teaspoon salt
- 1/4 teaspoon pepper
- 1/8 teaspoon each ground coriander, cumin and cinnamon
- 1/8 teaspoon cayenne pepper
- 1/4 cup all-purpose flour
- 1-1/4 cups water
- 1 cup unsweetened pineapple juice
- 1 medium tart apple, peeled and chopped

- 1/4 cup tomato sauce
- 1/2 cup sour cream
- Hot cooked noodles or rice, optional

Direction

- Brown meat, in batches, on all sides with oil in a Dutch oven, then take out of the pan and keep warm. Cook garlic and onion in drippings until onion is softened. Put in cayenne, cinnamon, cumin, coriander, pepper, salt and curry; cook and stir about 2 minutes. Sprinkle over with flour, then cook and stir about 2 to 3 minutes. Stir in tomato sauce, apple, pineapple juice and water.
- Put the meat back to Dutch oven; bring to a boil. Lower heat, then cover and simmer until meat is softened, about an hour. Take away from the heat, stirring in sour cream. Serve together with rice or noodles, if wanted.

Nutrition Information

- Calories: 310 calories
- Protein: 31g protein. Diabetic Exchanges: 4 lean meat
- Total Fat: 12g fat (4g saturated fat)
- Sodium: 533mg sodium
- Fiber: 2g fiber
- Total Carbohydrate: 18g carbohydrate (0 sugars
- Cholesterol: 95mg cholesterol

257. Curried Lamb Stir Fry

Serving: 4 servings. | Prep: 15mins | Cook: 0mins | Ready in:

Ingredients

- 1 teaspoon cornstarch
- 1/4 cup chicken broth
- 1 tablespoon soy sauce
- 1/4 teaspoon curry powder
- 12 ounces boneless lamb, cut into 1/8-inch strips
- 1 small onion, chopped
- 2 garlic cloves, minced
- 2 tablespoons vegetable oil, divided
- 1 small apple, chopped
- 1/2 cup chopped green pepper
- 1/2 cup sliced celery
- 1 can (8 ounces) sliced water chestnuts, drained
- 6 ounces fresh or frozen snow peas
- 1/4 teaspoon ground ginger
- Hot cooked rice

Direction

- Combine curry powder, soy sauce, broth, and cornstarch in a mixing bowl until no lumps remain; put to one side. Sauté garlic, onion, and lamb in 1 tablespoon oil in a wok or large skillet until meat turns brown. Take out and keep warm. Sauté ginger, peas, water chestnuts, celery, green pepper, and apple in the remaining oil in the same skillet until crisp-tender. Add cooked lamb mixture. Whisk broth mixture and pour into the skillet. Bring to a boil. Cook, stirring until thickened, about 2 minutes. Serve right away with rice.

Nutrition Information

- Calories: 264 calories
- Total Fat: 12g fat (0 saturated fat)
- Sodium: 198mg sodium
- Fiber: 0 fiber)
- Total Carbohydrate: 19g carbohydrate (0 sugars
- Cholesterol: 55mg cholesterol
- Protein: 20g protein. Diabetic Exchanges: 2 meat

258. Curried Lamb And Barley Grain

Serving: 4-6 servings. | Prep: 10mins | Cook: 01hours15mins | Ready in:

Ingredients

- CURRIED LAMB AND BARLEY:
- 1 pound ground lamb
- 1 large onion, chopped
- 1 cup medium pearl barley
- 1/2 cup sliced celery
- 1 tablespoon canola oil
- 3 cups chicken broth
- 1 to 2 tablespoons curry powder
- CUCUMBER SALSA:
- 1-1/2 cups coarsely chopped seeded cucumber
- 1/2 cup plain yogurt
- 1/4 cup snipped fresh parsley
- 1 tablespoon chopped green onion
- 1 tablespoon snipped fresh mint
- 2 teaspoons lemon juice
- 2 teaspoons olive oil
- 1 garlic clove, minced

Direction

- In a skillet, sauté onion, lamb, celery and barley in oil till barley is golden and lamb is browned. Add curry powder and broth; set to a boil. Pour into a 2-quart baking dish. Uncover and bake at 350° for approximately 1 and 1/4 to 1 and a half hours till barley is softened.
- In a small bowl, combine the salsa ingredients. Refrigerate, covered, for 1 hour. Serve with lamb.

Nutrition Information

- Calories: 336 calories
- Total Carbohydrate: 32g carbohydrate (4g sugars
- Cholesterol: 53mg cholesterol
- Protein: 19g protein.
- Total Fat: 15g fat (5g saturated fat)
- Sodium: 531mg sodium
- Fiber: 7g fiber)

259. Curried Lamb And Potatoes

Serving: 6 servings. | Prep: 30mins | Cook: 04hours00mins | Ready in:

Ingredients

- 6 garlic cloves, minced, divided
- 3 tablespoons curry powder, divided
- 2 tablespoons minced fresh gingerroot, divided
- 2 teaspoons garam masala, divided
- 1 teaspoon chili powder
- 1 teaspoon paprika
- 1 teaspoon dried thyme
- 1 teaspoon ground coriander, divided
- 1-1/2 teaspoons salt, divided
- 1 teaspoon pepper, divided
- 1/4 teaspoon ground cumin
- 1 tablespoon olive oil
- 2 pounds lamb shoulder blade chops
- 4 medium red potatoes, cut into 1/2-inch pieces
- 1 can (15 ounces) diced tomatoes, undrained
- 1 cup chicken broth
- 1 small onion, chopped
- Hot cooked brown rice and minced fresh cilantro, optional

Direction

- Mix olive oil, cumin, 1/2 tsp. pepper, 1/2 tsp. salt, 1/2 tsp. coriander, thyme and paprika, chili powder, 1 tsp. garam masala, 1 tbsp. ginger, 1 tbsp. curry powder and 3 garlic cloves in a big resealable plastic bag. Add lamb chops and seal bag; turn to coat. Refrigerate for 8 hours – overnight.
- In a 3-4-qt. slow cooker, put potatoes; put lamb into the slow cooker.

- In a blender, put leftover seasonings and garlic, onion, broth and tomatoes; cover. Process till blended. Put on potatoes and lamb; cook, with cover, for 4-5 hours on low till meat is tender. Remove meat from bones when meat is cool enough to handle; discard bones. Use 2 forks to shred meat. Strain the cooking juices and reserve potatoes; skim the fat. Put lamb, reserved potatoes and cooking juices back into slow cooker and heat through; serve with cilantro and rice, if desired.

Nutrition Information

- Calories: 337 calories
- Sodium: 935mg sodium
- Fiber: 5g fiber)
- Total Carbohydrate: 21g carbohydrate (4g sugars
- Cholesterol: 76mg cholesterol
- Protein: 22g protein.
- Total Fat: 19g fat (7g saturated fat)

260. Curry Lamb Stir Fry

Serving: 4 servings. | Prep: 15mins | Cook: 0mins | Ready in:

Ingredients

- 1 teaspoon cornstarch
- 1/4 teaspoon curry powder
- 1/4 cup chicken broth
- 1 tablespoon soy sauce
- 3/4 pound boneless lamb, cut into 1/8-inch strips
- 1 small onion, chopped
- 2 tablespoons canola oil, divided
- 2 garlic cloves, minced
- 1 small red apple, chopped
- 1/2 cup chopped green pepper
- 1/2 cup sliced celery
- 1 can (8 ounces) sliced water chestnuts, drained
- 6 ounces fresh or frozen snow peas
- 1/4 teaspoon ground ginger
- Hot cooked rice

Direction

- Combine curry powder and cornstarch in a small mixing bowl. Mix in soy sauce and broth until no lumps remain. Put to one side.
- Sauté onion and lamb in 1 tablespoon oil in a wok or large skillet until lamb turns brown. Add garlic, cook for another 1 minute. Take out and keep warm.
- Sauté ginger, peas, water chestnuts, celery, green pepper, and apple in remainder of oil in the same skillet until crisp-tender. Put in lamb mixture.
- Stir broth mixture well and pour into the skillet. Bring to a boil. Cook, stirring, until thickened, about 2 minutes. Serve over rice.

Nutrition Information

- Calories: 250 calories
- Total Fat: 12g fat (3g saturated fat)
- Sodium: 345mg sodium
- Fiber: 4g fiber)
- Total Carbohydrate: 19g carbohydrate (8g sugars
- Cholesterol: 47mg cholesterol
- Protein: 18g protein. Diabetic Exchanges: 2 lean meat

261. Favorite Irish Stew

Serving: 8 servings (2-1/2 quarts). | Prep: 20mins | Cook: 01hours45mins | Ready in:

Ingredients

- 1/3 cup plus 1 tablespoon all-purpose flour, divided
- 1-1/2 pounds lamb stew meat, cut into 1-inch cubes
- 3 tablespoons olive oil, divided

- 3 medium onions, chopped
- 3 garlic cloves, minced
- 4 cups reduced-sodium beef broth
- 2 medium potatoes, peeled and cubed
- 4 medium carrots, cut into 1-inch pieces
- 1 cup frozen peas
- 1 teaspoon salt
- 1 teaspoon dried thyme
- 1/2 teaspoon pepper
- 1/2 teaspoon Worcestershire sauce
- 2 tablespoons water

Direction

- In a big resealable plastic bag, add 1/3 cup of flour. Put in lamb, a few pieces at a time, and shake to coat well.
- Brown lamb in batches with 2 tbsp. oil in a Dutch oven. Take out and set aside. Sauté onions in the leftover oil in the same pan until softened. Put in garlic and cook for 1 minute more.
- Put in broth while stirring to loosen browned bits from pan. Put the lamb back to pan; bring to a boil. Lower heat, then cover and simmer until meat is softened, about an hour.
- Put in carrots and potatoes; cover and cook about 20 minutes. Stir in peas, then cook until vegetables are softened, about 5 to 10 minutes more.
- Put in Worcestershire sauce and seasonings. Mix water with the leftover flour until smooth, stirring into stew. Bring to a boil, then cook and stir until thickened, about 2 minutes.

Nutrition Information

- Calories: 271 calories
- Cholesterol: 58mg cholesterol
- Protein: 22g protein. Diabetic Exchanges: 2 lean meat
- Total Fat: 10g fat (2g saturated fat)
- Sodium: 618mg sodium
- Fiber: 4g fiber)
- Total Carbohydrate: 24g carbohydrate (7g sugars

262. Festive Rack Of Lamb

Serving: 2 servings. | Prep: 15mins | Cook: 15mins | Ready in:

Ingredients

- 2 tablespoons all-purpose flour
- 1 teaspoon salt
- 1/2 teaspoon pepper
- 1 rack of lamb (1-1/2 pounds and 8 ribs), trimmed
- 2 tablespoons butter
- 1 cup white wine or chicken broth
- 1 teaspoon grated lemon peel
- 1 garlic clove, minced
- 1/2 teaspoon dried rosemary, crushed
- 1 bay leaf

Direction

- In a shallow bowl, put pepper, salt and flour; coat lamb in flour mixture. Cook lamb in butter in a big skillet on medium high heat for 2 minutes per side; put onto a greased baking sheet.
- Bake without cover for 15-20 minutes at 375° till meat hits desired doneness(meat thermometer should read 170° for well-done, 160° for medium and 145° for medium-rare).
- Meanwhile, put bay leaf, rosemary, garlic, lemon peel and wine in skillet; boil. Cook for 8 minutes till liquid reduces by half.
- Take away lamb from oven; loosely cover with foil. Stand before slicing for 5 minutes; serve lamb with sauce.

Nutrition Information

- Calories: 480 calories
- Fiber: 0 fiber)
- Total Carbohydrate: 7g carbohydrate (1g sugars
- Cholesterol: 130mg cholesterol

- Protein: 30g protein.
- Total Fat: 27g fat (13g saturated fat)
- Sodium: 769mg sodium

263. Flavorful Lamb Chops

Serving: 6 servings. | Prep: 15mins | Cook: 30mins | Ready in:

Ingredients

- 1/2 cup orange juice
- 1/2 cup lime juice
- 2 tablespoons caraway seeds
- 2 teaspoons grated orange zest
- 6 lamb loin chops (about 1-3/4 pounds)
- 1 tablespoon canola oil
- 1/2 teaspoon salt
- 1/2 teaspoon pepper
- 1/2 cup chicken broth
- Fresh orange slices and parsley sprigs, optional

Direction

- Blend orange zest, caraway seeds, lime juice, and orange juice in a small bowl. Add half of the marinade to a big resealable plastic bag; put in lamb chops. Seal the bag and flip it to coat; put in the fridge overnight. Put a cover on and place the remaining marinade in the fridge.
- Drain the marinade from the lamb and discard. Brown both sides of the chops in oil in a non-stick skillet on medium-high heat until a thermometer registers 160 degrees. Flavor with pepper and salt. Take off the chops and keep them warm. Add in the saved marinade and broth into the skillet; boil. Bring the chops back into the pan; turn down the heat.
- Put the cover on and bring to a simmer for 20 minutes. Simmer, uncovered, for 10 more minutes. Serve the chops along with the pan juices. If desired, add parsley and oranges to decorate.

Nutrition Information

- Calories:
- Fiber:
- Total Carbohydrate:
- Cholesterol:
- Protein:
- Total Fat:
- Sodium:

264. Glazed Racks Of Lamb

Serving: 4 servings. | Prep: 10mins | Cook: 10mins | Ready in:

Ingredients

- 2 frenched racks of lamb (1-1/2 pounds each)
- 1/2 cup honey
- 1/2 cup cherry preserves
- 2 teaspoons olive oil
- 1 teaspoon lime juice

Direction

- Put the lamb into a greased foil-lined baking sheet, then drape a piece of heavy-duty foil atop bones to keep from overbrowning. Mix lime juice, oil, preserves and honey in a small bowl. Save 1/2 cup. Scoop half of remaining glaze atop lamb.
- Broil for 10 to 12 minutes at 4 to 6 in. from heat, basting once with the remaining glaze or until the meat reaches the doneness desired (for medium-rare, the internal temperature using a thermometer should be 145°; well-done, 170°; medium, 160°).
- Take out the lamb from oven and then cover loosely with foil. Allow to stand for five minutes prior to slicing. Brush with the reserved glaze.

Nutrition Information

- Calories: 512 calories
- Sodium: 94mg sodium
- Fiber: 0 fiber)
- Total Carbohydrate: 61g carbohydrate (59g sugars
- Cholesterol: 100mg cholesterol
- Protein: 30g protein.
- Total Fat: 17g fat (6g saturated fat)

265. Greek Shepherd's Pie

Serving: 6 servings. | Prep: 25mins | Cook: 35mins | Ready in:

Ingredients

- 5-1/2 cups cubed eggplant (about 1 large)
- 2 teaspoons salt
- 4 large potatoes, peeled and cubed
- 1/2 cup sour cream
- 1/4 cup butter
- 2 tablespoons all-purpose flour
- 1/4 cup vegetable oil
- 1 pound ground lamb
- 1/2 pound ground turkey
- 1 jar (26 ounces) meatless spaghetti sauce
- 2 tablespoons dried minced onion
- 2 tablespoons minced fresh parsley
- 1 teaspoon garlic powder
- 1/2 teaspoon dried rosemary, crushed
- 1/2 teaspoon dried basil
- 1/2 teaspoon pepper
- 1 cup (4 ounces) crumbled feta cheese

Direction

- Put eggplant in a strainer over a plate and toss with salt. Let the eggplant sit for 30 minutes. While waiting for eggplant, put potatoes covered with water in a large pot. Bring the potatoes to a boil, then decrease heat, cover, and cook until tender about 10-15 minutes. Drain and mash the potatoes with butter and sour cream. Rinse and drain the eggplant well. Toss the eggplant with flour. In a frying pan on medium heat, cook eggplant in oil until brown and all oil is absorbed. Place eggplant in a 3-qt. baking dish that has been sprayed with cooking spray. Cook turkey and lamb until not pink in the same frying pan on medium heat. Drain excess grease. Mix in seasonings, spaghetti sauce, parsley, and onion. Cook for 5 minutes or so until heated through. Dump mixture over eggplant and evenly spread feta cheese then mashed potatoes on top. Bake in a 350-degree oven, uncovered, until browning begins to appear on top, 35-45 minutes. Remove from oven and let cool for 10-15 minutes.

Nutrition Information

- Calories: 736 calories
- Protein: 31g protein.
- Total Fat: 39g fat (16g saturated fat)
- Sodium: 1302mg sodium
- Fiber: 9g fiber)
- Total Carbohydrate: 65g carbohydrate (16g sugars
- Cholesterol: 119mg cholesterol

266. Herb Crusted Rack Of Lamb

Serving: Makes 2 servings | Prep: | Cook: | Ready in:

Ingredients

- 1 large garlic clove
- 1/2 cup chopped fresh basil
- 1/3 cup freshly grated pecorino Romano cheese
- 1/3 cup plain dry breadcrumbs
- 2 tablespoons herbes de Provence*
- 1 1/2 tablespoons Dijon mustard
- 2 1/2 tablespoons olive oil
- 1 1 1/2-pound rack of lamb, trimmed

Direction

- Mince the garlic in a processor. Add in the next 5 ingredients. Process using on/off turns, just until the basil is finely chopped. Drizzle the oil over. Continue to process until the mixture is incorporated. Take note that this can be prepared 4 hours in advance. Just keep it in the fridge with cover and chill.
- Set the oven for preheating to 425°F. Spice up the lamb with a sprinkle of pepper and salt. Place it on a small rimmed baking sheet, positioning it bone side facing down. Press the breadcrumb mixture on the lamb to coat completely. Roast for about half an hour, until meat thermometer poked into center of lamb reaches 135°F for medium-rare. Allow the lamb to rest for 15 minutes.
- Place the lamb over the cutting board. Slice between bones into double chops or just individual. Distribute among 2 plates. Serve.

Nutrition Information

- Calories: 1249
- Fiber: 2 g(10%)
- Total Carbohydrate: 17 g(6%)
- Cholesterol: 212 mg(71%)
- Protein: 46 g(93%)
- Total Fat: 110 g(169%)
- Saturated Fat: 44 g(220%)
- Sodium: 713 mg(30%)

267. Herb Crusted Rack Of Lamb With Mushroom Sauce

Serving: 4 servings (1 cup sauce). | Prep: 25mins | Cook: 15mins | Ready in:

Ingredients

- 2 frenched racks of lamb (1-1/2 pounds each)
- 1 tablespoon steak seasoning
- 4-1/2 teaspoons olive oil
- 1 tablespoon Dijon mustard
- 1/3 cup panko (Japanese) bread crumbs
- 1 tablespoon minced fresh thyme or 1 teaspoon dried thyme
- 1 tablespoon minced fresh mint or 1 teaspoon dried mint
- 1 teaspoon Worcestershire sauce
- 1/2 teaspoon dried rosemary, crushed
- MUSHROOM SAUCE:
- 3/4 pound sliced fresh mushrooms
- 2 tablespoons olive oil
- 1/4 cup butter, divided
- 4 garlic cloves, minced
- 1/2 cup dry red wine or beef broth
- 1/4 cup beef broth
- 1/2 teaspoon honey
- 2 tablespoons minced chives, optional

Direction

- Sprinkle the steak seasoning over the lamb. Cook the lamb in oil in a large skillet on medium-high heat for 2 minutes per side. Use mustard to brush it.
- Blend rosemary, Worcestershire sauce, mint, thyme, and panko in a small bowl; press on the lamb. Place into a 15x10-inch baking pan that's greased. Bake without cover at 375 degrees until the meat reaches the desired degree of doneness or 15-20 minutes (for well-done: a thermometer should register 170 degrees; medium: 160 degrees; medium-rare: 145 degrees).
- Sauté the mushrooms in oil and 2 tablespoons of butter in a large skillet until they become tender. Put in the garlic; cook 1 more minute. Pour in wine and stir. Boil and cook until the liquid reduces by half. Take away from the heat. Stir in chives if desired, the remaining butter, honey, and broth.
- Take the lamb out from the oven and use the foil to cover loosely. Before cutting, allow to stand for 5 minutes. Serve together with the sauce.

Nutrition Information

- Calories: 532 calories
- Protein: 33g protein.

- Total Fat: 39g fat (14g saturated fat)
- Sodium: 861mg sodium
- Fiber: 1g fiber)
- Total Carbohydrate: 10g carbohydrate (2g sugars
- Cholesterol: 130mg cholesterol

268. Hungarian Lamb Stew

Serving: 9 servings. | Prep: 30mins | Cook: 02hours00mins | Ready in:

Ingredients

- 3 slices bacon, cut into 1-inch pieces
- 2 medium onions, thinly sliced
- 2 pounds lamb stew meat, cut into 1-inch cubes
- 2 tablespoons Hungarian paprika
- 1 teaspoon salt
- 1 teaspoon caraway seeds
- 1 garlic clove, minced
- 1 medium green pepper, sliced, divided
- 1 medium sweet red pepper, sliced, divided
- 1 cup water
- 3 medium potatoes, peeled and cut into 3/4-inch pieces
- 1 large tomato, sliced

Direction

- Cook bacon over medium heat in a Dutch oven until crispy. Transfer bacon to paper towels with a slotted spoon, saving bacon grease. Sauté onions in bacon grease until softened. Take onions out of the Dutch oven. Cook meat in grease over medium-high heat until all sides are browned.
- Place onions and bacon back into the pan along with half of the pepper, garlic, caraway, salt, and paprika. Pour in water. Bring everything in the pan to a boil. Lower heat; simmer mixture, covered, for 90 minutes. Pour in more water if needed.
- Whisk in remaining peppers and potatoes. Bring to a boil. Lower heat; simmer for 20 minutes. Put in tomatoes; simmer until vegetables and meat are tender for 10 more minutes. Adjust seasoning, if desired.

Nutrition Information

- Calories: 241 calories
- Sodium: 388mg sodium
- Fiber: 2g fiber)
- Total Carbohydrate: 15g carbohydrate (4g sugars
- Cholesterol: 71mg cholesterol
- Protein: 23g protein.
- Total Fat: 10g fat (4g saturated fat)

269. Irish Lamb Stew

Serving: 10 | Prep: 20mins | Cook: 2hours25mins | Ready in:

Ingredients

- 1 1/2 pounds thickly sliced bacon, diced
- 6 pounds boneless lamb shoulder, cut into 2 inch pieces
- 1/2 teaspoon salt
- 1/2 teaspoon ground black pepper
- 1/2 cup all-purpose flour
- 3 cloves garlic, minced
- 1 large onion, chopped
- 1/2 cup water
- 4 cups beef stock
- 2 teaspoons white sugar
- 4 cups diced carrots
- 2 large onions, cut into bite-size pieces
- 3 potatoes
- 1 teaspoon dried thyme
- 2 bay leaves
- 1 cup white wine

Direction

- Place the bacon into a big, deep skillet and cook over a medium-high heat until browned evenly. Drain the bacon, crumble it, and put aside.
- In a big mixing bowl, place flour, pepper, salt, and lamb, tossing to evenly coat the meat. Brown the meat using the pan with the bacon fat.
- Place the meat in a stockpot, leaving 1/4 cup of fat in the pan. Add yellow onion and garlic, then sauté until onion starts to turn golden. Deglaze the pan with 1/2 cup of water and add the onion-garlic mixture to the stockpot with sugar, beef stock, and pieces of bacon. Simmer while covered for 1 1/2 hours.
- Place in wine, bay leaves, thyme, potatoes, onions, and carrots. Turn the heat down and simmer, covered, for around 20 minutes until the vegetables become tender.

Nutrition Information

- Calories: 672 calories;
- Sodium: 1189
- Total Carbohydrate: 26.3
- Cholesterol: 163
- Protein: 46.4
- Total Fat: 39.3

270. Irish Stew

Serving: 6 | Prep: 15mins | Cook: 1hours45mins | Ready in:

Ingredients

- 1 tablespoon olive oil
- 2 pounds boneless lamb shoulder, cut into 1 1/2 inch pieces
- 1/2 teaspoon salt
- freshly ground black pepper to taste
- 1 large onion, sliced
- 2 carrots, peeled and cut into large chunks
- 1 parsnip, peeled and cut into large chunks (optional)
- 4 cups water, or as needed
- 3 large potatoes, peeled and quartered
- 1 tablespoon chopped fresh rosemary (optional)
- 1 cup coarsely chopped leeks
- chopped fresh parsley for garnish (optional)

Direction

- In a Dutch oven or big stockpot, heat the oil over medium heat. Put in pieces of lamb and cook, mixing softly, till evenly browned. Add pepper and salt to season.
- Put in parsnips, carrots and onion, and cook softly alongside of meat for several minutes. Mix in water. Place on the cover and let it come to boil prior to reducing the heat to low. Let it simmer for an hour or more, this will vary on the meat cut you used and the tenderness.
- Mix in potatoes, and let it simmer for 15 to 20 minutes, prior to putting in rosemary and leeks. Keep simmering without a cover, till potatoes are soft but remain whole. Jazz up with fresh parsley and serve piping hot in bowls.

Nutrition Information

- Calories: 609 calories;
- Total Carbohydrate: 43.4
- Cholesterol: 109
- Protein: 29.8
- Total Fat: 35.1
- Sodium: 325

271. Italian Leg Of Lamb

Serving: 11 servings. | Prep: 10mins | Cook: 02hours15mins | Ready in:

Ingredients

- 1/2 to 2/3 cup lemon juice
- 1/2 cup olive oil
- 2 tablespoons dried oregano
- 2 teaspoons ground mustard
- 1 teaspoon garlic powder
- 4 garlic cloves, minced
- 1 boneless leg of lamb (4 to 5 pounds)

Direction

- Mix seasonings, oil and lemon juice in a small bowl. Put 1/2 marinade into a big resealable plastic bag then add lamb; seal bag. Turn to coat; refrigerate it for a minimum of 2 hours to overnight. Cover; refrigerate leftover marinade.
- Drain marinade from lamb; discard. Put onto rack into shallow roasting pan, fat side up; bake for 2 1/4-3 hours at 325°, uncovered, till meat gets preferred doneness; 170° well-done, 160 for medium on a thermometer, occasionally basting using leftover marinade; before slicing, stand for 10-15 minutes.

Nutrition Information

- Calories:
- Sodium:
- Fiber:
- Total Carbohydrate:
- Cholesterol:
- Protein:
- Total Fat:

272. Italian Leg Of Lamb With Lemon Sauce

Serving: 12 servings (2 cups gravy). | Prep: 25mins | Cook: 02hours15mins | Ready in:

Ingredients

- 2/3 cup lemon juice
- 1/2 cup canola oil
- 2 tablespoons dried oregano
- 4 teaspoons chopped anchovy fillets
- 3 garlic cloves, minced
- 2 teaspoons ground mustard
- 1 teaspoon salt
- One 2-gallon resealable plastic bag
- 1 boneless leg of lamb (5 to 6 pounds), trimmed
- 1/4 cup all-purpose flour
- 1/4 cup cold water

Direction

- Mix the first 7 ingredients in a small bowl. In a 2-gal resealable plastic bag, put 2/3 cup marinade. Add lamb; seal bag. Turn to coat; refrigerate for 8 hours – overnight. Cover; refrigerate leftover marinade.
- Preheat an oven to 325°. Drain; remove marinade. Put leg of lamb onto a rack in a roasting pan; bake without cover for 2 1/4-2 3/4 hours, till meat gets desired doneness (meat thermometer should read 170° for well done, 160° for medium and 145° for medium-rare)
- Transfer meat to a serving platter and let it stand for 15 minutes prior slicing.
- Meanwhile, put loosened brown bits and drippings into a 2-cup measuring cup then skim fat. Add reserved marinade and enough water to get 1 3/4 cups.
- Mix cold water and flour till smooth in a small saucepan; mix in drippings slowly. Boil; mix and cook till thickened for 2 minutes; serve with lamb.

Nutrition Information

- Calories: 319 calories
- Sodium: 262mg sodium
- Fiber: 0 fiber)
- Total Carbohydrate: 3g carbohydrate (0 sugars
- Cholesterol: 115mg cholesterol
- Protein: 36g protein.
- Total Fat: 17g fat (5g saturated fat)

273. Lamb Broccoli Strudel

Serving: 6 servings. | Prep: 20mins | Cook: 45mins | Ready in:

Ingredients

- 1 pound ground lamb or pork
- 1 medium onion, chopped
- 2 cups chopped fresh broccoli, blanched
- 1 cup shredded part-skim mozzarella cheese
- 1/2 cup sour cream
- 1/4 cup dry bread crumbs
- 1 garlic clove, minced
- 1 teaspoon seasoned salt
- 1/2 teaspoon pepper
- 20 sheets phyllo dough (14 inches x 9 inches)
- 1/2 cup butter, melted

Direction

- Cook onion and lamb in a skillet on medium heat till not pink. Drain; cool. Mix pepper, seasoned salt, garlic, breadcrumbs, sour cream, cheese and broccoli in a big bowl; stir in onion and meat.
- Put 1 phyllo dough sheet onto waxed paper piece. Brush butter; keep layering with 9 extra dough sheets, brushing butter on each. Keep leftover dough covered in plastic wrap then a damp towel to avoid drying out. On dough, put 1/2 meat mixture. Roll up, starting at short end, jellyroll style.
- Put roll onto greased baking sheet, seam side down; repeat with leftover filling and dough. Brush leftover butter on tops of rolls. Bake at 350° till golden brown for 45-50 minutes. Cool before slicing for 10 minutes.

Nutrition Information

- Calories: 607 calories
- Protein: 25g protein.
- Total Fat: 35g fat (18g saturated fat)
- Sodium: 875mg sodium
- Fiber: 3g fiber)
- Total Carbohydrate: 50g carbohydrate (6g sugars
- Cholesterol: 119mg cholesterol

274. Lamb Chops With Mint Stuffing

Serving: 8 servings. | Prep: 20mins | Cook: 60mins | Ready in:

Ingredients

- 1/4 cup chopped onion
- 1/4 cup chopped celery
- 1/2 cup butter, cubed
- 2/3 cup fresh mint leaves, chopped and packed
- 4 cups white or brown bread, torn in 3/4-in. pieces
- Salt to taste
- Black pepper to taste
- 1 large egg, beaten
- 8 shoulder lamb chops
- 4 teaspoons creme de menthe, optional

Direction

- Sauté celery and onion in butter; mix with bread and mint. Season with pepper and salt. Add egg; lightly mix.
- Put lamb into shallow baking dish; if desired, brush using crème de menthe. Pile stuffing over chops; bake for 1 hour at 350°.

Nutrition Information

- Calories:
- Total Carbohydrate:
- Cholesterol:
- Protein:
- Total Fat:
- Sodium:
- Fiber:

275. Lamb Chops With Prunes

Serving: 4 servings. | Prep: 20mins | Cook: 20mins | Ready in:

Ingredients

- 8 lamb loin chops (1 inch thick)
- 1 tablespoon vegetable oil
- Salt and pepper to taste
- 3/4 cup orange juice, divided
- 2 tablespoons maple syrup
- 1/2 teaspoon ground ginger
- 1/4 teaspoon ground allspice
- 1 package (9 ounces) pitted dried plums
- 1-1/2 teaspoons cornstarch

Direction

- Cook chops in oil in a medium skillet until both sides are browned; season chops with pepper and salt. Drain well; place chops back into the skillet. Measure 1 tablespoon of orange juice and put to one side; transfer the rest of juice to the skillet. Add allspice, ginger, and syrup; cook over medium-low heat, covered, for 15 minutes, flipping once. Add prunes. Simmer, covered, until chops are tender. Transfer chops to a serving platter and keep them warm. Stir together the reserved orange juice and cornstarch; pour into the skillet. Heat over medium heat until mixture comes to a boil; cook for 2 minutes, stirring while cooking. Ladle over lamb to serve.

Nutrition Information

- Calories:
- Fiber:
- Total Carbohydrate:
- Cholesterol:
- Protein:
- Total Fat:
- Sodium:

276. Lamb Fajitas

Serving: 8 servings. | Prep: 15mins | Cook: 15mins | Ready in:

Ingredients

- 1 boneless leg of lamb or lamb shoulder (3 to 4 pounds)
- 1/2 cup canola oil
- 1/2 cup lemon juice
- 1/3 cup soy sauce
- 1/3 cup packed brown sugar
- 1/4 cup vinegar
- 3 tablespoons Worcestershire sauce
- 1 tablespoon ground mustard
- 1/2 teaspoon pepper
- 1 large green pepper, sliced
- 1 large sweet red pepper, sliced
- 1 large onion, sliced
- 16 flour tortillas (7 inches), warmed
- Chopped tomato and cucumber, optional

Direction

- Cut lamb to thin bite-sized strips. Mix pepper, mustard, Worcestershire, vinegar, sugar, soy sauce, lemon juice and oil in a big resealable plastic bag. Add lamb; seal bag. Turn to coat, refrigerate, occasionally turning, for 3 hours.
- Put marinade and lamb into big saucepan/Dutch oven; boil. Lower heat; cover. Simmer till meat is tender for 8-10 minutes. Add onion and peppers; cook till veggies are crisp tender for 4 minutes.
- Put veggies and meat on tortillas using slotted spoon; if desired, top with cucumber and tomato. Fold in tortilla's sides.

Nutrition Information

- Calories: 697 calories
- Sodium: 1251mg sodium

- Fiber: 1g fiber)
- Total Carbohydrate: 67g carbohydrate (12g sugars
- Cholesterol: 95mg cholesterol
- Protein: 40g protein.
- Total Fat: 30g fat (6g saturated fat)

- Protein: 28g protein.
- Total Fat: 34g fat (19g saturated fat)
- Sodium: 695mg sodium
- Fiber: 2g fiber)
- Total Carbohydrate: 30g carbohydrate (4g sugars
- Cholesterol: 165mg cholesterol

277. Lamb Noodle Stroganoff

Serving: 8-10 servings. | Prep: 20mins | Cook: 30mins | Ready in:

Ingredients

- 2 pounds ground lamb
- 2 garlic cloves, minced
- 1 can (16 ounces) tomato sauce
- 1 teaspoon salt
- 1/4 teaspoon pepper
- 1 package (12 ounces) medium noodles, cooked and drained
- 1 package (8 ounces) cream cheese, softened
- 2 cups sour cream
- 6 green onions, sliced
- 1-1/2 cups shredded cheddar cheese
- Paprika

Direction

- Cook garlic and lamb in a skillet until lamb is browned; drain well. Mix in pepper, salt, and tomato sauce. Simmer without covering for 10 minutes. Arrange noodles in an oiled 13x9-inch baking dish. Place meat mixture on top. Beat sour cream and cream cheese together in a small mixing bowl until no lumps remain; mix in onions. Spread cream cheese mixture over meat mixture. Bake without covering for half an hour at 350° until thoroughly heated. Scatter top with paprika and cheese; allow to sit for 5 minutes before serving.

Nutrition Information

- Calories: 549 calories

278. Lamb Ratatouille

Serving: 6 servings. | Prep: 30mins | Cook: 20mins | Ready in:

Ingredients

- 1 package (6.8 ounces) beef-flavored rice and vermicelli mix
- 2 tablespoons butter
- 2-1/2 cups water
- 3 medium tomatoes, peeled, seeded and chopped
- 1 medium zucchini, sliced
- 1-1/2 cups sliced fresh mushrooms
- 1 small onion, chopped
- 6 green onions, sliced
- 3 garlic cloves, minced
- 2 tablespoons olive oil
- 1 pound cooked lamb or beef, cut into thin strips

Direction

- Reserve the rice seasoning packet. Sauté rice mix in a big pan with butter until brown. Mix in the seasoning packet contents and water; boil. Lower heat; let it simmer for 15 minutes with cover.
- In the meantime, sauté vegetables in another pan with oil until tender-crisp. Put the vegetables and lamb in the rice; cover. Let it simmer for 5-10 minutes until the rice is tender and the meat is not pink.

Nutrition Information

- Calories: 369 calories
- Cholesterol: 76mg cholesterol
- Protein: 25g protein.
- Total Fat: 16g fat (6g saturated fat)
- Sodium: 580mg sodium
- Fiber: 3g fiber)
- Total Carbohydrate: 31g carbohydrate (6g sugars

279. Lamb And Potato Stew

Serving: 8 servings (2 quarts). | Prep: 5mins | Cook: 01hours30mins |Ready in:

Ingredients

- 2 pounds lean lamb stew meat, cut into 1-inch pieces
- 1/2 cup chopped onion
- 4 to 6 medium potatoes, peeled and diced
- 4 carrots, diced
- 1-1/4 cups water
- 1 can (14-1/2 ounces) diced tomatoes, undrained
- 1/2 cup diced celery
- 1-1/2 teaspoon salt
- 1/2 teaspoon pepper
- 1/2 teaspoon garlic powder
- 1/2 teaspoon dried thyme
- 1/2 teaspoon dried basil
- 1 to 2 bay leaves

Direction

- Combine all ingredients in a Dutch oven or large kettle. Bake, covered for 1.5 to 2.5 hours at 325° or until softened. Remove bay leaves before serving.

Nutrition Information

- Calories: 266 calories
- Protein: 26g protein.
- Total Fat: 6g fat (2g saturated fat)
- Sodium: 606mg sodium
- Fiber: 4g fiber)
- Total Carbohydrate: 26g carbohydrate (6g sugars
- Cholesterol: 74mg cholesterol

280. Lamb With Apricots

Serving: 8 servings. | Prep: 15mins | Cook: 01hours30mins |Ready in:

Ingredients

- 1 large onion, chopped
- 2 tablespoons olive oil
- 1 boneless lamb shoulder roast (2-1/2 to 3 pounds), cubed
- 1 teaspoon each ground cumin, cinnamon and coriander
- Salt and pepper to taste
- 1/2 cup dried apricots, halved
- 1/4 cup orange juice
- 1 tablespoon ground almonds
- 1/2 teaspoon grated orange zest
- 1-1/4 cups chicken broth
- 1 tablespoon sesame seeds, toasted

Direction

- Place the onion in a big skillet and sauté in oil until softened. Cook the lamb and put in the seasonings. Stir while it cooks for 5 minutes or until the meat becomes brown. Stir in the orange juice, apricots, orange zest and almonds.
- Place on a 2-1/2 quarts. baking dish. Mix in the broth. Let it bake at 350° while covered for 1-1/2 hours or until the lamb is tender. Top it off with sesame seeds.

Nutrition Information

- Calories: 280 calories
- Sodium: 198mg sodium

- Fiber: 2g fiber)
- Total Carbohydrate: 9g carbohydrate (6g sugars
- Cholesterol: 70mg cholesterol
- Protein: 19g protein.
- Total Fat: 19g fat (7g saturated fat)

281. Lamb With Raspberry Sauce

Serving: 8 servings. | Prep: 10mins | Cook: 20mins | Ready in:

Ingredients

- 2 cups fresh or frozen unsweetened raspberries
- 3/4 cup finely chopped seeded peeled cucumber
- 1/2 cup finely chopped peeled tart apple
- 2 tablespoons white grape juice
- 1 to 2 tablespoons sugar
- 4 garlic cloves, minced
- 3 tablespoons olive oil
- 8 lamb loin chops (1 to 1-1/2 inches thick and 6 ounces each)

Direction

- Put raspberries in a blender; cover and pulse into puree. Sieve pureed raspberries, discarding seeds; pour pureed raspberries into a small saucepan. Whisk in sugar, grape juice, apple, and cucumber. Bring to a boil. Lower heat; simmer without covering until apple and cucumber are tender for 5 to 7 minutes.
- In the meantime, sauté garlic in oil in a large skillet until tender. Put in lamb chops. Cook without covering for 7 to 10 minutes per side until desired doneness of lamb is reached (145° for medium-rare, 160° for medium, and 170° for well done). Spoon raspberry sauce over lamb to serve.

Nutrition Information

- Calories: 230 calories
- Protein: 22g protein. Diabetic Exchanges: 3 lean meat
- Total Fat: 12g fat (3g saturated fat)
- Sodium: 61mg sodium
- Fiber: 2g fiber)
- Total Carbohydrate: 7g carbohydrate (4g sugars
- Cholesterol: 68mg cholesterol

282. Leg Of Lamb

Serving: 9 | Prep: | Cook: | Ready in:

Ingredients

- 8 pounds whole leg of lamb
- salt to taste
- ground black pepper to taste
- 6 ounces prepared mustard
- 1 dash Worcestershire sauce
- 2 tablespoons all-purpose flour
- 4 cloves garlic, sliced (optional)

Direction

- Preheat an oven to 165°C/325°F.
- Pepper and salt lamb generously; smear mustard all over lamb. Sprinkle with fine coating of the flour. Put lamb into a roasting pan; put garlic slices over the top. Sprinkle Worcestershire sauce to taste.
- Roast without cover to desired doneness at 165°C/325°F; 20 minutes per pound to get pink roast. Transfer onto a heated platter; use drippings to create gravy by water and a little flour. Season using pepper and salt.

Nutrition Information

- Calories: 476 calories;
- Protein: 46.1
- Total Fat: 29.8

- Sodium: 329
- Total Carbohydrate: 2.8
- Cholesterol: 164

283. Leg Of Lamb Dinner

Serving: 10-12 servings. | Prep: 35mins | Cook: 02hours00mins | Ready in:

Ingredients

- 1 leg of lamb (5 to 7 pounds)
- 8 garlic cloves, cut into slivers
- 4 teaspoons minced fresh rosemary, divided
- 2 teaspoons ground mustard
- 1-1/2 teaspoons salt, divided
- 1 teaspoon chopped fresh mint or 1/4 teaspoon dried mint flakes
- 1/4 teaspoon pepper
- 1 tablespoon water
- 3 pounds red potatoes, cut into 1-inch slices
- 1 package (16 ounces) baby carrots
- 2 tablespoons olive oil
- 3 cups fresh or frozen peas
- 3 tablespoons cornstarch
- 1 cup beef broth
- 1/2 cup cold water
- 1/3 to 1/2 cup currant jelly

Direction

- From roast, remove thin fat layer. Create deep cuts in meat; in each, insert garlic sliver. Mix pepper, mint, 1 tsp. salt, mustard and 3 tsp. rosemary; mix in water. Rub on meat. Put onto rack in big roasting pan; bake at 350°, uncovered, for 1 1/2 hours.
- Meanwhile, toss salt, leftover rosemary, oil, carrots and potatoes in a big bowl; put into separate greased roasting pan. Bake at 350°, uncovered, for 1-3/4 hours.
- Use pan drippings to base roast; bake till meat gets desired doneness, 170° for well done, 160° for medium well, for 30 minutes – 2 hours.
- Put peas in veggie mixture; bake till veggies are tender and browned for 10 minutes. Transfer veggies and roast onto warm serving platter; keep warm.
- Into saucepan, strain pan drippings; skim fat. Mix cold water, broth and cornstarch till smooth in small bowl; add to drippings slowly. Mix in jelly. Boil; mix and cook till thick for 2 minutes. Serve with veggies and roast.

Nutrition Information

- Calories: 372 calories
- Cholesterol: 93mg cholesterol
- Protein: 31g protein.
- Total Fat: 10g fat (3g saturated fat)
- Sodium: 470mg sodium
- Fiber: 5g fiber)
- Total Carbohydrate: 39g carbohydrate (12g sugars

284. Lemon Herb Lamb Chops

Serving: 2 servings. | Prep: 5mins | Cook: 10mins | Ready in:

Ingredients

- 1/4 cup olive oil
- 1 tablespoon lemon juice
- 1 garlic clove, minced
- 1 teaspoon grated lemon peel
- 1/4 teaspoon salt
- 1/4 teaspoon dried basil
- 1/4 teaspoon dried rosemary, crushed
- 1/4 teaspoon pepper
- 2 lamb loin chops (1 inch thick and 6 ounces each)

Direction

- Mix the first 8 ingredients in a big ziplock bag; put in chops. Seal then turn the bag to coat the chops; chill for at least 2 hours to overnight.
- Drain and get rid of the marinade. Broil the chops for 4-9 minutes per side, three to four inches from heat until it reaches the preferred doneness. The thermometer should register 145 degrees F for medium-rare, 160 degrees F for medium, and 170°C for well-done.

Nutrition Information

- Calories: 303 calories
- Sodium: 238mg sodium
- Fiber: 0 fiber)
- Total Carbohydrate: 1g carbohydrate (0 sugars
- Cholesterol: 68mg cholesterol
- Protein: 22g protein.
- Total Fat: 23g fat (5g saturated fat)

285. Lemon Herb Leg Of Lamb

Serving: 12 servings. | Prep: 10mins | Cook: 01hours45mins |Ready in:

Ingredients

- 2 teaspoons lemon juice
- 1-1/2 teaspoons grated lemon peel
- 1 teaspoon garlic salt
- 1 teaspoon dried oregano
- 1 teaspoon dried thyme
- 1 teaspoon dried rosemary, crushed
- 1 teaspoon ground mustard
- 1 boneless leg of lamb (4 pounds), rolled and tied

Direction

- Mix initial 7 ingredients in a small bowl; rub on lamb leg. Cover; refrigerate overnight.
- Preheat an oven to 325°. Put lamb onto rack in shallow roasting pan; bake for 1 3/4-2 1/4 hours, uncovered, till meat gets desired doneness; 170° well-done, 160° medium and 145° for medium-rare on a thermometer.
- Before slicing, stand for 15 minutes.

Nutrition Information

- Calories: 198 calories
- Total Fat: 8g fat (3g saturated fat)
- Sodium: 225mg sodium
- Fiber: 0 fiber
- Total Carbohydrate: 0 carbohydrate (0 sugars
- Cholesterol: 92mg cholesterol
- Protein: 28g protein. Diabetic Exchanges: 4 lean meat.

286. Mediterranean Rack Of Lamb

Serving: 4 servings. | Prep: 15mins | Cook: 30mins | Ready in:

Ingredients

- 2 racks of lamb (1-1/2 pounds each)
- 1/4 cup grated lemon zest
- 1/4 cup minced fresh oregano or 4 teaspoons dried oregano
- 6 garlic cloves, minced
- 1 tablespoon olive oil
- 1/4 teaspoon salt
- 1/4 teaspoon pepper
- Fresh oregano and lemon slices, optional

Direction

- Preheat an oven to 375°. In a shallow roasting pan, put lamb. Mix pepper, salt, oil, garlic, oregano and lemon zest in small bowl; rub over lamb.
- Bake for 30-40 minutes till meat gets desired doneness (thermometer should read 145° for medium well; 140° for medium and 135° for medium rare). Before cutting, stand for 5

minutes; serve with lemon slices and fresh oregano if desired.

Nutrition Information

- Calories: 307 calories
- Protein: 30g protein.
- Total Fat: 19g fat (6g saturated fat)
- Sodium: 241mg sodium
- Fiber: 1g fiber)
- Total Carbohydrate: 3g carbohydrate (0 sugars
- Cholesterol: 100mg cholesterol

287. Mint Lamb Stew

Serving: 6 servings. | Prep: 40mins | Cook: 07hours00mins |Ready in:

Ingredients

- 1/2 cup all-purpose flour
- 1/2 teaspoon salt
- 1/4 teaspoon pepper
- 1-1/2 pounds lamb stew meat, cubed
- 2 shallots, sliced
- 2 tablespoons olive oil
- 1/2 cup red wine
- 2 cans (14-1/2 ounces each) beef broth
- 2 medium potatoes, cubed
- 1 large sweet potato, peeled and cubed
- 2 large carrots, cut into 1-inch pieces
- 2 medium parsnips, peeled and cubed
- 1 garlic clove, minced
- 1 tablespoon mint jelly
- 4 bacon strips, cooked and crumbled

Direction

- In a large resealable plastic bag, mix pepper, salt and flour. Put in the meat, a few pieces at a time; shake to coat. Brown shallots and meat in a large skillet with oil, working in batches.
- Move to a 5- or 6-qt. slow cooker. Pour wine into the skillet; stir to loosen browned bits from the pan. Allow to boil. Lower the heat; simmer without a cover for 1-2 minutes. Transfer into the slow cooker.
- Mix in garlic, parsnips, carrots, sweet potato, potatoes and broth. Cook with a cover on low till the meat is tender, or for 7-9 hours. Mix in jelly; drizzle over with bacon.

Nutrition Information

- Calories: 442 calories
- Protein: 31g protein.
- Total Fat: 13g fat (4g saturated fat)
- Sodium: 1016mg sodium
- Fiber: 5g fiber)
- Total Carbohydrate: 46g carbohydrate (11g sugars
- Cholesterol: 79mg cholesterol

288. Mint Pesto Lamb Chops

Serving: 8 servings. | Prep: 40mins | Cook: 20mins | Ready in:

Ingredients

- 2 cups pomegranate juice
- 1 cup balsamic vinegar
- PESTO:
- 1/4 cup fresh mint leaves
- 1/4 cup fresh cilantro leaves
- 8 garlic cloves, peeled
- 1 teaspoon salt
- 1 teaspoon pepper
- 1/4 cup olive oil
- LAMB:
- 8 double-cut lamb rib chops (2 inches thick and 4 ounces each)
- 1 tablespoon olive oil

Direction

- Combine the vinegar and pomegranate juice in a large saucepan and let it boil over medium

heat; cook the mixture until it evaporates and reduces to half a cup.
- For the meantime, make the pesto. Place together the pepper, salt, garlic, cilantro and mint in a small food processor; pulse with cover until chopped. While processing, add the oil little by little in a stable stream.
- Coat the chops using the pesto. In a big ovenproof skillet, cook it in oil all over until the lamb turns brown.
- Allow to bake inside the oven without placing any cover at 450° for 15-20 minutes or until the meat achieves your preferred doneness (for medium-rare, a thermometer should reach 145°; medium, 160°; well-done, 170°). Top it off with a drizzle of pomegranate sauce.

Nutrition Information

- Calories: 238 calories
- Total Carbohydrate: 15g carbohydrate (13g sugars
- Cholesterol: 45mg cholesterol
- Protein: 15g protein. Diabetic Exchanges: 2 lean meat
- Total Fat: 13g fat (3g saturated fat)
- Sodium: 352mg sodium
- Fiber: 0 fiber

289. Old Fashioned Lamb Stew

Serving: 10-12 servings. | Prep: 20mins | Cook: 03hours00mins | Ready in:

Ingredients

- 1/4 cup all-purpose flour
- 1 teaspoon salt
- 1/2 teaspoon pepper
- 3 pounds boneless lamb, cut into 3-inch pieces
- 2 tablespoons canola oil
- 1 can (28 ounces) diced tomatoes, undrained
- 1 medium onion, cut into eighths
- 1 tablespoon dried parsley flakes
- 2 teaspoons dried rosemary, crushed
- 1/4 teaspoon garlic powder
- 4 large carrots, cut into 1/2-inch pieces
- 4 medium potatoes, peeled and cut into 1-inch pieces
- 1 package (10 ounces) frozen peas
- 1 can (4 ounces) mushroom stems and pieces, drained

Direction

- Combine pepper, salt, and flour in a large resealable plastic bag; working in batches (a few pieces at a time), put lamb pieces into the bag and turn to coat evenly. Cook lamb in oil in a Dutch oven until browned; drain well. Stir in garlic powder, rosemary, parsley, onion, and tomatoes. Simmer, covered, for 2 hours.
- Put in potatoes and carrots; cook, covered, until meat is tender for 1 more hour. Put in mushrooms and peas; cook until thoroughly heated. Thicken mixture if you wish.

Nutrition Information

- Calories: 273 calories
- Fiber: 4g fiber
- Total Carbohydrate: 22g carbohydrate (7g sugars
- Cholesterol: 74mg cholesterol
- Protein: 27g protein.
- Total Fat: 8g fat (2g saturated fat)
- Sodium: 426mg sodium

290. Orange Blossom Lamb

Serving: 4 servings. | Prep: 5mins | Cook: 25mins | Ready in:

Ingredients

- 8 lamb rib chops (6 to 7 ounces each and 1-thick)
- 2 tablespoons butter

- 1 can (6 ounces) orange juice concentrate, thawed
- 1 medium onion, sliced
- 1 to 2 teaspoons soy sauce
- 1 teaspoon salt
- Dash pepper

Direction

- Brown the lamb chops in butter on medium heat in a big skillet. Add leftover ingredients; stir well. Lower heat; cover. Simmer till meat is tender, flipping once, for 20-25 minutes. Serve: Put sauce on lamb.

Nutrition Information

- Calories: 442 calories
- Fiber: 1g fiber)
- Total Carbohydrate: 20g carbohydrate (18g sugars
- Cholesterol: 151mg cholesterol
- Protein: 45g protein.
- Total Fat: 20g fat (9g saturated fat)
- Sodium: 847mg sodium

291. Pasta Lamb Skillet

Serving: 8 servings. | Prep: 15mins | Cook: 0mins | Ready in:

Ingredients

- 1 package (8 ounces) small pasta
- 12 ounces ground lamb
- 1 cup chopped onion
- 2 garlic cloves, minced
- 1 tablespoon olive oil
- 1 medium zucchini, quartered and thinly sliced (1-1/4 cups)
- 1 can (14-1/2 ounces) diced tomatoes, undrained
- 1 cup sliced fresh mushrooms
- 3 tablespoons minced fresh basil or 1 tablespoon dried basil
- 1/2 teaspoon pepper
- 1/4 to 1/2 teaspoon seasoned salt
- 1/4 cup sliced ripe olives

Direction

- Follow package directions to cook pasta. Cook garlic, onion and lamb in oil in a big skillet on medium heat till veggies are tender and meat isn't pink anymore; drain. Put aside; keep warm.
- Mix seasoned salt, pepper, basil, mushrooms, tomatoes and zucchini in same skillet; cover. Cook for 5 minutes on medium heat till veggies are tender. Drain the pasta. Add olives, lamb mixture and pasta to skillet and heat through.

Nutrition Information

- Calories: 228 calories
- Protein: 12g protein.
- Total Fat: 9g fat (3g saturated fat)
- Sodium: 176mg sodium
- Fiber: 3g fiber)
- Total Carbohydrate: 27g carbohydrate (4g sugars
- Cholesterol: 28mg cholesterol

292. Plum Glazed Lamb

Serving: 6 servings. | Prep: 5mins | Cook: 01hours45mins | Ready in:

Ingredients

- 1 bone-in leg of lamb (4 to 5 pounds)
- Salt and pepper to taste
- 2 cans (15 ounces each) plums, pitted
- 2 garlic cloves
- 1/4 cup lemon juice
- 2 tablespoons reduced-sodium soy sauce

- 2 teaspoons Worcestershire sauce
- 1 teaspoon dried basil

Direction

- Preheat an oven to 325°. Put lamb onto rack, fat side up, in shallow baking pan; season with pepper and salt. Bake for 1 3/4-2 1/4 hours, uncovered, till meat gets desired doneness; 170° for well-done, 160° for medium and 145° for medium-rare on a thermometer.
- Meanwhile, drain the plums; save 1/2 cup syrup. Cover and process basil, Worcestershire sauce, soy sauce, lemon juice, garlic, reserved syrup and plums till smooth in a food processor; put 1/2 plum sauce aside.
- Baste the lamb every 15 minutes through the final hour of roasting. Simmer reserved sauce for 5 minutes in a small saucepan; serve with meat.

Nutrition Information

- Calories: 338 calories
- Fiber: 2g fiber)
- Total Carbohydrate: 23g carbohydrate (18g sugars
- Cholesterol: 137mg cholesterol
- Protein: 39g protein.
- Total Fat: 10g fat (4g saturated fat)
- Sodium: 283mg sodium

293. Rack Of Lamb

Serving: 4 servings | Prep: 15mins | Cook: |Ready in:

Ingredients

- 1 rack of lamb (2 lb.)
- 1 cup A.1. Garlic & Herb Marinade

Direction

- Arrange lamb rack in a shallow dish, meat side down. Stream marinade over lamb. Allow lamb to marinate in the fridge, flipping every 1 1/2 hours.
- Turn oven to 375°F to preheat. Take lamb out of the marinade; dispose used marinade. Arrange meat in a shallow roasting pan.
- Bake lamb in the preheated oven until its internal temperature reaches 160°F for 30 to 45 minutes. Take out of the oven; allow to stand, covered, for 15 minutes before serving.

Nutrition Information

- Calories: 220
- Total Carbohydrate: 8 g
- Protein: 21 g
- Total Fat: 11 g
- Sodium: 620 mg
- Sugar: 4 g
- Cholesterol: 70 mg
- Saturated Fat: 4 g
- Fiber: 1 g

294. Rack Of Lamb With Figs

Serving: 6-8 servings. | Prep: 30mins | Cook: 45mins | Ready in:

Ingredients

- 2 racks of lamb (2 pounds each)
- 1 teaspoon salt, divided
- 1 cup water
- 1 small onion, finely chopped
- 1 tablespoon canola oil
- 1 garlic clove, minced
- 2 tablespoons cornstarch
- 1 cup port wine or 1/2 cup grape juice plus 1/2 cup reduced-sodium beef broth
- 10 dried figs, halved
- 1/4 teaspoon pepper
- 1/2 cup coarsely chopped walnuts, toasted

Direction

- Use 1/2 tsp. of salt to rub lamb. On a rack set in a roasting pan coated with grease, arrange lamb with meat side facing up. Bake at 375 degrees without a cover until reaching desired doneness (for medium-rare, a thermometer should register 145 degrees; medium, 160 degrees and well-done, 170 degrees), about 45 to 60 minutes.
- Transfer to a serving platter and use foil to cover loosely. Put 1 cup of water into the roasting pan, then stir to loosen any browned bits from pan. Strain the mixture with a fine sieve, then put drippings aside.
- Sauté onion in a small saucepan with oil until soft. Put in garlic and cook for 1 minute more. Stir in cornstarch until combined, then put in leftover salt, pepper, figs, drippings and wine gradually. Bring the mixture to a boil. Lower heat to moderately low and cook without a cover for 10 minutes, until sauce is thickened and figs are soft, while stirring sometimes.
- Sprinkle walnuts over lamand serve together with fig sauce.

Nutrition Information

- Calories: 363 calories
- Sodium: 362mg sodium
- Fiber: 3g fiber)
- Total Carbohydrate: 23g carbohydrate (14g sugars
- Cholesterol: 66mg cholesterol
- Protein: 23g protein.
- Total Fat: 16g fat (4g saturated fat)

295. Rack Of Lamb With Fresh Herbs

Serving: 4 servings. | Prep: 15mins | Cook: 30mins | Ready in:

Ingredients

- 1 tablespoon coarsely chopped fresh parsley or 1 teaspoon dried parsley flakes
- 1 tablespoon olive oil
- 2 garlic cloves, minced
- 1 teaspoon minced fresh rosemary or 1/4 teaspoon dried rosemary, crushed
- 1 teaspoon minced fresh thyme or 1/4 teaspoon dried thyme
- 1/4 teaspoon salt
- 1/4 teaspoon Montreal steak seasoning
- 1/4 teaspoon pepper
- 2 frenched racks of lamb (1-1/2 pounds each)
- 1/4 cup pomegranate seeds

Direction

- Set the oven to 375° and start preheating. Mix the first 8 ingredients in a small bowl. On a rack in a shallow roasting pan, put lamb; and rub the lamb with herb mixture.
- Bake until meat reaches the doneness as desired, about 30-40 minutes (for those who like well-done meat, a thermometer should read 170°; for medium, 160°; for medium-rare, 145°). Allow to sit 5 minutes before cutting. Serve with pomegranate seeds.

Nutrition Information

- Calories:
- Protein:
- Total Fat:
- Sodium:
- Fiber:
- Total Carbohydrate:
- Cholesterol:

296. Roast Lamb With Plum Sauce

Serving: 11 servings. | Prep: 30mins | Cook: 02hours30mins | Ready in:

Ingredients

- 1 leg of lamb (5 to 6 pounds)
- 3 garlic cloves, slivered
- 1/2 cup thinly sliced green onions
- 1/4 cup butter
- 1 jar (12 ounces) plum jam
- 1/2 cup chili sauce
- 1/4 cup white grape juice
- 1 tablespoon lemon juice
- 1/2 teaspoon ground allspice
- 1 tablespoon dried parsley flakes

Direction

- Remove thin fat covering from roast. In meat, make slits; insert a garlic sliver into each. Put onto a rack in big roasting pan; bake for 1 1/2 hours at 325°, uncovered.
- Meanwhile, to make plum sauce, sauté onions in butter till tender in a medium saucepan. Add allspice, lemon juice, grape juice, chili sauce and jam; boil, occasionally mixing. Simmer for 10 minutes, uncovered.
- Use sauce to baste roast; bake for 1 hour, occasionally basting with plum sauce, till meat gets desired doneness (170° for well-done, 160° for medium on a thermometer). Boil leftover sauce; mix in parsley. Stand roast for 10-15 minutes then carve; serve roast with leftover sauce.

Nutrition Information

- Calories: 300 calories
- Total Carbohydrate: 25g carbohydrate (22g sugars
- Cholesterol: 104mg cholesterol
- Protein: 26g protein.
- Total Fat: 11g fat (5g saturated fat)
- Sodium: 253mg sodium
- Fiber: 0 fiber)

297. Roast Leg Of Lamb

Serving: 12 | Prep: 15mins | Cook: 1hours45mins | Ready in:

Ingredients

- 4 cloves garlic, sliced
- 2 tablespoons fresh rosemary
- salt to taste
- ground black pepper to taste
- 5 pounds leg of lamb

Direction

- Set oven to 350°F (175°C) to preheat.
- Make slits every 3 to 4 inches over top of the lamb's leg, deep enough to push slices of garlic down into the meat. Liberally sprinkle pepper and salt over top of lamb to season; arrange several fresh rosemary sprigs over top and bottom of the lamb. Position lamb on a roasting pan.
- Roast lamb for about 1-3/4 to 2 hours in preheated oven until desired doneness is reached. Do not overcook the lamb. Keep the lamb meat slightly pink for the best flavor. Allow meat to stand for at least 10 minutes before cutting to serve.

Nutrition Information

- Calories: 382 calories;
- Cholesterol: 136
- Protein: 35.8
- Total Fat: 25.3
- Sodium: 136
- Total Carbohydrate: 0.4

298. Roast Leg Of Lamb With Rosemary

Serving: 6 | Prep: 15mins | Cook: 1hours20mins | Ready in:

Ingredients

- 1/4 cup honey
- 2 tablespoons prepared Dijon-style mustard
- 2 tablespoons chopped fresh rosemary
- 1 teaspoon freshly ground black pepper
- 1 teaspoon lemon zest
- 3 cloves garlic, minced
- 5 pounds whole leg of lamb
- 1 teaspoon coarse sea salt

Direction

- Mix garlic, lemon zest, ground black pepper, rosemary, mustard and honey well in a small bowl; apply to lamb. Cover; marinate overnight in the fridge.
- Preheat an oven to 230°C/450°F.
- Put lamb onto a rack in a roasting pan; sprinkle salt to taste.
- Bake for 20 minutes at 230°C/450°F; lower heat to 200°C/400°F. Roast to get medium-rare for 55-60 minutes; internal temperature should be at least 63°C/145°F using a meat thermometer. Rest roast for 10 minutes; carve.

Nutrition Information

- Calories: 922 calories;
- Total Fat: 64.6
- Sodium: 631
- Total Carbohydrate: 13.6
- Cholesterol: 261
- Protein: 67.9

---

299. Roast Rack Of Lamb With Herb Sauce

Serving: 4 servings (1-3/4 cups sauce). | Prep: 35mins | Cook: 35mins | Ready in:

Ingredients

- 1/4 cup minced fresh rosemary
- 1-1/2 teaspoons coarsely ground pepper
- 1-1/2 teaspoons salt
- 2 racks of lamb (1-1/2 pounds each)
- 1 tablespoon olive oil
- SAUCE:
- 3/4 cup fresh parsley leaves
- 2/3 cup fresh basil leaves
- 1/3 cup each fresh cilantro leaves, mint leaves, oregano leaves and thyme leaves
- 1/3 cup coarsely chopped fresh chives
- 1/3 cup chopped shallots
- 2 garlic cloves, crushed
- 3 tablespoons grated lemon peel
- 1/2 cup lemon juice
- 2 tablespoons Dijon mustard
- 3/4 teaspoon salt
- 1/2 teaspoon pepper
- 1/3 cup olive oil

Direction

- Mix salt, pepper and rosemary; rub on lamb. Refrigerate for 8 hours or overnight, covered.
- Preheat an oven to 375°. Put lamb, fat side up, into a shallow roasting pan; drizzle with oil.
- Roast for 35-45 minutes till meat gets desired doneness (170°: well-done, 160°: medium, 145°: medium-rare on a thermometer). Take off lamb from oven; use foil to tent. Let sit for 10 minutes then serve.
- Meanwhile, pulse garlic, shallots and herbs till herbs are chopped in a food processor. Add pepper, salt, mustard, lemon juice and lemon peel; process till blended. In a steady stream, gradually add oil while processing; serve lamb with sauce.

Nutrition Information

- Calories:
- Protein:
- Total Fat:
- Sodium:
- Fiber:
- Total Carbohydrate:
- Cholesterol:

300. Rosemary Leg Of Lamb

Serving: 10-12 servings. | Prep: 10mins | Cook: 01hours30mins | Ready in:

Ingredients

- 4 garlic cloves, minced
- 1 to 2 tablespoons minced fresh rosemary or 1 teaspoon dried rosemary, crushed
- 1 teaspoon salt
- 1/2 teaspoon pepper
- 1 bone-in leg of lamb (7 to 9 pounds), trimmed
- 1 teaspoon cornstarch
- 1/4 cup beef broth

Direction

- Preheat an oven to 350°. Mix pepper, salt, rosemary and garlic in a small bowl; rub on meat. Put onto rack in the big roasting pan.
- Bake for 1 1/2-2 1/2 hours, uncovered, till meat gets desired doneness; 170° well done, 160° medium and 145° for medium rare on a thermometer. Before slicing, stand for 10 minutes.
- Meanwhile, put loosened brown bits and pan drippings in a small saucepan and skim fat. Mix broth and cornstarch till smooth; whisk into drippings. Boil; mix and cook till thick for 1-2 minutes; serve with lamb.

Nutrition Information

- Calories: 220 calories
- Total Fat: 8g fat (4g saturated fat)
- Sodium: 268mg sodium
- Fiber: 0 fiber)
- Total Carbohydrate: 1g carbohydrate (0 sugars
- Cholesterol: 119mg cholesterol
- Protein: 33g protein.

301. Rosemary Roasted Lamb

Serving: 10 servings. | Prep: 10mins | Cook: 02hours05mins | Ready in:

Ingredients

- 1/2 cup olive oil
- 3 garlic cloves, minced
- 1 tablespoon kosher salt
- 1 tablespoon minced fresh rosemary
- 1 leg of lamb (7 to 9 pounds)

Direction

- Preheat the oven to 425 degrees. Mix rosemary, oil, salt, and garlic in a small bowl; massage over the lamb then cover. Chill the lamb overnight. Arrange the lamb on a rack in a shallow roasting pan with the fat-side up.
- Bake for 20 minutes without cover. Lower heat to 350 degrees; bake for another 1 3/4-2 1/4 hours or until the preferred doneness. Thermometer should register 170 degrees for well-done, 160 degrees for medium, and 145 degrees for medium-rare; use the pan juices to baste the lamb occasionally. Let it sit for 15 minutes then slice.

Nutrition Information

- Calories: 357 calories
- Protein: 40g protein.
- Total Fat: 21g fat (6g saturated fat)
- Sodium: 629mg sodium
- Fiber: 0 fiber)
- Total Carbohydrate: 0 carbohydrate (0 sugars
- Cholesterol: 143mg cholesterol

302. Rosemary Seasoned Lamb

Serving: 12 servings. | Prep: 10mins | Cook: 01hours45mins | Ready in:

Ingredients

- 2 tablespoons chopped fresh rosemary
- 1 teaspoon coarsely ground pepper
- 3/4 teaspoon salt
- 1/2 teaspoon ground mustard
- 1/2 teaspoon dried oregano
- 1/2 teaspoon garlic powder
- 1/4 teaspoon white pepper
- 1/8 teaspoon cayenne pepper
- 1 boneless leg of lamb (about 4 pounds)

Direction

- Mix seasonings in a spice mill/blender with cover till coarsely ground. Untie leg of lamb; unroll. On both sides of the meat, rub spice blend. Reroll; tie using kitchen string.
- In shallow a roasting pan, put onto a rack; bake without cover for 1 3/4-2 1/4 hours at 350° till meat gets desired doneness (170° for well-done, 160° for medium and 145° for medium-rare on a thermometer). Stand for 10-15 minutes; slice.

Nutrition Information

- Calories: 181 calories
- Total Carbohydrate: 0 carbohydrate (0 sugars
- Cholesterol: 81mg cholesterol
- Protein: 25g protein. Diabetic Exchanges: 3 lean meat.
- Total Fat: 8g fat (3g saturated fat)
- Sodium: 209mg sodium
- Fiber: 0 fiber)

303. Rosemary Rubbed Lamb Chops

Serving: 4-6 servings. | Prep: 30mins | Cook: 15mins | Ready in:

Ingredients

- 2 frenched racks of lamb (1-1/2 pounds each)
- 2 tablespoons olive oil
- 2 tablespoons Dijon mustard
- 4 garlic cloves, minced
- 1 tablespoon minced fresh rosemary
- 1 tablespoon minced fresh marjoram
- 1 teaspoon soy sauce
- 1/2 teaspoon salt
- 1/4 teaspoon pepper

Direction

- Slice each rack of lamb into individual chops using a sharp knife. Mix the remaining ingredients in a small bowl and then massage onto each side of the chops; transfer onto a rack in a shallow roasting pan. Cover the pan and chill for two hours.
- Bake while uncovered for 14 to 16 minutes at 400° or until the meat reaches the doneness desired (for medium-rare, a thermometer should indicate 145°; well-done, 170°; medium, 160°).

Nutrition Information

- Calories: 139 calories
- Total Carbohydrate: 2g carbohydrate (0 sugars
- Cholesterol: 33mg cholesterol
- Protein: 10g protein.
- Total Fat: 10g fat (2g saturated fat)
- Sodium: 405mg sodium
- Fiber: 0 fiber)

304. Sauerbraten Lamb Shanks

Serving: 6 servings (about 6 cups gravy). | Prep: 60mins | Cook: 02hours00mins | Ready in:

Ingredients

- 7-1/2 cups water
- 2 cups white vinegar
- 1 large onion, sliced

- 1 medium lemon, sliced
- 1/2 cup sugar
- 3 bay leaves
- 1-1/2 teaspoons whole peppercorns
- 5 whole allspice
- LAMB SHANKS:
- 6 lamb shanks (20 ounces each)
- 3 garlic cloves, sliced
- 6 tablespoons all-purpose flour
- 1/3 cup plus 2 tablespoons canola oil, divided
- 2 large onions, thinly sliced
- 3 medium carrots, sliced
- 9 gingersnap cookies, crushed
- 1 tablespoon beef bouillon granules
- 6 tablespoons cornstarch
- 1/3 cup cold water

Direction

- Boil initial 8 ingredients in a Dutch oven. Lower heat; simmer for 2 minutes, uncovered. Fully cool. Strain 1/2 marinade and cover; refrigerate.
- In the lamb shanks, cut slits and put into slits with slices of garlic. In a big shallow nonmetallic bowl, arrange lamb shanks and put in leftover marinade. Place a cover and chill overnight.
- Drain marinade from lamb; discard. In a shallow bowl, put flour; coat lamb shanks in flour. Brown shanks in batches in 1/3 cup oil on all sides in a stockpot. Remove; put aside.
- Sauté onions in leftover oil in the same pan; add reserved marinade. Put shanks in pan; boil. Lower heat; cover. Simmer for 1 3/4 hours then add carrots; boil. Lower heat; cover. Simmer till carrots are tender for 15-20 minutes.
- Put shanks on a cutting board. From cooking juices, skim fat; mix in bouillon and cookie crumbs. Mix water and cornstarch till smooth in a small bowl; mix into juices slowly. Boil; mix and cook till thick for 1-2 minutes. Put meat in gravy; heat through.

Nutrition Information

- Calories: 791 calories
- Total Carbohydrate: 42g carbohydrate (20g sugars
- Cholesterol: 199mg cholesterol
- Protein: 55g protein.
- Total Fat: 44g fat (12g saturated fat)
- Sodium: 623mg sodium
- Fiber: 3g fiber)

305. Skillet Lamb Chops

Serving: 2 servings. | Prep: 5mins | Cook: 40mins | Ready in:

Ingredients

- 2 lamb shoulder blade chops (8 ounces each)
- 2 tablespoons canola oil
- 1/2 cup warm water
- 1 teaspoon lemon juice
- 1 teaspoon dried minced onion
- 1/2 teaspoon dried oregano
- 1/4 teaspoon salt
- 1/8 teaspoon pepper

Direction

- Brown the lamb chops in oil in a big skillet. Add leftover ingredients; boil. Lower heat; cover. Simmer till meat attains the desired doneness (for well-done 170° on a thermometer, 160° for medium and 145° for medium rare) for 30-35 minutes.

Nutrition Information

- Calories: 288 calories
- Total Carbohydrate: 1g carbohydrate (0 sugars
- Cholesterol: 56mg cholesterol
- Protein: 14g protein.
- Total Fat: 25g fat (7g saturated fat)
- Sodium: 332mg sodium
- Fiber: 0 fiber)

306. Slow Cook Lamb Chops

Serving: 4 servings. | Prep: 10mins | Cook: 05hours30mins | Ready in:

Ingredients

- 4 bacon strips
- 4 lamb shoulder blade chops, trimmed
- 2-1/4 cups thinly sliced peeled potatoes
- 1 cup thinly sliced carrots
- 1/2 teaspoon dried rosemary, crushed
- 1/4 teaspoon garlic powder
- 1/4 teaspoon salt
- 1/4 teaspoon pepper
- 1/4 cup chopped onion
- 2 garlic cloves, minced
- 1 can (10-3/4 ounces) condensed cream of mushroom soup, undiluted
- 1/3 cup 2% milk
- 1 jar (4-1/2 ounces) sliced mushrooms, drained

Direction

- Bind the lamb chops in bacon then secure using toothpicks; put in a 3-quart slow cooker. Cook for 1 1/2 hours on High with cover.
- Take the chops out then remove the bacon and toothpicks; drain the liquid in the cooker. Put carrot and potatoes then place the lamb chops on top. Sprinkle garlic, rosemary, onion, garlic powder, pepper, and salt.
- Mix milk and soup in a small bowl; put in mushrooms. Pour the mixture on top of the chops; cover. Cook for 4-6 hours on Low until the veggies and meat are tender.

Nutrition Information

- Calories:
- Sodium:
- Fiber:
- Total Carbohydrate:
- Cholesterol:
- Protein:
- Total Fat:

307. Slow Cooked Lamb Chops

Serving: 4 servings. | Prep: 10mins | Cook: 04hours00mins | Ready in:

Ingredients

- 1 medium onion, sliced
- 1 teaspoon dried oregano
- 1/2 teaspoon dried thyme
- 1/2 teaspoon garlic powder
- 1/4 teaspoon salt
- 1/8 teaspoon pepper
- 8 lamb loin chops (about 1-3/4 pounds)
- 2 garlic cloves, minced

Direction

- Put onion into a 3-quart slow cooker. Mix pepper, salt, garlic powder, thyme, and oregano together; rub lamb chops with the spice mixture. Arrange lamb chops over onion. Place garlic atop chops. Cook, covered, for 4 to 6 hours on low setting until meat is tender.

Nutrition Information

- Calories: 201 calories
- Total Carbohydrate: 5g carbohydrate (2g sugars
- Cholesterol: 79mg cholesterol
- Protein: 26g protein.
- Total Fat: 8g fat (3g saturated fat)
- Sodium: 219mg sodium
- Fiber: 1g fiber)

308. Spice Rubbed Lamb Chops

Serving: 2 servings. | Prep: 15mins | Cook: 5mins | Ready in:

Ingredients

- 2 teaspoons lemon juice
- 2 teaspoons Worcestershire sauce
- 1-1/2 teaspoons pepper
- 1-1/4 teaspoons ground cumin
- 1-1/4 teaspoons curry powder
- 1 garlic clove, minced
- 1/2 teaspoon sea salt
- 1/2 teaspoon onion powder
- 1/2 teaspoon crushed red pepper flakes
- 4 lamb rib chops
- 1 tablespoon olive oil

Direction

- Mix initial 9 ingredients; spread on chops. Refrigerate overnight, with cover.
- Preheat an oven to 450°. Heat oil in an oven-safe skillet on medium high heat; brown the chops for 2 minutes on each side. Put into oven; roast for 3-4 minutes or to desired doneness (a thermometer reads 160 degrees for medium and 145 degrees for medium-rare.

Nutrition Information

- Calories: 290 calories
- Cholesterol: 90mg cholesterol
- Protein: 29g protein. Diabetic Exchanges: 4 lean meat
- Total Fat: 17g fat (4g saturated fat)
- Sodium: 620mg sodium
- Fiber: 2g fiber)
- Total Carbohydrate: 5g carbohydrate (1g sugars

309. Spiced Lamb Stew With Apricots

Serving: 5 servings. | Prep: 30mins | Cook: 05hours00mins | Ready in:

Ingredients

- 2 pounds lamb stew meat, cut into 3/4-inch cubes
- 3 tablespoons butter
- 1-1/2 cups chopped sweet onion
- 3/4 cup dried apricots
- 1/2 cup orange juice
- 1/2 cup chicken broth
- 2 teaspoons paprika
- 2 teaspoons ground allspice
- 2 teaspoons ground cinnamon
- 1-1/2 teaspoons salt
- 1 teaspoon ground cardamom
- Hot cooked couscous
- Chopped dried apricots, optional

Direction

- Set a large frying pan, put lamb and brown it in butter in batches. Use a slotted spoon to move it to a 3-qt. slow cooker. In exactly the same frying pan, sauté onion in drippings till tender. Mix in seasonings, broth, orange juice and apricots; drizzle over lamb.
- Cook on high heat with a cover for 5-6 hours or till meat is tender. Serve with couscous. Drizzle chopped apricots on top if desired.

Nutrition Information

- Calories: 404 calories
- Protein: 38g protein.
- Total Fat: 17g fat (8g saturated fat)
- Sodium: 975mg sodium
- Fiber: 5g fiber)
- Total Carbohydrate: 24g carbohydrate (15g sugars
- Cholesterol: 136mg cholesterol

310. Spinach Stuffed Lamb

Serving: 8-10 servings. | Prep: 30mins | Cook: 01hours15mins | Ready in:

Ingredients

- 3 tablespoons minced garlic
- 1 tablespoon olive oil
- 2 packages (10 ounces each) frozen chopped spinach, thawed and squeezed dry
- 2 logs (4 ounces each) fresh goat cheese, crumbled
- 3/4 teaspoon salt, divided
- 1/4 teaspoon pepper, divided
- 1 boneless butterflied leg of lamb (4 to 5 pounds), trimmed
- 3 garlic cloves, slivered
- 3 tablespoons minced fresh rosemary

Direction

- Sauté minced garlic for 2-3 minutes in oil in a small skillet. Take off heat; mix in 1/8 tsp. pepper, 1/2 tsp. salt, cheese and spinach.
- Untie lamb. So it lies flat, open; flatten to 3/4-in. thick. Spread meat within 1-in. of edges with spinach mixture. Roll up lamb beginning at 1 short side. Tuck ends in; at 2-in. intervals, tie with kitchen string. Create slits on outside of meat with a sharp knife; insert garlic slivers. Sprinkle leftover pepper and salt and rosemary.
- Put onto rack in shallow roasting pan, seam side down; cover. Bake for 1 hour at 425°. Uncover; bake, basting with pan juices occasionally, till thermometer reads 160° and browned for 15-30 minutes. Stand before slicing for 10-15 minutes.

Nutrition Information

- Calories: 343 calories
- Total Fat: 18g fat (9g saturated fat)
- Sodium: 404mg sodium
- Fiber: 1g fiber)
- Total Carbohydrate: 3g carbohydrate (1g sugars
- Cholesterol: 128mg cholesterol
- Protein: 40g protein.

311. Spring Lamb Supper

Serving: 4 servings. | Prep: 20mins | Cook: 0mins | Ready in:

Ingredients

- 1 pound boneless lamb, cut into cubes
- 2 teaspoons olive oil
- 2 cups thinly sliced yellow summer squash
- 1/2 pound fresh mushrooms, sliced
- 2 medium tomatoes, seeded and chopped
- 1/2 cup sliced green onions
- 3 cups cooked brown rice
- 1 teaspoon salt
- 1/2 teaspoon garlic powder
- 1/2 teaspoon pepper
- 1/2 teaspoon dried rosemary, crushed

Direction

- Sauté lamb in a large skillet with oil till not pink anymore; using a slotted spoon, take lamb out of the skillet. In the same skillet, stir-fry onions, tomatoes, mushrooms and squash till tender, or for 2-3 minutes. Turn the lamb back to the skillet. Mix in seasonings and rice; cook while stirring till heated through.

Nutrition Information

- Calories: 376 calories
- Sodium: 659mg sodium
- Fiber: 6g fiber)
- Total Carbohydrate: 44g carbohydrate (5g sugars
- Cholesterol: 63mg cholesterol
- Protein: 27g protein.

- Total Fat: 11g fat (3g saturated fat)

312. Squash And Lentil Lamb Stew

Serving: 8 servings (2-1/2 quarts). | Prep: 30mins | Cook: 06hours00mins |Ready in:

Ingredients

- 1 can (13.66 ounces) coconut milk
- 1/2 cup creamy peanut butter
- 2 tablespoons red curry paste
- 1 tablespoon hoisin sauce
- 1 teaspoon salt
- 1/2 teaspoon pepper
- 1 can (14-1/2 ounces) chicken broth
- 3 teaspoons olive oil, divided
- 1 pound lamb or beef stew meat (1 to 1-1/2 inches)
- 2 small onions, chopped
- 1 tablespoon minced fresh gingerroot
- 3 garlic cloves, minced
- 1 cup dried brown lentils, rinsed
- 4 cups cubed peeled butternut squash (about 1 pound)
- 2 cups chopped fresh spinach
- 1/4 cup minced fresh cilantro
- 1/4 cup lime juice

Direction

- Blend together the first 7 ingredients in a 5- or 6-qt. slow cooker. Place a large skillet on medium heat and heat 2 teaspoons of oil; cook lamb in batches until brown. Put into the slow cooker.
- In the same skillet on medium heat, sauté onions for 4-5 minutes in the remaining oil until tender. Include in garlic and ginger; cook while stirring for 1 minute. Put into the slow cooker. Mix in squash and lentils. Cook on low heat with a cover for 6-8 hours, until lentils and meat are tender. Mix in spinach until wilted. Mix in lime juice and cilantro. For freezing option, place cooled stew in freezer containers. For use, place in refrigerator overnight to partially unfreeze. In a saucepan, heat through while occasionally stirring and including in a little broth if needed.

Nutrition Information

- Calories: 411 calories
- Protein: 23g protein.
- Total Fat: 21g fat (11g saturated fat)
- Sodium: 777mg sodium
- Fiber: 6g fiber)
- Total Carbohydrate: 34g carbohydrate (7g sugars
- Cholesterol: 38mg cholesterol

313. Tangy Lamb Tagine

Serving: 8 servings. | Prep: 40mins | Cook: 08hours00mins |Ready in:

Ingredients

- 3 pounds lamb stew meat, cut into 1-1/2-inch cubes
- 1 teaspoon salt
- 1 teaspoon pepper
- 4 tablespoons olive oil, divided
- 6 medium carrots, sliced
- 2 medium onions, chopped
- 6 garlic cloves, minced
- 2 teaspoons grated lemon zest
- 1/4 cup lemon juice
- 1 tablespoon minced fresh gingerroot
- 1-1/2 teaspoons ground cinnamon
- 1-1/2 teaspoons ground cumin
- 1-1/2 teaspoons paprika
- 2-1/2 cups reduced-sodium chicken broth
- 1/4 cup sweet vermouth
- 1/4 cup honey
- 1/2 cup pitted dates, chopped
- 1/2 cup sliced almonds, toasted

Direction

- Sprinkle pepper and salt over the lamb. Brown meat in batches in a Dutch oven with 2 tablespoons of oil. Move the meat to a 4 or 5-quart slow cooker using a slotted spoon.
- Sauté lemon zest, carrots, garlic, and onion in a Dutch oven with the remaining oil until tender-crisp. Put in paprika, lemon juice, cumin, cinnamon, and ginger; cook and stir for another 2 minutes. Move to the slow cooker.
- Mix in date, broth, honey, and vermouth; cover. Cook for 8-10 hours on low until the meat is tender. Scatter top with almonds.

Nutrition Information

- Calories: 440 calories
- Protein: 38g protein.
- Total Fat: 19g fat (4g saturated fat)
- Sodium: 620mg sodium
- Fiber: 4g fiber)
- Total Carbohydrate: 28g carbohydrate (21g sugars
- Cholesterol: 111mg cholesterol

314. Tender Lamb With Mint Salsa

Serving: 4 servings. | Prep: 15mins | Cook: 20mins | Ready in:

Ingredients

- 1 tablespoon plus 2 teaspoons olive oil
- 2 garlic cloves, minced
- 1 teaspoon each dried basil, thyme and rosemary, crushed
- 1/2 teaspoon salt
- 1/4 teaspoon pepper
- 2 racks of lamb (1 to 1-1/2 pounds each)
- SALSA:
- 1 cup minced fresh mint
- 1 small cucumber, peeled, seeded and chopped
- 1/2 cup seeded chopped tomato
- 1/3 cup finely chopped onion
- 1/3 cup chopped sweet yellow pepper
- 1 jalapeno pepper, seeded and chopped
- 3 tablespoons lemon juice
- 2 tablespoons sugar
- 2 garlic cloves, minced
- 3/4 teaspoon ground ginger
- 1/4 teaspoon salt

Direction

- Mix seasonings, garlic and oil in a small bowl. Massage atop lamb. Put in a roasting pan, then cover and chill for one hour. Mix the salsa ingredients in a bowl, cover and then chill until serving.
- Bake the lamb while uncovered for 30 to 35 minutes at 375° or until the meat reaches the doneness desired (for medium-rare, the internal temperature from the thermometer should be 145°; well-done, 170°; medium, 160°). Take out from oven and loosely cover with foil. Leave to stand for 5 to 10 minutes prior to cutting. Serve together with salsa.

Nutrition Information

- Calories: 283 calories
- Protein: 21g protein.
- Total Fat: 16g fat (4g saturated fat)
- Sodium: 510mg sodium
- Fiber: 2g fiber)
- Total Carbohydrate: 14g carbohydrate (8g sugars
- Cholesterol: 66mg cholesterol

315. Traditional Lamb Stew

Serving: 4 servings. | Prep: 10mins | Cook: 60mins | Ready in:

Ingredients

- 1-1/2 pounds lamb stew meat
- 2 tablespoons olive oil, divided
- 3 large onions, quartered
- 3 medium carrots, cut into 1-inch pieces
- 4 small potatoes, peeled and cubed
- 1 can (14-1/2 ounces) beef broth
- 1 teaspoon salt
- 1/4 teaspoon pepper
- 1 tablespoon butter
- 1 tablespoon all-purpose flour
- 1-1/2 teaspoons minced fresh parsley
- 1-1/2 teaspoons minced chives
- 1/2 teaspoon minced fresh thyme

Direction

- Brown meat in 1 tbsp. oil till meat isn't pink in a Dutch oven on medium heat. Use a slotted spoon to remove; put aside. Add leftover oil, carrots and onions to pan; cook, occasionally mixing, till onions are tender for 5 minutes. Add lamb, pepper, broth, salt and potatoes; boil.
- Take off heat; cover. Bake at 350° till veggies and meat are tender for 50-60 minutes.
- Remove veggies and meat into a big bowl with a slotted spoon; put aside. Keep warm. Put pan juices into separate bowl; put aside.
- Melt butter on medium heat in a Dutch oven; mix in flour till smooth. Whisk in pan juices slowly; boil. Mix and cook till thick for 2 minutes. Mix in veggies, meat, thyme, chives and parsley; heat through.

Nutrition Information

- Calories:
- Fiber:
- Total Carbohydrate:
- Cholesterol:
- Protein:
- Total Fat:
- Sodium:

316. Vegetable Stew

Serving: about 8-10 servings (3-1/2 quarts). | Prep: 5mins | Cook: 01hours45mins | Ready in:

Ingredients

- 1-1/2 pounds lean boneless lamb or pork, cut into 1-inch cubes
- 2 tablespoons vegetable oil
- 1 medium onion, chopped
- 2 medium potatoes, peeled and cubed
- 1 medium leek, sliced
- 6 cups beef broth
- 2 tablespoons tomato paste
- 1 teaspoon salt
- 1/2 teaspoon dried thyme
- 1/4 teaspoon pepper
- 4 cups chopped cabbage
- 2 to 3 cups cauliflower florets
- 3 carrots, sliced
- 1 celery rib, sliced
- 1 package (9 ounces) frozen cut green beans, thawed
- Minced fresh parsley
- Cornstarch and water, optional

Direction

- Brown meat in oil on medium high heat in a Dutch oven. Add onion. Cook till tender; drain. Add next 7 ingredients; cover. Simmer for 1 hour till meat is tender. Add parsley, beans, celery, carrots, cauliflower and cabbage; cover. Simmer for 30 minutes till veggies are tender. Thicken with cornstarch dissolved in water if desired.

Nutrition Information

- Calories: 141 calories
- Sodium: 595mg sodium
- Fiber: 3g fiber
- Total Carbohydrate: 12g carbohydrate (4g sugars

- Cholesterol: 32mg cholesterol
- Protein: 12g protein.
- Total Fat: 5g fat (1g saturated fat)

317. West Virginia Shepherd's Pie

Serving: 6 servings. | Prep: 40mins | Cook: 30mins | Ready in:

Ingredients

- 4 medium potatoes, peeled and cubed
- 2 medium parsnips, peeled and cubed
- 3/4 cup evaporated milk
- 2 tablespoons butter
- 1 teaspoon salt
- 1 teaspoon pepper, divided
- 2 eggs
- 1 teaspoon dried mint
- 1 teaspoon dried rosemary, crushed
- 1 teaspoon Worcestershire sauce
- 1/4 teaspoon ground allspice
- 1 pound ground lamb
- 1/2 cup chopped onion
- 1/4 cup chopped celery
- 1 tablespoon olive oil
- 1/2 cup fresh peas

Direction

- In a big saucepan, put parsnips and potatoes, and add water to cover. Boil it. Lower the heat, put a cover on and cook until soft, about 15-20 minutes. Strain, mash the potato mixture. Add 1/2 teaspoon pepper, salt, butter, and milk; mash until blended.
- Mix the leftover pepper, allspice, Worcestershire sauce, rosemary, mint, and eggs together in a big bowl. Crumble over the mixture with lamb and stir thoroughly.
- Cook celery and onion with oil in a big frying pan over medium heat until soft. Add the lamb mixture, stir and cook until the lamb is not pink anymore; strain.
- In an 11x7-inch baking dish coated with cooking spray, put the lamb mixture; sprinkle peas over. Spread over the peas with the potato mixture. Bake without a cover at 375° until turning golden brown, about 30-35 minutes.

Nutrition Information

- Calories: 402 calories
- Sodium: 538mg sodium
- Fiber: 4g fiber)
- Total Carbohydrate: 35g carbohydrate (9g sugars
- Cholesterol: 140mg cholesterol
- Protein: 20g protein.
- Total Fat: 20g fat (9g saturated fat)

318. Wyoming Lamb Stew

Serving: 6 servings. | Prep: 30mins | Cook: 02hours00mins | Ready in:

Ingredients

- 5 bacon strips, diced
- 1/4 cup all-purpose flour
- 1 teaspoon salt
- 1/2 teaspoon pepper
- 6 lamb shanks (about 6 pounds)
- 1 can (28 ounces) diced tomatoes, undrained
- 1 can (14-1/2 ounces) beef broth
- 1 can (8 ounces) tomato sauce
- 2 cans (4 ounces each) mushroom stems and pieces, drained
- 2 medium onions, chopped
- 1 cup chopped celery
- 1/2 cup minced fresh parsley
- 2 tablespoons prepared horseradish
- 1 tablespoon cider vinegar
- 2 teaspoon Worcestershire sauce
- 1 garlic clove, minced

Direction

- Cook bacon over medium heat in a Dutch oven until crispy. Transfer bacon to paper towels to drain with a slotted spoon, saving drippings. Set bacon aside for garnish; chill in the fridge.
- Combine pepper, salt, and flour in a big resealable plastic bag; put in lamb shanks, one by one, and shake until well coated. Cook shanks in the reserve bacon drippings until all sides are browned; drain. Put in the rest of ingredients. Bring to a boil.
- Bake, covered, for 2 to 2.5 hours at 325° until meat is very tender; skim fat. Sprinkle top with the reserved bacon to garnish.

Nutrition Information

- Calories: 569 calories
- Protein: 49g protein.
- Total Fat: 31g fat (13g saturated fat)
- Sodium: 1423mg sodium
- Fiber: 5g fiber)
- Total Carbohydrate: 21g carbohydrate (9g sugars
- Cholesterol: 171mg cholesterol

319. Zesty Herbed Lamb Chops

Serving: 4 servings. | Prep: 15mins | Cook: 15mins | Ready in:

Ingredients

- 1/2 cup fresh mint leaves
- 1/4 cup minced fresh oregano
- 1/4 cup packed fresh parsley sprigs, stems removed
- 1/4 cup lemon juice
- 3 tablespoons water
- 6 garlic cloves
- 1 tablespoon olive oil
- 1/4 teaspoon salt
- Dash pepper
- LAMB CHOPS:
- 8 lamb loin chops (3 ounces each)
- 1/2 teaspoon salt
- 1/2 teaspoon pepper
- 1 tablespoon olive oil

Direction

- Blend the first nine ingredients in a food processor; pulse with a cover until blended. Put aside half of the sauce. Brush chops with remaining sauce; drizzle with pepper and salt.
- In a big greased skillet, cook each side of the chops with oil over medium heat for 7-10 minutes or until reaching desired doneness (a thermometer should indicate 145° for medium-rare; 160° for medium and 170° for well-done). Serve the dish with reserved mint sauce.

Nutrition Information

- Calories: 236 calories
- Protein: 22g protein.
- Total Fat: 14g fat (3g saturated fat)
- Sodium: 509mg sodium
- Fiber: 1g fiber)
- Total Carbohydrate: 5g carbohydrate (0 sugars
- Cholesterol: 68mg cholesterol

Chapter 8: Easter Lamb Recipes

***

320. Bacon Wrapped Leg Of Lamb With Red Wine Reduction

Serving: 6 | Prep: 20mins | Cook: 1hours40mins | Ready in:

Ingredients

- 1 (4 pound) leg of lamb
- 3 cloves garlic, slivered
- 2 tablespoons olive oil
- 1 tablespoon lemon juice
- 1 teaspoon minced fresh rosemary
- 6 slices bacon
- 1 small onion, minced
- 1/2 cup dry red wine
- 1 cup beef stock
- 1 teaspoon tomato paste
- salt and ground black pepper to taste

Direction

- Prepare the leg of lamb by trimming the thin membrane and excess fat, then place it in a roasting pan. Cut slits in meat and insert slivered garlic in the slits. In a bowl, pour the lemon juice, olive oil, and rosemary. Mix and brush mixture on the lamb. Place bacon slices on the meat, and for 30 minutes leave the meat at room temperature.
- Preheat the oven to 165°C (325°F).
- Roast the lamb for 1/2 an hour and when an instant-read thermometer poked in thickest location in leg, do not touch bone, registers 65°C (145°F) it is medium rare. Roast it for 1 1/2-1 3/4 hours when it reaches 70°C (160°F) it is medium. Move the lamb out of the oven and on a serving platter. Place an aluminum foil on top loosely, and let the meat rest.
- Remove the excess grease from the drippings in the pan by skimming. Heat the pan on medium heat. Add in onions; stir and sauté for 5 minutes until it turns translucent. Add in wine, stir it with drippings and scrape the food stuck to the bottom of the pan and dissolve. Add in the stock and boil, reduce to low heat. Add tomato paste, stir and simmer. Reduce the sauce to about 1 cup. Add salt and black pepper to season. Strain the sauce to make it smoother.

Nutrition Information

- Calories: 442 calories;
- Total Fat: 27.6
- Sodium: 324
- Total Carbohydrate: 3.2
- Cholesterol: 132
- Protein: 39

321. Baked Lamb Chops

Serving: 6 | Prep: 10mins | Cook: 45mins | Ready in:

Ingredients

- 3 eggs
- 3 teaspoons Worcestershire sauce
- 12 (5.5 ounce) lamb chops
- 2 cups dry bread crumbs

Direction

- Preheat the oven to 190°C (375°F).
- Mix the Worcestershire sauce with eggs in a medium bowl; mix well. Dip the lamb chop into the sauce, and dredge lightly into the bread crumbs. Place them in a baking dish of 9x13-inch.
- Bake for 20 minutes at 190°C (375°F), flip the chops over, then cook until reaching the desired doneness, about another 20 minutes.

Nutrition Information

- Calories: 738 calories;
- Total Fat: 45.2
- Sodium: 462
- Total Carbohydrate: 26.7
- Cholesterol: 270

- Protein: 52.4

322. Braised Lamb Shank With Vegetables

Serving: 7 | Prep: 20mins | Cook: 2hours |Ready in:

Ingredients

- 7 (1 pound) lamb shanks
- 2 tablespoons vegetable oil
- water to cover
- 1 1/2 pounds potatoes, peeled and diced
- 1 1/2 pounds carrots, peeled and diced
- 1 1/2 pounds onions, peeled and diced
- 1 ounce all-purpose flour
- 2 ounces butter, melted

Direction

- Heat a big saucepan with oil over medium high heat. Brown the shanks in oil for about 20 minutes. Fill with water enough to cover, adjust the heat to low and simmer for about an hour.
- Add the onions, carrots and potatoes. Let it simmer for about an hour. Combine the flour into melted butter in a small bowl to make a roux, and stir the mixture into simmering dish to make it thick.

Nutrition Information

- Calories: 695 calories;
- Protein: 57.8
- Total Fat: 33.5
- Sodium: 216
- Total Carbohydrate: 39.3
- Cholesterol: 196

323. Braised Lamb With Radishes And Mint

Serving: 4 | Prep: 10mins | Cook: 3hours33mins |Ready in:

Ingredients

- 1 tablespoon kosher salt
- 1 teaspoon black pepper
- 1 teaspoon paprika
- 1/4 teaspoon cayenne pepper
- 4 (10 ounce) lamb shoulder chops
- 1 tablespoon olive oil
- 1/3 cup sherry vinegar
- 2 tablespoons white sugar
- 4 oil-packed anchovy fillets
- 1 1/2 cups low-sodium chicken broth
- 2 teaspoons minced fresh rosemary
- 1/4 teaspoon ground cinnamon
- 2 bunches breakfast radishes, rinsed and trimmed
- 5 fresh mint leaves, finely sliced
- 1 tablespoon cold butter

Direction

- Preheat an oven to 135°C/275°F.
- Mix together cayenne pepper, paprika, pepper and salt. On a work surface, place lamb chops; press seasoning on both sides of the lamb chops.
- Heat oil in big ovenproof skillet on high heat; brown lamb well for 3-4 minutes per side on both sides. Take out chops from pan; lower the heat to low. Add anchovies, sugar and vinegar; mix and cook, breaking up anchovies. Turn the heat to medium; keep mixing for about 3 minutes till mixture reduces to syrup consistency. Mix in chicken broth; put heat on high. Add cinnamon and rosemary; simmer. Place browned lamb chops into the pan; add radishes among the chops then cover.
- In preheated oven, put skillet; slowly roast for 1 1/2 hours. Flip chops; keep roasting for another 1 1/2 hours till meat starts to separate from bone and just tender. Flip chops again.

- Put oven temperature on 220°C/425°F; uncover skillet. Roast for 15-20 minutes till meat is fork tender and falls off the bone; take skillet out of the oven.
- Put radishes and lamb onto serving platter. Put pan on the stove above medium high heat; simmer sauce, skimming off surface fat till thick and slightly reduced. Take off the heat. Add butter and sliced mint; keep mixing till butter melts. Scoop sauce on top radishes and lamb.

Nutrition Information

- Calories: 530 calories;
- Total Fat: 36.2
- Sodium: 1759
- Total Carbohydrate: 9.1
- Cholesterol: 158
- Protein: 39.4

324. Broiled And Slow Roasted Butterflied Leg Of Lamb With Cumin And Garlic

Serving: 14 | Prep: | Cook: | Ready in:

Ingredients

- 1/4 cup olive oil
- 8 cloves garlic, minced
- 2 1/2 teaspoons salt
- 1 teaspoon pepper
- 2 tablespoons ground cumin
- 1 tablespoon dried oregano
- 1 (8 pound) leg of lamb, boned and butterflied to a more or less even thickness, 4 3/4 to 5 1/2 pounds trimmed weight, fell and most fat removed
- 1 lemon, juiced
- Minced fresh parsley, cilantro or mint (optional)

Direction

- Combine oregano, cumin, pepper, salt, garlic and oil. Add it on both sides of the lamb and spread out; let it stand until the meat comes to room temperature for 1 hour.
- Put the oven rack on upper-middle or upper position (based on the thickness of lamb) and turn on the broiler to preheat on high for 10 minutes at least.
- Arrange lamb on a large wire rack over a roasting pan lined with foil, cut side up. Broil for about 8 minutes while moving the pan to evenly brown the whole surface. Flip the lamb; broil for about 8 minutes longer until the other side is well-browned. Turn off the broiler; take the lamb off the oven and set aside to rest for 10 minutes.
- Turn on the oven to 325° to heat. Insert a meat thermometer into the lamb's thickest part; put it back to the oven. Roast until the thermometer reads a rosy pink 140°, for a total of 50 minutes to 1 hour. After 30 minutes, be sure to check lamb a few times. Lower the heat to 170° if the lamb gets done earlier before serving.
- When the lamb is taken off the oven, immediately add a squeeze of lemon juice and use fresh herbs to sprinkle. Carve, slice across the grain if possible. Transfer to a platter; serve with a drizzle of accumulated juices.

Nutrition Information

- Calories: 336 calories;
- Total Carbohydrate: 2.2
- Cholesterol: 106
- Protein: 29.5
- Total Fat: 22.8
- Sodium: 494

325. Cassandra's Yummy Lamb Chops

Serving: 2 | Prep: 1Day25mins | Cook: 35mins | Ready in:

Ingredients

- 2 lamb chops
- 2 bulbs roasted garlic
- 1/2 teaspoon dried thyme
- salt and ground black pepper to taste
- 1 1/2 cups olive oil for marinating
- 1 cup red wine
- 3 tablespoons olive oil
- 1 small onion, chopped

Direction

- Put lamb chops in a shallow dish; smear both sides with roasted garlic. Season with pepper, salt and thyme. Cover with 1 1/2 cups olive oil; keep in the fridge for 1 night.
- Take the marinade and chops out of the dish, scrape off the oil which will partially have solidified in the fridge. Return the chops to the dish, cover with red wine. Keep in the fridge for 4 hours.
- In a large heavy skillet, over medium-high heat, heat 3 tablespoons of olive oil. Sauté chopped onion until it becomes tender. Transfer lamb chops to the skillet, cook with a cover for 8-10 minutes on each side.

Nutrition Information

- Calories: 699 calories;
- Cholesterol: 60
- Protein: 19.6
- Total Fat: 49.3
- Sodium: 58
- Total Carbohydrate: 25.1

326. Chef John's Roasted Leg Of Lamb

Serving: 8 | Prep: 20mins | Cook: 1hours45mins | Ready in:

Ingredients

- 1/4 cup pomegranate molasses
- 4 cloves garlic, minced
- 1 tablespoon chopped fresh rosemary
- 1 tablespoon kosher salt
- 2 teaspoons freshly ground black pepper
- 1 teaspoon Aleppo pepper
- 1 teaspoon dried mint
- 1 teaspoon ground cumin
- 1 (5 pound) boneless leg of lamb, butterflied
- kitchen twine
- salt to taste
- water as needed
- 1 tablespoon pomegranate molasses, or as needed

Direction

- In a bowl, stir together cumin, Aleppo pepper, mint, black pepper, kosher salt, rosemary, garlic and a quarter cup of pomegranate molasses.
- On work surface, place butterflied leg of the lamb, fatty side facing down. Make two deep slashes in each fleshy ends of meat. Turn lamb over; cut across surface of fat, about 10 to 20 shallow slashes.
- Coat meat-side of lamb completely by spreading 3/4 of pomegranate molasses mixture over. Fold the meat together. Invert into the large bowl. Spread over fatty side of meat with the remaining pomegranate mixture. Wrap bowl in the plastic wrap. Place in the refrigerator for 8 hours to overnight.
- Start preheating the oven to 350°F (175°C). In a roasting pan, position a roasting rack in bottom.
- Discard lamb from the marinade. Remove any excess marinade. Then gather the roast; arrange on the work surface, fatty side up. Tie

the middle section of roast using the kitchen twine to cinch roast together. Repeat ties 4 times along the roast length.
- Put in salt to season the roast. Place into the prepared roasting pan. Cover bottom of pan by pouring water below rack.
- In the prepared oven, roast for 105 mins until slightly pink in the middle and hot. The instant-read thermometer should register at least 135°F (57°C) when inserted into the middle. Let rest for 15 mins. Then place onto a plate; brush the remaining pomegranate molasses over.

Nutrition Information

- Calories: 326 calories;
- Total Fat: 20.6
- Sodium: 804
- Total Carbohydrate: 1.2
- Cholesterol: 115
- Protein: 31.9

327. Easter Leg Of Lamb

Serving: 6 | Prep: 35mins | Cook: 1hours | Ready in:

Ingredients

- Marinade:
- 1 (16 ounce) container plain yogurt
- 4 sprigs fresh rosemary, leaves stripped
- 1/2 bunch fresh parsley, stems removed
- 1/2 head garlic, peeled and smashed
- 1 1/2 lemons, zested
- 1/2 (6 pound) leg of lamb
- For roasting:
- 2 large onions, quartered
- 1/4 cup olive oil
- 3 tablespoons kosher salt
- 3 tablespoons ground black pepper
- 4 sprigs fresh rosemary, leaves stripped
- 1/2 bunch fresh parsley, stems removed
- 1/2 head garlic
- 1 1/2 lemons, zested

Direction

- In a big bowl, mix zest of 1 1/2 lemons, smashed garlic, 1/2 bunch of parsley, 4 rosemary sprigs and yogurt; put leg of lamb in yogurt mixture. Mix to coat. Cover; refrigerate for 24-48 hours.
- Preheat oven to 200°C/400°F the next day. Spread onions onto bottom of roasting pan. Take lamb from marinade. Rinse; pat dry. Put aside.
- Process zest of 1 1/2 lemons, 1/2 garlic head, 1/2 bunch of parsley, 4 rosemary sprigs, pepper, salt and olive oil till it makes a smooth paste in a food processor. Rub paste on leg of lamb; put over onions in roasting pan.
- In preheated oven, bake for 20 minutes. Lower temperature to 165°C/325°F; bake for 40-50 minutes for medium or to desired doneness. An inserted instant-read thermometer in middle should read 70°C/160°F.

Nutrition Information

- Calories: 707 calories;
- Total Fat: 49.4
- Sodium: 3073
- Total Carbohydrate: 21.9
- Cholesterol: 161
- Protein: 47.1

328. Easy Leg Of Lamb

Serving: 8 | Prep: 10mins | Cook: 2hours30mins | Ready in:

Ingredients

- 1 (5 1/2 pound) boneless leg of lamb, tied in netting
- 20 cloves garlic, or more to taste
- garlic powder, or to taste
- 10 fresh rosemary sprigs

Direction

- Start preheating the oven at 325°F (165°C).
- Make 20 deep slits evenly apart around the leg of lamb without cutting to the netting. Press a garlic clove into each slit. Rub the lamb with garlic powder. Cut rosemary sprigs under netting evenly around the lamb. Arrange the lamb in a roasting pan.
- Roast in prepared oven for about 2 to 2 1/2 hours until the center is reddish-pink and juicy for medium-rare. An instant-read thermometer should show 130°F (54°C) when inserted into the center. Wrap in aluminum foil; let the meat stand until thermometer shows 135°F (57°C) before slicing.

Nutrition Information

- Calories: 346 calories;
- Total Carbohydrate: 3.4
- Cholesterol: 126
- Protein: 36.4
- Total Fat: 19.8
- Sodium: 93

329. Easy Roast Leg Of Lamb

Serving: 4 | Prep: 30mins | Cook: 1hours | Ready in:

Ingredients

- 1 (4 pound) leg of lamb, deboned and tied
- 1 tablespoon ground black pepper
- 1 teaspoon salt
- 5 cloves garlic, cut into slivers
- 2 sprigs fresh rosemary
- 1 (15 ounce) can tomato sauce

Direction

- Start preheating the oven to 375°F (190°C).
- Rub pepper and salt all over the leg of lamb. Make small holes in the lamb with a small knife, approximately 1-in. separately. Press into each hole with slivers of garlic, approximately 1/2-in. beneath the surface. In a roasting pan, put the meat. You can secure the rosemary against the lamb with the string from it, or you can cut the rosemary from the stalk and rub and sprinkle over all the sides of the meat.
- Bake in the preheated oven for 45 minutes, and then lower the heat to 325°F (160°C), and keep baking for 15 minutes until the internal temperature of the meat reaches a minimum of 160°F (70°C). If you want the meat to be well-done, bake until the internal temperature is 170°F (75°C).

Nutrition Information

- Calories: 500 calories;
- Sodium: 1220
- Total Carbohydrate: 8
- Cholesterol: 201
- Protein: 52.2
- Total Fat: 28

330. Farikal

Serving: 4 | Prep: 2hours | Cook: 2hours | Ready in:

Ingredients

- 8 ounces sliced lamb meat
- 1 head cabbage, cored and sliced
- 2 cups water
- 1 1/2 tablespoons whole black peppercorns
- salt to taste

Direction

- In base of soup pot or Dutch oven, set a layer of the sliced lamb. Put layer of cabbage on top. Redo layering as many times as possible. Into small portion of cheesecloth, bind the peppercorns, and put in the middle of casserole. Put water on everything, and place lid to cover.

- Boil, then let simmer for 2 hours on low heat. Discard package of peppercorns then serve.

Nutrition Information

- Calories: 123 calories;
- Cholesterol: 22
- Protein: 11
- Total Fat: 2
- Sodium: 70
- Total Carbohydrate: 18.3

331. Grecian Lamb Caesar Salad

Serving: 6 | Prep: 15mins | Cook: 12mins | Ready in:

Ingredients

- 1 pound boneless lamb meat, cut into bite-sized pieces
- 5 cups romaine lettuce - washed, dried and torn into bite-sized pieces
- 1 cup canned garbanzo beans, drained
- 1/2 cup sliced red onion
- 1/2 cup bottled Caesar salad dressing
- 1/2 cup crumbled feta cheese

Direction

- Preheat the oven broiler.
- On a medium baking sheet, place lamb meat and broil 8-12 minutes until the internal temperature reaches 160°F or 63°C, flipping once. Take away from heat and let cool.
- Mix cooked lamb together with Caesar salad dressing, red onion, garbanzo beans and romaine lettuce in a big bowl. Put feta cheese on top.

Nutrition Information

- Calories: 346 calories;
- Sodium: 607
- Total Carbohydrate: 13.4
- Cholesterol: 76
- Protein: 20.4
- Total Fat: 23.1

332. Greek Orange Roast Lamb

Serving: 4 | Prep: 30mins | Cook: 1hours | Ready in:

Ingredients

- 1 large orange, juiced
- 3 tablespoons dark French mustard
- 3 tablespoons olive oil
- 4 teaspoons dried oregano
- salt and pepper to taste
- 10 potatoes, peeled and cut into 2-inch pieces
- 1 (3 pound) half leg of lamb, bone-in
- 5 cloves garlic

Direction

- Preheat the oven to 190°C or 375°Fahrenheit.
- Beat pepper, orange juice, salt, mustard, oregano, and olive oil in a big bowl; toss in potatoes to coat in mixture of orange juice. Use a slotted spoon to move the potatoes to a big roasting pan.
- Make slashes on the meat then put garlic cloves in the slashes. Massage the remaining orange juice mixture form bowl on the lamb. Put the lamb over the potatoes in the roasting pan. Pour any remaining orange juice mixture on the lamb if there's any.
- Roast for an hour in the preheated oven until the meat is cooked to medium and the potatoes are tender. An inserted meat thermometer in the thickest meat part should register 60°C or 140°Fahrenheit. While roasting, check every 20-30 minutes. If the potatoes are drying pour in a bit of hot water. If the lamb is cooked before the potatoes, move it to a serving platter or cutting board.

Tent potatoes with foil as it finishes to bake in oven.

Nutrition Information

- Calories: 912 calories;
- Total Carbohydrate: 103.2
- Cholesterol: 137
- Protein: 51.4
- Total Fat: 32.5
- Sodium: 312

333. Grilled Lamb With Brown Sugar Glaze

Serving: 4 | Prep: 15mins | Cook: 10mins | Ready in:

Ingredients

- 1/4 cup brown sugar
- 2 teaspoons ground ginger
- 2 teaspoons dried tarragon
- 1 teaspoon ground cinnamon
- 1 teaspoon ground black pepper
- 1 teaspoon garlic powder
- 1/2 teaspoon salt
- 4 lamb chops

Direction

- Combine the salt, garlic powder, pepper, cinnamon, tarragon, ginger and brown sugar in a medium bowl. Rub lamb chops using the seasonings, and put on a plate. Cover, and keep in the fridge for an hour.
- Set the grill to high heat for preheating.
- Brush the grill grate lightly using oil, and position the lamb chops on the grill. Cook the chops for 5 minutes per side, or to preferred doneness.

Nutrition Information

- Calories: 241 calories;
- Total Carbohydrate: 15.8
- Cholesterol: 56
- Protein: 14.6
- Total Fat: 13.1
- Sodium: 339

334. Lamb Chops In Duck Sauce

Serving: 6 | Prep: 25mins | Cook: 1hours20mins | Ready in:

Ingredients

- 3 pounds lamb chops
- 2 tablespoons Worcestershire sauce
- 1 tablespoon adobo seasoning
- cayenne pepper to taste
- salt and pepper to taste
- 1 1/2 cups duck sauce

Direction

- Preheat the oven to 175°C (350°F).
- In a medium baking dish, organize the lamb chops, then coat evenly with cayenne pepper, adobo seasoning and Worcestershire sauce. Add pepper and salt for seasoning.
- Bake in preheated oven for 1 hour.
- Cover the lamb chops with duck sauce, then keep baking for 15 to 20 minutes to internal temperature of 65°C (145°F).

Nutrition Information

- Calories: 819 calories;
- Total Fat: 60.7
- Sodium: 407
- Total Carbohydrate: 28.2
- Cholesterol: 168
- Protein: 37.3

335. Lamb Chops With Mint Oil

Serving: 4 | Prep: 20mins | Cook: 4mins | Ready in:

Ingredients

- 8 lamb chops
- 2 tablespoons olive oil, divided
- 2 teaspoons chopped fresh rosemary
- salt and ground black pepper to taste
- Mint Oil:
- 1/4 cup mint leaves
- 3 tablespoons extra-virgin olive oil
- 1 tablespoon lemon juice
- 1 teaspoon lemon zest

Direction

- Brush a tablespoon of olive oil on lamb chops; add salt, pepper and rosemary to season. Refrigerate to marinate for 15 minutes up to 2 hours.
- In skillet, heat leftover tablespoon of olive oil. Let lamb chops cook to brown, for 2 to 3 minutes on each side. An inserted instant-read thermometer in the middle must read 63 ° C or 145 ° F.
- Use a blender to mix lemon zest, lemon juice, 3 tablespoons of the extra-virgin olive oil and mint leaves; process till smooth. Sprinkle on top of lamb chops.

Nutrition Information

- Calories: 508 calories;
- Sodium: 126
- Total Carbohydrate: 0.5
- Cholesterol: 112
- Protein: 28.4
- Total Fat: 42.9

336. Lamb L'Arabique

Serving: 5 | Prep: 20mins | Cook: 2hours | Ready in:

Ingredients

- 2 tablespoons olive oil, divided
- 2 pounds lamb shanks
- 1 large onion, quartered
- 4 cloves garlic, chopped
- 6 cups roma (plum) tomatoes, chopped
- 1 (15 ounce) can chickpeas (garbanzo beans), drained
- 1 cup cooked lentils
- 1 tablespoon ground cumin
- 1 teaspoon ground cinnamon
- 1/4 teaspoon ground nutmeg
- 1/8 teaspoon crushed red pepper flakes
- 1 teaspoon finely chopped green chile peppers
- 1 dash hot pepper sauce

Direction

- Over medium-high heat, heat one tablespoon of oil in a large skillet and add lamb shanks. Sauté until browned lightly. Take out from the skillet and put in a deep casserole dish. Sauté garlic and onion in the skillet until tender. Mix in lentils, chickpeas and tomatoes. Season the mixture with hot pepper sauce, chile peppers, red pepper flakes, nutmeg, cinnamon and cumin. Combine thoroughly and let the flavors blend for about 3 minutes on medium heat.
- Preheat an oven to 190 degrees C (375 degrees F).
- Take out the browned shanks from the casserole for a second and then place the vegetable mixture into a casserole dish. Replace the shanks atop vegetable mixture.
- Cover the dish and then bake for 2 hours at 190 degrees C (375 degrees F) or until the lamb is receding from the bone and is cooked through.

Nutrition Information

- Calories: 586 calories;
- Sodium: 292
- Total Carbohydrate: 33.8
- Cholesterol: 122
- Protein: 42.7
- Total Fat: 31.5

337. Lamb Ribs With Honey And Wine

Serving: 6 | Prep: 10mins | Cook: 1hours10mins | Ready in:

Ingredients

- 3 1/2 pounds lamb ribs
- 2 onions, chopped
- 1 cup dry white wine
- 1/4 cup soy sauce
- 1/4 cup fresh lemon juice
- 1 tablespoon honey
- 1 tablespoon olive oil
- 2 teaspoons minced garlic
- 1 teaspoon ground cinnamon
- 1 teaspoon salt
- 1 teaspoon ground black pepper

Direction

- Place the lamb in a baking dish, 9x13-inch in size.
- In a small bowl, mix pepper, salt, cinnamon, garlic, olive oil, honey, lemon juice, soy sauce, white wine and onions. Combine thoroughly and put the mixture on the entire lamb. Cover using plastic wrap and refrigerate to marinate for an hour.
- Preheat the oven to 200 °C or 400 °F.
- In the prepped oven, let the lamb roast for an hour and 10 minutes till soft and browned.

Nutrition Information

- Calories: 507 calories;

- Total Carbohydrate: 10.2
- Cholesterol: 112
- Protein: 25.8
- Total Fat: 36.8
- Sodium: 1077

338. Leg O' Lamb With Lemon And Rosemary

Serving: 8 | Prep: 10mins | Cook: 1hours30mins | Ready in:

Ingredients

- 1 (6 pound) leg of lamb, at room temperature
- 1/4 cup butter, softened
- 6 cloves garlic, halved
- 4 sprigs fresh rosemary, chopped
- 1/2 teaspoon freshly ground black pepper
- 1 (6 ounce) can frozen lemonade concentrate, thawed
- 1 (1 ounce) package dry onion and mushroom soup mix

Direction

- Set the oven for preheating to 325°F (165°C).
- Spread the butter generously over the lamb and distribute the garlic clove halves on top of the meat. Spice it up with a sprinkle of pepper and rosemary. Position the lamb on a rack set inside a roasting pan.
- Roast the lamb inside the preheated oven for an hour.
- Combine the dry soup mix and lemonade concentrate together in a bowl, pour on top of the lamb and roast 30 minutes more. A meat thermometer poked into the thickest part of the lamb should reach 120°F/58°C for medium-rare or 145°F/68°C for medium-well. Let the roast stand for about 20 minutes before slicing.

Nutrition Information

- Calories: 500 calories;
- Total Fat: 30.6
- Sodium: 360
- Total Carbohydrate: 15.8
- Cholesterol: 154
- Protein: 38.6

339. Mint Crusted Rack Of Lamb

Serving: 4 | Prep: 20mins | Cook: 20mins | Ready in:

Ingredients

- 1 cup fresh mint leaves
- 2 cloves garlic, sliced
- 2 tablespoons olive oil
- 1/2 cup plain bread crumbs
- salt and ground black pepper to taste
- 1 pinch cayenne pepper, or to taste
- 1 1/2 tablespoons finely grated Parmigiano-Reggiano cheese
- 1/4 cup Dijon mustard
- 2 teaspoons honey
- 2 tablespoons extra virgin olive oil
- 2 teaspoons rice vinegar
- 2 teaspoons honey
- 1 teaspoon Dijon mustard
- 1 pinch salt and freshly ground black pepper to taste
- 2 (1 1/4 pound) racks of lamb, trimmed
- 1 teaspoon vegetable oil
- salt and pepper to taste

Direction

- Set the oven for preheating to 400°F (200°C).
- Prepare a baking sheet lined with a foil.
- Fill a pot with water and let it boil, then put the mint leaves and cook for about 10 seconds.
- Move the mint leaves to a bowl of water with ice; immerse for 30 seconds, drain excess water and squeeze dry.
- Mix together the cayenne pepper, black pepper, salt, bread crumbs, olive oil and garlic with blanched mint in a food processor or you can also use a blender. Blend for 20 seconds to half a minute, until the texture turns crumbly and fine.
- Place the mint mixture on a big bowl; mix in Parmigiano-Reggiano cheese, put aside.
- Combine 2 teaspoons honey and a quarter cup of Dijon mustard in a small bowl, put aside.
- Mix together the black pepper, salt, a teaspoon of Dijon mustard, 2 teaspoons honey, rice vinegar and extra-virgin olive oil in a lidded jar. Shake the vinaigrette vigorously for about 30 seconds, until blended. Put the vinaigrette aside.
- Cut a half inch to an inch slits between each bone of the lamb racks to achieve even roasting of the meat.
- Spice up each rack using black pepper and salt all over.
- Heat the vegetable oil in skillet placed over high heat. Add the meat and cook each lamb rack for 2 to 3 minutes per side, until it turns brown.
- Arrange the lamb racks on the baking sheet lined with foil.
- Brush over each rack the honey–mustard mixture. Top it off with a sprinkle of mint mixture and sprinkle the sides of each rack as well.
- Pop it in the preheated oven and let it bake for about 20 minutes, until the top turns brown and medium rare in the middle. An instant-read thermometer poked in the center should register 125 to 130°F (52 to 54°C). Take it out from the oven and allow to rest for 10 minutes before serving. Finish by drizzling with honey mustard vinaigrette.

Nutrition Information

- Calories: 681 calories;
- Sodium: 625
- Total Carbohydrate: 20.2
- Cholesterol: 122

- Protein: 29
- Total Fat: 52.9

340. Nita's Lamb, Green Beans And Tomatoes

Serving: 4 | Prep: 20mins | Cook: 1hours | Ready in:

Ingredients

- 1 tablespoon olive oil
- 1 1/2 pounds lamb stew meat
- 1 large onion, chopped
- 2 pounds fresh green beans, washed and trimmed
- 1 (15 ounce) can tomato sauce
- 1 cup water
- salt and pepper to taste
- 2 teaspoons chopped fresh mint leaves

Direction

- In a large skillet, heat the oil over medium-high heat. Add onion and lamb, cook until the meat gets browned; mix in beans, cook and stir from time to time for 10 minutes.
- Stir in mint, pepper, salt, water, and tomato sauce. Turn down the heat to low, put on a cover and let simmer until cooked through and the beans become tender, about an hour.

Nutrition Information

- Calories: 273 calories;
- Protein: 26.9
- Total Fat: 8.9
- Sodium: 616
- Total Carbohydrate: 25.1
- Cholesterol: 65

341. Paddy's Chile Verde

Serving: 8 | Prep: 30mins | Cook: 4hours15mins | Ready in:

Ingredients

- 4 pounds fresh tomatillos, husks removed
- 2 large onions (keep the skin on)
- 2 poblano peppers
- 1 head garlic
- 3 chipotle peppers in adobo sauce
- 2 (12 fluid ounce) cans or bottles lager-style beer
- 1 tablespoon ground cumin
- 1 tablespoon salt
- 1 tablespoon ground black pepper
- 4 tablespoons vegetable oil
- 4 pounds cubed lamb stew meat

Direction

- Preheat oven's broiler, place the rack about 6 inches away from the heat source.
- On a baking sheet, arrange garlic, poblano peppers, onions, and tomatillos.
- Cook the vegetables under the broiler for 3 to 5 minutes on each side, until the skins on side near the heat source are charred; turn to cook the other side until equally charred.
- Remove and discard the stems and seeds from the peppers, and the root and outer skin from the garlic and onion.
- In a blender, combine pepper, salt, cumin, lager-style beer, chipotle peppers in adobo sauce, garlic, poblano peppers, onion, and some of the tomatillos until about half full; work in batches. Hold the lid down, pulse a few times, then leave the blender on to puree until mixture smoothens. Transfer into a slow cooker.
- In a large saucepan, heat oil. Cook and stir cubed lamb in the hot oil for about 5 minutes, until all sides are evenly browned. Transfer into the slow cooker.
- Cook for 4 hours on High.

Nutrition Information

- Calories: 487 calories;
- Protein: 41.9
- Total Fat: 22.4
- Sodium: 1011
- Total Carbohydrate: 24.6
- Cholesterol: 124

---

342. Pistachio Crusted Rack Of Lamb

Serving: 4 | Prep: 10mins | Cook: 35mins | Ready in:

Ingredients

- 2 racks of lamb, trimmed
- 1 teaspoon herbes de Provence
- salt and ground black pepper to taste
- 1 tablespoon vegetable oil
- 2/3 cup chopped pistachio nuts
- 2 tablespoons dry bread crumbs
- 1 tablespoon melted butter
- 1 teaspoon olive oil
- salt and ground black pepper to taste
- 3 tablespoons Dijon mustard

Direction

- Turn oven to 400°F (200°C) to preheat. Line aluminum foil over a baking sheet. Liberally season each lamb rack with black pepper, salt, and herbes de Provence.
- Heat oil over high heat in a large skillet. Put lamb into the skillet, cook for 6 to 8 minutes until all sides are browned. Remove lambs to a baking sheet lined with aluminum foil; put to one side.
- In a mixing bowl, combine pistachios with black pepper, a pinch of salt, olive oil, butter, and breadcrumbs. Smear mustard over the fat side of each lamb rack. Press pistachio mixture on top of mustard. Bake lamb rack for 20 to 25 minutes in the preheated oven until crust turns golden but center is still pink. Remove lamb to a serving plate and allow to sit for 10 minutes before cutting to serve.

Nutrition Information

- Calories: 619 calories;
- Total Fat: 39.8
- Sodium: 652
- Total Carbohydrate: 10.3
- Cholesterol: 164
- Protein: 53.1

---

343. Portofino Lamb And Artichoke Risotto

Serving: 6 | Prep: 20mins | Cook: 30mins | Ready in:

Ingredients

- 2 tablespoons olive oil
- 1 tablespoon butter
- 1/2 cup chopped shallots
- 2 cups uncooked Arborio rice
- 1/2 cup red wine
- 6 cups chicken broth - heated and divided
- 3/4 cup grated Asiago cheese
- 2 cups diced leftover roast lamb
- 1 clove garlic, minced
- 1 (6.5 ounce) jar marinated artichoke hearts, undrained and chopped

Direction

- Set a large saucepan and heat the butter and oil over medium heat. Add in the onions or you can use shallots; sauté and stir for 2 to 3 minutes. Pour in the rice, mixing well for about 1 minute to coat.
- Pour the wine in the rice mixture and let it absorb by the rice for about 2 to 3 minutes. Mix in the broth a half cup in every addition and wait until the rice fully absorbs each half a cup before adding the next half cup. Repeat

this method until you have fully consumed all but reserving 1/4 cup of broth for later use.
- Check the rice after about 20 minutes, it should be soft but firm. Turn the heat off. Add and stir in the remaining quarter cup of broth, artichoke hearts, garlic, leftover lamb, and the cheese. Stir thoroughly to blend well with the rice and place on warm serving dinner plates to serve.

Nutrition Information

- Calories: 611 calories;
- Total Fat: 24
- Sodium: 1000
- Total Carbohydrate: 59.6
- Cholesterol: 87
- Protein: 32.6

344. Rack Of Lamb With Strawberry Mint Sauce

Serving: 4 | Prep: 20mins | Cook: 40mins | Ready in:

Ingredients

- Sauce:
- 2 cups fresh strawberries, hulled and halved
- 1 lemon, zested and juiced
- 1 lemon, juiced
- 1/4 cup water
- 2 tablespoons honey
- salt and cayenne pepper to taste
- 1/4 cup freshly sliced mint leaves
- Lamb:
- 1 (8 bone) rack of lamb, fully trimmed
- kosher salt to taste
- freshly ground black pepper to taste
- cayenne pepper to taste
- 2 tablespoons Dijon mustard
- 1 tablespoon finely minced green onions
- 1/4 cup fine plain bread crumbs
- 2 tablespoons melted butter
- 1/4 teaspoon salt

Direction

- In a pot, simmer the halved strawberries, honey, cayenne pepper, salt, the juice from the 2 lemons, zest from one lemon, and water over medium-high heat. Once the strawberries start to release their liquid, start to break down, and soften, adjust the heat to medium-low; cook and stir the mixture occasionally for 10 minutes until the fruit is very soft. Remove the mixture from the heat. Pass it through the fine mesh strainer.
- Set the oven to 475°F (245°C) to preheat. Use a foil to line the shallow baking pan, bringing their ends up and over the sides of the baking pan.
- Season the rack of lamb on both sides liberally with freshly ground black pepper, cayenne pepper, and kosher salt. Arrange the lamb onto the prepared pan. Roast the lamb in the hot oven for 10 minutes until seared. Remove the pan from the oven. Adjust the temperature of the oven to 375°F (190°C).
- Set the oven to 375°F (190°C) to preheat.
- In a small bowl, mix the onions and mustard. In a separate bowl, pour the melted butter into the breadcrumbs; stir until the mixture looks like wet sand. Season the mixture with salt.
- Generously coat the top of the lamb with the mustard mixture. Sprinkle the crumb mixture onto the mustard mixture, pressing it down to make a crumb crust.
- Roast the rack for 15 minutes until the internal temperature of the lamb reaches 125°F (50°C). Allow the rack to rest for 10 minutes before slicing it between its ribs; cut the ribs into four 2-rib serving or two 4-rib servings.
- Stir the thinly sliced mint into the strawberry sauce before serving. Drizzle a small pool of sauce onto the serving plates. Arrange the ribs on the sauce, serve.

Nutrition Information

- Calories: 470 calories;

- Sodium: 609
- Total Carbohydrate: 24.4
- Cholesterol: 115
- Protein: 22
- Total Fat: 32.5

345. Roast Leg Of Lamb With Orange Juice And White Wine

Serving: 10 | Prep: 10mins | Cook: 1hours30mins | Ready in:

Ingredients

- 1/2 cup orange juice
- 1 cup white wine
- 1/4 cup olive oil
- 3 cloves garlic, minced
- 2 tablespoons chopped fresh thyme
- 2 tablespoons chopped fresh rosemary
- ground black pepper to taste
- 1 (6 pound) bone-in leg of lamb, trimmed
- salt and black pepper

Direction

- Blend together the pepper, fresh thyme and rosemary, garlic, olive oil, white wine and orange juice in a blender. Transfer the mixture into a big, resealable plastic bag, and put in the lamb. Coat meat using the marinade, squeeze to release the excess air and secure the bag. Place the bag inside the fridge for 8 hours or up to overnight to marinate.
- Take the lamb out from the refrigerator at least half an hour before roasting. Pat it dry using a paper towel. Liberally season with pepper and salt on each sides of the meat.
- Set the oven for preheating to 425°F (220°C). Position two racks inside the oven - a middle rack to support the lamb, and a lower rack to hold the roasting pan to catch the drippings. Put the empty roasting pan inside the oven while you're preheating the oven.
- Position the meat directly on the middle rack, fattiest side facing up for the fat to melt into the meat while the lamb cooks. Place the roasting pan under the meat so it will catch the drippings. Roast the lamb for half an hour, and then adjust the heat to 300°F (150°C). Continue to roast in the oven for about 10 to 12 minutes each pound until an instant-read thermometer poked into the middle reaches between 130 to 135°F (54 to 57°C). Take the meat out from the oven, cover loosely using a foil. Put the meat aside to rest for 10 to 15 minutes.

Nutrition Information

- Calories: 383 calories;
- Total Fat: 25.1
- Sodium: 313
- Total Carbohydrate: 2.5
- Cholesterol: 111
- Protein: 30.6

346. Roasted Lamb With Root Vegetables

Serving: 8 | Prep: 20mins | Cook: 1hours50mins | Ready in:

Ingredients

- 1 (6 pound) leg of lamb
- 5 cloves garlic, minced
- 2 teaspoons coarsely ground black pepper
- 1 teaspoon crushed red pepper flakes
- 1 bay leaf, crushed
- 1 tablespoon chopped fresh rosemary
- 1/2 cup olive oil
- 2 tablespoons balsamic vinegar
- 2 tablespoons honey
- 2 tablespoons coarse salt, or as needed
- 8 carrots, peeled and trimmed
- 16 small potatoes, unpeeled
- 1 large beet, peeled and cut into wedges

- 1 yam, peeled and cut into wedges
- 8 baby turnips, peeled
- 2 tablespoons olive oil
- salt to taste

Direction

- Let the lamb's leg rest at room temperature for 1 hour before cooking.
- Start preheating the oven at 400°F (200°C). Arrange the oven rack in the lower third of the oven.
- In a small bowl, combine honey, vinegar, 1/2 cup of olive oil, rosemary, bay leaf, red pepper flakes, pepper, and garlic. Massage the mixture over the lamb, then flavor with 2 tablespoons of coarse salt. Put aside. Arrange turnips, yam, beet, potatoes, and carrots in a large roasting pan. Mix with 1 pinch of salt and 2 tablespoons of olive oil. Place the seasoned leg of lamb on top of the vegetables.
- In the prepared oven, roast the lamb for 20 minutes, then lower the oven temperature to 325°F (165°C). Keep roasting to reach your desired doneness, about 90 minutes for medium-rare. An instant-read thermometer should show 130°F (54°C) when inserted into the center.
- Before carving, bring the lamb's leg to a cutting board, covered with aluminum foil, for 30 minutes. Arrange the vegetables on a serving platter and cover with aluminum foil to maintain warmth until ready to serve.

Nutrition Information

- Calories: 927 calories;
- Total Fat: 39.1
- Sodium: 2019
- Total Carbohydrate: 96.1
- Cholesterol: 137
- Protein: 49

347. Slow Roast Leg Of Lamb

Serving: 6 | Prep: 10mins | Cook: 7hours15mins | Ready in:

Ingredients

- 3 carrots, coarsely chopped
- 1 head garlic, split but not peeled
- 1 (5 pound) leg of lamb
- 1 1/4 cups red wine
- 1 1/4 cups lamb stock
- salt and freshly ground black pepper to taste

Direction

- Preheat an oven to 120°C/250°F.
- In a roasting pan big enough for leg of lamb, put garlic and carrots. Put lamb over; add lamb stock and wine. Put roasting pan onto stove; heat till liquid boils on medium low heat. Tightly cover roasting pan with aluminum foil. Put into oven (to protect your hands, use oven mitts).
- In preheated oven, roast for 7 hours till inserted instant-read thermometer in middle reads 54°C/130°F, for medium; remove from oven.
- Put oven temperature on 200°C/400°F; put lamb into 2nd roasting pan.
- Roast lamb for 15-20 minutes, uncovered, till skin is crispy. Before slicing, rest.
- Put cooking juices from 1st roasting pan into saucepan as lamb rests. Boil; simmer for 5 minutes till reduced into gravy. Season with pepper and salt.

Nutrition Information

- Calories: 474 calories;
- Total Fat: 12.1
- Sodium: 1590
- Total Carbohydrate: 10.2
- Cholesterol: 137
- Protein: 63.7

348. Spice Crusted Roast Rack Of Lamb With Cilantro Mint Sauce

Serving: 4 | Prep: 20mins | Cook: 15mins | Ready in:

Ingredients

- 1 1/2 tablespoons coriander seeds
- 1 1/2 tablespoons caraway seeds
- 1 1/2 tablespoons cumin seeds
- 1 teaspoon cayenne pepper
- 1 (8 bone) rack lamb ribs
- salt and ground black pepper to taste
- 1 tablespoon olive oil
- 2 small bunches fresh mint
- 1 bunch fresh cilantro
- 1 lime, juiced
- 1 tablespoon agave nectar
- 1 tablespoon rice wine vinegar
- 2 cloves garlic
- salt and ground black pepper to taste
- 1/2 cup extra-virgin olive oil

Direction

- Preheat oven to 200°C/400°F.
- On medium high heat, heat a dry saucepan. Add cumin seeds, caraway and coriander. Toast for 2 minutes till smoky. Put into mortar and pestle. Grind spices together roughly.
- On both lamb sides, rub spices. Pat down to create a crust. Use pepper and salt to season.
- In an oven-proof skillet, heat 1 tbsp. olive oil on medium high heat. Put lamb in, fat side down. Cook for 5 minutes, flipping halfway till both sides are browned. Put skillet into oven immediately.
- In preheated oven, roast lamb for 8 minutes till not red in the middle. An inserted instant-read thermometer in the middle should register 54°C/130°F. Take out of oven. Let rest for 5 minutes.
- In a food processor, mix garlic, vinegar, agave nectar, lime juice, cilantro and mint. Use pepper and salt to season. Process till chopped finely. Drizzle in 1/2 cup olive oil slowly while blending to create sauce.
- Slice lamb rack. On each serving, spoon coriander and mint sauce.

Nutrition Information

- Calories: 699 calories;
- Sodium: 164
- Total Carbohydrate: 11.1
- Cholesterol: 98
- Protein: 23.5
- Total Fat: 63

349. Stuffed Leg Of Lamb

Serving: 8 | Prep: 35mins | Cook: 40mins | Ready in:

Ingredients

- 1 (5 pound) boneless leg of lamb
- salt and black pepper to taste
- 1 (10 ounce) bag fresh spinach leaves
- 6 ounces goat cheese, or more if needed
- 2 teaspoons pine nuts
- kitchen twine
- 1 cup all-purpose flour
- 1 tablespoon salt
- 1 tablespoon ground black pepper
- 1 teaspoon dried thyme
- 1 teaspoon fennel seeds
- 1 tablespoon sesame oil

Direction

- If any, remove twine/plastic netting from around lamb leg; on cutting board, open up the roast. Put boned roast side up. Cut away extra fatty areas with sharp paring knife; cut 1/2-in. deep silts with sharp knife in the meat, 2-in. apart, to help meat lie flat. Use sturdy plastic wrap piece/cut-apart food storage bag to cover meat; use a mallet/edge of small plate

to pound meat till roast is 10-14-in. square and 3/4-in. thick everywhere.
- Preheat oven to 200°C/400°F.
- Sprinkle pepper and salt on upper side of meat; within 1/2-in. of edges, spread spinach leaves over the top of roast. Break goat cheese up; evenly sprinkle on spinach. Sprinkle pine nuts on top of cheese.
- Roll up roast to a tight cylinder; tie roast together at 2-in. intervals with kitchen twine; it is okay if a bit of stuffing protrudes from roast's sides.
- Mix fennel seeds, thyme, 1 tbsp. pepper, 1 tbsp. salt and flour in flat dish; firmly press tied roast to coat all sides in flour mixture.
- Heat sesame oil in heavy ovenproof/cast iron skillet on medium-high heat till oil shimmers; sear all roast sides and ends till golden brown in color. Lay roast in skillet; put into preheated oven. Roast for 40 minutes till internal temperature is 65°C/145°F for medium or to preferred doneness level. Take out of oven; use a doubled aluminum foil sheet to cover. Rest for 10-15 minutes prior to slicing in a warm area.

Nutrition Information

- Calories: 485 calories;
- Sodium: 1092
- Total Carbohydrate: 14.6
- Cholesterol: 132
- Protein: 39.2
- Total Fat: 29.2

350. Stuffed Leg Of Lamb With Balsamic Fig Basil Sauce

Serving: 6 | Prep: 50mins | Cook: 1hours | Ready in:

Ingredients

- 1/2 cup coarsely chopped prunes
- 1/4 cup currants
- 2 tablespoons creme de cassis liqueur
- 1 1/2 tablespoons minced fresh rosemary
- 1 1/2 tablespoons minced fresh thyme
- 1/2 teaspoon ground coriander
- 1 1/4 teaspoons salt
- 1 teaspoon freshly ground black pepper
- 1 (4 pound) boneless leg of lamb, rolled and tied
- 1/2 cup chopped roasted and salted almonds
- 2 tablespoons chopped fresh mint
- 3 cloves garlic, cut into thirds
- 2 tablespoons olive oil
- 1/2 cup balsamic vinegar
- 5 tablespoons butter
- 3 tablespoons honey
- 1/3 cup thinly sliced, stemmed Calimyrna figs
- 5 teaspoons chopped fresh basil
- 6 leaves mint
- 6 leaves basil

Direction

- Warm up oven to 200°C or 400°F.
- In a small bowl, mix the chopped currants and prunes with the crème de cassis, and then set aside. Combine thyme, rosemary, salt, coriander, and pepper in another small bowl, and set aside.
- On a work surface, untie and unroll the lamb and lay it out flat. Make sure lamb is evenly thick and slightly rectangular in shape by trimming off excess fat and cutting out any thick parts open. Drizzle with half of the herb mixture. Combine the chopped mint and almonds into the prune mixture and spread evenly over the lamb. Roll it up starting with one of the short sides, and tie at 1-inch intervals with a kitchen twine. On the top of the lamb, cut nine slits about an inch deep and insert a slice of garlic in each slit. Rub lamb with olive oil and drizzle with the remaining herb mixture.
- On a rack set in a roasting pan, place lamb with seam-side up. Roast lamb in the preheated oven until desired doneness is achieved. To get a medium-rare result, roast until inserted thermometer at the center reads

140°F or 60°C. Remove from the oven and cover with a foil. Allow lamb to rest for about 15 minutes.
- In a small saucepan over high heat, bring balsamic vinegar to a boil while lamb is resting. Boil for about 4-5 minutes, or until vinegar has reduced by half. Once vinegar is reduced, mix in the sliced figs, butter, and honey. Mix until butter is melted, remove from heat, mix in chopped basil, and set aside.
- Remove twine from the cooked lamb and then cut into about 1/2-inch thick slices to serve. Arrange on a warm serving platter, sprinkle with fig sauce, and garnish with some mint and basil leaves.

Nutrition Information

- Calories: 631 calories;
- Sodium: 649
- Total Carbohydrate: 29.2
- Cholesterol: 147
- Protein: 38.2
- Total Fat: 39.7

Chapter 9: Awesome Lamb Recipes

***

351. A Vegetable Stew Tabakh Rohoo

Serving: 8 | Prep: 40mins | Cook: 1hours15mins | Ready in:

Ingredients

- 1 tablespoon ghee (clarified butter)
- 1 pound lamb meat, cut into small pieces
- Spice Mix:
- 1 teaspoon ground allspice
- 1/2 teaspoon ground cinnamon
- 1/4 teaspoon ground cloves
- 1/4 teaspoon ground nutmeg
- 1 pinch ground cardamom
- 2 onions, sliced
- 1 potato, peeled and sliced
- 1 pound eggplant, peeled and cubed
- 1 pound zucchini, thickly sliced
- 2 pounds tomatoes, cubed
- 1 green chile pepper
- salt to taste
- 1 tablespoon tomato paste
- 1/4 cup water
- 6 cloves cloves garlic, crushed
- salt to taste
- 3 tablespoons dried mint
- 1 tablespoon ghee (clarified butter), melted (optional)

Direction

- In a large pot, heat the ghee over medium-high heat, put in the lamb meat. Cook and stir until browned evenly. Add cardamom, nutmeg, cloves, cinnamon, and allspice to season. Mix well.
- Put a layer of onion on top of the lamb, do not mix. Top with layers of tomatoes, zucchini, eggplant, and potato.
- Repeat the process till you have used all the vegetables up, ending with tomatoes on top. In the center of the tomatoes, put the chile pepper. Season with salt. Next, dilute the tomato paste in the water, pour over the greens. Boil, reduce the heat to low, stew for 1 hour till the vegetables are tender.
- Use pestle and mortar to crush the dried mint, a pinch of salt, and garlic together. Combine with 2 tablespoons of liquid from the pot, and place by spoonfuls over the greens in the pot, do not stir. Stew for 5 minutes more.
- Remove the stew to a serving dish or a wide bowl by tipping the pot gently to let it slip out into the plate while still maintaining its layers. Dust with ghee if you like.

Nutrition Information

- Calories: 174 calories;
- Sodium: 54
- Total Carbohydrate: 21.3
- Cholesterol: 35
- Protein: 11.5
- Total Fat: 5.8

352. Algerian Couscous

Serving: 10 | Prep: 30mins | Cook: 1hours7mins | Ready in:

Ingredients

- 1/4 cup olive oil, or more as needed, divided
- 8 mutton chops, fat removed
- 4 chicken drumsticks
- 1 pinch salt and ground black pepper to taste
- 3 onions, quartered
- water to cover
- 2 tablespoons ground turmeric
- 2 tablespoons ground cumin
- 2 tablespoons ground coriander
- 3 potatoes, cut into chunks
- 3 turnips, cut into chunks
- 3 carrots, sliced lengthwise and cut into chunks
- 1 (6 ounce) can tomato paste
- 2 tablespoons ras el hanout
- 1 (7 ounce) can chickpeas, drained
- 2 zucchini, sliced lengthwise and cut into chunks
- 5 sprigs cilantro, chopped
- Couscous:
- 3 cups water
- 2 cups couscous
- 1 tablespoon butter
- 3 tablespoons harissa

Direction

- Put 3 tbsp. of olive oil in a large pot and heat it over medium-high heat. Season the chicken drumsticks and mutton chops with salt and pepper. Working in batches, cook them in hot oil for 2 minutes per side together with the onions until browned. Transfer them into the large plate.
- Use a wooden spoon to scrape the pot's bottom so that the browned bits will be released. Place the chicken and mutton chops back into the pot. Cover them with enough water. Add the coriander, turmeric, and cumin. Cover the pot and bring it back to a boil. Adjust the heat to medium and simmer the mixture for 20 minutes.
- Mix in turnips, carrots, and potatoes. Cover and simmer the mixture for 10 minutes until the vegetables start to soften. Stir in ras el hanout and tomato paste. Cook the mixture for 10 minutes. Mix in cilantro, chickpeas, and zucchini. Cover and cook for 5 minutes until the zucchini is tender.
- Boil 3 cups of water in a saucepan. Remove it from the heat. Mix in butter and couscous. Cover the saucepan and allow it to stand for 5-10 minutes until the water is completely absorbed. Use a fork to fluff the couscous. Mix in 1 tbsp. of olive oil. Transfer the mixture into the serving dish.
- Ladle 2 scoops of the cooking liquid into the bowl. Stir in harissa until smooth.
- Scoop the vegetables into the serving plate. Place the chicken and mutton into the separate plate. Serve them together with the harissa sauce, couscous, and remaining cooking liquid from the pot.

Nutrition Information

- Calories: 492 calories;
- Total Fat: 15.8
- Sodium: 358
- Total Carbohydrate: 57.3
- Cholesterol: 72
- Protein: 30.5

353. American Gyros

Serving: 8 | Prep: 15mins | Cook: 40mins | Ready in:

Ingredients

- 1 pound ground lamb
- 1 pound ground beef
- 1/2 cup finely diced yellow onion
- 4 cloves garlic, crushed
- 1 tablespoon minced fresh rosemary
- 2 teaspoons dried oregano
- 2 teaspoons kosher salt, or to taste
- 1 teaspoon fresh ground black pepper
- 1 teaspoon cumin
- 1 teaspoon paprika
- 1/8 teaspoon ground cinnamon
- 1/8 teaspoon cayenne pepper
- 2 tablespoons dry bread crumbs
- 1 tablespoon olive oil

Direction

- Preheat the oven to 175°C or 350°F. Grease a 9-inch by 13-inch baking dish. Place parchment paper up to the sides of the dish. Flip the parchment paper until the greased side is up.
- In a mixing bowl, put the ground beef and lamb; mix in bread crumbs, onions, cayenne pepper, garlic, cinnamon, rosemary, paprika, oregano, cumin, pepper, and salt until well blended. Press the meat mixture on the prepared baking dish firmly in an even layer that reaches the edges. It should be fairly dense and packed.
- Bake for 40-45 minutes in the preheated oven at 350°F until nicely brown. An instant-read thermometer inserted in the middle should register at least 70°C or 160°F. Let it cool down to room temperature then move to a plate. Use a sheet of plastic wrap to cover then place in the refrigerator for 1-2 hours.
- Slice the meat crosswise into 3 portions on a cutting board. Cut each portion into 1/8-in pieces as desired.
- On medium-high heat, heat oil in a pan; cook meat slices for 2 minutes on each side until brown.

Nutrition Information

- Calories: 255 calories;
- Total Fat: 17.8
- Sodium: 549
- Total Carbohydrate: 3.4
- Cholesterol: 72
- Protein: 19.3

354. Anna's Amazing Goulash

Serving: 12 | Prep: 30mins | Cook: 2hours | Ready in:

Ingredients

- 5 thick slices bacon, diced
- 1 cup beef stew meat, cut into 1 1/2 inch pieces
- 1 pound lamb stew meat, cut into 1 1/2 inch pieces
- 1 pound pork stew meat, cut into 1 1/2 inch pieces
- 2 tablespoons unsalted butter
- 2 onions, chopped
- 1 bulb garlic, peeled and minced
- 1 cup all-purpose flour
- 1 teaspoon caraway seeds
- 3 tablespoons Hungarian sweet paprika
- 1 1/2 teaspoons red pepper flakes
- 1 cup red wine vinegar
- 1 (14.5 ounce) can peeled and diced tomatoes
- 5 cups beef stock
- 1 (12 fluid ounce) can or bottle beer
- 1/2 tablespoon salt
- 3 cups water
- 2 red bell peppers, chopped
- 3 potatoes, peeled and cubed
- 1 parsnip, chopped
- 3 stalks celery, chopped
- 4 carrots, chopped

- 1 cup dry bread crumbs
- 1/2 medium head cabbage, chopped
- 1 cup green peas

Direction

- On medium high heat, fry bacon for 5-10 minutes till well browned in a big skillet. Remove bacon from skillet with a slotted spoon. Put aside. Sauté meat in small batches in bacon fat till browned. Set stew meats aside with a slotted spoon as well.
- In bacon fat, melt butter in same skillet on medium heat. Add garlic and onion. Sauté for 5 minutes. Mix crushed red pepper flakes, paprika, caraway seeds and flour in. Mix for 2 minutes till flour melts. Whisk tomato and vinegar in. It will be very thick.
- Put reserved meat, reserved bacon, red bell peppers, water, salt, beer and beef stock in. Boil. Lower heat to low. Simmer, covered, for 45 minutes. Mix carrots, celery, parsnip and potatoes in. Simmer for 30 minutes more, covered, till veggies are tender.
- Mix breadcrumbs in till stew thickens. Add peas and cabbage. Simmer for another 5 minutes. Let soup cool slightly and refrigerate overnight then reheat then serve for best results.

Nutrition Information

- Calories: 537 calories;
- Sodium: 687
- Total Carbohydrate: 41.9
- Cholesterol: 80
- Protein: 26.2
- Total Fat: 28.4

355. Ash E Anar (Persian Pomegranate Soup)

Serving: 8 | Prep: 15mins | Cook: 1hours5mins | Ready in:

Ingredients

- Broth:
- 4 tablespoons olive oil
- 2 large sweet onions, chopped
- 6 cloves garlic, minced
- 3/4 cup yellow split peas
- 2 quarts chicken stock
- 2 tablespoons ground black pepper
- 1 tablespoon ground turmeric
- 2 1/4 teaspoons mild paprika
- 3/4 teaspoon cayenne pepper
- 1/4 teaspoon ground fennel seeds
- 1 cinnamon stick
- Meatballs:
- 1 1/2 pounds ground lamb
- 1/4 cup minced onion
- 2 tablespoons minced fresh mint
- 2 tablespoons minced fresh parsley
- 1 clove garlic, minced
- 1 cup basmati rice
- 1/2 cup minced fresh parsley
- 1/2 cup minced fresh mint
- 1/4 cup pomegranate molasses
- 1 tablespoon honey
- Garnish:
- 2 cups pomegranate seeds
- 1/4 cup heavy whipping cream, or more to taste

Direction

- Put oil in the heavy stockpot and heat it over medium-high heat. Stir in chopped onions and cook for 5 minutes until soft. Add the garlic and cook for 2 more minutes until browned. Mix in split peas and cook for 1 minute until the peas have a bit of color.
- Add the chicken stock into the pot. Stir in a cinnamon stick, paprika, turmeric, fennel seeds, cayenne, and pepper. Boil the soup. Lower the heat and let it simmer for 20 minutes until the peas are tender.
- While waiting for the soup, start preparing the meatballs. Combine mint, garlic, minced onion, parsley, and lamb. Shape the mixture into walnut-sized meatballs and drop them

into the simmering soup. Let it cook for 10 more minutes until their center is no longer pink.
- Remove the cinnamon stick from the soup and discard it. Stir in mint, honey, basmati rice, pomegranate molasses, and parsley. Cook for 20 minutes longer until the rice softens.
- Distribute soup into the bowls and garnish each with cream and pomegranate seeds.

Nutrition Information

- Calories: 451 calories;
- Total Fat: 22.5
- Sodium: 741
- Total Carbohydrate: 45.4
- Cholesterol: 68
- Protein: 19.1

356. Atlas Mountain Soup

Serving: 4 | Prep: 15mins | Cook: 45mins | Ready in:

Ingredients

- 3/4 cup chopped dried apricots
- 2 tablespoons olive oil
- 2 cloves garlic, minced
- 2 teaspoons ground cinnamon
- 2 teaspoons ground cumin
- 2 teaspoons paprika
- 1 pound ground lamb
- 4 stalks celery, cut into 1/2 inch pieces
- 1 large green bell pepper, sliced
- 1 pound tomatoes, coarsely chopped
- 1 lemon
- 1 1/4 cups water
- 1 tablespoon white sugar
- salt and black pepper to taste

Direction

- Leave the apricots to soak for 2 hours or more in water, until soft; strain.
- Place a heavy, large saucepan on medium heat; heat olive oil. Cook in paprika, cumin, cinnamon and garlic; stir for 1 minute. Turn to medium-high heat; crumble in ground lamb; using a wooden spoon, brake it up and stir until well browned, for a few minutes. Mix in the tomato, green pepper, celery and strained apricots.
- Shave 5-6 rind strips off the lemon with a vegetable peeler; transfer to the soup with lemon juice. Mix in sugar and water. Bring to boil; then lower the heat to medium-low; gently simmer with a cover for 30 minutes. Season with pepper and salt.

Nutrition Information

- Calories: 405 calories;
- Total Fat: 23.1
- Sodium: 110
- Total Carbohydrate: 31.3
- Cholesterol: 76
- Protein: 22.6

357. Aunt Louise's Baked Kibbeh

Serving: 8 | Prep: 20mins | Cook: 45mins | Ready in:

Ingredients

- 1 cup bulgur wheat
- 2 cups boiling water
- 1/2 cup finely chopped onion, divided
- 2 teaspoons salt, divided
- 1 1/2 teaspoons dried basil
- 1/2 teaspoon ground black pepper
- 1 pound ground beef
- 1 pound ground lamb, divided
- 1/2 cup pine nuts
- 1/4 stick salted butter
- 1/2 cup cherry tomatoes, or to taste
- 1/4 cup fresh mint leaves, or to taste

Direction

- In a big bowl, put in the bulgur and fill it with enough boiling water to submerge the bulgur. Let it sit for about 30 minutes until the bulgur have soaked up the water.
- Preheat your oven to 350°F (175°C).
- Add the basil, 1/4 cup of onion, pepper and 1 1/2 teaspoons of salt into the soaked bulgur and give it a mix. Put in 1/2 pound of lamb and ground beef and mix it thoroughly. Separate the meat mixture into 2 equal portions. Flatten 1 portion of the meat mixture on the bottom of a 7x12-inch baking dish.
- On a piece of waxed paper, flatten the other portion of the meat mixture into a rectangle in the same size as the baking dish. Put it aside for the top layer.
- In a skillet, put in the remaining 1/2 pound of lamb and 1/4 cup of onion and sauté it for about 5 minutes until it turns brown in color. Drain off the excess fat from the skillet. Add the remaining 1/2 teaspoon of salt and pine nuts; mix well. Spread a spoonful of the lamb-pine nut mixture evenly on top of the meat layer in the bottom of the baking dish.
- Flip the other meat layer upside down to cover the lamb-pine nut layer. Remove the waxed paper. Create diamond patterns on the top meat layer by cutting it diagonally about 3 inches away from each other in both directions. Push a small amount of butter to the center of each of the diamonds.
- Put it in the preheated oven and let it bake for about 40 minutes until it turns golden brown in color. Top it with mint and cherry tomatoes.

Nutrition Information

- Calories: 364 calories;
- Sodium: 663
- Total Carbohydrate: 16.1
- Cholesterol: 80
- Total Fat: 23.4
- Protein: 23.2

358. Awesome Herb Roast Leg Of Lamb

Serving: 4 | Prep: 10mins | Cook: 50mins | Ready in:

Ingredients

- 1 clove garlic, minced
- 1 teaspoon salt
- 1 teaspoon ground black pepper
- 1/2 teaspoon ground ginger
- 1/2 teaspoon ground dried thyme
- 1/2 teaspoon dried sage
- 1/2 teaspoon dried marjoram
- 1 tablespoon reduced-sodium soy sauce
- 1 tablespoon vegetable oil
- 1 bay leaf
- 2 pounds leg of lamb

Direction

- Preheat an oven to 150°C/300°F.
- In a bowl, mix marjoram, sage, thyme, ginger, pepper, salt and garlic. Mix vegetable oil and soy sauce into garlic mixture till loosely-paste like; add bay leaf.
- On all sides, cut slits into lamb; rub herb mixture on entire lamb surface, massaging into slits. Put lamb into roasting pan.
- Roast lamb for 50 minutes for rare till red in center and browned outside; an inserted instant-read thermometer in middle should read 52°C/125°F. Loosely cover lamb with aluminum foil; cool before carving for 20 minutes.

Nutrition Information

- Calories: 276 calories;
- Total Fat: 17.8
- Sodium: 781
- Total Carbohydrate: 1.3
- Cholesterol: 91
- Protein: 26.3

359. Bacon Wrapped Mushroom Meatloaf

Serving: 20 | Prep: 20mins | Cook: 1hours30mins | Ready in:

Ingredients

- 1 pound ground beef chuck
- 1 pound ground pork
- 1 pound ground lamb
- 1 cup chopped button mushrooms
- 1 cup bread crumbs
- 3 eggs
- 3 tablespoons minced garlic
- 2 tablespoons dried thyme
- 1 tablespoon soy sauce
- 1 tablespoon mushroom-flavored soup base
- 1 tablespoon dried parsley
- 1 tablespoon dried sage
- 1 pound bacon strips

Direction

- Set the oven at 350°F (175°C) and start preheating.
- In a large bowl, thoroughly combine sage, parsley, soup base, soy sauce, thyme, garlic, eggs, bread crumbs, mushrooms, lamb, pork and beef together; form into 2 loaves. Wrap the loaves with bacon strips to completely cover. Arrange loaves on a baking sheet.
- Bake for 90 minutes to 2 hours in the preheated oven, or till the loaves are not pink in the center anymore. An instant-read thermometer should read at least 160°F (70°C) when inserted into the center.

Nutrition Information

- Calories: 210 calories;
- Total Fat: 13.4
- Sodium: 368
- Total Carbohydrate: 5.1
- Cholesterol: 80
- Protein: 16.5

360. Bamieh (Middle Eastern Okra Stew)

Serving: 8 | Prep: 20mins | Cook: 2hours | Ready in:

Ingredients

- 2 tablespoons vegetable oil
- 2 large onions, chopped
- salt and ground black pepper to taste
- 2 pounds cubed lamb stew meat
- 3 tablespoons ground cinnamon
- 1 1/2 teaspoons ground cumin
- 1 1/2 teaspoons ground coriander
- 1 1/2 tablespoons garlic paste
- 5 (14.5 ounce) cans canned diced tomatoes, drained
- 1 1/2 tablespoons tomato paste
- 2 beef bouillon cubes
- 4 cups boiling water
- 2 pounds frozen sliced okra

Direction

- Heat vegetable oil in big pot on medium heat. Mix black pepper, salt and onion in. Mix and cook for about 10 minutes till onion is light golden brown and soft.
- Add garlic paste, coriander, cumin, cinnamon and lamb. Cook for 10-15 minutes on medium heat till lamb begins to brown, occasionally mixing. Mix tomato paste and tomatoes in; mix and cook for 5 more minutes.
- In 4 cups boiling water, melt beef bouillon cubes. Put broth into pot with lamb. Mix okra in. Cover okra with water if needed; cover. Simmer, occasionally mixing, for 30 minutes. Uncover. Cook till stew hits preferred thickness and lamb is very tender for another 45 minutes – 1 hour.

Nutrition Information

- Calories: 262 calories;
- Total Carbohydrate: 22.6
- Cholesterol: 53
- Protein: 21.6
- Total Fat: 8.3
- Sodium: 779

361. Bhuna Gosht

Serving: 6 | Prep: 15mins | Cook: 50mins | Ready in:

Ingredients

- 1/4 cup cooking oil
- 3 pods green cardamom
- 1 pod black cardamom
- 2 bay leaves
- 1 cinnamon stick
- 6 large onions, sliced thin
- 6 cloves garlic
- 1 (1/2 inch) piece fresh ginger root, peeled and julienned
- 2 teaspoons Kashmiri red chili powder
- 1 teaspoon ground cumin
- 1/2 teaspoon ground turmeric
- salt, to taste
- 2 tomatoes, pureed
- 2 pounds lamb chops, rinsed and patted dry
- 2 tablespoons water
- 3 green chile peppers, halved lengthwise
- 1/4 cup cilantro leaves, for garnish

Direction

- Put the oil in a big skillet and set over medium heat. Add the black cardamom pods, green cardamom pods, cinnamon stick and bay leaves in the hot oil, frying them until you smell the nice aroma. Mix in the ginger, garlic and onions in the mixture. Adjust the heat to low and continue to cook until the onions turned golden brown; spice it off using the salt, red chili powder, cumin and turmeric. Stir in the tomatoes and continue to cook for roughly additional 5 minutes until the oil separates from the gravy.
- Put the lamb chops with the mixture in the skillet and adjust the heat to medium-low. Stir while it cooks for roughly 20 minutes until the lamb is halfway done and the sauce produces a glaze on the outside of the meat. Drizzle the water over the mixture. Cook the lamb while covered for additional 15 to 20 minutes until it the meat is tender. Take the cover off and drop the cilantro leaves and green chile peppers. Adjust the heat to high and allow to cook for additional 3 to 5 minutes. Serve while it is hot.

Nutrition Information

- Calories: 453 calories;
- Total Fat: 30.4
- Sodium: 90
- Total Carbohydrate: 20.5
- Cholesterol: 90
- Protein: 25.6

362. Boxty With Liver And Bacon

Serving: 6 | Prep: 25mins | Cook: 26mins | Ready in:

Ingredients

- 1 cup self-rising flour
- 5 tablespoons milk
- 1 pound potatoes, peeled and coarsely grated
- salt and freshly ground black pepper to taste
- 2 tablespoons butter, divided
- 2 tablespoons vegetable oil, divided
- 3 tablespoons all-purpose flour
- 1 teaspoon dried mixed herbs
- 8 ounces lamb's liver, cut into thin strips
- 8 slices bacon
- 6 ounces shredded cabbage

Direction

- In a bowl, sift self-rising flour; mix in milk. Squeeze excess moisture from grated potatoes then stir in. Flavor with pepper and salt.
- In a large skillet, melt 1 teaspoon oil with 1 1/2 teaspoon butter over medium heat. Spread 1/4 potato mixture in skillet; cook for 3-4 mins each side, until golden brown. Repeat 3 times with the rest of oil, butter, and potato mixture. On a plate, stack potato pancakes and keep warm.
- In a bowl, mix pepper, salt, mixed herbs, and all-purpose flour. In the flour mixture, roll liver strips until coated evenly.
- In the skillet, heat the rest of 2 teaspoons of oil. Cook while stirring liver strips until golden brown in the hot oil, about 2-3 mins.
- In the same skillet, cook bacon slices until evenly browned, turning occasionally, about 10 mins. Remove bacon slices on paper towels to drain.
- In a large pot, add lightly salted water and bring to a boil. Put in cabbage and cook for 3 mins, until wilted. Drain.
- Add liver, bacon and cabbage on top of potatoes pancakes and flavor with black pepper. Serve.

Nutrition Information

- Calories: 353 calories;
- Total Fat: 16.9
- Sodium: 641
- Total Carbohydrate: 35.1
- Cholesterol: 135
- Protein: 15

363. Braised Lamb Shoulder Chops

Serving: 6 | Prep: 20mins | Cook: 3hours10mins | Ready in:

Ingredients

- 1 tablespoon olive oil
- 2 pounds lamb shoulder chops, or more to taste
- salt and ground black pepper to taste
- 1 small yellow onion, sliced
- 4 cloves garlic, minced
- 2 tablespoons chopped fresh rosemary
- 1 cup beef broth
- 1 cup red wine
- 2 tablespoons cornstarch
- 1/2 cup water
- 1 tablespoon Worcestershire sauce

Direction

- Preheat oven to 150°C (300°F).
- In a skillet, heat the olive oil over medium-high heat. Add pepper and salt to season the lamb chops. Sear the lamb in hot oil about 1 to 2 minutes on each side, until browned. Transfer the chops to a dish to drain, saving the drippings in skillet.
- Sauté the garlic and onion in the reserved drippings for 5 minutes until soft.
- Move the drained lamb chops to a baking dish; put in onion mixture. Sprinkle onto the chops with the rosemary. Add the red wine and beef broth in the baking dish. Cover the dish using aluminum foil.
- Bake for 3 hours in the preheated oven.
- Transfer the lamb to a serving platter. Drain the liquid carefully from the baking dish into a saucepan, then put over medium heat. Beat the water and cornstarch in a bowl with a whisk to ensure that there are no lumps left; mix into the liquid in the saucepan. Put in Worcestershire sauce, then cook for 5 minutes, until liquid thickens into a gravy.

Nutrition Information

- Calories: 360 calories;
- Sodium: 258
- Total Carbohydrate: 5.9
- Cholesterol: 90
- Protein: 23.3

- Total Fat: 23.1

364. Butter Lamb Gravy

Serving: 6 | Prep: 25mins | Cook: 35mins | Ready in:

Ingredients

- 2 pounds boneless lamb shoulder, cut into 1 inch pieces
- 1/2 teaspoon garam masala
- salt to taste
- 2 tablespoons butter, divided
- 1 onion, chopped
- 1/2 teaspoon ground turmeric (optional)
- 1/2 teaspoon minced ginger
- 1/2 teaspoon minced garlic
- 1/2 teaspoon cayenne pepper, or to taste
- 1 tablespoon tomato paste
- 1 cup water
- 1/2 cup heavy cream
- 1 tablespoon honey
- 1 cup chopped fresh cilantro

Direction

- Use salt and garam masala to season lamb. Heat 1 tbsp. butter in big skillet on medium heat; fry lamb cubes till browned, constantly mixing. Take out of skillet; put aside.
- Melt leftover butter in same skillet on medium heat. Add onion; mix and cook for 5 minutes till onion is translucent and soft.
- Mix garlic, ginger and turmeric in; mix and cook for 1 minute. Mix tomato paste and cayenne in till well blended; mix water in. Simmer; put lamb back in skillet. Simmer for 20 minutes on low heat till lamb is tender.
- Mix honey and cream in; put on serving dish. Garnish with cilantro.

Nutrition Information

- Calories: 321 calories;
- Sodium: 115
- Total Carbohydrate: 8.2
- Cholesterol: 115
- Protein: 22.9
- Total Fat: 21.8

365. Candice's Lamb Cannelloni With Mint Pesto

Serving: 6 | Prep: 20mins | Cook: 25mins | Ready in:

Ingredients

- 1 (8 ounce) package lasagna noodles
- 2 teaspoons vegetable oil
- 10 ounces ground lamb
- 1 teaspoon dried sage
- 1 teaspoon thyme
- 1/2 teaspoon salt
- 1/4 teaspoon pepper
- 1 (5.5 ounce) package crumbled goat cheese
- 1 bunch fresh mint
- 1/4 cup pine nuts
- 6 tablespoons olive oil

Direction

- Let a big pot of slightly-salted water come to a rolling boil. Allow the pasta to cook in boiling water without a cover for 12 minutes till cooked completely yet remain firm to the bite. Drain thoroughly in colander place in sink. Halve every sheet width-wise.
- In a skillet, heat vegetable oil over moderate heat; let the lamb cook in hot oil for 7 to 10 minutes till equally browned. Add pepper, salt, thyme and sage to season. Take off heat; into the cooked lamb, mix goat cheese. Into the middle of every of lasagna sheets, scoop approximately a tablespoon of lamb mixture and roll into a cylinder; set on plate.
- In a blender, process olive oil, pine nuts and mint till finely chopped yet not liquefied; sprinkle on top of rolls, serve.

Nutrition Information

- Calories: 490 calories;
- Sodium: 357
- Total Carbohydrate: 29.5
- Cholesterol: 52
- Protein: 20.3
- Total Fat: 33

366. Cephalonian Meat Pie

Serving: 12 | Prep: 1hours | Cook: 2hours | Ready in:

Ingredients

- 8 cups all-purpose flour
- 1/3 cup olive oil
- 1/2 cup dry white wine
- 2 cups water
- 1/2 teaspoon salt
- 1/4 cup olive oil
- 1 onion, finely chopped
- 2 cloves garlic, minced
- 1 pound boneless lamb shoulder, cut into 1-inch cubes
- 1 pound boneless pork shoulder, cut into 1-inch cubes
- 1/4 cup tomato paste
- 1/4 cup dry white wine
- 3/4 cup water
- 1 cup grated Greek Kefalotiri or Parmesan cheese
- 1 potato, peeled and cut into 1/2-inch cubes
- 1/2 cup long grain rice
- 1 teaspoon minced parsley
- 1 teaspoon chopped fresh mint or spearmint
- 1/2 teaspoon dried marjoram
- salt and pepper to taste
- 1 egg, beaten

Direction

- In a large bowl, prepare the dough placing flour. Create a well in the center and put in salt, water, white wine, and 1/3 cup of olive oil. Use your hands to mix together for a few minutes to shape a smooth dough. Wrap in plastic wrap and put in the refrigerator while you move on with the recipe.
- Over medium heat, in a large saucepan, heat olive oil. Stir in garlic and onion, then cook for a few minutes until the onion is tender and turns transparent. Stir in pork and lamb; increase the heat to medium-high and keep cooking for about 5 minutes until the onion starts to brown.
- Blend in tomato paste until the meat is covered. Mix in white wine and simmer for 1 minute. Add water and heat to a simmer. Lower the heat to medium-low and simmer, covered, for about 45 minutes until softened.
- Once the meat is done, turn off the heat and let cool while making the crust.
- Start preheating the oven to 450°F (230°C). Lightly grease olive oil onto a 9x13-inch glass baking dish.
- Cut the dough into 2 pieces, with one piece larger than the other. On a floured surface, roll out the large piece until it is large enough to fit the base of the baking dish and come up the sides of the pan; press into the baking dish. Form the smaller piece of dough into a rectangle to use as the top crust; put aside.
- Stir rice, potato, and Kefalotiri cheese into the meat mixture. Flavor with pepper, salt, marjoram, mint, and parsley. Add egg and beat until well-blended. Transfer this mixture into the baking dish and top with the leftover piece of dough. Brush the top with olive oil and a little water.
- Bake pie in the prepared oven for 1 hour until deep golden brown.

Nutrition Information

- Calories: 691 calories;
- Sodium: 398
- Total Carbohydrate: 75.8
- Cholesterol: 76
- Protein: 28.6
- Total Fat: 28.1

367. Chalau

Serving: 6 | Prep: 30mins | Cook: 2hours | Ready in:

Ingredients

- 1/2 cup vegetable oil
- 1 large onion, finely chopped
- 2 cloves garlic, minced
- 1 1/2 pounds cubed lamb stew meat
- 1 1/2 cups water
- salt to taste
- freshly ground black pepper to taste
- 1/4 teaspoon cayenne pepper, or to taste
- 1 teaspoon ground cumin
- 3 cups chopped fresh spinach
- 2 tablespoons chopped fresh cilantro
- 1/4 cup cooking oil
- 3 cups uncooked basmati rice
- 6 cups water

Direction

- In a big heavy skillet, heat 1/2 cup of oil on moderately low heat. Put in onion and fry gently until it is transparent. Raise heat to moderate then put in garlic and stew meat. Cook mixture until the outside of meat is browned, while stirring often. Pour in water and use cumin, cayenne pepper, pepper and salt to season. Bring to a simmer and lower heat to low. Place a cover on pan and keep on cooking for 1 1/2-2 hours.
- In a big saucepan, heat 1/4 cup of oil on moderately high heat. Put in rice and cook for 5 minutes while stirring often. Put in 6 cups of water and bring to a boil. Lower heat to low and cook for 30 minutes, covered loosely, until rice is softened.
- Put into the meat mixture with cilantro and spinach, then cook for 10-15 more minutes. Mound on a platter with the rice and scoop over top with some of the lamb stew. Put in a separate serving bowl with leftover stew.

Nutrition Information

- Calories: 740 calories;
- Total Fat: 34.6
- Sodium: 88
- Total Carbohydrate: 77
- Cholesterol: 74
- Protein: 30.9

368. Chef John's Lamb Moussaka Burger

Serving: 4 | Prep: 40mins | Cook: 25mins | Ready in:

Ingredients

- 2 tablespoons olive oil
- 1 yellow onion, diced
- 1 teaspoon salt
- 2 cups diced eggplant
- 3 cloves garlic, crushed
- 1 teaspoon freshly ground black pepper
- 1/2 teaspoon cumin
- 1/4 teaspoon ground cinnamon
- 1/4 teaspoon dried oregano
- 2 teaspoons tomato paste
- 1 1/2 tablespoons olive oil
- 2 tablespoons flour
- 1 cup cold milk
- 1 pinch ground nutmeg
- 1 pinch cayenne pepper
- 1 pinch freshly ground black pepper
- 1/2 cup grated Parmesan cheese
- 1 pound ground lamb
- salt to taste
- 8 slices tomato
- 1 tablespoon chopped fresh mint
- 1 tablespoon rice vinegar
- 1 tablespoon olive oil, or as needed
- 4 hamburger buns, split and toasted

Direction

- On medium-high heat, heat 2tbsp olive oil in a pan; add diced onion and a teaspoon of salt. Cook and stir for 5mins until the onion is a bit translucent; put in eggplant. Turn to medium heat, cook and stir for another 3-5mins until the eggplant is soft and opaque.
- Mix oregano, garlic, cinnamon, cumin, and a teaspoon of black pepper into the eggplant mixture. Cook while stirring regularly for a minute until aromatic; put tomato paste. Cook and stir for 2mins until completely heated. Move to a plate then cool through; use a plastic wrap to cover. Place in the refrigerator for at least 15mins until chilled.
- On medium-high heat, mix flour and 1 1/2tbsp olive oil together in a pot for 2-3mins until bubbling and golden; add milk. Let it simmer while stirring constantly for 3-5mins until it forms into a thick and smooth sauce. Add nutmeg and a pinch each of cayenne and black pepper to season; take off heat. Mix in Parmesan cheese until it melts.
- In a bowl, mix a pinch of salt, chilled eggplant mixture, and lamb together; shape into 4 patties then put on a plate. Use a plastic wrap to cover then place in the refrigerator until ready to cook.
- In a shallow bowl, put tomato slices then season with chopped mint and a pinch each of black pepper and salt; toss in rice vinegar to coat.
- On medium-high heat, heat a tablespoon of olive oil in a big pan. Cook burgers for 4mins on each side until the center is a bit pink. An inserted instant-read thermometer in the middle should register 60°C or 140°Fahrenheit for medium.
- Slather the preferred amount of cheese sauce on each side of the hamburger buns; put burgers on the bottom bun. Add two slices of tomato on top then put the top bun.

Nutrition Information

- Calories: 620 calories;
- Cholesterol: 90
- Protein: 31.2
- Total Fat: 37.3
- Sodium: 1133
- Total Carbohydrate: 39.9

369. Crostini Alla Fiorentina

Serving: 4 | Prep: 5mins | Cook: 20mins | Ready in:

Ingredients

- 3 tablespoons olive oil
- 1 teaspoon chopped onion
- 1 teaspoon celery, chopped
- 1 chopped carrot
- 2 cloves garlic, pressed
- 4 ounces chicken livers, rinsed and sliced into strips
- 4 ounces lamb or pork livers, rinsed and cut into strips
- 1/2 cup red wine
- 1 tablespoon tomato puree
- 2 tablespoons chopped fresh parsley
- 3 anchovy fillets, chopped
- 2 tablespoons chicken stock or water
- salt and pepper to taste
- 1 tablespoon butter, or as needed
- 1 tablespoon capers

Direction

- Place a skillet on the stove and turn on to low heat then put the oil. Add in the garlic, carrot, celery and onion; stir and cook for about 5 minutes until onions are softened.
- Pat dry the lamb and chicken liver, then add in to the skillet. Cook on low heat until every sides turned to brown in color. Stir in the red wine over the liver, and let it evaporate in a minute. Mix in the pepper, salt, chicken stock, anchovies, half of parsley, and tomato puree. Cover with a lid and gently boil for 20 minutes and mix in the left parsley, capers and butter.
- Puree the liver mixture using a hand-held blender. Send it to a food processor if you

don't have a hand-held blender and mix blend well until becomes smooth. Put it back to the skillet, and mix in the left parsley, capers and butter.

Nutrition Information

- Calories: 224 calories;
- Total Fat: 16.1
- Sodium: 273
- Total Carbohydrate: 2.5
- Cholesterol: 212
- Protein: 11.7

370. Curried Ground Lamb With Quinoa, Swiss Chard, And Fiddle Ferns

Serving: 5 | Prep: 15mins | Cook: 40mins | Ready in:

Ingredients

- 1 cup fiddlehead ferns
- 1/2 pound ground lamb
- 4 cups chopped Swiss chard
- 1 carrot, cut into 1/4 inch rounds
- 1 stalk celery, chopped
- 1/2 onion, chopped
- 1/2 cup frozen peas
- 2 cups lamb stock
- 1 cup quinoa
- 2 tablespoons curry powder
- 2 cloves garlic, pressed
- salt and ground black pepper to taste

Direction

- Boil a pot of water then add fiddlehead ferns; cook for about 5mins until tender. Drain.
- On medium-high heat, heat a 9-in cast iron pan; add lamb. Cook and stir for 5-7mins until crumbly and brown. Put in peas, chard, onion, celery and carrot; cook for about 10mins while mixing from time to time, until the veggies are soft and the chard wilts.
- Stir in curry powder, quinoa and lamb stock into the lamb mixture; cover then boil. Turn to low heat then let it simmer for about 15mins until most of the moisture is absorbed and the quinoa is tender.
- Take pan off from heat then mix in garlic and fiddlehead ferns into the lamb-quinoa mixture; sprinkle pepper and salt to season. Let it stand for 5mins then serve.

Nutrition Information

- Calories: 263 calories;
- Cholesterol: 30
- Protein: 15.6
- Total Fat: 8.8
- Sodium: 154
- Total Carbohydrate: 31.5

371. Curried Stew With Lamb

Serving: 8 | Prep: 40mins | Cook: 2hours20mins | Ready in:

Ingredients

- 1 cup yogurt
- 1 tablespoon minced garlic
- 2 pounds lamb sirloin, cut into cubes
- 2 cups water
- 1 cup uncooked rice
- 1 tablespoon vegetable oil
- 1 large onion, grated
- 1/2 teaspoon ground cloves
- 1/2 teaspoon ground ginger
- 1/2 teaspoon ground cumin
- 3/4 teaspoon ground cayenne pepper
- 3 tablespoons curry powder
- 2/3 cup slivered almonds, toasted
- 1 cup currants
- 8 cups vegetable broth

Direction

- In the medium-sized bowl, mix the garlic and yogurt. Mix in lamb cubes till coated. Keep covered and chilled in the refrigerator overnight.
- In the sauce pan, boil the water. Put in the rice and mix. Lower the heat, keep covered and let it simmer for 20 minutes. Take out of the heat, and put aside.
- Heat the oil on medium-high heat in the big skillet. Sauté the onions till becoming soft. Mix in the marinated lamb mixture. Use the curry powder, cayenne, cumin, ginger, and cloves. Mix in the raisins, lower the heat, and let simmer for 2 hours. Mix in the vegetable stock and cooked rice. Simmer again, and cook 5 minutes longer.

Nutrition Information

- Calories: 623 calories;
- Sodium: 550
- Total Carbohydrate: 44.7
- Cholesterol: 86
- Protein: 26.1
- Total Fat: 38.1

372. Diced Lamb With Roasted Vegetables And Couscous

Serving: 2 | Prep: 30mins | Cook: 20mins | Ready in:

Ingredients

- 1 sprig fresh rosemary, chopped
- 1/4 cup chopped fresh mint leaves
- 1 hot chile pepper, minced
- 1 clove garlic, minced
- 2 limes, juiced
- 6 tablespoons olive oil, divided
- salt and pepper to taste
- 3/4 pound boneless lamb, cut into 1/2-inch cubes
- 1 eggplant, peeled and cubed
- 1 red bell pepper, cut into 1 inch pieces
- 1 yellow bell pepper, cut into 1 inch pieces
- 2 green onions, chopped
- 1 tablespoon butter
- 1 (10 ounce) box couscous
- 1 1/2 cups boiling water
- 1 lime, juiced

Direction

- Mix the salt and pepper to taste, chili pepper, rosemary, juices from 2 limes, 2 tbsp. of olive oil, mint, and garlic. Add the lamb to the mixture and coat it well. Let it marinate inside the fridge for at least 1 hour or overnight.
- Set the oven to 350°F or 175°C for preheating.
- Mix the red and yellow peppers, onions, eggplant, and 3 tbsp. of olive oil until well coated. Spread the vegetables in a single layer onto the large baking sheet. Roast the vegetables for 20 minutes until tender.
- Put 1 tbsp. of olive oil in a skillet and heat it over medium heat. Get the lamb from the marinade and add it to the skillet, discarding the marinade. Cook and stir for 10 minutes until the lamb is no longer pink.
- In the meantime, put butter in a small saucepan and melt it over medium heat. Add the couscous. Stir the mixture briefly until well coated. Pour in water. Cook and stir until it starts to boil. Cover the pan and put it aside for 10 minutes until the water is completely absorbed. Use a fork to fluff the couscous. Mix in juice from a lime.
- Serve the vegetables and lamb over the couscous.

Nutrition Information

- Calories: 1216 calories;
- Sodium: 86
- Total Carbohydrate: 135.8
- Cholesterol: 96
- Protein: 47.3

- Total Fat: 54.5

373. Eggplant And Lamb Stew

Serving: 6 | Prep: 15mins | Cook: 2hours | Ready in:

Ingredients

- 2 tablespoons butter
- 1 1/2 pounds lamb shoulder
- 2 large eggplants, peeled and chopped
- 2 large tomatoes, chopped
- 2 large onions, chopped
- 2 green bell peppers, chopped
- 10 cloves garlic, chopped
- 1 tablespoon tomato paste
- 1/2 cup water
- 1 teaspoon allspice
- 2 teaspoons salt
- 1 teaspoon ground black pepper

Direction

- Melt butter in a large pot that is set over medium heat. Brown all the sides of the lamb. Stir in garlic, eggplants, onions, tomatoes, and green bell peppers. Cook and stir until they are browned lightly and tender.
- Blend the water and tomato paste in a small bowl. Stir the mixture into the pot with lamb. Season the lamb with salt, pepper, and allspice. Lower the heat. Simmer the mixture for 1 1/2 hours while occasionally stirring it until the meat can be shred easily using the fork. You can add a little amount of water as needed to keep the ingredients moist.

Nutrition Information

- Calories: 292 calories;
- Total Fat: 16.2
- Sodium: 871
- Total Carbohydrate: 20.8
- Cholesterol: 68

- Protein: 18.2

374. Egyptian Bamia

Serving: 4 | Prep: 15mins | Cook: 2hours | Ready in:

Ingredients

- 1/4 cup olive oil
- 1 large onion, finely chopped
- 1 pound boneless lamb shoulder, cut into 1-inch pieces
- salt and ground black pepper to taste
- 1 (8 ounce) can tomato sauce
- 2 cups water, or as needed to cover
- 1 (10 ounce) package frozen okra, thawed

Direction

- In big saucepan, heat olive oil on medium heat; mix and cook for about 7 minutes till onion is translucent. Mix black pepper, salt and lamb in. Mix and cook for 5-10 minutes more till lamb is lightly browned.
- Mix water and tomato sauce in; season with black pepper and salt. Boil lamb mixture; lower heat to low. Simmer lamb in the sauce for minimum of 1 hour till very tender; add more water if needed. Occasionally mix.
- Preheat an oven to 175°C/350°F.
- Mix okra in lamb mixture, adding extra water if needed; boil. Spoon bamia into 2-qt. baking dish. Adjust black pepper and salt. Use foil to cover dish.
- In preheated oven, bake for about 45 minutes till okra is tender. Uncover at final 10 minutes of baking.

Nutrition Information

- Calories: 339 calories;
- Total Fat: 25.7
- Sodium: 337
- Total Carbohydrate: 11.2

- Cholesterol: 58
- Protein: 16.9

375. Fasolia (Green Bean Stew)

Serving: 4 | Prep: 10mins | Cook: 1hours20mins | Ready in:

Ingredients

- 1 (17.5 ounce) package lamb neck
- 1 tablespoon butter
- 1/2 cup chopped onion
- 4 cloves garlic, chopped
- 3 cups water
- 1 1/2 cups tomato sauce
- 1 teaspoon salt
- 1/2 teaspoon ground allspice
- 1/4 teaspoon ground black pepper
- 1 pound green beans
- 2 potatoes (or to taste), thinly sliced (optional)

Direction

- Melt the butter on medium heat in a big skillet; cook and whisk the lamb neck bones in the hot butter for 7-10 minutes till brown. Put in the garlic and onion; cook and whisk for 7-10 minutes till brown.
- In the small-sized bowl, whisk together the pepper, allspice, salt, tomato sauce and water; add to skillet and boil. Lower the heat to medium low, put the cover onto the skillet, and cook for roughly 45 minutes till meat is pulled away from neck bones.
- Add the potatoes and green beans to skillet so they are in liquid, replace the cover, and keep cooking for roughly 15 minutes till potatoes become thoroughly cooked and beans soften. Take out and get rid of the bones prior to serving.

Nutrition Information

- Calories: 178 calories;
- Protein: 5.9
- Total Fat: 3.3
- Sodium: 1103
- Total Carbohydrate: 34.8
- Cholesterol: 8

376. Gigot D'Agneau Au Four (Roast Lamb With Beans)

Serving: 8 | Prep: 15mins | Cook: 40mins | Ready in:

Ingredients

- 1 (3 pound) leg of lamb
- 6 cloves garlic, peeled
- 2 tablespoons butter, softened
- salt and ground black pepper to taste
- 4 (14 ounce) cans cannellini beans, drained and rinsed
- 1 tablespoon chopped fresh parsley

Direction

- Set oven to 220° C (425° F) and start preheating.
- In a big baking dish, place the leg of lamb. Use a sharp knife to prick in 6 places; fill the slits with garlic cloves. Brush lamb with butter. Put in pepper and salt to season.
- Place in the preheated oven and roast 25 minutes, basting frequently with juices. Spread cannellini beans around the lamb, tossing to coat with juices. Keep roasting 15 minutes longer until the temperature inside the lambs is 71° C (160 ° F) for medium and beans are warmed through.
- Let lamb stand about 10 minutes then slice. Top with chopped parsley, place beans on the side to serve.

Nutrition Information

- Calories: 363 calories;

- Sodium: 505
- Total Carbohydrate: 28.3
- Cholesterol: 73
- Protein: 26.6
- Total Fat: 14.9

377. Grape Leaves Aleppo

Serving: 32 | Prep: 45mins | Cook: 1hours15mins | Ready in:

Ingredients

- 1 cup uncooked white rice
- 2 pounds ground lamb
- 2 (16 ounce) jars grape leaves, drained and rinsed
- 1 teaspoon salt
- 1 teaspoon ground black pepper
- 1 tablespoon ground allspice
- 6 cloves garlic, sliced
- 1 cup lemon juice
- 2 kalamata olives (optional)

Direction

- Soak the rice in cold water, then drain. Combine the pepper, salt, allspice, rice and ground lamb in a big bowl until well combined. Put approximately 1 tbsp. of the meat mixture onto the middle of each leaf. Fold the leaf over once, then flip in the edges on each side and roll the leaf to close.
- In a big pot, stack the leaf-rolls, then use garlic slices to cover each layer. Pour just enough water to cover the rolls, then pour lemon juice. Add olives into the pot for the flavoring, if preferred. Put a plate over the rolls to help them remain under water.
- Let it boil, then lower the heat, put on cover and let it simmer for 1 hour and 15 minutes. Taste the rice if it's done. The grape leaves taste even better after letting it sit for a couple of hours. Serve.

Nutrition Information

- Calories: 101 calories;
- Total Fat: 4.5
- Sodium: 902
- Total Carbohydrate: 9.2
- Cholesterol: 19
- Protein: 6.5

378. Greek Burgers

Serving: 8 | Prep: 25mins | Cook: 10mins | Ready in:

Ingredients

- 1/2 cup mayonnaise
- 1 teaspoon minced garlic
- 2 pounds ground lamb
- 1/4 cup breadcrumbs
- 1 cup trimmed, diced fennel bulb
- 3 tablespoons shallots, minced
- 1 teaspoon dried oregano
- 1/2 teaspoon salt
- ground black pepper to taste
- 1 tablespoon olive oil
- 8 hamburger buns

Direction

- Blend together minced garlic and mayonnaise in a small bowl. Cover; put in the fridge for at least 1 hour.
- Set grill to high heat and start preheating.
- Combine together salt, oregano, shallot, fennel, breadcrumbs, and lamb. Shape into 3/4-in.-thick patties; sprinkle black pepper on top of each.
- Use olive oil to brush grate; put the burgers on grill. Cook until done, about 3-5 minutes on each side, turning once. Place onto buns and serve with garlic mayonnaise.

Nutrition Information

- Calories: 479 calories;

- Total Fat: 30.4
- Sodium: 559
- Total Carbohydrate: 26.2
- Cholesterol: 81
- Protein: 23.9

379. Greek Hamburgers

Serving: 4 | Prep: 20mins | Cook: 10mins |Ready in:

Ingredients

- 1 pound ground beef
- 1 (4 ounce) container crumbled feta cheese
- 2 ounces goat cheese
- 2 tablespoons fresh lemon juice
- 2 tablespoons extra-virgin olive oil
- 1 tablespoon dried oregano
- 1 clove garlic, minced
- 1/2 cup Greek yogurt
- 1/4 cup diced cucumber
- 3 tablespoons fresh lemon juice

Direction

- In a large bowl, use hands together to combine garlic, oregano, olive oil, 2 tablespoons of lemon juice, goat cheese, feta cheese, and ground beef. Shape meat into 4 patties.
- In a bowl, mix together 3 tablespoons of lemon juice, cucumber, and Greek yogurt.
- Heat a frying pan for about 2 minutes on medium heat; cook burgers for about 5 minutes on each side to the desired doneness. An instant-read thermometer should display 70°C (160°F) when inserted into the center. Finally, serve the burgers with yogurt sauce.

Nutrition Information

- Calories: 469 calories;
- Total Fat: 37.3
- Sodium: 471
- Total Carbohydrate: 5.4

- Cholesterol: 112
- Protein: 27.6

380. Gyroll

Serving: 4 | Prep: 25mins | Cook: 35mins |Ready in:

Ingredients

- 1 tablespoon olive oil
- 1 pound ground lamb
- 6 cloves garlic, crushed
- 1 large onion, sliced
- 1 tablespoon dried oregano
- 2/3 teaspoon ground cumin
- 2 teaspoons salt
- 2 teaspoons freshly ground black pepper
- 1 dash hot pepper sauce
- 2/3 cup chopped fresh parsley
- 1 pound pizza crust dough
- 6 ounces feta cheese
- 1/2 zucchini, diced
- 8 ounces chopped black olives
- 1/2 teaspoon garlic powder

Direction

- Preheat oven to 450 °F (230 °C).
- In a large skillet, heat oil over medium-high heat. Brown the meat with onion, garlic, cumin, oregano, salt, hot pepper sauce and pepper. Add in parsley when meat is almost done, and cook till the parsley wilts. Take away mixture from heat and allow to cool.
- Roll pizza dough out to form a rectangle of 18 x 12 inches (with the long side laid out left-to-right in front of you). Evenly spread out black olives, zucchini and feta cheese over the dough, leaving 3 inches from the edges of the crust uncovered. Spread the top with the cooled meat mixture, but still keep the edges of dough uncovered.
- Beginning with the edge closest to you, roll up the whole thing till it is all rolled up. You can do this by using the uncovered edge of dough

at the end as a 'strip' to stick to the roll and seal it, making sure that both ends are pressed down and sealed. Sprinkle with garlic powder and bake in the preheated oven for 5 minutes. Then, decrease heat to 350 °F (175 °C) and bake for about 30 minutes until it has the color of golden brown.

Nutrition Information

- Calories: 694 calories;
- Total Fat: 32.9
- Sodium: 2952
- Total Carbohydrate: 66.6
- Cholesterol: 95
- Protein: 32.5

381. H'rira Onctueuse A L'Agneau (Rich And Creamy Harira Soup)

Serving: 8 | Prep: 45mins | Cook: 1hours3mins | Ready in:

Ingredients

- 3 tablespoons vegetable oil
- 1 1/3 pounds lamb leg, cubed
- 2 large potatoes, cubed
- 1 pound tomatoes, diced
- 1 pound zucchini, chopped
- 2 onions, finely chopped
- 1 cup dried chickpeas, soaked overnight and drained
- 2 carrots, cut into 1-inch strips
- 1 stalk celery, thinly sliced
- 1 bunch fresh mint, finely chopped
- 1 bunch fresh cilantro, finely chopped
- 1 teaspoon ground ginger
- 1/4 teaspoon ground cinnamon
- 1 pinch saffron
- cold water to cover
- 1 (7 ounce) can tomato puree
- salt and freshly ground black pepper to taste

Direction

- In a big pot, heat the oil on high heat. Put the lamb and cook and stir for 3 to 5 minutes, until it becomes brown. Lower the heat to medium, then put carrots, chickpeas, onions, zucchini, tomatoes and potatoes. Mix in the saffron, cinnamon, ginger, cilantro, mint and celery. Pour water to cover and let it simmer for 15 minutes.
- Turn down the heat to low. Mix in enough water to cover and tomato puree. Let it simmer for about 45 minutes, adding more water as it is absorbed, until the chickpeas become soft. Move the lamb onto a plate with a slotted spoon. Using an immersion blender, puree the chickpea mixture until it becomes smooth. Sprinkle pepper and salt to season. Sprinkle pepper and salt to season the lamb. Stir it back into the pot.

Nutrition Information

- Calories: 323 calories;
- Sodium: 184
- Total Carbohydrate: 43
- Cholesterol: 29
- Protein: 18.5
- Total Fat: 9.7

382. Helga's Russian Borscht

Serving: 6 | Prep: 30mins | Cook: 2hours20mins | Ready in:

Ingredients

- 2 tablespoons canola oil
- 1 pound lamb stew meat, cut into 1/2-inch cubes
- 1 onion, peeled and finely chopped
- 3 1/2 quarts beef broth
- 1/4 cup red wine vinegar

- 2 tablespoons lemon juice
- 1 1/4 pounds cabbage, cored and shredded
- 1 1/2 pounds ripe tomatoes, diced
- 2 pounds beets, peeled and diced (tops reserved)
- 2 bay leaves
- 1 teaspoon salt
- 1/2 teaspoon freshly ground black pepper
- 1 pint sour cream
- 1/4 cup chopped dill

Direction

- In a large stockpot, heat canola oil over medium-high heat until it's very hot. Next, put the cubed lam in; sear until well browned. Then add onion, cook for about 2 minutes, until transparent and softened.
- Pour in the lemon juice, vinegar, and beef broth; add pepper, salt, bay leaves, the diced beets, tomatoes, and cabbage. Boil over high heat, then reduce to medium-low heat; next, cover and simmer for about 2 hours, until the beets and lamb are tender.
- Cut the beet tops, and stir into the borscht, continue to simmer for 15 minutes more. Season with and pepper and salt to taste. Ladle the soup into soup bowls, decorate with a touch of sour cream, and dust with dill.

Nutrition Information

- Calories: 528 calories;
- Protein: 28.3
- Total Fat: 32.5
- Sodium: 763
- Total Carbohydrate: 33
- Cholesterol: 72

383. Irish Shepherd's Pie

Serving: 8 | Prep: 25mins | Cook: 1hours10mins | Ready in:

Ingredients

- 1 tablespoon olive oil
- 1 tablespoon butter
- 1 onion, diced
- 2 pounds lean ground lamb
- 1/3 cup all-purpose flour
- salt and ground black pepper to taste
- 2 teaspoons minced fresh rosemary
- 1 teaspoon paprika
- 1/8 teaspoon ground cinnamon
- 1 tablespoon ketchup
- 3 cloves garlic, minced
- 2 1/2 cups water, or as needed
- 1 (12 ounce) package frozen peas and carrots, thawed
- 2 1/2 pounds Yukon Gold potatoes, peeled and halved
- 1 tablespoon butter
- 1 pinch ground cayenne pepper
- 1/4 cup cream cheese
- 1/4 pound Irish cheese (such as Dubliner®), shredded
- salt and ground black pepper to taste
- 1 egg yolk
- 2 tablespoons milk

Direction

- Start preheating the oven to 190°C (375°F).
- In a Dutch oven, heat the olive oil and butter on medium heat. Whisk in the ground lamb and the onion; cook and crumble the meat for about 10 minutes until the meat is browned.
- Whisk in the flour until combined, then whisk in garlic, ketchup, cinnamon, paprika, rosemary, black pepper, and salt; cook while stirring for 2-3 minutes until the garlic fragrant.
- Mix in the water and scrape up any brown bits from the bottom of the oven. Lower the heat to medium-low and simmer the mixture while stirring for about 5-6 minutes until thick.
- Take the lamb mixture away from heat and whisk in carrots and peas until combined.
- Into the bottom of a 9x13-inch baking dish, spread the lamb mixture, then put aside.

- Put potatoes in a big pan of salted water. Boil; lower the heat to medium and cook for about 15 minutes until they are soft. Strain well and move the potatoes back to the pan.
- Add the Irish cheese, cream cheese, cayenne pepper, and butter to the potatoes. Mash until they are well combined and smooth. Add black pepper and salt to taste.
- In a small bowl, stir together the milk and the egg yolk; stir the egg mixture to the mashed potato mixture.
- Evenly spread the mashed potatoes on top of the lamb mixture in the baking dish to cover.
- Bake for about 25-30 minutes in the preheated oven until the sauce bubbles up around the edges and the top becomes golden brown.

Nutrition Information

- Calories: 517 calories;
- Protein: 29.2
- Total Fat: 28.3
- Sodium: 301
- Total Carbohydrate: 37.2
- Cholesterol: 132

384. Irish Stew, My Way

Serving: 8 | Prep: 30mins | Cook: 3hours | Ready in:

Ingredients

- 2 tablespoons olive oil
- 1 small sweet onion, diced
- 1/4 teaspoon salt
- 1/2 teaspoon freshly ground black pepper
- 1 tablespoon dried Italian seasoning
- 3 cloves garlic, crushed
- 1 pound cubed lamb stew meat
- 1 pound cubed pork stew meat
- 1 (14.5 ounce) can beef broth
- 3 carrots, cut into 1/2 inch pieces
- 1 medium turnip, quartered and cut into 1/2 inch pieces
- 2 parsnips, peeled and cut into 1/2 inch pieces
- 1 red bell pepper, seeded and cut into 1 inch pieces
- 1 yellow bell pepper, seeded and cut into 1 inch pieces
- 1 green bell pepper, seeded and cut into 1 inch pieces
- 1 medium sweet onion, cut into large chunks
- 2 stalks celery, cut into 1/2 inch pieces
- 1 (12 fluid ounce) can beer
- 8 small red potatoes, quartered
- 2 tablespoons cornstarch

Direction

- Heat olive oil in big skillet on medium heat. Put 1 onion in skillet; season with Italian seasoning, pepper and salt. Mix garlic in, then mix and cook till tender. Mix pork and lamb in. Cook till evenly browned. Lower heat to low; add beef broth and simmer for 30 minutes.
- Put skillet mixture in big pot; mix celery, leftover onion, parsnips, turnip, carrots and yellow, green and red bell pepper in. Add beer and cover. Cook on low heat for 2 hours.
- Take out 1/2 cup of stew liquid. Mix potatoes into pot; cook till potatoes are tender for 30 minutes. Mix cornstarch into reserved liquid 15 minutes before serving. To thicken, mix into stew.

Nutrition Information

- Calories: 424 calories;
- Sodium: 334
- Total Carbohydrate: 46.1
- Cholesterol: 61
- Protein: 24.9
- Total Fat: 14.7

385. Italian Lamb Stew

Serving: 6 | Prep: 25mins | Cook: 1hours10mins | Ready in:

Ingredients

- 2 tablespoons olive oil
- 1 1/2 pounds boneless lamb shoulder, cut into 1-inch cubes
- salt and ground black pepper to taste
- 5 cloves garlic, sliced thin
- 1/2 cup red wine
- 1/2 cup chicken broth
- 4 cups peeled, chopped tomatoes
- 1 teaspoon dried oregano
- 1 bay leaf
- 4 potatoes, peeled and cut into 1-inch pieces
- 2 cups fresh green beans, trimmed
- 1 red bell pepper, seeded and cut into 1-inch pieces
- 2 small zucchini, sliced
- 3 tablespoons chopped fresh parsley

Direction

- In a Dutch oven or in a large heavy-bottom pot, heat olive oil. Sprinkle lamb with salt and pepper to season and cook in hot oil for 2 to 3 minutes until brown in color. Add garlic and cook, for 1 minute, remember to stir while cooking. Pour chicken broth and red wine into the pan; bring to a boil, remember to use a wooden spoon to scrape out all the browned bits in the bottom of the pot while boiling. Lower the heat to medium low; and add bay leaf, oregano and tomatoes to the pot. Bring to a gentle boil for about 45 minutes until the lamb is softened.
- Raise the heat to medium-high. Add zucchini, red pepper, green bean and potatoes to the pot. Cook for an additional 15 to 20 minutes until vegetables are softened. Scatter parsley over soup. Remove bay leaf and add salt and pepper to season. Serve.

Nutrition Information

- Calories: 389 calories;
- Total Carbohydrate: 38
- Cholesterol: 58
- Protein: 20.3
- Total Fat: 16.7
- Sodium: 283

386. JG's Irish Lamb Stew

Serving: 6 | Prep: 45mins | Cook: 2hours35mins | Ready in:

Ingredients

- 4 slices bacon, chopped
- 2 pounds cubed lamb stew meat
- salt and ground black pepper to taste
- 2 stalks celery, sliced
- 1 carrot, chopped
- 1 red onion, chopped
- 4 cloves garlic, chopped
- 2 tablespoons chopped fresh rosemary
- 1 tablespoon chopped fresh thyme
- 1 tablespoon chopped fresh oregano
- 1 (12 fluid ounce) can or bottle Irish stout beer (such as Guinness®), divided
- 1 (14.5 ounce) can fire-roasted diced tomatoes, with juice
- 4 cups beef stock, or as needed
- 1 cup pearl barley, rinsed
- 1 pound small red potatoes, cubed
- 2 carrots, sliced
- 1 rutabaga, peeled and cubed
- 1 (10 ounce) package sliced fresh mushrooms
- 3 tablespoons all-purpose flour, or as needed

Direction

- In a big pot, cook chopped bacon on medium heat, stirring often, for 10 minutes until bacon is crisp and brown. Take out using a slotted spoon. Leave drippings in the pot. Put aside.
- Sprinkle lamb with black pepper and salt. In several batches, brown meat well in bacon drippings on medium heat. Don't overcrowd

the pan. Put aside lamb. In bacon drippings, sauté oregano, thyme, rosemary, garlic, red onion, chopped carrot, and celery for 5 minutes until onion is translucent and soft. Pour almost all the stout beer into the pan but keep 1/4 cup in a small bowl and put aside. Boil mixture. Cook for 10 minutes until stout beer reduces to about half. Scrape and melt any brown flavor bits on the pot's bottom into liquid.

- Mix in cooked lamb meat and bacon to the stew. Mix in fire-roasted tomatoes with juices. Cover with enough beef stock. Boil. Lower heat to simmer. Cook for 1 hour 45 minutes. Mix in pearl barley. Simmer for another 15 minutes. Mix in mushrooms, rutabaga, sliced carrots, and red potatoes. Simmer for 30 minutes until potatoes are tender.
- To make the consistency of the stew thick, mix flour into the reserved 1/4 cup stout beer until smooth. Mix mixture into stew. Simmer for 5 minutes until thick.

Nutrition Information

- Calories: 615 calories;
- Total Fat: 26.6
- Sodium: 522
- Total Carbohydrate: 57.1
- Cholesterol: 99
- Protein: 36.9

387. Juggernauts Meatloaf

Serving: 12 | Prep: 25mins | Cook: 1hours30mins | Ready in:

Ingredients

- 1 pound ground lamb
- 1 pound ground chicken
- 1/2 pound ground pork
- 1 egg
- 1 1/2 cups rolled oats
- 1 cup finely chopped onion
- 1/2 cup finely chopped green bell pepper
- 1/4 cup raisins
- 1/4 cup chopped carrots
- 1/4 cup ketchup
- 3 tablespoons hot pepper sauce, or to taste
- 3 cloves garlic, minced
- 1 tablespoon curry powder
- 1 tablespoon dried oregano, or to taste
- 1 tablespoon dried rosemary, or to taste

Direction

- Preheat the oven to 220 degrees C (425 degrees F). Grease two 9x5-in. loaf pans.
- In the big bowl, combine pork, chicken and ground lamb together till 3 meats become combined totally; combine in rosemary, oregano, curry powder, garlic, hot pepper sauce, ketchup, carrots, raisins, green pepper, onion, rolled oats, and egg. Split mixture in half; shape each half into the loaf, and add to prepped loaf pans.
- Bake in preheated oven for 60 minutes; lower the heat to 150 degrees C (300 degrees F) and bake for half an hour more. Tilt pans to let the grease to gather at the pan's corner; pour off grease. Let meat loaves to cool down for 10 minutes prior to taking out of the pans. Cook till the food is no less than 71 degrees C (160 degrees F), check using the instant-read thermometer.

Nutrition Information

- Calories: 232 calories;
- Sodium: 209
- Total Carbohydrate: 13.8
- Cholesterol: 76
- Protein: 20.7
- Total Fat: 10.3

388. Kentucky Burgoo

Serving: 20 | Prep: 1hours10mins | Cook: 9hours10mins | Ready in:

Ingredients

- 5 pounds bone-in mutton shoulder or leg, cut into 1 pound pieces
- 2 teaspoons salt
- 1 tablespoon Italian seasoning
- 3 pounds baking potatoes, peeled and cubed
- 1 pound carrots, peeled and sliced
- 2 (15 ounce) cans crushed tomatoes
- 2 teaspoons extra-virgin olive oil or canola oil
- 1 small onion, chopped
- 2 cups medium salsa
- 1 (15 ounce) can tomato sauce
- 1/2 cup packed brown sugar
- 1/4 cup hickory smoke flavored barbeque sauce
- 1 (15.25 ounce) can whole kernel corn, drained
- 1 (14.5 ounce) can green beans, drained
- 1 (16 ounce) package frozen lima beans, thawed
- 1 (10 ounce) package frozen okra
- 1 (46 fluid ounce) can tomato juice

Direction

- Day 1: Place meat in a big heavy pot, add water to. Add 1tsp salt, Italian seasoning, and water to cover the meat. Let it simmer for an hour over medium heat.
- Turn on the oven to 190°C (375°F) to preheat. Take the meat out of stock. Place the stock inside the fridge for later use. Separate the bones from the meat, throw out bones, and put the meat inside a roasting pan. Let it roast in heated oven for 1 1/2 hour or until when poked with a fork it is tender. Using an aluminum foil, cover the pan and place it inside the fridge.
- Day 2: Take out stock from the fridge, skim off the thickened white fat on the top and discard it. In a heavy stock pot, pour in 4 cups of stock and add 1 can crushed tomatoes, carrots, potatoes, and 1 tsp salt. Let it cook for 20 minutes over medium-high heat, stirring from time to time. Let it cool for a little and then refrigerate.
- Preheat oven to 150°C or 300°F. In a small frying pan, heat olive oil over medium heat and add onion. Cook the onion and stir until translucent, 5-8 minutes. Put to the side. Take the meat out of fridge and add the rest of the stock to the pan. Place a lid or some aluminum foil on the roasting pan.
- Place the meat in heated oven for 1 1/2 hours to cook. Take the meat out of oven and pour in tomato sauce, salsa, 1 can crushed tomatoes, brown sugar, onion, and barbecue sauce. Proceed with roasting for an additional 1 1/2 hours. Let it cool a little and place it inside the fridge overnight.
- Day 3: In a big stock pot or Dutch oven portable roaster, combine the vegetable mixture from day 2 with the meat, green beans, corns, lima beans, tomato juice, and okra. Cook at 150°C (or 300°F) if using a roaster or simmer, if a stock pot is being used, over medium-low heat, stirring from time to time.

Nutrition Information

- Calories: 532 calories;
- Total Carbohydrate: 49.7
- Cholesterol: 82
- Protein: 28.2
- Total Fat: 25.6
- Sodium: 975

389. Kreatopita Argostoli

Serving: 12 | Prep: | Cook: | Ready in:

Ingredients

- 24 sheets phyllo dough
- 4 cups cooked white rice

- 1 clove garlic, minced
- 3 cups cubed cooked lamb
- 1 lemon, juiced
- 2 potatoes, peeled and quartered
- 4 hard-cooked eggs, quartered
- 2 tablespoons lemon zest
- 2 tablespoons chopped fresh parsley
- 2 tablespoons chopped fresh mint leaves
- 1 1/2 cups crumbled feta cheese
- 1/2 cup olive oil
- 1 cup beef broth
- 1 tablespoon chopped fresh oregano
- 1/2 teaspoon ground black pepper
- 1 egg, beaten
- 1/2 cup butter, melted

Direction

- Preheat an oven to 165°C/325°F. Boil a big pot of salted water. Add potatoes; cook for 15 minutes till tender yet firm. Drain and cool; chop.
- Brush melted butter on 9x13-in. pan lightly. Put 1 phyllo sheet into pan; brush butter lightly. Add phyllo sheets, lightly brushing butter on each (doesn't need to fully cover every phyllo sheet in butter), till you get 12 in total.
- Spread cooked rice on phyllo; sprinkle minced garlic. In an even layer, add lamb; sprinkle lemon juice. Put 1 cup diced potatoes on lamb.
- Arrange 1/4 eggs; sprinkle lemon zest, mint and parsley. Add the crumbled feta cheese.
- Add beef broth and olive oil; sprinkle pepper and oregano then add beaten egg.
- Put leftover 12 phyllo sheets over, lightly brushed in melted butter.
- Bake at 165°C/325°F for 40-50 minutes. Put temperature on 175°C/350°F at final 10 minutes. Remove from oven; cool for 15 minutes on a rack. Cut to squares or diamonds; serve warm.

Nutrition Information

- Calories: 543 calories;
- Total Fat: 29.4
- Sodium: 575
- Total Carbohydrate: 43.4
- Cholesterol: 172
- Protein: 25.8

390. Lamb (Gosht) Biryani

Serving: 8 | Prep: 25mins | Cook: 1hours | Ready in:

Ingredients

- 2 1/2 cups basmati rice
- 1/4 cup cooking oil
- 8 whole cloves
- 4 black cardamom pods
- 4 cinnamon sticks
- 4 large onions, sliced thin
- 1 tablespoon garlic paste
- 1 tablespoon ginger paste
- 1/4 cup chopped fresh cilantro leaves
- 3 tablespoons chopped fresh mint leaves
- 1 pound lamb chops
- salt to taste
- 3 tomatoes, chopped
- 4 green chile peppers, halved lengthwise
- 2 teaspoons ground red pepper
- 2 tablespoons plain yogurt
- 2 tablespoons lemon juice
- 7 1/2 cups water
- 1 teaspoon salt
- 1 tablespoon vegetable oil
- 1 onion, sliced
- 1/2 teaspoon saffron
- 2 tablespoons warm milk

Direction

- In a big container, place basmati rice; pour in some inches of cool water to cover. Allow to stand for 30 minutes. Drain.
- In a big skillet, heat 1/4 cup oil on medium heat. In the hot oil, fry cinnamon sticks, cardamom pods and the cloves for 1 minute until fragrant. Put in onion, cook while stirring

5 minutes till onions are slightly browned. Mix ginger paste and garlic paste into onion mixture; cook 1 minute longer till ginger and garlic are fragrant. Sprinkle the mixture with mint and cilantro; cook 1 more minute.

- Put lamb chops in the skillet and season with salt. Cook while stirring the lamb 20 minutes until beginning to brown.
- Mix ground red pepper, green chile peppers and tomatoes into the mixture. Keep cooking 10 minutes till the oil starts to detach from the gravy. Put in lemon juice and yogurt. Put on cover and cook 15 minutes till lamb is tender. Add water if necessary to prevent the mixture from being too dry.
- In a saucepan, boil 1 teaspoon salt, 7 1/2 cups water, and rice until rice is almost done but a little chewy, about 10-15 minutes. Drain to remove excess water if there is.
- In a small skillet, heat 1 tablespoon oil. In the hot oil, fry sliced onion until slightly browned.
- In the bottom of a deep pot accompanied with a lid, layer about half of the rice. Scoop lamb masala over the rice. Spread lamb masala with fried onion. Layer the rest of rice atop. In a small bowl, combine warm milk and saffron; spread over the top rice layer. Put on lid to cover the pot. Place pot over low heat and cook 15 minutes till rice is well cooked.

Nutrition Information

- Calories: 544 calories;
- Total Fat: 25
- Sodium: 429
- Total Carbohydrate: 64.3
- Cholesterol: 43
- Protein: 16.5

391. Lamb Braised In Pomegranate

Serving: 6 | Prep: 15mins | Cook: 2hours30mins |Ready in:

Ingredients

- 3 pounds lamb shoulder blade chops
- salt and freshly ground pepper to taste
- 1 tablespoon vegetable oil
- 1 onion, sliced
- 1 pinch salt
- 4 cloves garlic, sliced
- 2 cups pomegranate juice
- 1/3 cup aged balsamic vinegar
- 1/4 teaspoon dried rosemary
- 8 fresh mint leaves
- 1/4 teaspoon red pepper flakes
- 1 tablespoon honey, or more to taste
- salt and ground black pepper to taste
- 2 tablespoons pomegranate seeds
- 1 tablespoon sliced fresh mint leaves
- 1 tablespoon pumpkin seeds

Direction

- Preheat an oven to 150 degrees C (300 degrees F). Season the lamb chops generously with black pepper and salt.
- Over high heat, heat vegetable oil in a Dutch oven and then put the lamb chops into the Dutch oven. Cook for about 8 minutes until the chops are browned on all sides. Place the lamb onto a plate and lower the heat to medium.
- Add a dash of salt and onion into Dutch oven and mix. Let to cook for about 3 minutes until the onions become slightly golden. Mix in the garlic and let to cook for 30 seconds.
- Add the pomegranate juice to Dutch oven and then scrape off the browned bits from the pot's bottom. Add in the balsamic vinegar, raise the heat to high and heat to boil.
- Mix red pepper flakes, mint leaves and rosemary into the pomegranate juice mixture. Continue boiling for about 10 minutes until

the liquid is decreased by half. Place back the lamb and any accumulated juices into the Dutch oven. Ladle the pomegranate mixture on top of the lamb and then cover.
- Cook for about 2 hours in prepped oven until the meat becomes fork tender. Place the lamb onto a plate and position the Dutch oven over the stovetop on high heat. Heat the pomegranate mixture to boil. Cook while skimming the fat that accumulates about 5 minutes until the liquid is decreased by 1/3.
- Mix in honey and then add black pepper and salt to taste. Place the lamb back into the Dutch oven and mix to combine. Stud with pumpkin seeds, sliced mint leaves and pomegranate seeds.

Nutrition Information

- Calories: 546 calories;
- Cholesterol: 134
- Protein: 34.9
- Total Fat: 34.1
- Sodium: 190
- Total Carbohydrate: 23.3

392. Lamb Chops With Minted Yogurt Sauce

Serving: 4 | Prep: 15mins | Cook: 15mins | Ready in:

Ingredients

- 8 (3/4-inch thick) rib lamb chops
- 1/2 ounce Crosse & Blackwell® Mint Sauce, divided
- 1 cup Greek-style plain yogurt
- 6 tablespoons Crisco® 100% Extra Virgin Olive Oil, divided
- 1 tablespoon chopped fresh parsley
- 1 teaspoon minced garlic
- 1/2 teaspoon salt
- 1/2 teaspoon pepper

Direction

- In a big resealable plastic bag, mix 1/4 cup mint sauce and lamb chops; seal bag. To coat chops, turn; chill for 30 minutes.
- Whisk leftover 1/4 cup mint sauce, pepper, salt, garlic, parsley, leftover 1/4 cup olive oil and yogurt till combined in medium bowl; chill till serving.
- Heat leftover olive oil on medium heat in big skillet. Put lamb chops in skillet; cook till internal temperature is 145°F for 3-5 minutes per side. Cover; rest for 3 minutes. Serve it with minted yogurt sauce.

Nutrition Information

- Calories: 605 calories;
- Total Carbohydrate: 2.5
- Cholesterol: 124
- Protein: 31.4
- Total Fat: 51.2
- Sodium: 411

393. Lamb Korma

Serving: 6 | Prep: 10mins | Cook: 1hours15mins | Ready in:

Ingredients

- 2 1/4 pounds cubed lamb meat
- 4 teaspoons olive oil, divided
- 1 brown onion, chopped
- 1 red potato, peeled and cubed
- 1/2 cup curry powder
- 1/2 cup water
- 1/3 cup coconut milk
- 1/3 cup drained canned chickpeas (garbanzo beans)

Direction

- Add the lamb into bowl and sprinkle 2 tsp. of

the olive oil on the lamb; whisk till becoming coated.
- Heat leftover 2 tsp. of the olive oil in the sauce pan on low heat; cook and stir the onion 10-15 minutes till becoming tender. Take the sauce pan out of the heat and put potato into the onion.
- Heat the big skillet on medium heat; cook and stir the lamb, working in the small batches, approximately 5 minutes on each batch till becoming brown. Move the browned lamb to the onion mixture.
- Mix the curry to the onion-lamb mixture and cook on medium heat for 60 seconds. Pour water into onion-lamb mixture and boil. Lower the heat to low, keep sauce pan covered, and let simmer approximately 45 minutes till the potatoes soften and the lamb becomes thoroughly cooked.
- Whisk the chickpeas and coconut milk into the onion-lamb mixture and let simmer approximately 5 minutes till becoming thoroughly heated.

Nutrition Information

- Calories: 301 calories;
- Protein: 28.1
- Total Fat: 13.8
- Sodium: 102
- Total Carbohydrate: 17.4
- Cholesterol: 80

394. Lamb Lover's Pilaf

Serving: 6 | Prep: 10mins | Cook: 20mins | Ready in:

Ingredients

- 2 tablespoons vegetable oil, divided
- 1 1/2 pounds boneless lamb stew meat cut into 1/2 inch strips
- 1/2 teaspoon Greek-style seasoning
- 1 onion, chopped
- 2 stalks celery, minced
- 1 cup dry bulgur wheat
- 1 1/2 cups chicken broth
- 1 pinch ground cinnamon
- 1 pinch ground allspice
- 1/4 cup raisins
- 1/4 cup slivered almonds

Direction

- In a big skillet, heat 1 tbsp. of oil over moderately high heat. Use Greek seasoning to season the lamb strips and sauté them in the hot oil until browned. Take out of the skillet and put aside.
- Lower heat to moderate and heat leftover tablespoon of oil. Sauté celery and onion until soft, then put in bulgur wheat and keep on cooking for 5 more minutes, while stirring frequently.
- Stir in allspice, cinnamon, broth and reserved lamb. Lower heat to low and simmer with a cover until liquid is absorbed, about 15-20 minutes. Use raisins and almonds to decorate and serve.

Nutrition Information

- Calories: 297 calories;
- Total Fat: 12.4
- Sodium: 89
- Total Carbohydrate: 26.6
- Cholesterol: 54
- Protein: 21.4

395. Lamb Madras Curry

Serving: 8 | Prep: 30mins | Cook: 2hours | Ready in:

Ingredients

- Curry Paste
- 1 1/2 tablespoons coriander seeds
- 1 1/2 teaspoons cumin seeds

- 1/2 teaspoon salt
- 5 whole dried red chile peppers
- 6 fresh curry leaves
- 3 tablespoons garlic paste
- 2 teaspoons ginger paste
- 1 1/2 teaspoons ground turmeric
- 2 1/4 pounds lamb meat, cut into 1 1/2 inch cubes
- 1/2 cup ghee (clarified butter), melted
- 1/4 cup vegetable oil
- 4 onion, sliced 1/4 inch thick
- 1 (13.5 ounce) can coconut milk
- 2 cups water, divided
- 1 teaspoon fennel seeds
- 6 cardamom pods
- 1 cinnamon stick
- 1 1/2 teaspoons garam masala
- 1 teaspoon sugar
- 3 tablespoons warm water
- 1 tablespoon tamarind paste

Direction

- On medium low heat, toast coriander seeds until they start to pop and brown. Repeat toasting method with cumin seeds then with dried red peppers. Put each ingredient in a spice grinder/food processor when finished. Add salt. Grind into a fine powder. Mix with ginger and garlic to make a thick paste.
- Sprinkle turmeric on lamb. Lightly stir to coat. Toast fennel seeds like earlier. Put aside. On medium heat, heat a Dutch oven with vegetable oil and ghee. Cook onions for 10 minutes until golden brown. Mix in curry paste. Fry for a minute. Mix in meat. Fry for another minute. Put 1 cup water and 2/3 of a coconut milk can. Boil. Lower heat to low. Simmer for about 10 minutes.
- Mix in 1 cup water, toasted fennel seeds, cinnamon stick, cardamom pods and leftover coconut milk. Cover, with the lid ajar, then return to a simmer, cook for about 1 1/2 hours until lamb is tender. Occasionally stir. Thin using water if sauce is too thick as it cooks.
- When lamb becomes tender, mix in tamarind paste melted in 3 tbsp. water, sugar, and garam masal. Cook for 5 minutes longer until sauce thickens. Take out cardamom pods and cinnamon stick. Serve.

Nutrition Information

- Calories: 519 calories;
- Sodium: 479
- Total Carbohydrate: 16.2
- Cholesterol: 116
- Protein: 28.6
- Total Fat: 37.1

396. Lamb Merguez Sausage Patties

Serving: 4 | Prep: 10mins | Cook: 10mins | Ready in:

Ingredients

- 1 teaspoon salt
- 1/4 teaspoon fennel seeds
- 1 teaspoon ground cumin
- 1/2 teaspoon ground cinnamon
- 1/2 teaspoon ground coriander
- 1/4 teaspoon ground turmeric
- 3 cloves garlic, peeled
- 2 tablespoons harissa, or to taste (see Ingredient note)
- 1 tablespoon tomato paste
- 1 pound lean ground lamb
- 1 tablespoon olive oil

Direction

- Pound fennel seeds and salt till fine in a mortar and pestle. Mix garlic cloves, turmeric, coriander, cinnamon and cumin into salt mixture; grind to make a thick paste. Mix tomato paste and harissa sauce in till combined.
- Use a fork to mix spice paste and ground lamb in big bowl. Cover; refrigerate overnight.

- Shape sausage to patties. Heat olive oil in big skillet on medium-high heat and cook patties for 5-8 minutes on each side, varying from patties' size, till not pink inside anymore.

Nutrition Information

- Calories: 268 calories;
- Total Fat: 19.2
- Sodium: 718
- Total Carbohydrate: 2.8
- Cholesterol: 76
- Protein: 19.9

397. Lamb Shoulder Vindaloo

Serving: 4 | Prep: 5mins | Cook: 1hours15mins | Ready in:

Ingredients

- 1 tablespoon olive oil
- 1/8 teaspoon brown mustard seeds
- 1/4 teaspoon whole black peppercorns
- 1 pinch whole fenugreek seeds
- 1 1/4 pounds lamb shoulder chops
- 1 (3 ounce) package curry sauce (such as Sukhi's®)
- 2 leaves basil, torn

Direction

- Over moderately-high heat, heat a big skillet. Into hot pan, add olive oil and heat till shimmering. In hot oil, let mustard seeds cook for about a minute till they start to pop; instantly put in fenugreek seeds and peppercorns.
- Into skillet, slowly place lamb chops in one layer; put in basil and curry sauce and mix. Let sauce come to boil, cover skillet with a tight-fitting lid, lower heat to low, and cook for 60 to 70 minutes till lamb is softened.
- Take lid off skillet. Keep cooking while mixing for 10 to 15 minutes longer till majority of liquid has been cooked down and meat is browned on every side.

Nutrition Information

- Calories: 485 calories;
- Total Fat: 42.2
- Sodium: 152
- Total Carbohydrate: 0.9
- Cholesterol: 105
- Protein: 23.7

398. Lamb Stew In An Hour

Serving: 6 | Prep: 20mins | Cook: 35mins | Ready in:

Ingredients

- 2 tablespoons olive oil
- 2 1/2 pounds lamb, cut into 1-inch cubes
- 2 cups water
- 1 cup corn kernels, pureed in a blender
- 1 1/2 tablespoons chicken soup base
- 1 bay leaf
- 1 tablespoon dried marjoram
- 1 tablespoon dried parsley
- 1 teaspoon dried chives
- 1 tablespoon ground allspice
- salt and ground black pepper to taste
- 2 cups water
- 8 new potatoes, cut into chunks
- 16 baby carrots
- 1 small onion, cut into wedges

Direction

- In a pressure cooker, heat olive on medium heat. Cook and stir the lamb in the heated oil and cook for 10 minutes until brown. Stir in black pepper, 2 cups water, salt, pureed corn, allspice, chicken soup base, chives, bay leaf, parsley, and marjoram.
- Secure lid onto the pressure cooker and increase pressure to full. Adjust the heat to

medium-low to maintain the pressure consistent. Cook for 25 minutes.
- Relieve pressure from cooker. Put onion, potatoes, carrots, and two cups water in the lamb mixture.
- Secure lid on the cooker and increase pressure to full. Adjust heat to medium-low to keep pressure consistent; cook for 8 minutes more.

Nutrition Information

- Calories: 479 calories;
- Sodium: 644
- Total Carbohydrate: 29.8
- Cholesterol: 108
- Protein: 32.8
- Total Fat: 25.5

399. Lamb Stew With Green Beans

Serving: 12 | Prep: 30mins | Cook: 1hours30mins | Ready in:

Ingredients

- 3 tablespoons olive oil
- 1 large onion, chopped
- 1 stalk celery, chopped
- 3 pounds boneless lamb shoulder, cut into 2 inch pieces
- 1 (8 ounce) can tomato sauce
- 3 cups hot water
- 2 pounds fresh green beans, trimmed
- 1 tablespoon chopped fresh parsley
- 1/2 teaspoon dried mint
- 1/2 teaspoon dried dill weed
- 1 pinch ground cinnamon
- 1 pinch white sugar
- salt and pepper to taste

Direction

- In a large pot over medium heat, heat oil. Add celery and onion and sauté in hot oil until golden in color. Stir in lamb and cook until browned evenly. Stir in water and tomato sauce. Lower the heat and simmer for about 60 minutes.
- Stir in green beans. Add pepper, salt, sugar, cinnamon, dill, mint and parsley to season. Continue to cook until beans are softened.

Nutrition Information

- Calories: 363 calories;
- Protein: 20.6
- Total Fat: 27.9
- Sodium: 272
- Total Carbohydrate: 7.8
- Cholesterol: 82

400. Lamb Tagine

Serving: 4 | Prep: 45mins | Cook: 2hours | Ready in:

Ingredients

- 3 tablespoons olive oil, divided
- 2 pounds lamb meat, cut into 1 1/2 inch cubes
- 2 teaspoons paprika
- 1/4 teaspoon ground turmeric
- 1/2 teaspoon ground cumin
- 1/4 teaspoon cayenne pepper
- 1 teaspoon ground cinnamon
- 1/4 teaspoon ground cloves
- 1/2 teaspoon ground cardamom
- 1 teaspoon kosher salt
- 1/2 teaspoon ground ginger
- 1 pinch saffron
- 3/4 teaspoon garlic powder
- 3/4 teaspoon ground coriander
- 2 medium onions, cut into 1-inch cubes
- 5 carrots, peeled, cut into fourths, then sliced lengthwise into thin strips
- 3 cloves garlic, minced
- 1 tablespoon freshly grated ginger

- 1 lemon, zested
- 1 (14.5 ounce) can homemade chicken broth or low-sodium canned broth
- 1 tablespoon sun-dried tomato paste
- 1 tablespoon honey
- 1 tablespoon cornstarch (optional)
- 1 tablespoon water (optional)

Direction

- Into a bowl, add diced lamb, toss with 2 tbsp. olive oil, and put aside. In a big resealable bag, toss coriander, garlic powder, saffron, ginger, salt, cardamom, cloves, cinnamon, cayenne, cumin, turmeric, and paprika; stir well. Put the lamb into the bag, and coat well by tossing around. Keep in the refrigerator for no less than 8 hours or overnight will be better.
- In a heavy bottomed and big pot on medium high heat, heat 1 tbsp. of olive oil. Put in a third of the lamb, and brown them well. Transfer to a dish, and repeat the process with the rest of the lamb. Put in carrots and onions to the pot and cook for 5 minutes. Mix in the ginger and fresh garlic; keep cooking for an extra 5 minutes. Bring the lamb back to the pot and whisk in the honey, tomato paste, chicken broth and lemon zest. Boil, then lower heat to low, keep it covered, and simmered till the meat becomes soft or for 1 1/2 to 2 hours, mixing once in a while.
- You may thicken the tagine using a mixture of water and cornstarch if the consistency of it is too thin at the last 5 minutes of cooking.

Nutrition Information

- Calories: 423 calories;
- Protein: 35.8
- Total Fat: 20.5
- Sodium: 1129
- Total Carbohydrate: 23.6
- Cholesterol: 109

401. Lamb And Bulgur Soup (Shorba Freek)

Serving: 6 | Prep: 10mins | Cook: 1hours | Ready in:

Ingredients

- 1 tablespoon olive oil
- 3/4 pound lamb shoulder with bones, cut into pieces
- 1 small onion, diced
- 2 cloves garlic, chopped
- 2 cinnamon sticks
- 1 cup canned garbanzo beans, drained
- 1 (14.5 ounce) can whole peeled tomatoes with juice
- 1/4 cup bulgur (cracked wheat), uncooked
- 7 cups water
- salt and pepper to taste
- 1/4 cup chopped fresh parsley
- 1/2 teaspoon dried mint

Direction

- In a stock pot, heat oil over medium-high heat. Add cinnamon, garlic, onion, and lamb. Lightly sprinkle with pepper and salt to season. Cook until onions are nearly tender and meat turns brown, stirring constantly while cooking. Mix in garbanzo beans and water; bring to a boil.
- Simmer over low heat, removing scum from the top on occasion, for 45 to 60 minutes. In the meantime, transfer tomatoes to a food processor or blender and process into smooth puree.
- Once meat is tender enough, take out using a slotted spoon. Pick out any bones and fat, and add meat back into the pot. Throw the bones and fat away. Pick out cinnamon sticks. Add bulgur wheat and tomato puree. Simmer until bulgur is puffed and softened, or for about 10 minutes.
- Pour soup into a soup tureen and top with mint and parsley.

Nutrition Information

- Calories: 194 calories;
- Sodium: 238
- Total Carbohydrate: 18.6
- Cholesterol: 29
- Protein: 10.7
- Total Fat: 9

402. Lamb And Okra Stew

Serving: 6 | Prep: 20mins | Cook: 45mins | Ready in:

Ingredients

- 2 tablespoons extra-virgin olive oil
- 1/4 cup crushed garlic
- 2 pounds cubed leg of lamb meat
- 1 teaspoon ground cumin
- 1 teaspoon chopped fresh mint
- 1 teaspoon ground dried turmeric
- 1 teaspoon chopped fresh rosemary
- 2 (14.5 ounce) cans diced tomatoes, drained
- 2 tablespoons tomato paste
- 1 pound baby okra
- 1 teaspoon lemon juice
- 1 cup water
- 1 tablespoon butter
- 1 cup thin egg noodles
- 2 cups long grain rice
- 2 cups chicken broth
- 2 cups water
- 1 pinch salt and pepper to taste
- 1 teaspoon olive oil

Direction

- In a big skillet, heat olive oil over medium heat. Cook the garlic until it turns transparent. Put the cubed lamb. Cook it until all of its side turns brown. Season it with rosemary, turmeric, mint and cumin. Let it cook for another 5 minutes. Put the okra, tomato paste and the diced tomatoes. Stir the mixture of the water and the lemon juice in the skillet. Cover it and for 45 minutes, let it simmer over low heat.
- In a saucepan, melt the butter over medium heat. Put the egg noodles. Sauté until it is toasted. Put the water and the chicken broth. Bring it to a boil. Mix the rice in. For about 15 minutes, cover and let simmer until the rice is tender over low heat. Season it with pepper and salt. Mix olive oil in. Top the lamb stew on the rice pilaf and serve.

Nutrition Information

- Calories: 552 calories;
- Total Fat: 19.1
- Sodium: 325
- Total Carbohydrate: 67
- Cholesterol: 72
- Protein: 25.5

403. Lamb And Winter Vegetable Stew

Serving: 8 | Prep: 30mins | Cook: 1hours | Ready in:

Ingredients

- 2 tablespoons vegetable oil
- 1 pound lamb stew meat, cubed
- 2 cups beef broth
- 1 cup dry red wine
- 2 cloves garlic, minced
- 1 tablespoon chopped fresh thyme
- 1/4 teaspoon salt
- 1/4 teaspoon black pepper
- 1 bay leaf
- 2 cups peeled, seeded, and sliced butternut squash
- 1 cup peeled, sliced parsnips
- 1 cup peeled, chopped sweet potatoes
- 1 cup sliced celery
- 1 medium onion, thinly sliced
- 1/2 cup sour cream
- 3 tablespoons all-purpose flour

Direction

- In a big saucepan, heat oil, and brown lamb meat on every side. Drain fat, and mix in wine and beef broth. Add bay leaf, pepper, salt, thyme and garlic to season. Boil the mixture. Lower heat, put cover on, and let simmer for 20 minutes.
- Stir in onion, celery, sweet potatoes, parsnips and squash. Boil, then lower heat and let simmer for half an hour, or till vegetables are soft.
- Mix flour and sour cream in small bowl. Slowly mix in half cup hot stew mixture.
- Into saucepan, mix sour cream mixture. Get rid of bay leaf, and keep cooking and mixing till thickened.

Nutrition Information

- Calories: 208 calories;
- Protein: 11
- Total Fat: 8.9
- Sodium: 321
- Total Carbohydrate: 16.2
- Cholesterol: 33

404. Lancashire Hot Pot

Serving: 6 | Prep: 20mins | Cook: 2hours | Ready in:

Ingredients

- 1 tablespoon vegetable oil
- 12 ounces chopped onion
- 1 1/2 pounds cubed leg of lamb meat
- 2 1/2 pounds potatoes, peeled and thinly sliced
- 2 tablespoons chopped fresh thyme
- 1 ounce butter
- 2 cups chicken or lamb stock

Direction

- Place a large skillet on medium-high heat; heat oil. Sauté in onion till deep golden and soft. Take away from the skillet; set aside. Put lamb into the skillet; fry for 12-15 minutes, working in batches if needed, till rich chestnut brown in color. Strain fat; reserve.
- Set the oven at 375°F (190°C) and start preheating.
- Spread 1/2 of the potatoes onto the bottom of a 13x9-in. baking sheet. Flavor with pepper and salt. Arrange onions and browned lamb on top; sprinkle thyme over and season to taste. Spread the remaining potatoes on top to cover; season to taste; dot with butter. Transfer stock over all.
- Bake for 1 1/2-2 hours in the preheated oven. Note: Add more stock as needed if the casserole is drying out while cooking. Use aluminum foil to cover if the casserole is browned too quickly.

Nutrition Information

- Calories: 365 calories;
- Sodium: 302
- Total Carbohydrate: 38.4
- Cholesterol: 58
- Protein: 17.1
- Total Fat: 16.3

405. Low Carb Lamb Burgers

Serving: 4 | Prep: 5mins | Cook: 10mins | Ready in:

Ingredients

- 1 pound ground lamb
- 1 tablespoon soy sauce
- 1/3 cup chopped onion
- salt and ground black pepper to taste
- 1/8 cup avocado oil
- 1/3 cup crumbled feta cheese (optional)

Direction

- In a bowl, put onion, soy sauce, and lamb. Use pepper and salt to season to taste. Combine using your hands to blend. Shape the lamb mixture into 4 patties.
- In a skillet, heat avocado oil over medium heat. Cook the lamb patties for 5-8 minutes per side until turning brown. An instant-read meat thermometer should display a minimum of 145°F (65°C) when you insert it into the middle of a patty. Sprinkle feta cheese over and enjoy.

Nutrition Information

- Calories: 296 calories;
- Total Fat: 20.9
- Sodium: 524
- Total Carbohydrate: 3.1
- Cholesterol: 95
- Protein: 22.9

406. Mama's Lamb Roast

Serving: 4 | Prep: 10mins | Cook: 1hours30mins | Ready in:

Ingredients

- 1 1/2 cups white wine
- 4 cloves garlic, crushed
- 1 tablespoon dried parsley
- 1 1/2 teaspoons salt
- 1 (4 pound) leg of lamb

Direction

- Set the oven to 175°C or 350°F to preheat.
- In a bowl, combine together salt, parsley, garlic and white wine. Put in a big roasting pan the leg of lamb and drizzle lamb evenly with white wine mixture.
- In the preheated oven, roast the lamb about 1 hour and 30 minutes to your wanted degree of doneness, while turning lamb over halfway through, until the internal temperature of lamb reaches 65°C or 145°F for medium. Take lamb out of the oven and use a doubled aluminum foil sheet to cover. Allow lamb to rest in a warm place for 10-15 minutes prior to slicing.

Nutrition Information

- Calories: 563 calories;
- Cholesterol: 183
- Protein: 52.3
- Total Fat: 28.7
- Sodium: 1012
- Total Carbohydrate: 3.6

407. Margaret's Keftedes (Greek Meatballs)

Serving: 4 | Prep: 25mins | Cook: 30mins | Ready in:

Ingredients

- 4 slices white bread, torn into pieces
- 2 tablespoons milk
- 1 clove garlic
- 1 onion, quartered
- 4 teaspoons dried mint
- 1 teaspoon salt
- ground black pepper to taste
- 1/2 pound ground beef
- 1/2 pound ground lamb
- 4 eggs
- 1/2 cup all-purpose flour for dredging
- vegetable oil for frying

Direction

- In a large bowl, moisten bread pieces with milk. Put aside. In a food processor, mince garlic. Put in pepper, salt, mint and onion. Process until onion is chopped finely. Put onion mixture into the moist bread in the bowl, along with eggs, lamb and beef. Using

your hands, mix until they are blended thoroughly.
- Roll to form mixture into the balls measuring 1 1/2-2-inch in diameter. In a shallow pan, put flour, then coat the balls by rolling in the flour. Shake off all the excess flour. Arrange meatballs onto a baking sheet or plate, slightly flatten by pressing. It will prevent the meatballs from rolling away.
- In a large skillet, heat 1-in. oil over medium heat. Put in meatballs, 8 or 10 at a time; cook for 10 mins until no longer pink in the middle and browned nicely outside; drain on the paper towel-lined plate. Repeat with the remaining meatballs.

Nutrition Information

- Calories: 522 calories;
- Total Fat: 31.5
- Sodium: 893
- Total Carbohydrate: 28.6
- Cholesterol: 259
- Protein: 29.7

408. Marinated Lamb Chislick

Serving: 4 | Prep: 10mins | Cook: 10mins | Ready in:

Ingredients

- 1/2 cup Worcestershire sauce
- 1 teaspoon liquid smoke flavoring
- 1/2 teaspoon lemon pepper
- 1 1/4 pounds cubed lamb stew meat
- 1 tablespoon creamy salad dressing (such as Miracle Whip™)
- 1 tablespoon thousand island salad dressing
- 1 teaspoon Worcestershire sauce
- 1 teaspoon yellow mustard
- 1 teaspoon ketchup
- 1/2 teaspoon onion powder

Direction

- Whisk lemon pepper, liquid smoke, and 1/2 cup Worcestershire sauce in a bowl, then pour into a plastic resealable bag. Add the lamb cubes, coat with the marinade, squeeze out any excess air, then seal the bag. Marinate the meat inside the refrigerator for around 1 hour. Make the dipping sauce by whisking onion powder, ketchup, mustard, 1 teaspoon Worcestershire sauce, and salad dressings into a small bowl, and keep in the refrigerator until about to serve.
- Heat up the oven's broiler beforehand and set the rack in the middle of the oven. Use nonstick cooking spray to coat the broiler pan.
- In a colander placed in the sink, drain the lamb cubes, throwing away the marinade, then place the cubes into the prepped broiler pan. Cook in the oven until cooked to the doneness you prefer, roughly 10-15 minutes for medium.
- Put the lamb cubes onto a plate that has been covered with paper towels. Serve the dish hot with dipping sauce with toothpicks. Don't reheat since lamb loses flavor once reheated.

Nutrition Information

- Calories: 77 calories;
- Total Fat: 4.2
- Sodium: 494
- Total Carbohydrate: 8.8
- Cholesterol: 6
- Protein: 1

409. Marinated, Breaded Lamb Chops With Rosemary And Garlic

Serving: 6 | Prep: 15mins | Cook: 35mins | Ready in:

Ingredients

- 1 cup Worcestershire sauce
- 1/4 cup soy sauce

- 3 cloves garlic, chopped
- 1 sprig fresh rosemary, bruised
- 6 lamb chops
- 2 eggs
- 1 cup bread crumbs

Direction

- In a non-reactive bowl, combine rosemary, garlic, soy sauce and Worcestershire sauce. Put lamb chops into the marinade and flip. Chill without a cover in the fridge for one and a half to three hours; flipping once or twice during marination.
- Set oven to 190°C (or 375°F) and start preheating. Prepare a greased 13x9x2" glass baking dish.
- Take lamb chops out of the marinade and put aside. Get rid of rosemary sprig. Stir eggs into the remaining marinade. Spread breadcrumbs on a large plate.
- Dunk lamb chops into the egg-marinade mixture, then roll into bread crumbs to evenly coat. Arrange lamb chops in greased baking dish. Get rid of egg-marinade mixture.
- Bake and flip over lamb chops, 20 minutes. Bake for another 15 minutes or to preferred doneness.

Nutrition Information

- Calories: 316 calories;
- Sodium: 1244
- Total Carbohydrate: 23.2
- Cholesterol: 118
- Protein: 19.4
- Total Fat: 15.6

410. McIntire's Lamb Stew

Serving: 6 | Prep: 30mins | Cook: 6hours | Ready in:

Ingredients

- 1 pound boneless lamb shoulder, cut into 2 inch pieces
- 2 cups diced carrots
- 5 large potatoes, peeled and diced
- 1/2 sweet yellow onion, chopped
- 3 cloves garlic, minced
- 2 cups beef stock
- 1 pinch seasoned salt (such as LAWRY'S®), or to taste
- ground black pepper to taste
- 1 pinch paprika, or to taste
- 1 pinch dried thyme, or to taste
- 1 (1.5 fluid ounce) jigger Irish whiskey (such as Jameson®)
- 1 cup frozen peas

Direction

- Cook Irish whiskey, thyme, paprika, pepper, seasoned salt, beef stock, garlic, onion, potatoes, carrots and lamb shoulder in a slow cooker for 6-7 hours on low. 15 minutes before serving, add peas.

Nutrition Information

- Calories: 513 calories;
- Total Fat: 17.1
- Sodium: 192
- Total Carbohydrate: 64.3
- Cholesterol: 54
- Protein: 22.1

411. Mediterranean Lamb Burgers

Serving: 4 | Prep: 35mins | Cook: 10mins | Ready in:

Ingredients

- 1 pound ground lamb
- 1/2 pound ground beef
- 3 tablespoons chopped fresh mint
- 1 teaspoon minced fresh ginger root

- 1 teaspoon minced garlic
- 1 teaspoon salt
- 1/2 teaspoon ground black pepper
- 1 (16 ounce) container Greek yogurt
- 1/2 lemon, zested
- 1 clove garlic, minced
- 1/2 teaspoon salt
- 1 large sweet onion, cut into 1/2-inch slices
- 4 slices green tomato
- 4 ciabatta sandwich rolls, sliced horizontally
- 1 (8 ounce) package feta cheese, sliced
- 8 baby arugula leaves

Direction

- Preheat outdoor grill to medium high heat; oil grate lightly.
- Mix pepper, 1 tsp. salt, 1 tsp. garlic, ginger, mint, ground beef and ground lamb till just combined in big bowl. Evenly divide to 4 portions; shape to big patties. Put aside. Mix 1/2 tsp. salt, 1 garlic clove, lemon zest and Greek yogurt in a bowl. Cover; refrigerate.
- On preheated grill, cook beef and lamb patties, 3-4 minutes each side for well done, till cooked to preferred degree of doneness. An inserted instant-read thermometer in the middle should read 70°C/160°F. Put green tomato and onion slices on grill; cook, 1 minute per side, till lightly charred.
- Spread yogurt sauce on sliced ciabatta rolls. Make each burger by putting patty on roll; divide feta cheese slices on patties. Top with 2 arugula leaves, grilled onion, grilled tomato slice then top with other half of roll.

Nutrition Information

- Calories: 808 calories;
- Protein: 50
- Total Fat: 47.8
- Sodium: 2031
- Total Carbohydrate: 42.4
- Cholesterol: 187

412. Mellas Family Lamb Stuffed Zucchini (Koosa)

Serving: 4 | Prep: 30mins | Cook: 1hours25mins | Ready in:

Ingredients

- 2 large zucchini
- 1 (28 ounce) can chopped tomatoes with juice
- 2 tablespoons tomato paste
- 3/4 cup water
- 1/4 teaspoon ground cinnamon
- 1 tablespoon olive oil
- 1/2 cup chopped onion
- 1 pound ground lamb
- 3/4 cup basmati rice
- 2 tablespoons olive oil
- 1/2 cup water
- 2 tablespoons dried mint
- 2 teaspoons salt

Direction

- Slice each of the zucchinis into 2 equal pieces and remove the flesh and seeds from each halved zucchini using a thin and sharp knife; reserve the round 1/2-inch zucchini shells.
- In a big and oven-proof Dutch oven, mix the tomatoes, juice, cinnamon, tomato paste and 3/4 cup of water together. Let it simmer and cook for about 20 minutes over medium heat until it is thick in consistency.
- In a small skillet, put in 1 tablespoon of olive oil and let it heat up. Mix in the onion and let it cook for about 5 minutes until it is soft. Mix the lamb, dried mint, 2 tablespoons of olive oil, salt, rice, 1/2 cup of water and cooked onion together in a big bowl. Mix it thoroughly. Gently fill each of the zucchini shells with the prepared lamb mixture. Put the stuffed zucchini shells into the simmering tomato mixture.
- Cover the Dutch oven and put it inside a preheated oven. Let it bake for about 1 hour until the rice has softened. In case the sauce is

too thin, just let it simmer on the stove until you get the preferred consistency. Cut the baked stuffed zucchini shells into 1-inch rounds and drizzle it with the tomato mixture on top then serve.

Nutrition Information

- Calories: 511 calories;
- Total Fat: 26.6
- Sodium: 1593
- Total Carbohydrate: 44.8
- Cholesterol: 76
- Protein: 26.2

413. Mensaf (Jordanian Lamb Stew)

Serving: 8 | Prep: 15mins | Cook: 55mins | Ready in:

Ingredients

- 4 tablespoons olive oil
- 2 pounds boneless lamb shoulder, cut into 2 inch pieces
- 8 cups water
- 2 cups uncooked white rice
- 1/4 cup pine nuts
- 6 pita bread rounds
- 1 cup salted goat's milk (jameed el-kasih)

Direction

- On medium-high heat, put a tablespoon of olive oil in the pressure cooker. Place the lamb and cook until all sides are brown; take the lamb out. Place a cooking rack in the pressure cooker, set the lamb on top. Add 4 cups water in the cooker. Secure with a lid and put the pressure regulator on the vent pipe. Set to maximum pressure on high heat. Lower to medium-high heat and cook for 40 minutes. Adjust the heat accordingly to maintain a slow but stable rocking movement.
- Take off heat and let the pressure release naturally. Remove and debone the lamb, keep the meat warm. Throw bones away. Transfer the pan broth in a bowl and put aside.
- On medium-high heat, combine rice, leftover 4 cups water, and a tablespoon olive oil in a saucepan; boil. Mix, lower heat, secure lid, and let it simmer for 20 minutes until the rice absorbs all the moisture.
- On medium heat, pour the leftover 2 tbsp. olive oil in a pan. Cook and stir in pine nuts for 5 minutes until deep brown.
- In a big pan, add goat's milk, the reserved two cups broth, and lamb. Let it simmer on medium heat for half an hour until the lamb absorbs some of the mixture.
- Place pita bread on a big platter, add rice on top. Arrange the lamb over the rice and pour the leftover milk mixture. Add pine nuts on top. Serve.

Nutrition Information

- Calories: 544 calories;
- Sodium: 263
- Total Carbohydrate: 59.8
- Cholesterol: 61
- Protein: 23.4
- Total Fat: 22.6

414. Moroccan Lamb Tagine (Mrouzia)

Serving: 12 | Prep: 30mins | Cook: 1hours20mins | Ready in:

Ingredients

- 1/2 cup water
- 1 tablespoon paprika
- 1 1/2 teaspoons ras el hanout (optional)
- 1 teaspoon ground black pepper
- 1 teaspoon ground cinnamon
- 1 teaspoon ground coriander

- 1/2 teaspoon ground cloves
- 1/2 teaspoon ground nutmeg
- 1/2 teaspoon ground cardamom
- 1/4 teaspoon cayenne pepper, or more to taste
- 1/4 teaspoon ground turmeric
- salt to taste
- 1/4 teaspoon red pepper flakes (optional)
- 3 pounds lamb shoulder, trimmed and cut into cubes
- 1/2 cup butter
- 2 medium onions, finely chopped
- 1 shallot, finely chopped
- 2 cloves garlic, finely chopped
- 2 cinnamon sticks
- 3 cups chicken stock, or more as needed
- 2 cups whole blanched almonds
- 1 cup diced carrots
- 1 cup chopped dried apricots
- 1/2 cup raisins
- 1/2 cup pitted, chopped prunes (optional)
- 1/3 cup honey
- 1 tablespoon lemon juice, or more to taste

Direction

- In a small bowl, mix salt, turmeric, cayenne pepper, cardamom, nutmeg, cloves, coriander, cinnamon, black pepper, ras el hanout, paprika, and water. If you want the dish to be spicier, add red pepper flakes.
- Place lamb cubes into the large bowl and thoroughly coat with the spice mix. Cover and transfer to a refrigerator for 8 hours to overnight.
- In a Dutch oven, add butter and melt. Add cinnamon sticks, garlic, shallots, and onions. Sauté for 6 to 8 minutes. Add in the lamb with the spice mixture. Pour in chicken stock until covered and bring to a boil. Reduce to low heat and simmer for 1 to 1 1/2 hours, or until tender. If lamb looks dry, add more chicken stock. Add honey, prunes, raisins, apricots, carrots, and almonds to the Dutch oven. Simmer for 15 to 30 minutes until lamb is fully tender, almonds are slightly soft, and carrots are cooked. Squeeze on some lemon juice. Add salt to season.

Nutrition Information

- Calories: 494 calories;
- Total Fat: 32.2
- Sodium: 295
- Total Carbohydrate: 34.7
- Cholesterol: 79
- Protein: 21.6

415. Moroccan Shepherd's Pie

Serving: 4 | Prep: 20mins | Cook: 1hours15mins | Ready in:

Ingredients

- cooking spray
- 1 tablespoon olive oil
- 1 pound cubed lamb stew meat
- 1 teaspoon ground cumin, divided
- 1/2 teaspoon salt, divided
- 1 1/2 cups chopped onion
- 4 garlic cloves, minced
- 1 tablespoon tomato paste
- 1 1/2 (10.5 ounce) cans low-sodium chicken broth
- 1/2 cup water
- 2 tablespoons olives, or to taste
- 1/3 cup raisins
- 2 tablespoons honey
- 1/2 teaspoon cayenne pepper
- 1/4 teaspoon ground turmeric
- 1/2 teaspoon ground cinnamon, divided
- 1 cup frozen green peas
- 4 cups peeled and chopped sweet potatoes
- 1 large egg, lightly beaten

Direction

- Set the oven at 175°C (350°F) to preheat. Spray the cooking spray onto 4 10-ounce ramekins dish.

- Set the heat to medium-high and heat a big skillet. Put in oil and swirl to coat.
- Evenly drizzle 1/4 tsp of salt and half a tsp of cumin over the lamb. Cook while stirring the lamb in hot oil for about 4 minutes, until all sides are browned. Move the lamb to a bowl. Add onion to the same skillet, cook while stirring for about 3 minutes, until the onion is slightly tender. Put in garlic and cook for about half a minute, until fragrant.
- Whisk the tomato paste into the onion mixture for about half a minute, until it is evenly coated. Add water and broth to the onion mixture. Bring the mixture to a boil, use a wooden spoon to scrap the skillet to loosen browned bits of food. Transfer the lamb back to the skillet.
- Mix 1/8 tsp of cinnamon, turmeric, cayenne pepper, honey, raisins, olives, and the remaining half a tsp of cumin into the lamb mixture. Lower the heat and simmer while stirring occasionally for about half an hour, until the flavors have blended and the lamb is fully cooked. Take away from heat and mix in peas.
- In a big pot, boil the sweet potatoes with salted water. Lower the heat to medium-low and simmer for about 10 minutes, until the potatoes are softened. Drain and let it cool for 5 minutes. Move the sweet potatoes to a bowl and scatter with 3/8 tsp of cinnamon and 1/4 tsp of salt. Use a hand mixer to beat the potato mixture on high speed until smooth. Put in egg and beat until incorporated.
- Scoop the lamb mixture into each ramekin; spread the sweet potato mixture on top of the lamb mixture. Arrange the ramekins onto the baking sheet.
- Bake for about 25 minutes in the preheated oven, until bubbling.

Nutrition Information

- Calories: 425 calories;
- Total Fat: 10.2
- Sodium: 586
- Total Carbohydrate: 60.3
- Cholesterol: 102
- Protein: 25.5

416. Mozzarella Stuffed Leg Of Lamb

Serving: 8 | Prep: 15mins | Cook: 1hours30mins | Ready in:

Ingredients

- 2 cups small dried bread cubes or plain croutons
- 1/2 cup shredded mozzarella cheese
- 2 teaspoons finely chopped mint leaves
- 1/2 cup Heinz® Chili Sauce
- 1 (3 pound) boneless, butterflied leg of lamb, trimmed
- 3/4 teaspoon salt
- 3/4 teaspoon pepper

Direction

- Turn the oven to 325°F (160°C) to preheat. Mix chili sauce, mint, cheese, and bread cubes together until fully blended.
- Place the meat with the fat-side turning down and sprinkle pepper and salt over all. Evenly spread bread mixture over, leaving a border of 1-inch (2.5-cm) at one end. Beginning from the smaller end, roll the meat up in jellyroll style.
- Tie kitchen string around the rolled roast. Bring to a rack fitted in a roasting pan and roast for 1 1/2 hours until a meat thermometer displays 160°F (70°C) for medium doneness or 140°F (60°C) for rare, basting sometimes. Let the roast sit for 10 minutes. Cut into thick slices. Create 8 servings.

Nutrition Information

- Calories: 251 calories;
- Total Fat: 12.9

- Sodium: 596
- Total Carbohydrate: 10.8
- Cholesterol: 70
- Protein: 21.4

417. Mum's Mutton Curry

Serving: 5 | Prep: 20mins | Cook: 1hours | Ready in:

Ingredients

- 1 clove garlic, peeled
- 1 (2 inch) piece fresh ginger root, peeled
- 1/4 cup vegetable oil
- 1 (3 inch) cinnamon stick
- 1/2 teaspoon cumin seeds
- 1 star anise pod
- 8 kaffir lime leaves
- 2 pounds mutton, cubed
- 10 shallots, sliced
- 2 large tomatoes, chopped
- 5 tablespoons curry powder
- 1/2 cup coconut milk
- salt to taste
- 4 cups water
- 4 large potatoes, peeled and cubed

Direction

- In a food processor, mix ginger and garlic. Blend into a paste and put aside.
- In a large skillet, heat oil over medium heat. Put in the lime leaves, anise pod, cumin seeds, and cinnamon stick. Add shallots, continue to cook and stir for about 5 minutes or until it starts to brown. Add the ginger-garlic paste, stir. Cook and stir for a few minutes longer, then stir in tomatoes and the mutton. Over low heat, simmer while covered for a half-hour.
- Stir in water, coconut milk, and the curry powder; put in the potato. Season with salt to taste. Simmer, covered, for another 30 minutes or until the mutton and potato are soft.

Nutrition Information

- Calories: 724 calories;
- Cholesterol: 118
- Protein: 47.2
- Total Fat: 26.8
- Sodium: 195
- Total Carbohydrate: 77.2

418. NO YOLKS® Lamb Stew

Serving: 4 | Prep: 10mins | Cook: 1hours15mins | Ready in:

Ingredients

- 6 ounces NO YOLKS® Dumplings
- 1 tablespoon olive oil
- 1 pound lamb stew meat in 1 1/2-inch chunks
- 2 leeks, white part only, chopped
- 2 cloves garlic, minced
- 1/3 cup dry red wine
- 1 (14.5 ounce) can crushed tomatoes
- 1 cup beef broth
- 1/4 teaspoon pepper
- 1 teaspoon crushed dried rosemary
- 1 teaspoon salt
- 2 cups frozen cut green beans, thawed

Direction

- Cook noodles following package directions.
- In a big heavy bottomed pot place over medium heat, heat oil. Add lamb half at a time in hot oil and cook until all sides all browned. When done, remove from the pot. In the same pot, add wine, garlic and leeks, make sure to scrape all browned bits from the bottom of pot. Cook, stirring occasionally, for 2 minutes. Add rosemary, pepper, broth and tomatoes. Bring to a simmer, transfer lamb back to the pot and cook, covered, for 60 minutes over low heat. Stir in salt and green beans. Place on top of noodles and serve.

Nutrition Information

- Calories: 475 calories;
- Sodium: 994
- Total Carbohydrate: 50.2
- Cholesterol: 64
- Protein: 27.1
- Total Fat: 16.4

419. Never Fail Boneless Leg Of Lamb

Serving: 12 | Prep: 25mins | Cook: 1hours20mins | Ready in:

Ingredients

- 9 cloves garlic, divided
- 1/4 cup Dijon mustard
- 5 sprigs fresh rosemary, divided
- 1 tablespoon balsamic vinegar
- 1 teaspoon salt, divided
- 1/2 teaspoon freshly ground black pepper, divided
- 1 (4 pound) boneless leg of lamb, or more to taste
- 3 pounds ripe tomatoes, cored and diced into 1-inch pieces
- 1 Spanish onion, sliced
- 1/2 cup honey, divided
- 1/4 cup olive oil
- 3 sprigs fresh thyme

Direction

- Prepare the oven by preheating to 450°F (230°C).
- In a small food processor, combine 1/4 teaspoon pepper, 1/2 teaspoon salt, vinegar, leaves from 2 sprigs of rosemary, Dijon mustard, and 4 cloves garlic. Process them into a paste. Crush the rest of garlic.
- Cut excess fat from the lamb and transfer to a large roasting pan.
- In a large bowl, mix the rest of pepper and salt, remaining crushed garlic, olive oil, 1/4 cup honey, onion, and tomatoes. Stir well.
- Put rosemary-mustard paste over the top of the lamb and spread. Place the tomato mixture around the lamb. Insert the rest of the rosemary and thyme sprigs evenly up against the leg of lamb. Shower with the rest of 1/4 cup honey.
- Place in the preheated oven and bake for 20 minutes. Lower the oven temperature to 375°F (175°C). Keep on roasting for 1 hour to 1 hour and 15 minutes until an instant-read thermometer poked into the lamb registers at least 130°F (54°C).
- Place the lamb onto a cutting board, use aluminum foil to cover it, and allow it to rest for 10-15 minutes. Get rid of thyme and rosemary stems. Bring the roasting pan back to the oven to keep the tomato mixture warm.
- Cut and arrange lamb on a plate. Scoop the warm pan juices and tomato mixture on top.

Nutrition Information

- Calories: 299 calories;
- Sodium: 371
- Total Carbohydrate: 21.7
- Cholesterol: 62
- Protein: 18.7
- Total Fat: 15.8

420. Nova Scotia Style Donair

Serving: 15 | Prep: 40mins | Cook: 2hours30mins | Ready in:

Ingredients

- 4 pounds ground beef
- 1 pound ground lamb
- 5 teaspoons all-purpose flour (optional)
- 4 teaspoons salt
- 5 teaspoons dried oregano

- 2 1/2 teaspoons dry mustard
- 2 1/2 teaspoons garlic powder
- 2 1/2 teaspoons cracked black pepper
- 2 1/2 teaspoons cayenne pepper
- 2 teaspoons crushed dried chile pepper
- 1 1/2 teaspoons paprika
- 1 teaspoon Italian seasoning
- Sauce:
- 1 (12 fluid ounce) can evaporated milk
- 3/4 cup white sugar
- 2 teaspoons garlic powder
- 3 tablespoons white vinegar, or as needed
- 15 pita bread rounds
- 2 tomatoes, chopped, or more to taste
- 1 onion, chopped

Direction

- Start preheating the oven to 300°F (150°C). Coat a large baking pan with sides with oil.
- In a bowl, put Italian seasoning, paprika, chile pepper, cayenne pepper, black pepper, 2 1/2 teaspoons of garlic powder, dry mustard, oregano, salt, flour, lamb and beef. Using your hands, knead all the ingredients together for 10 mins until the paste forms. Shape meat mixture into a large loaf form. Put into prepared pan.
- Bake in prepared oven for 120 mins or until the middle is no longer pink. The instant-read thermometer should register at least 160°F (70°C) when inserted into middle. Take out meat from the oven. Allow meat to cool completely on drip rack to let fat and juices drain. Place meat in the refrigerator for 6 hours or up to overnight.
- In a small bowl, stir together 2 teaspoons of garlic powder, sugar and evaporated milk. Stir in the vinegar gradually until the mixture has just thickened.
- Slice the donair meat into 1/8-1/4-in. thick strips. In a skillet, fry the meat strips over medium-high heat, in single-sandwich batches, until the edges of meat start to crisp. Take out of the pan. Rub one pita round quickly and lightly with water. In the same frying pan, fry pita for one min or until it is just warm, turning once.
- Spread half a tablespoon sauce mixture over the pita. Place donair meat on top. Decorate with more sauce, tomato, and onion; do the same with the remaining pita and meat.

Nutrition Information

- Calories: 511 calories;
- Sodium: 1004
- Total Carbohydrate: 44.9
- Cholesterol: 103
- Protein: 32.7
- Total Fat: 21.6

421. Oven Roasted Boneless Leg Of Lamb

Serving: 6 | Prep: 10mins | Cook: 1hours30mins | Ready in:

Ingredients

- 2/3 cup extra virgin olive oil
- 1/4 cup lemon juice
- 1/4 cup lime juice
- 2 tablespoons minced garlic
- 1/2 teaspoon dried mint flakes
- 1/2 teaspoon dried oregano
- 1/2 teaspoon dried marjoram
- 3/4 teaspoon dried thyme
- 1/2 teaspoon crushed rosemary
- 1/2 teaspoon ground nutmeg
- 1/2 teaspoon ground cinnamon
- 1/2 teaspoon ground ginger
- 1/4 teaspoon ground white pepper
- 1/4 teaspoon salt
- 2 1/4 pounds boneless leg of lamb
- cooking spray
- 3 white potatoes, cut into large chunks (optional)
- 3 large carrots, cut into large chunks (optional)
- 2 tablespoons vegetable oil

Direction

- Combine salt, white pepper, ginger, cinnamon, nutmeg, rosemary, thyme, marjoram, oregano, mint, garlic, lime juice, lemon juice, and olive oil in a bowl. Cover with plastic wrap; chill marinade in the refrigerator for at least 1 hour.
- Pierce lamb in several places evenly; put into a gallon-sized freezer bag. Pour marinade over the lamb, squeeze to discard the excess air from the bag, and seal the bag. Let marinate in the refrigerator for 8 hours to overnight.
- Start preheating the oven at 325°F (165°C). Grease a shallow roasting pan with cooking spray.
- Take the lamb out of marinade; shake to discard the excess liquid. Save 2 tablespoons of marinade; discard the leftover.
- Arrange the lamb in the middle of the greased roasting pan.
- Mix carrots and potatoes in a large bowl. Spread the saved marinade and vegetable oil over the vegetables; toss to blend. Pour vegetables around the lamb. Use aluminum foil to cover the roasting pan.
- Roast lamb in prepared oven for about 80 minutes until an instant-read thermometer shows 140°F (60°C) when inserted into the center. Uncover the foil and keep cooking for extra 10 minutes until firm and meat is hot and seems slightly pink in the center. Let the lamb rest for 10 minutes before slicing to serve.

Nutrition Information

- Calories: 558 calories;
- Cholesterol: 69
- Protein: 21.5
- Total Fat: 42.1
- Sodium: 178
- Total Carbohydrate: 23.6

422. Oven Roasted Lamb Ribs

Serving: 4 | Prep: 35mins | Cook: 1hours30mins | Ready in:

Ingredients

- 4 pounds lamb ribs
- 1/2 cup lemon juice
- 3 tablespoons molasses
- 3 tablespoons white vinegar
- 2 tablespoons mustard
- 2 tablespoons ketchup
- 1 tablespoon ground cinnamon
- 1 tablespoon curry powder
- 1 tablespoon ground cumin
- 1 tablespoon salt
- 1 tablespoon ground black pepper
- 1 onion, quartered
- 2 small tomatoes, quartered
- 2 small thin-skinned sweet peppers, cored and seeded
- 1 cup finely chopped parsley
- 9 cloves garlic, minced
- 1 1/2 teaspoons cayenne pepper

Direction

- Rinse ribs well. Submerge in a big bowl of water, changing water after every half an hour for 2 hours, to get rid of extra fat. Let drain and pat it dry using paper towels.
- In a big, deep bowl, mix pepper, salt, cumin, curry powder, cinnamon, ketchup, mustard, vinegar, molasses and lemon juice.
- In a food processor, mix cayenne pepper, garlic, parsley, sweet peppers, tomatoes and onion; pulse to create a paste.
- In a bowl, mix the onion paste into lemon juice mixture. Put the lamb ribs; coat by flipping. Cover in plastic wrap. Refrigerate to marinate for a minimum of 10 hours.
- Preheat the oven to 150 °C or 300 °F.
- With aluminum foil, line a big baking sheet and place a rack over. On the rack, set the ribs.
- In the prepped oven, let the ribs bake for 1 1/2 to 2 hours till fat has released and meat is soft.

Using aluminum foil, cover the ribs and allow to sit for 5 minutes prior to serving.

Nutrition Information

- Calories: 819 calories;
- Sodium: 2088
- Total Carbohydrate: 33
- Cholesterol: 190
- Protein: 46.9
- Total Fat: 56.1

423. Pakistani Lamb Curry

Serving: 6 | Prep: 20mins | Cook: 40mins | Ready in:

Ingredients

- 2 tablespoons ghee
- 1 large onion, chopped
- 1 (28 ounce) can crushed tomatoes
- 1/2 cup water
- 1 (4 inch) piece ginger, peeled and roughly chopped
- 6 cloves garlic, chopped
- 2 pounds cubed leg of lamb meat
- 1 tablespoon salt, or to taste
- 1 tablespoon ground paprika
- 1 tablespoon ground turmeric
- 1 tablespoon ground coriander
- 1 tablespoon ground cumin
- 1 tablespoon ground cayenne pepper, or to taste
- 2 small serrano peppers, finely chopped, or to taste (optional)
- 1 tablespoon water, or as needed
- 2 tablespoons chopped fresh cilantro, or to taste
- 2 teaspoons garam masala

Direction

- Set a skillet on medium heat; heat ghee. Include in onion; cook while stirring for 5-7 minutes, or till translucent and soft. Move into a blender. Include in garlic, ginger, water and tomatoes; purée till smooth.
- Transfer the puréed sauce into a saucepan over medium heat. Include in cayenne pepper, cumin, coriander, turmeric, paprika, salt and lamb. Turn the heat down to medium-low; simmer for around 30 minutes, or till tender and pulled apart easily with a fork.
- In a small food processor, put in serrano peppers; grind with 1 tablespoon of water till the mixture forms a paste. Include into the lamb; keep simmering for around 5 minutes, or till all flavors are well combined. Stir in garam masala and cilantro.

Nutrition Information

- Calories: 288 calories;
- Protein: 20.3
- Total Fat: 16.5
- Sodium: 1387
- Total Carbohydrate: 16.9
- Cholesterol: 72

424. Pastry Wrapped Lamb Rack

Serving: 4 | Prep: 30mins | Cook: 15mins | Ready in:

Ingredients

- 1 tablespoon olive oil
- 1 small shallot, minced
- 1/2 cup fresh morel mushrooms, sliced
- 1/2 cup fresh oyster mushrooms, stemmed and sliced
- 2 tablespoons dry white wine
- 1 teaspoon ground cumin
- 1 teaspoon paprika
- 1 teaspoon dried oregano
- 2 teaspoons brown sugar
- 1 teaspoon garlic powder
- 1 teaspoon dried parsley flakes

- 2 teaspoons ground black pepper
- 2 teaspoons kosher salt
- 1 rack of lamb, trimmed and frenched
- 1 sheet frozen puff pastry, thawed
- 2 egg yolk, beaten
- 3/4 cup demi-glace
- 2 tablespoons butter
- 2 tablespoons chopped fresh parsley

Direction

- Heat olive oil on medium high heat in a skillet. Whisk in oyster mushrooms, morel and minced shallot; cook till mushrooms turn soft and lightly-browned. Add white wine, and cook till evaporated. Scrape mushrooms onto a plate, and put aside to cool down. At the same time, in a bowl, whisk the salt, pepper, parsley flakes, garlic powder, brown sugar, oregano, paprika and cumin together. Coat lamb rack with the spice mixture and put aside.
- Preheat the oven to 175 degrees C (350 degrees F). Use the aluminum foil to line the baking sheet and grease it slightly.
- Spread mushroom mixture evenly on one side of puff pastry. Slice a slit 2 in. away from one edge of puff pastry for each bone on lamb rack. Carefully poke bones through slits and wrap pastry around lamb rack, pressing edges of pastry together to seal them. Add to prepped baking sheet and use the beaten egg yolk to brush. Keep lamb in the refrigerator for 10 minutes prior to baking.
- Bake lamb in preheated oven for roughly 15 minutes or till pastry becomes puffed and golden-brown. Take out, and allow it to stand for 5 minutes prior to slicing. When lamb is resting, simmer demi-glace in a small-sized saucepan. Stir in butter till dissolved. Sprinkle demi-glace on sliced lamb chops, and drizzle with the chopped fresh parsley to decorate.

Nutrition Information

- Calories: 946 calories;
- Sodium: 2314
- Total Carbohydrate: 47.9

- Cholesterol: 212
- Protein: 42.1
- Total Fat: 63.9

425. Paul's Apple, Lamb And Lentil Soup

Serving: 6 | Prep: 30mins | Cook: 2hours | Ready in:

Ingredients

- 3 pounds lamb shoulder steak
- 1 pound lamb neck bones
- 1 (16 ounce) package dried lentils
- 2 medium yellow onion, chopped
- 5 cloves cloves garlic, finely chopped
- 2 teaspoons fresh thyme leaves, finely chopped
- 2 Red Delicious apples - peeled, cored and diced
- 1 cup Cabernet Sauvignon wine
- 1 cup fresh cilantro leaves, chopped
- salt and freshly ground black pepper

Direction

- Trim lamb shoulder steak from the bones. Put bones aside. Slice steak to 1-in. cubes. Put aside. Put neck and shoulder bones in a big stockpot; cover with water. Simmer the bones on medium-high heat for 1-1 1/2 hours. Take bones out of stockpot and throw away. Keep liquid.
- In the stockpot, add thyme, garlic, onions, lentils and cubed lamb. Cook for 15 minutes on medium heat. Add wine and apples to stockpot. Cook for 15 minutes more until lamb and lentils are tender. Season with pepper and salt. Serve in bowls, topped with cilantro.

Nutrition Information

- Calories: 746 calories;
- Cholesterol: 197

- Protein: 81.3
- Total Fat: 16.9
- Sodium: 209
- Total Carbohydrate: 56.8

426. Punjabi Lamb Korma With Onion Cilantro Salad

Serving: 6 | Prep: 30mins | Cook: 2hours27mins | Ready in:

Ingredients

- Lamb Korma:
- 1/2 cup whole milk yogurt
- 1/2 cup almonds
- 1/4 cup ghee (clarified butter)
- 3 yellow onions, thinly sliced
- 1 pound boneless lamb shoulder, cut into 1-inch pieces
- 1/2 teaspoon cayenne pepper
- 1 pinch salt to taste
- 1 cup water
- 1/2 teaspoon garam masala
- 1/2 teaspoon ground cardamom
- 1/4 teaspoon ground mace
- Onion Cilantro Salad:
- 2 red onions, thinly sliced
- 2 tablespoons chopped fresh cilantro
- 1 tablespoon lemon juice, or more to taste
- salt to taste

Direction

- In a blender or food processor, blend almonds and yogurt together till the mixture forms a smooth and creamy paste.
- Set a large, wide-bottomed pan on medium heat; include in ghee and melt. Cook while stirring in yellow onions for 10-15 minutes, or till evenly browned. Include in lamb; cook while stirring from time to time for around 6 minutes, or till browned slightly. Stir in salt and cayenne pepper; cook for 2 minutes.
- Mix in the prepared yogurt-almond paste. Boil the mixture; lower the heat; simmer for 2-3 hours, or till the meat becomes very tender. Mix in mace, cardamom and garam masala; simmer for 10 more minutes.
- In a bowl, combine cilantro and red onions; include in salt and lemon juice; stir well. Serve the salad alongside the lamb korma.

Nutrition Information

- Calories: 330 calories;
- Total Fat: 23.2
- Sodium: 94
- Total Carbohydrate: 17.9
- Cholesterol: 63
- Protein: 14.7

427. Rack Of Lamb With Blueberry Sauce

Serving: 4 | Prep: 20mins | Cook: 40mins | Ready in:

Ingredients

- 2 (8 bone) racks of lamb, fully trimmed
- salt and ground black pepper to taste
- 1 tablespoon vegetable oil
- 2 teaspoons Dijon mustard
- 1 teaspoon minced fresh rosemary
- 1/8 teaspoon ground cinnamon
- 1/8 teaspoon ground cumin
- 1/3 cup sliced shallot
- 1 pinch salt
- 1 cup fresh blueberries
- 1 cup dry red wine
- 1 pinch ground black pepper
- 1 tablespoon balsamic vinegar
- 1 tablespoon butter, or more as needed

Direction

- Preheat the oven to 190 °C or 375 °F.

- Liberally season the lamb with black pepper and salt. In an oven-proof skillet, heat the oil over moderately-high heat. Scorch the lamb on every side for 3 to 5 minutes each side till nicely browned. Switch off heat. Take off the lamb to a platter.
- In a small bowl, combine together cumin, cinnamon, rosemary and Dijon mustard. Scatter the mustard mixture thin on a single layer on every lamb rack.
- Into the same skillet, put a pinch of salt and chopped shallots. Cook and mix over medium-heat for 5 minutes till shallots start to lose moisture and turn soft and browned. Put the blueberries and continue to cook for 2 minutes. Mix in the red wine, switch off heat, and to deglaze the pan, mix the mixture.
- Into a skillet, put lamb racks and interlace rib bones together to force the lamb racks near to each other, retaining lamb bone "zipper" in the middle. Into the middle of skillet, put lamb racks. Add a pinch of black pepper to season.
- In the prepped oven, put the skillet and let the lamb roast for 20 minutes till inner temperature attains 52 °C or 125 °F for medium-rare.
- Take the lamb off to a chopping board to allow to sit for 5 minutes.
- Into the blueberry sauce, sprinkle the balsamic vinegar; put a pinch of salt. Set the heat to moderately-high and simmer for 4 minutes to cook down sauce by 1/2. Switch off the heat and mix in butter. Once butter is liquified, taste seasonings and put additional salt if necessary.
- Cut the racks into portions of 2 ribs each. Top with spoonful of blueberry sauce and serve.

Nutrition Information

- Calories: 831 calories;
- Total Fat: 62.1
- Sodium: 238
- Total Carbohydrate: 10.4
- Cholesterol: 202
- Protein: 44.9

428. Roasted Orange Leg Of Lamb

Serving: 8 | Prep: 20mins | Cook: 2hours50mins | Ready in:

Ingredients

- 1 tablespoon olive oil
- 1 tablespoon seasoned salt, or as needed
- 1 (3 pound) leg of lamb
- 1 cup all-purpose flour
- 1 tablespoon dry mustard
- 1 cup fresh orange juice, or more as needed
- 1 onion, chopped
- 1/2 cup water, or more as needed

Direction

- Set the oven to 260°C or 500°F to preheat. Use olive oil to coat a roasting pan.
- Rub over leg of lamb with seasoned salt.
- In a bowl, combine together mustard and flour, then rub mixture over leg of lamb. Remove to the prepped roasting pan.
- In the preheated oven, roast leg of lamb for 20 minutes, until browned.
- Lower the temperature of oven to 160°C or 325°F. Put into roasting pan with water, onion and orange juice. Keep on baking lamb for 2 1/2 hours while basting with water and orange juice after each half an hour, until tender.

Nutrition Information

- Calories: 247 calories;
- Sodium: 397
- Total Carbohydrate: 18.4
- Cholesterol: 66
- Protein: 23.6
- Total Fat: 8.1

429. Rob's Lamb Curry Pie

Serving: 8 | Prep: 1hours | Cook: 50mins | Ready in:

Ingredients

- Filling:
- 3 tablespoons olive oil
- 3 cloves garlic
- 1 (3/4 inch thick) slice fresh ginger root, coarsely chopped
- 1 tablespoon red curry paste
- 1/2 cup fresh cilantro leaves
- 1/2 teaspoon ground cumin
- 1/2 teaspoon ground turmeric
- 1/2 teaspoon cayenne pepper
- 1/4 teaspoon ground cinnamon
- 3 red onions, chopped
- 1 eggplant, chopped
- 3/4 cup chopped celery
- 1 large red bell pepper, chopped
- 3 cups diced leftover roast lamb
- Sauce:
- 1 1/2 cups milk
- 3 tablespoons butter
- 1/2 cup sweet white wine
- 3 tablespoons all-purpose flour
- salt to taste
- Crust:
- 1 cup all-purpose flour
- 1/2 teaspoon salt
- 1 tablespoon curry powder
- 6 tablespoons shortening
- 3 tablespoons cold water, or as needed

Direction

- Preheat the oven to 190 degrees C (375 degrees F). Grease big baking dish or pie dish.
- Add the cinnamon, cayenne pepper, turmeric, cumin, cilantro, curry paste, ginger, garlic and olive oil to work bowl of the food processor, and blend into a paste. Add curry paste to the big mixing bowl, and whisk along with the red bell pepper, celery, eggplant and red onions to coat all vegetables with the curry mixture. Move vegetables to the big skillet on medium heat, and cook and stir approximately 7 minutes till veggies soften. Mix in cooked lamb, and cook and stir 2-3 minutes longer till lamb becomes hot and coated with the spice mixture. Switch off heat under skillet.
- Heat the wine, butter and milk on medium heat in the sauce pan till butter melts and mixture becomes hot yet not boiling. Stir 3 tbsp. of the flour to hot milk mixture, and cook, stirring continuously, till sauce becomes thick. Turn heat under skillet of the veggies and lamb to medium, and cook and stir approximately 2 minutes till becoming hot; add sauce to veggies and lamb, and combine by stirring. Use salt to season to taste, and add hot filling to prepped pie dish.
- For making the crust, whisk curry powder, half tsp. of the salt, and 1 cup of flour together in the bowl till becoming combined through. Chop in shortening using the pastry cutter till mixture looks like coarse crumbs. Drizzle with water, and whisk lightly till dough just comes together. Shape into the rough ball, put onto the floured work surface, and roll out to the crust to fit pie plate. Lay crust on top of plate and lamb filling, crimp it to dish using the fork, and cut a few slits in crust's top.
- Bake in preheated oven approximately 35 minutes till crust turns golden brown and filling is hot. Allow it to cool down 7-10 minutes prior to serving.

Nutrition Information

- Calories: 518 calories;
- Total Carbohydrate: 23.4
- Cholesterol: 93
- Protein: 26
- Total Fat: 34.2
- Sodium: 301

430. Rosemary And Lamb Crispy Roast Potatoes

Serving: 4 | Prep: 15mins | Cook: 45mins | Ready in:

Ingredients

- 4 large baking potatoes, peeled and quartered
- 1/2 teaspoon dried rosemary
- 1/2 cup lamb roast drippings, cooled to room temperature
- salt to taste

Direction

- Start preheating the oven to 425°F (220°). In a big pan, put potatoes and cover with enough water. Boil it and cook until partially cooked, about 10 minutes.
- In a big tub that has a lid, put the potatoes and add the lamb drippings. Use salt and rosemary to season. Close the lid and shake to blend to the potatoes. Put them on a baking sheet.
- Put in the preheated oven and bake until crisp and turning dark brown, or about 45 minutes.

Nutrition Information

- Calories: 352 calories;
- Total Fat: 1.9
- Sodium: 35
- Total Carbohydrate: 64.6
- Cholesterol: 35
- Protein: 20

431. Scotch Broth II

Serving: 8 | Prep: 30mins | Cook: 3hours55mins | Ready in:

Ingredients

- 2 1/4 pounds leg of lamb
- 8 cups water
- 3 onions, chopped
- 3 turnips, chopped
- 2 carrots, chopped
- 1 tablespoon whole black peppercorns
- 1/2 cup barley
- 1 carrot, diced
- 2 onions, minced
- 1 leek, chopped
- 1 stalk celery, diced
- 2 turnips, diced

Direction

- To prepare the stock, in a big pot, place water, peppercorns, 2 carrots, 3 turnips, 3 onions, and lamb shanks. Boil it, lower the heat, put a cover on and simmer for 3 hours. Skim the top as needed.
- Take out the shanks and any meat that falls off the bones and let cool briefly. Strip the meat off the bones and finely cut, and then put a cover on and chill. Drain the stock, remove the vegetables. Let the stock cool and chill until the fat floats on top and you can remove it, about overnight.
- Add water to slightly cover the barley and bath for 1 hour.
- In a big pan, pour the stock and lightly reheat. Add turnip, celery, leek, onion, more carrot, and the drained barley. Boil it, lower the heat and simmer just until the vegetables and barley have cooked, about 30 minutes. Put the meat back to the pan and bring to a simmer for 5 minutes. Season thoroughly and enjoy with parsley.

Nutrition Information

- Calories: 366 calories;
- Cholesterol: 92
- Protein: 27.5
- Total Fat: 17.6
- Sodium: 171
- Total Carbohydrate: 24.4

432. Simplified Cassoulet

Serving: 15 | Prep: | Cook: | Ready in:

Ingredients

- 3 pounds boneless lamb shoulder roast, cut into 11/2-inch cubes (or a combination of lamb and boneless pork shoulder roast)
- 3 tablespoons olive oil
- Salt and freshly ground black pepper
- 1 pound mild Italian sausages
- 1 cup water for sausages
- 1/2 pound kielbasa, cut into 6 pieces
- 1 1/2 pounds boneless duck breast halves
- 1 (14.5 ounce) can chicken broth
- 2 cups water
- 1 cup full-bodied dry red wine
- reserved duck fat
- 2 large onions, cut into medium dice
- 6 garlic cloves, minced
- 2 ounces thinly sliced prosciutto, minced
- 2 teaspoons dried thyme
- 1 (14.5 ounce) can diced tomatoes
- 6 (16 ounce) cans white beans, drained
- 3 cups fresh bread crumbs (process sliced bread in a food processor or blender)
- 3 tablespoons butter, melted
- 1/3 cup minced fresh parsley

Direction

- Arrange oven rack to lower middle position; set the oven to 450° and start heating.
- Arrange lamb cubes in a bowl. Add 2 tablespoons of oil on top and generously sprinkle salt and pepper to season, flip until well coated.
- In a large heavy roasting pan set over 2 burners, combine remaining 1 tablespoon oil, 1 cup water and Italian sausages. Cover the pan with heavy-duty foil and set the heat to medium high. Cook for about 5 minutes until the raw color of the sausage is no longer visible. Remove foil (reserve it) and keep cooking until water fully evaporates. Add smoked sausages and cook for 5 to 8 more minutes until browned, remember to flip frequently while cooking. Move to a plate to cool. When sausage is safe to handle, cut in to bite size chunks. Cut smoked sausages by half lengthwise. Set aside.
- Generously sprinkle salt and pepper over duck breasts, lower the heat under roasting pan and arrange duck breasts skin side down and cook for 10 to 12 minutes until skin turns to a mahogany brown color and fat is rendered out.
- Flip dusk breasts and cook for an additional 5 minutes until cooked through. Remove duck from pan. Drain off all excess fat from the pan and reserve. Divide each breast into 4 pieces by slicing crosswise.
- Return roasting pan to medium high heat. Add lamb cubes and cook for 8 to 10 minutes until a brown crust creates on two sides, remember to flip one time while cooking.
- Move lamb to a big ovenproof pot; set roasting pan aside. Add wine and broth mixture to lamb and use reserved foil to cover, remember to press the foil down until it almost touches the meat, seal foil around the top of pot, remember to leave a small opening for steam to get out. Bring to a simmer and simmer for a couple minutes until alcohol is burned off. Seal the foil completely, and cover the pot with its lid. Bake for 75 minutes until meat becomes very tender, remember not to check the pot.
- In the meantime, reheat roasting pan over medium high heat. Add enough amount of saved duck fat or olive oil to equal 2 tablespoons. Add garlic and onions, sauté for about 5 minutes until softened. Add thyme and prosciutto and sauté for 1-2 more minutes until flavors are well combined. Add beans and tomatoes and simmer for about 10 minutes until flavors are well blended. Remove from heat.
- Move broth and cooked lamb to roasting pan. Add sausages, duck and enough water until mixture resembles a soupy and moist casserole. You can allow cassoulet mixture to stand at room temperature for a maximum of 2 hours.

- An hour prior to serving, arrange oven rack to lower middle position; set the oven to 350° and start heating. Bring cassoulet to a simmer.
- Combine parsley, melted butter and breadcrumbs; dust on top of cassoulet. Bake for another 45 minutes until stew is bubbly and crumbs turn golden in color. Allow to stand for 5 minutes. Serve.

Nutrition Information

- Calories: 572 calories;
- Sodium: 789
- Total Carbohydrate: 48.2
- Cholesterol: 97
- Protein: 38.2
- Total Fat: 23.8

433. Slow Cooker Lamb Chops

Serving: 6 | Prep: 15mins | Cook: 4hours30mins | Ready in:

Ingredients

- 1/2 cup red wine
- 1/2 sweet onion, roughly chopped
- 3 tablespoons honey
- 2 tablespoons Dijon mustard
- 2 tablespoons lemon juice
- 4 garlic cloves, minced
- 1 tablespoon ground thyme
- 1 tablespoon dried rosemary
- 2 teaspoons ground basil
- 1 teaspoon salt
- 1 teaspoon coarse ground black pepper
- 1/4 cup tapioca starch
- 1 1/2 pounds sirloin lamb chops, room temperature

Direction

- In a slow cooker, mix onion and red wine.
- Whisk pepper, salt, basil, rosemary, thyme, garlic, lemon juice, mustard and honey till well blended in a small bowl. Add tapioca starch; whisk till combined well. Sit for 5 minutes minimum till thickened.
- Dip lamb chops in mustard mixture; massage till coated fully.
- Put chops on onion and red wine mixture in slow cooker in 1 layer; put leftover mustard mixture over.
- Cover slow cooker; cook on low for 4 1/2 hours till inserted instant-read thermometer in middle of chop reads minimum of 54°C/130°F.

Nutrition Information

- Calories: 209 calories;
- Total Carbohydrate: 18.5
- Cholesterol: 44
- Protein: 13
- Total Fat: 7.7
- Sodium: 550

434. Slow Cooker Leg Of Lamb

Serving: 8 | Prep: 15mins | Cook: 6hours | Ready in:

Ingredients

- 1 small lemon
- 2 tablespoons chopped fresh rosemary
- 5 cloves garlic, minced
- 1 tablespoon chopped fresh thyme
- 1 tablespoon chopped fresh parsley
- 1 tablespoon olive oil
- 1 teaspoon sea salt
- 1 teaspoon ground black pepper
- 1/4 teaspoon onion powder
- 1 (3 pound) leg of lamb
- 1/2 cup vegetable broth

Direction

- Use a mortar to grate lemon zest; add onion powder, black pepper, sea salt, olive oil, parsley, thyme, garlic, and rosemary. Use a pestle to grind into a paste.
- Pat the lamb dry and knead herb mixture all over the lamb. Transfer the lamb to a 3-qt slow cooker and squeeze the juice of a lemon over the lamb. Pour in broth and cover.
- Cook for 6-8 hours on low.

Nutrition Information

- Calories: 205 calories;
- Total Fat: 12.6
- Sodium: 300
- Total Carbohydrate: 2.8
- Cholesterol: 69
- Protein: 19.9

435. Slow Cooker Roasted Leg Of Lamb

Serving: 6 | Prep: 10mins | Cook: 5hours | Ready in:

Ingredients

- 1 (3 pound) bone-in leg of lamb, or more to taste
- 1/2 cup red wine
- 1 lemon, juiced
- 2 tablespoons raw honey
- 2 tablespoons Dijon mustard
- 3 cloves garlic, minced
- 1 tablespoon apple cider vinegar
- 1 tablespoon dried rosemary
- 1 teaspoon dried thyme
- 1 teaspoon sea salt
- 1/2 teaspoon fresh cracked pepper

Direction

- Let lamb leg cool to room temperature, approximately 2 hours.

- Add wine in a slow cooker. In a mixing bowl, combine pepper, sea salt, thyme, rosemary, vinegar, garlic, mustard, honey, and lemon juice until a thick paste is formed. Rub paste into lamb with your hands; carefully put into the slow cooker.
- Cook lamb for 5 hours on low setting, covered. An instant-read thermometer pinned near the bone registers 145°F (65°C). Allow lamb to sit for 15 to 20 minutes before serving.

Nutrition Information

- Calories: 285 calories;
- Cholesterol: 100
- Protein: 25.6
- Total Fat: 14
- Sodium: 465
- Total Carbohydrate: 10.5

436. Special Mutton Leg Roast For Eid Ul Azha

Serving: 12 | Prep: 5mins | Cook: 2hours15mins | Ready in:

Ingredients

- 1 (5 pound) leg of lamb, trimmed of excess fat
- 4 cups plain yogurt
- 4 tablespoons ginger-garlic paste
- 3 tablespoons lemon juice
- 2 tablespoons ground red chile pepper
- 2 tablespoons chaat masala
- 2 tablespoons garam masala
- 1 tablespoon salt, or to taste
- 1 tablespoon red pepper flakes
- 1 tablespoon ground turmeric
- 1 tablespoon ground black pepper
- 1 tablespoon ground cumin
- 1 tablespoon ground coriander
- 1 cup vegetable oil

Direction

- Make deep slashes approximately 2 inches apart across the lamb.
- In a mixing bowl, combine coriander, cumin, black pepper, turmeric, red pepper flakes, salt, garam masala, chaat masala, ground red chile, lemon juice, ginger-garlic paste, and yogurt. Stir until well incorporated. Spoon marinade liberally all over the lamb in a dish; flip over; baste with more marinade. Chill, covered, for 3 hours to overnight.
- Heat oil over medium heat in a large cast-iron. Gently lay lamb leg into the bottom of the pot. Cover the pot with lid; lay a heavy weight atop the lid. Turn heat to low and cook for 60 minutes. Turn over the leg; cook for 1 more hour.
- Keep cooking for about 15 minutes longer or until meat is golden and tender, juices in the pot is mostly vaporized, and oils begin to accumulate at the edges of the lamb. An instant-read thermometer inserted into the center of the lamb should register 130°F (54°C). Remove cooked lamb to a serving dish to serve.

Nutrition Information

- Calories: 449 calories;
- Total Fat: 32
- Sodium: 1000
- Total Carbohydrate: 10.2
- Cholesterol: 88
- Protein: 25.9

437. Spring Lamb Sliders

Serving: 4 | Prep: 15mins | Cook: 3hours10mins | Ready in:

Ingredients

- 1 (3 1/2) pound bone-in lamb shoulder roast
- Kosher salt and freshly ground black pepper
- 1 tablespoon vegetable oil
- 1 onion, cut in large dice
- 4 cloves garlic, minced
- 1 cup chicken broth
- 1/2 cup cider vinegar
- 1/4 cup honey
- 1/4 teaspoon red pepper flakes
- 2 tablespoons fresh sliced mint
- 12 slider buns

Direction

- Set oven to 165° C (325° F) and start preheating. Season pepper and salt on all sides of roast.
- In a Dutch oven, heat oil on high heat. Beginning with the meat side down, brown all sides of roast; cook for 4-5 minutes or until browned well. Flip over and cook for 4-5 minutes, or until the bone side has been browned. When second side browns, arrange garlic and chopped onions around the roast. Onion will start to be translucent once roast browns. Add red pepper flakes, honey, cider vinegar and chicken broth and mix together, tossing to coat all sides of the roast.
- For the meat side up, put a cover on the pot and put into the center rack of preheated oven. Roast for 3 hours, or till meat is fork tender.
- Use a spoon to remove excess fat then break up the meat into small strips; arrange in a pot. Get rid of bones. Strain broth into the pot of picked meat. Cook on medium heat until simmering. Mix in chopped fresh mint.
- Arrange on toasted slider rolls to serve.

Nutrition Information

- Calories: 959 calories;
- Total Fat: 49
- Sodium: 474
- Total Carbohydrate: 498.4
- Cholesterol: 204
- Protein: 58.3

438. Stuffed Greek Leg Of Lamb

Serving: 8 | Prep: 15mins | Cook: 1hours30mins | Ready in:

Ingredients

- 1 (3 1/2) pound leg of lamb, butterflied
- olive oil, or as needed
- 2 tablespoons chopped fresh oregano
- 2 tablespoons chopped fresh basil
- 1 (12 ounce) jar marinated artichoke hearts, drained and chopped
- 1 (8 ounce) package crumbled feta cheese
- 1 (6 ounce) jar sun-dried tomatoes packed in oil, drained and chopped
- 3 cloves garlic, minced
- salt and ground black pepper to taste

Direction

- Preheat the oven to 175°C or 350°Fahrenheit.
- Arrange the lamb leg with the inside facing you on a cutting board; evenly drizzle top of lamb with olive oil. Scatter basil and oregano all over the lamb, then top with garlic, artichoke hearts, sun-dried tomatoes, and feta cheese. Sprinkle pepper and salt to season.
- Roll the lamb leg around the stuffing then tie with kitchen twine to avoid unrolling. Use aluminum foil to wrap the lamb then put in a baking dish.
- Roast to your preferred doneness in the preheated oven or 90 minutes until the internal temperature reaches 70°C or 150°Fahrenheit to get a medium. Put aside and rest for 10 minutes in a warm place before carving. Save pan juices to serve.

Nutrition Information

- Calories: 389 calories;
- Sodium: 602
- Total Carbohydrate: 11.5
- Cholesterol: 105
- Protein: 29.6
- Total Fat: 25.7

439. The Shorba Freekeh Of Algeria

Serving: 8 | Prep: 30mins | Cook: 3hours | Ready in:

Ingredients

- 2 large tomatoes, cut into chunks
- 2 onions, cut into chunks
- 1 serrano pepper, cut into chunks
- 1 Anaheim pepper, cut into chunks
- 1/2 zucchini, cut into chunks
- 3 cloves garlic
- 1/4 cup olive oil
- 1 pound lamb stew meat, cut into 1-inch cubes
- 3/4 pound ground beef
- 2 teaspoons salt
- 2 cubes vegetable bouillon, or more to taste
- 2 teaspoons ground cumin
- 1 teaspoon ground black pepper
- 1 teaspoon paprika
- 1/2 teaspoon ground coriander
- 1/4 teaspoon ground turmeric
- 1/4 teaspoon cayenne pepper
- 2 1/2 quarts water
- 1 (6 ounce) can tomato paste
- 1/2 cup finely ground freekeh
- 2 cups green peas
- 2 tablespoons butter
- 1 bunch cilantro, coarsely chopped
- 1 lemon, cut into wedges, or more to taste

Direction

- In a blender, process together garlic, zucchini, Anaheim pepper, serrano pepper, onions and tomatoes until vegetables are pureed totally.
- In a big pot, heat olive oil on moderate heat. Cook beef and lamb on hot oil together with a pinch of salt while stirring sometimes, for 25 minutes, until all sides of lamb is browned and cooked through.

- Stir into lamb mixture with cayenne pepper, turmeric, coriander, paprika, black pepper, cumin, vegetable bouillon and vegetable puree. Bring mixture to a simmer and lower heat to moderately low. Cook and stir sometimes for 35 minutes, until flavors start to combine.
- Pour into lamb mixture with water and tomato paste, then bring to a simmer. Lower heat to moderately low and cook for 1 1/2 hours, until lamb begins to tenderize. Put in freekeh and simmer for a half hour, until freekeh is blended into soup.
- Stir into soup with butter and peas. Take pot away from the heat and stir into soup with cilantro. Scoop into bowls with soup and squeeze lemon juice into bowls.

Nutrition Information

- Calories: 375 calories;
- Total Fat: 22.5
- Sodium: 835
- Total Carbohydrate: 24.3
- Cholesterol: 62
- Protein: 20.9

440. Tim's Lamb Stew

Serving: 10 | Prep: 30mins | Cook: 2hours | Ready in:

Ingredients

- 1 (14.5 ounce) can beef broth
- 2 pounds lamb stew meat, cubed
- 1 1/2 tablespoons chopped fresh parsley
- 1 teaspoon dried thyme
- salt and pepper to taste
- 2 pounds potatoes, peeled and sliced
- 1 1/2 pounds carrots, peeled and diced
- 1 medium onion, finely chopped
- 6 tablespoons all-purpose flour
- 1/4 cup corn oil

Direction

- Combine thyme, parsley, lamb and beef broth in a big saucepan over medium heat. Add salt and pepper to season and cook, covered, for 30 minutes, remember to stir occasionally while cooking.
- Stir onion, carrots and potatoes into lamb mixture. Lower the heat to low and cook, covered, for 90 minutes until all vegetables are softened.
- Combine oil and flour in a small bowl until smooth. Stir into the stew mixture and cook for 5 minutes until mixture thickens.

Nutrition Information

- Calories: 293 calories;
- Total Fat: 10.7
- Sodium: 245
- Total Carbohydrate: 27.1
- Cholesterol: 59
- Protein: 21.9

441. Tomato Bredie

Serving: 6 | Prep: 30mins | Cook: 2hours | Ready in:

Ingredients

- 1 tablespoon vegetable oil
- 3 1/2 pounds lamb or mutton breast chops, chopped into portions
- 2 tablespoons cake flour
- 1 large onion, chopped
- 2 1/4 pounds fresh tomatoes, chopped
- 1 teaspoon salt
- 1/2 teaspoon freshly ground black pepper
- 6 whole white peppercorns
- 2 bay leaves
- 1 teaspoon brown sugar
- 1 tablespoon white vinegar
- 1 dash Worcestershire sauce
- 1 cube beef bouillon cube

- 2 medium potatoes, quartered (optional)

Direction

- Heat oil in a large, heavy-bottomed saucepan over medium-high heat. Press meat in flour to coat, and fry in heated oil until all sides are browned.
- Mix in onion; cook for about 5 minutes until onions are tender. Stir in tomatoes. Season with beef bouillon cube, Worcestershire sauce, vinegar, brown sugar, bay leaves, white peppercorns, black pepper, and salt. Lower heat; simmer, covered, for 1 hour and 15 minutes. Whisk occasionally to prevent food from sticking to the bottom of the pot.
- Mix in potatoes; keep cooking until meat is tender and potatoes are cooked through, for 45 minutes longer.

Nutrition Information

- Calories: 531 calories;
- Total Fat: 31.2
- Sodium: 633
- Total Carbohydrate: 25.3
- Cholesterol: 134
- Protein: 36.8

442. Tunisian Lamb With Saffron (Keleya Zaara)

Serving: 4 | Prep: 25mins | Cook: 30mins | Ready in:

Ingredients

- 1/4 cup vegetable oil
- 1 1/2 pounds cubed lamb stew meat
- 1 1/2 teaspoons saffron
- salt and pepper to taste
- 1 large onion, chopped
- 1 cup water
- 1/2 cup chopped fresh parsley
- 1 tablespoon butter
- 1 lemon, cut into wedges

Direction

- Place a large skillet on medium-high heat; heat in vegetable oil. Cook in lamb for about 5 minutes, until evenly browned on every side. Season with pepper, salt and saffron; mix in everything but 1/4 cup of the onion; pour in water. Bring to boil, the place a cover; lower the heat to medium-low; keep simmering for about 15 minutes, till the lamb becomes soft
- Uncover the frying pan; stir in butter; leave the sauce to reduce to the needed consistency, about 5-10 minutes. Season with pepper and salt; transfer into a serving dish. Sprinkle on top with parsley and the remaining chopped onions. Use lemon wedges to garnish. Serve.

Nutrition Information

- Calories: 336 calories;
- Total Fat: 23.2
- Sodium: 81
- Total Carbohydrate: 7.1
- Cholesterol: 88
- Protein: 26

443. Upside Down (Maqluba)

Serving: 6 | Prep: 30mins | Cook: 1hours10mins | Ready in:

Ingredients

- 7 cups water
- 2 onions, chopped
- 1 tablespoon chopped garlic
- 1 teaspoon ground cinnamon
- 1 teaspoon ground turmeric
- 2 teaspoons garam masala
- 1 pinch salt and ground black pepper to taste
- 2 cups cooking oil
- 2 cups lamb meat, cut into small pieces

- 1 large eggplant, cut into 3/4-inch slices
- 2 zucchini, cut into 1/4-inch slices
- 1 cup broccoli
- 1 cup cauliflower
- 1 1/2 cups jasmine rice
- 1 (16 ounce) container plain yogurt

Direction

- In a big pot, boil the pepper, salt, garam masala, turmeric, cinnamon, garlic, onion and water. Put in lamb; turn heat to low and let simmer for about 15 - 20 minutes. Remove lamb from liquid; put aside. Pour liquid into bowl.
- Meanwhile, in a deep, big skillet, heat oil on moderate heat. Fry slices of eggplant in hot oil, ensure to space pieces apart, until both sides turn brown; transfer onto paper towels lined plate and let drain. Fry cauliflower and zucchini in the same manner. Cook broccoli in oil till hot and transfer onto a plate lined with paper towel and let drain.
- Arrange lamb in layer on big pot's bottom. Place cauliflower, broccoli, zucchini and eggplant in layers over lamb. Add rice on top of vegetables and meat, gently shake the pot to let rice settle in dish. Add reserved lamb's cooking liquid on top of mixture till covered fully. Pour in water if necessary.
- Simmer with cover on low heat about 30 to 45 minutes, till rice is tender and liquid is soaked in. Uncover the pot. Put a big platter on top of pot and invert pot making dish "upside down" onto platter. Serve with yogurt alongside.

Nutrition Information

- Calories: 1019 calories;
- Sodium: 152
- Total Carbohydrate: 58.3
- Cholesterol: 50
- Protein: 24.3
- Total Fat: 78.1

444. Whitechapel Shepherd's Pie

Serving: 4 | Prep: 45mins | Cook: 25mins | Ready in:

Ingredients

- 1 stalk celery, chopped
- 3 carrots, peeled and chopped
- 1 parsnip, peeled and diced
- 1 small rutabaga, chopped
- 1/4 cup frozen green peas
- 1 pound ground lamb
- 1 onion, chopped
- 1 clove garlic, chopped
- 1 (8 ounce) can tomato sauce
- 1 teaspoon salt
- 1/2 teaspoon ground black pepper
- 1/4 teaspoon dried thyme
- 1/4 teaspoon dried sage
- 1/2 cup milk, or as needed
- 3 cups prepared mashed potatoes
- 2 tablespoons grated Parmesan cheese

Direction

- Preheat the oven to 350° F (175° C).
- In a large saucepan, add the peas, rutabaga, parsnip, carrots, and celery then cover with 1 inch of water. Boil, cover, then steam for 15 minutes, or till vegetables become softened.
- In the meantime, in a big frying pan, crumble the ground lamb over medium heat. Put in garlic and onion; cook and mix until lamb has no pink left. Drain off any grease. Mix in the tomato sauce and steamed vegetables. Season with sage, thyme, pepper and salt. Move all to a greased 7x11-inch baking dish.
- To make the mashed potatoes spreadable, whisk them with as much milk as needed. Spread them atop the casserole then decorate with a scatter of Parmesan cheese.
- In the preheated oven, bake for 25 minutes, till the casserole is heated through and the top becomes browned.

Nutrition Information

- Calories: 476 calories;
- Total Carbohydrate: 51.4
- Cholesterol: 84
- Protein: 27.5
- Total Fat: 18.1
- Sodium: 1529

Index

A
Ale 7,204,236

Apple 4,8,93,266

Apricot 3,5,6,7,32,128,179,194

Arborio rice 213

Artichoke 3,7,21,213

Asparagus 4,77

B
Bacon 7,201,225,226

Barley 3,6,45,167

Basil 4,7,83,97,218

Beans 3,5,7,8,33,138,212,235,250

Beef 5,6,110,160

Beer 3,5,23,127

Black pepper 176

Blackberry 5,120

Blueberry 8,267

Bread 6,8,162,255

Broccoli 6,176

Broth 8,222,270

Burger 4,5,6,7,8,83,84,85,87,89,91,92,101,107,145,230,236,253,256

Butter 3,4,5,7,22,39,80,125,203,228

C
Cabbage 4,6,53,143

Cardamom 3,9

Carrot 4,10,55

Champ 4,84,85

Chard 3,7,17,232

Cheddar 36,58,63,64

Cheese 4,6,89,145

Cherry 3,16

Chicken 5,106,114

Chipotle 3,6,10,11,16,20,145

Chocolate 3,40

Chutney 6,158,163

Cloves 3,21

Couscous 4,5,7,74,128,220,233

Cream 8,238

Crostini 7,231

Crumble 55,56,69,163,199

Cucumber 3,4,13,91

Cumin 5,7,122,203

Currants 10

Curry 3,4,6,8,41,55,93,168,247,261,265,269

D
Dab 90

Dal 4,87

Dijon mustard 10,12,14,17,19,83,87,88,100,107,117,118,120,122,124,152,153,160,171,172,189,191,211,213,214,262,267,268,272,273

Duck 7,208

Dumplings 261

E
Egg 3,4,5,7,40,56,57,64,65,124,234

F
Fat 4,9,11,12,13,14,15,16,17,18,19,20,21,22,23,24,25,26,27,28,29,30,31,32,33,34,35,36,37,38,39,40,41,42,43,44,45,46,47,48,49,50,51,52,53,54,55,56,57,58,59,60,61,62,63,64,65,66,67,68,69,70,71,72,73,74,75,76,77,78,79,80,81,82,83,84,85,86,87,88,89,90,91,92,93,94,95,96,97,98,99,100,101,102,10

3,104,105,106,107,108,109,110,111,112,113,114,115,116,117,118,119,120,121,122,123,124,125,126,127,128,129,130,131,132,133,134,135,136,137,138,139,140,141,142,143,144,145,146,147,148,149,150,151,152,153,154,155,156,157,158,159,160,161,162,163,164,165,166,167,168,169,170,171,172,173,174,175,176,177,178,179,180,181,182,183,184,185,186,187,188,189,190,191,192,193,194,195,196,197,198,199,200,201,202,203,204,205,206,207,208,209,210,211,212,213,214,215,216,217,218,219,220,221,222,223,224,225,226,227,228,229,230,231,232,233,234,235,236,237,238,239,240,241,242,243,244,245,246,247,248,249,250,251,252,253,254,255,256,257,258,259,260,261,262,263,264,265,266,267,268,269,270,272,273,274,275,276,277,278,279

Fennel 6,154

Feta 3,4,5,6,10,40,89,91,128,139,150

Fig 5,6,7,142,186,218

Freekeh 8,275

French bread 17

G

Garlic 3,5,7,8,10,21,22,127,130,133,186,203,255

Grain 6,167

Gravy 3,7,31,228

H

Ham 8,237

Harissa 33

Herbs 6,187

Honey 5,6,7,111,140,148,210

I

Irish stout 36,76,241

J

Jam 256

Jelly 4,10,96

Jerusalem artichoke 21

Jus 3,20,172

L

Lamb 1,3,4,5,6,7,8,9,10,11,12,13,14,15,16,17,18,19,20,21,22,23,24,25,26,27,28,29,30,31,32,33,34,35,36,40,41,42,45,46,47,48,49,50,51,52,53,54,55,56,57,58,59,62,64,66,68,72,73,75,76,77,79,80,81,82,83,84,85,86,87,88,89,90,91,92,93,94,95,96,97,98,99,100,101,102,103,106,107,108,109,110,111,112,113,114,115,116,117,118,119,120,121,122,123,124,125,126,127,128,129,130,131,133,135,136,137,138,139,140,141,142,144,145,146,147,148,149,150,151,152,153,154,155,156,157,158,159,160,161,162,163,164,165,166,167,168,169,170,171,172,173,174,175,176,177,178,179,180,181,182,183,184,185,186,187,188,189,190,191,192,193,194,195,196,197,199,200,201,202,203,204,205,206,207,208,209,210,211,212,213,214,215,216,217,218,219,224,227,228,230,232,233,234,235,241,244,245,246,247,248,249,250,251,252,253,254,255,256,257,258,260,261,262,263,264,265,266,267,268,269,270,272,273,274,275,276,277

Lancashire 8,253

Leek 4,55

Lemon 5,6,7,98,107,111,141,154,175,181,182,210

Lime 5,112

M

Madeira 22

Mango 6,158

Meat 3,4,5,6,7,8,31,38,42,48,49,55,56,59,65,67,69,71,128,129,132,146,156,222,225,229,242,254

Mince 4,62,172,198,203

Mint 3,4,5,6,7,8,10,12,19,86,90,96,97,113,130,139,161,176,183,197,202,209,211,214,217,228,246

Mozzarella 8,260

Mushroom 6,7,172,225

Mustard 3,6,14,148,152

Mutton 4,8,74,261,273

N

Nut 9,10,11,12,13,14,15,16,17,18,19,20,21,22,23,24,25,26,27,28,29,30,31,32,33,34,35,36,37,38,39,40,41,42,43,44,45,46,47,48,49,50,51,52,53,54,55,56,57,58,59,60,61,62,63,64,65,66,67,68,69,70,71,72,73,74,75,76,77,78,79,80,81,82,83,84,85,86,87,88,89,90,91,92,93,94,95,96,97,98,99,100,101,102,103,104,105,106,107,108,109,110,111,112,113,114,115,116,117,118,119,120,121,122,123,124,125,126,127,128,129,130,131,132,133,134,135,136,137,138,139,140,141,142,143,144,145,146,147,148,149,150,151,152,153,154,155,156,157,158,159,160,161,162,163,164,165,166,167,168,169,170,171,172,173,174,175,176,177,178,179,180,181,182,183,184,185,186,187,188,189,190,191,192,193,194,195,196,197,198,199,200,201,202,203,204,205,206,207,208,209,210,211,212,213,214,215,216,217,218,219,220,221,222,223,224,225,226,227,228,229,230,231,232,233,234,235,236,237,238,239,240,241,242,243,244,245,246,247,248,249,250,251,252,253,254,255,256,257,258,259,260,261,262,263,264,265,266,267,268,269,270,272,273,274,275,276,277,278,279

O

Oil 7,11,44,58,88,150,209,246

Okra 7,8,225,252

Olive 3,4,5,6,17,89,110,128,142,147,150,246

Onion 3,5,8,21,92,110,267,274

Orange 3,4,5,6,7,8,20,84,86,127,150,184,207,215,268

P

Paprika 178

Parmesan 17,46,47,229,230,231,278

Parsley 3,12

Pasta 5,6,136,185

Pastrami 5,100

Pastry 3,8,50,265

Peas 3,38

Pecan 3,16

Peel 14,18,20,65,91,96,120,123

Pepper 4,5,66,69,82,139,180

Pesto 6,7,183,228

Pie 3,4,6,7,8,36,68,146,151,164,171,199,229,239,259,264,269,278

Pistachio 3,7,15,213

Pizza 3,5,37,133,134,135

Plum 6,151,185,187

Pomegranate 4,7,8,94,222,245

Port 3,4,5,7,17,94,115,116,213

Potato 3,5,6,8,9,12,38,52,68,103,154,167,179,270

Prune 6,177

Pulse 26,133

Pumpkin 3,10

Q

Quinoa 7,232

R

Radish 7,202

Raspberry 6,144,180

Ratatouille 6,178

Rice 4,5,10,53,54,135

Risotto 7,213

Roast lamb 14,18,23,156,188,216,218,224,264

Rosemary 3,5,6,7,8,10,29,98,117,148,153,154,188,190,191,210,255,270

S

Saffron 3,8,10,11,277

Sage 5,118

Salad 4,6,7,8,60,145,207,267

Salsa 4,7,90,91,197

Salt 13,38,82,110,111,120,152,176,177,179,185,271

Sausage 3,5,8,22,114,248

Savory 4,57

Savoy cabbage 143

Sea salt 26

Seasoning 73

Sherry 12

Sirloin 5,100

Soup 3,4,7,8,45,72,222,223,238,251,266

Spaghetti 3,51

Spinach 4,5,7,60,110,136,195

Squash 4,5,7,54,125,196

Steak 4,5,85,98

Stew 4,5,6,7,8,55,57,73,74,75,76,77,78,79,142,146,160,165,168,173,174,179,183,184,194,196,197,198,199,219,225,232,234,235,240,241,249,250,252,256,258,261,276

Strawberry 7,214

Stuffing 6,176

Sugar 7,19,125,126,129,130,131,135,136,137,139,142,143,144,146,147,149,150,151,152,154,156,158,186,208

Sweetbread 6,157

Swiss chard 17,18,232

Syrup 9

T

Tabasco 52,81

Tahini 99

Tapenade 22

Thyme 5,111,117

Tomato 3,4,6,7,8,16,22,56,97,147,156,212,276

Turkey 3,38

Turnip 10

V

Vegetables 3,7,15,202,215,233

W

Walnut 3,12

Wine 3,4,7,29,95,201,210,215

Worcestershire sauce 36,41,46,47,50,67,68,87,97,110,115,122,149,151,163,169,172,177,180,186,194,199,201,208,227,255,256,276,277

Z

Zest 7,129,200

L

lasagna 228

Conclusion

Thank you again for downloading this book!

I hope you enjoyed reading about my book!

If you enjoyed this book, please take the time to share your thoughts and post a review on Amazon. It'd be greatly appreciated!

Write me an honest review about the book – I truly value your opinion and thoughts and I will incorporate them into my next book, which is already underway.

Thank you!

If you have any questions, **feel free to contact at:** *author@tempehrecipes.com*

Nancy Woods

tempehrecipes.com

Printed in Great Britain
by Amazon